Backcountry Crucibles

Studies in Eighteenth-Century America and the Atlantic World

co-sponsored by the Lawrence Henry Gipson Institute for Eighteenth-Century Studies, Lehigh University

General Editor: Scott Paul Gordon, *Lehigh University*

Publishing rich, innovative scholarship that extends and enlarges the field of early American studies, *Studies in Eighteenth-Century America and the Atlantic World* embraces interdisciplinary work in eighteenth-century transatlantic literature, history, visual arts, material culture, religion, education, law, and medicine.

Recent Titles in This Series

Jewel A. Smith, *Music, Women, and Pianos: The Moravian Young Ladies' Seminary in Antebellum Bethlehem, Pennsylvania (1815-1860)*

Charles K. Jones, *Francis Johnson (1792-1844): Chronicle of a Black Musician in Early Nineteenth-Century Philadelphia*

Steven Craig Harper, *Promised Land: Penn's Holy Experiment, The Walking Purchase, and the Dispossession of Delawares, 1600-1763*

Patricia D'Antonio, *Founding Friends: Families, Staff, and Patients at the Friends Asylum in Early Nineteenth-Century Philadelphia*

Robert W. Brockway, *A Wonderful Work of God: Puritanism and the Great Awakening*

Daniel J. Weeks, *Not for Filthy Lucre's Sake: Richard Saltar and the Antiproprietary Movement in East New Jersey, 1665-1707*

Michael V. Kennedy and William G. Shade, eds., *The World Turned Upside-Down: The State of Eighteenth-Century American Studies at the Beginning of the Twenty-First Century*

Carol A. Traupman-Carr, ed., *"Pleasing to Our Use": David Tannenberg and the Organs of the Moravians*

Hywel M. Davies, *Transatlantic Brethren: Rev. Samuel Jones (1735-1814) and His Friends: Baptists in Wales, Pennsylvania, and Beyond*

Edward H. Davidson and William J. Scheick, *Paine, Scripture and Authority: The Age of Reason as Religious and Political Idea*

Richard K. Matthews, ed., *Virtue, Corruption and Self-Interest: Political Values in the Eighteenth Century*

http://www.lehigh.edu/library/lup/

Ironfounder, from *The Book of Trades* (White-Hall, [Pa.], 1807).

Rare Books Division, the New York Public Library,
Astor, Lenox and Tilden Foundations.

Backcountry Crucibles

The Lehigh Valley from Settlement to Steel

Edited by

Jean R. Soderlund
and
Catherine S. Parzynski

Bethlehem: Lehigh University Press

© 2008 by Rosemont Publishing & Printing Corp.

All rights reserved. Authorization to photocopy items for internal or personal use, or the internal or personal use of specific clients, is granted by the copyright owner, provided that a base fee of $10.00, plus eight cents per page, per copy is paid directly to the Copyright Clearance Center, 222 Rosewood Drive, Danvers, Massachusetts 01923. [978-0-934223-80-5/08 $10.00 + 8¢ pp, pc.]

Associated University Presses
2010 Eastpark Boulevard
Cranbury, NJ 08512

The paper used in this publication meets the requirements of the American National Standard for Permanence of Paper for Printed Library Materials Z39.48-1984

Library of Congress Cataloging-in-Publication Data

Backcountry crucibles : the Lehigh Valley from settlement to steel / edited by Jean R. Soderlund and Catherine S. Parzynski.
  p. cm.
  Includes bibliographical references and index.
  ISBN-13: 978-0-934223-80-5 (alk. paper)
  ISBN-10: 0-934223-80-7 (alk. paper)
  1. Lehigh River Valley (Pa.)—Civilization—18th century. 2. Lehigh River Valley (Pa.)—Civilization —19th century. 3. Lehigh River Valley (Pa.)—Social Conditions. 4. Ethnology —Pennsylvania—Lehigh River Valley—History. 5. Lehigh River Valley (Pa.) Commerce—History. 6. Bethlehem Region (Pa.)—Civilization—18th century. 7. Bethlehem Region (Pa.)—Civilization—19th century. 8. Bethlehem Region (Pa.) —Social Conditions. 9. Ethnology—Pennsylvania—Bethlehem Region—History. 10. Bethlehem Region (Pa.)—Commerce–History. I. Soderlund, Jean R., 1947- II. Parzynski, Catherine S.
  F157.L6B33 2008
  974.8'27–dc
               2006102073

PRINTED IN THE UNITED STATES OF AMERICA

Contents

List of Illustrations — 9

Introduction — 11

Part I: The Transatlantic Context of European Settlement

Immigrant Kin and Indentured Servants: Fuel for Economic Growth in Colonial Pennsylvania — 25
 MARIANNE S. WOKECK

Pennsylvania: "Hell for Preachers"?: Religion and the German Colonists — 52
 MICHAEL G. BAYLOR

Gender Prescriptions in Eighteenth-Century Bethlehem — 74
 BEVERLY PRIOR SMABY

Religion, Expansion, and Migration: The Cultural Background to Scottish and Irish Settlement in the Lehigh Valley — 104
 NED C. LANDSMAN

Domestic, Dependent, Nations: The Colonial Origins of a Paradox — 125
 GREGORY EVANS DOWD

Part II: Settlement at the Forks: Economic Development and Religious Conflict

Perfection in the Mechanical Arts: The Development of Moravian Industrial Technology in Bethlehem, Pennsylvania, 1741-1814 — 161
 STEPHEN H. CUTCLIFFE and KAREN Z. HUETTER

Religious Conflict and Violence in German Communities during the Great Awakening — 185
 AARON SPENCER FOGLEMAN

The Wheels of Commerce: Market Networks in the Lehigh and
Musconetcong Valleys, 1735-1800   208
  MICHAEL V. KENNEDY

Part III: Politics in the New Republic

From Print Shop to Congress and Back: Easton's Thomas J. Rogers
and the Rise of Newspaper Politics   227
  JEFFREY L. PASLEY

"Perpetual Motion – Perpetual Change – A Boundless Ocean
Without a Shore": Democracy in Pennsylvania and the Consequences
of the Triumph of the People, 1800-1820   255
  ANDREW SHANKMAN

Part IV: Industrialization and De-Industrialization in the Countryside

Fine-tuning the Forks: Transformation of the Lehigh River   275
  AUGUSTINE NIGRO

The Improbable Success of Bethlehem Steel   295
  JOHN K. SMITH

Bethlehem Social Elites, "The Steel," and the Saucon Valley
Country Club   315
  ROGER D. SIMON

Gender and Economic Decline: The Pennsylvania Anthracite Region,
1920-1970   329
  THOMAS DUBLIN and WALTER LICHT

Contributors   341

Index   345

List of Illustrations

1.	Ironfounder, from *The Book of Trades*, 1807	Frontispiece
2.	German and Irish immigration to the Delaware Valley, 1720–1774	27
3.	*Rotterdam van de Maas te zien*, by Gerrit Groenewegen	29
4.	Title page of Gottlieb Mittelberger's *Journey to Pennsylvania in the Year 1750 and Return to Germany in the Year 1754*	54
5.	Count Nicolaus Ludwig von Zinzendorf	76
6.	Moravian love feast in Herrnhut, Germany	81
7.	*Paxton Expedition*, 1764	112
8.	A treaty scene by Benjamin West	132
9.	Monocacy industrial area	166
10.	The Bethlehem industrial area along Monocacy Creek	169
11.	William Duane, 1802	256
12.	Lehigh Canal, Lock No. 1, at Mauch Chunk	286
13.	The Lehigh River flood of June 5, 1862	288
14.	Bethlehem Steel Company in 1900	298
15.	Bethlehem Steel worker in the crucible steel plant	301
16.	Bethlehem Steel workers who produced alloy steels	301

17.	Women workers during World War I	305
18.	Growth of Steel Production Capacity, 1900–1950	309
19.	Area in which Bethlehem had shipping cost advantage over Pittsburgh	310
20.	The Linderman mansion in Bethlehem	317
21.	President Woodrow Wilson with Charles Schwab	317
22.	Saucon Valley Country Club	322

Introduction

PENNSYLVANIA HAS RECEIVED MUCH ATTENTION from United States historians, in large part because of the seminal role that Philadelphia played in the nation's early economic and political development. The colony's reputation for tolerance and diversity, rooted in William Penn's Quakerism, drew large numbers of settlers to the burgeoning colony, and most entered through the "city of brotherly love." With the fertile soil and temperate climate of Penn's patent, immigrants eager to improve their lot in life dubbed Pennsylvania the "best poor man's country." Yet by focusing so often on urban centers such as Philadelphia, historians have slighted the political, cultural, and economic contributions of the periphery.[1] Rural studies of the Delaware Valley have focused on a specific era, thus cannot provide an understanding of long-term growth.[2] This collection of essays attempts to balance the scales. By focusing attention on the "backcountry," in this case the Lehigh Valley in particular and the Delaware Valley more generally, we gain a more complete view of mid-Atlantic regional development, in which Philadelphia, of course, played a part.

The history of the Lehigh Valley is significant both for the intrinsic importance of the events that occurred there and as a model of regional cultural, economic, and political development beyond coastal cities. This volume of fourteen original essays places the Lehigh Valley in the larger context of Atlantic cultural and commercial development. The collection highlights a series of backcountry crucibles: conflict over land between Native Americans and Europeans resulting in the Seven Years' War; the influx of settlers from Germany and the British Isles; early industrial growth and commercial networks; tax rebellion and party politics; and the rise and fall of coal and steel. Metaphorically, the word "crucible" represents the clash of peoples and issues, as different cultural groups struggled for control, formed a new society, and developed a thriving yet constantly changing economy in a region removed from the Atlantic coast. Symbolically, "crucible" evokes the centrality, for more than two centuries, of iron and steel.

Although until recently American historians have emphasized major cities as cultural and economic centers, the United States remained primarily rural until well into the twentieth century. In 1790, only five percent of the population lived in towns of more than 2,500 residents. This volume explores the vitality of cultural, economic, and political life beyond Philadelphia and New York. The Lehigh Valley emerges as a place where events integral to the nation's history occurred, but even more importantly as an example of regional growth outside major cities. The Lehigh Valley's unique location, close enough to two metropolitan centers to market grain, iron, coal, and steel, yet distant enough to develop its own cultural life, offers a regional model persisting for more than two centuries heretofore unexplored in American historical scholarship. This long-term persistence of cultural and economic patterns, including the capacity to adapt to global economic change, makes the Lehigh Valley's history particularly intriguing.

The Transatlantic Context of European Settlement

Pennsylvania's history of cultural and ethnic diversity began early. Explorer Henry Hudson had initially established a Dutch claim to the area in 1609. Unable to provide sufficient numbers of settlers, the Dutch were soon supplanted by the Swedes. They established the first permanent European settlement in Pennsylvania in 1643 on Tinicum Island in the Delaware River. In 1655, Dutch forces regained control of the territory, only to be ousted by the English nine years later. England's Charles II ultimately granted the region to William Penn in 1681. Under his control, Pennsylvania became a haven for a specific group of religious outcasts, the Society of Friends. The religious freedom that Penn promised was not just limited to Welsh, Irish, and English Quakers, as people of all religions could worship in his colony. German Lutherans, Reformed, and sectarians such as Mennonites, Moravians, Dunkers, and Schwenkfelders flowed into the colony to seek promised religious freedom, economic opportunity, and political participation. Scots-Irish settlers also came in large numbers from the 1720s through the American Revolution, with similar goals. Because land proximate to Philadelphia had already been taken up, this second wave of immigrants settled the backcountry, including the Forks of the Delaware, now the Lehigh Valley.

The initial essays in this collection provide context for this settlement, from Marianne Wokeck's insightful discussion of the redemptioner system to Gregory Evans Dowd's careful exposition of English views on Native American rights to land and political sovereignty. Wokeck argues in "Immigrant Kin and Indentured Servants: Fuel for Economic Growth in Colonial Pennsylvania" that the availability of immigrant labor, especially servants, allowed Pennsylvania to finance its own growth. Quaker Pennsylvania offered settlers a quiet and stable environment. It also provided a first generation willing to assist newcomers, particularly relatives of already established émigrés. The key innovation, according to Wokeck, that brought labor to Pennsylvania was the *redemptioner* system. This process offset the prohibitive expenses of emigrating from Germany by creating a credit system, thus permitting many hopefuls to enter the colony. Prospective servants were consequently the actual "fuel" that ignited Pennsylvania's westward expansion. They functioned in a variety of ways: as product for investors, workers for farmers, and tamers of open spaces.

Whether German or English, rich or poor, bound or free, all immigrants to Pennsylvania brought with them social and cultural baggage that shaped the ways in which they dealt with conditions in the New World. Michael Baylor investigates the claim of Gottlieb Mittelberger, a Lutheran educator and church organist touring Pennsylvania between 1750 and 1754, that Pennsylvania was "hell for preachers." German immigrants, according to Baylor, carried their complex religious culture from Europe to the New World. But because circumstances were different in America, Old and New World values were not a perfect fit. The Treaty of Westphalia (1648) legally acknowledged just three Christian denominations within the Holy Roman Empire: the Evangelical/Lutheran church, the Reformed/ Calvinist church, and the Roman Catholic church. The various princes of Germany chose from these three religions, and their people were compelled to follow that belief. Germans like Mittelberger who accepted state-supported religion found things much different in Pennsylvania. In its tolerant and diverse religious environment, with no taxes to support an official church, according to Mittelberger, Germans turned their backs on religion, a situation German Lutheran, Calvinist, and Roman Catholic preachers found "hellish." On the other hand, Baylor argues that sectarian groups like the Mennonites or Moravians reveled in the religious freedom, considering Penn's colony – without persecuting rulers – more heaven than hell.

In "Gender Prescriptions in Eighteenth-Century Bethlehem," Beverly Prior Smaby explores some of the unique beliefs of the Moravian sect (*Unitas Fratrum*), which figured prominently in Lehigh Valley settlement. From the late 1720s to the 1760s, under the leadership of Count Nicholas Ludwig von Zinzendorf, Moravians extended comparatively impressive power to women in the *Gemeine* (Moravian Church). Like the Quakers, Zinzendorf believed the secondary status under which women labored because of the sins of the first woman, Eve, were cancelled by the love and loyalty shown by Christ's mother, Mary, in the New Testament. This positive attitude toward the contributions of women to the church reached its peak during the 1740s, then declined as Zinzendorf's views changed in the 1750s, according to Smaby, and especially after his death in 1760, when Moravians abandoned their former leader's liberal policies. This is not surprising, says Smaby, since the male majority of the church had never been truly comfortable with Zinzendorf's innovations. Smaby's essay reminds us of the wide range of beliefs and social practices immigrants brought to Pennsylvania, the freedom they found here to practice and evangelize their ideals, and the impact institutionalization of their religion had on those beliefs.

In "Religion, Expansion, and Migration: The Cultural Background to Scottish and Irish Settlement in the Lehigh Valley," historian Ned Landsman probes how Old World religious customs aided Scots-Irish settlers in assimilating to the New World. Landsman maintains that the Presbyterianism this ethnically complex group brought with them from Scotland provided a cultural background particularly suited to life in Pennsylvania's backcountry. The religious unity of Presbyterianism combined with the Scots-Irish "culture of migration," allowed these settlers to thrive on the frontier. They were already familiar with existing in small dispersed communities, and with living on the move. Unlike the German sectarians of Baylor's article, these Scots-Irish clung to, rather than abandoned, the established religion of their homeland.

As Landsman clarifies, the Scottish and Irish settlers had direct contact with Native Americans in the Lehigh, Susquehanna, and Ohio valleys because they willingly migrated to the frontier. As a result, in the 1750s, the settlers "faced the consequences not only of their own aggressive settlement but of imperial disputes and of high-handed diplomacy in the colony over the previous several decades." The Paxton massacres of 1763, in which Scots-Irish settlers murdered peaceful Christian Indians at Conestoga, climaxed violence that enflamed the Pennsylvania backcountry, from the Ohio to Lehigh valleys, at mid-century.

Gregory Evans Dowd places these events at the center of his essay, "Domestic, Dependent, Nations: The Colonial Origins of a Paradox," which explores the evolution of concepts of Indian sovereignty in both the British colonies that became the United States and in Canada. Despite the use of the word "treaty" in some negotiations with Native Americans, the British never recognized their sovereignty. Rather, until about 1760, the Crown considered Indians its subjects, like other residents of the realm. The Seven Years' War and Pontiac's War, which followed, tore apart earlier understandings for colonists and the government alike. While Indian nations maintained their sovereignty and fought to retrieve lost lands, many Euro-Americans considered them traitors, enemies, and rebels. The British government approached, with the Proclamation of 1763, the concept of limited sovereignty – of a domestic, dependent, nation – a status the U.S. government confirmed informally after the Revolution and more formally with John Marshall's Supreme Court opinions of 1831-32.

Clearly, although Pennsylvania and more specifically the Lehigh Valley offered settlers new opportunities, experiences, and adventures, even those who had fled from previous persecutions remained very much attached to their original places, ideals, and prejudices. Even in William Penn's "holy experiment," people failed to surmount imperial contests for power. Thus Pennsylvania took the center of what Lawrence Henry Gipson called "the Great War for Empire," the Seven Years' War.

Settlement at the Forks: Economic Development and Religious Conflict

Before 1737, European settlers filtered into the Lehigh Valley as a result of increasing immigration from Great Britain and Europe, including the Scots Irish who established Craig's and Hunter's settlements in the late 1720s. James Logan and fellow investors set up the Durham Ironworks in northern Bucks County after privately purchasing the four-square-mile tract in 1726 from Nutimus and other native leaders. None of these land claims rested on a secure legal foundation, however, because the Pennsylvania government had not yet acquired the region from its Lenape residents. In 1737, the land fraud of the Walking Purchase opened the Lehigh Valley to European settlement.[3] A tragic turning point in colonial history, it led directly to the Seven Years' War less than two decades later. Forcing many Lenapes from eastern Pennsylvania, the Walking Purchase marked the end of William Penn's policy of fair dealing with the Delaware Valley's native peoples. The Pennsylvania proprietor had initiated peaceful contact with Indians of the Lehigh Valley through the Swedish negotiator Lars Cock as early as 1682.[4] After Penn's death in 1718, however, his sons Thomas and John, aided by provincial secretary James Logan, adopted a devious, heavy-handed approach to gain the fertile countryside of northern Bucks and what in 1752 became Northampton County.

European settlement proceeded rapidly, with independent family farms and communal Moravian missionary towns. In 1760, about 10,000 people inhabited the region. This number grew to approximately 15,000 in 1778 and 24,000 in 1790.[5] In the 1740s, many Lenapes moved west to the Susquehanna and Ohio valleys, while others remained in the Lehigh Valley, joining Moravian missions. The founding of Bethlehem in 1741 by missionaries from central Europe distinguished the region from other parts of British America. The Moravians (*Unitas Fratrum*) organized town residents into "choirs" based on sex, age, and marital status, setting up a closed communal economy with industries ranging from gristmills to tanning. As Stephen H. Cutcliffe and Karen Z. Huetter show, Bethlehem's fifty crafts made it a unique proto-industrial site. The industries on Monocacy Creek and nearby farms supported missionaries who took Moravian beliefs to Indians and German settlers throughout the mid-Atlantic region. The Moravian approach met considerable success among the Lenapes and Mahicans, of whom about five hundred converted between 1742 and 1764. The Moravians founded a new village, Gnadenhütten, where Christian Indians and missionaries lived; the Lenape town Meniolagomekah welcomed the European preachers. The Moravians learned the Indians' languages, translated hymns and scripture, and resided among the native people. Until 1760, under Count Nicholas Ludwig von Zinzendorf's leadership, the Moravian emphasis on women's spiritual authority particularly appealed to Indian women, who often resisted more patriarchal Christian forms.[6]

The *Unitas Fratrum* also evangelized the recent German immigrants to Pennsylvania and adjacent colonies, who received little attention from Reformed and Lutheran hierarchies back in Europe. As Aaron Spencer Fogleman demonstrates, the Moravian missionaries took the German settlements by storm, adding to the more general religious havoc of the Great Awakening. Lutherans and Reformed congregations fought Moravian ecumenism and radical spirituality with violence and propaganda. Michael V. Kennedy places the development of Moravian Bethlehem into the larger context of colonial economic growth. He challenges the transition to capitalism thesis that the backcountry, in this case Pennsylvania's Lehigh Valley, first created a subsistence economy and entered commercial networks in the late eighteenth century. Kennedy demonstrates that enterprises such as the Durham Ironworks and gristmills served as commercial centers across the countryside, purchasing wheat, butter, firewood, and labor from farm families and selling them manufactures and imported goods.

Politics in the New Republic

In the years following the end of the American Revolution, political consensus was much pursued but rarely achieved. Problems plagued the callow republic. Not the least of these were economic depression and political unrest. Though the colonials had managed to come together and defeat the superior British forces, still a great deal of disagreement existed after the peace over who should rule and how? Two factions ultimately filled this power gap, the Federalists under George Washington and Alexander Hamilton, and the Democratic Republicans under Thomas Jefferson. The Federalists championed a strong federal government and rule by the "few," while Jefferson's supporters called for strong state governments and a more inclusive type of leadership. These two groups battled for control of the new nation. Class, regional, and ethnic divisions greatly complicated the situation. Citizens of the United States not only had to decide which group best met their needs, they also had to determine which group remained truest to the principles of the Revolution. This was no easy task for people working out the meaning of popular sovereignty, and who worried that threats existed everywhere to their new republic.

In his contribution, "From Print Shop to Congress and Back," Jeffrey L. Pasley examines the influence of newspapers on the nascent party system at the turn of the nineteenth century. To modern eyes these early newspapers seem confusing and uninformative. Using the career of printer/editor Thomas J. Rogers of Easton as his guide, Pasley argues that common printers, like Rogers, were able to exert tremendous sway over the political choices of their readers. Editors like Rogers were "professional politicians" in that they managed, directed, and actually defined political belief and action within their regions. They wielded impressive authority for their parties, in Rogers's case the Jeffersonian Democratic Republicans, and were so powerful, in fact, that many gentlemen politicians cried out against what they called the "tyrannies of the printers." These critics charged that men like Rogers were driven by avarice and would lead the average reader astray. Liberty and democracy could not possibly survive, they said, with such riff-raff controlling the mass of voters.

The next essay also deals with a challenge to urban political elites, as Andrew Shankman examines the rise of the Snyderites to political dominance in the first twenty years of the nineteenth century. After George Washington left the presidency Americans increasingly turned their backs on his Federalist party and looked instead to Thomas Jefferson. The Jeffersonians were an amalgam of factions, however, including the competing Democrats and Tertium Quids of Philadelphia, who disagreed on such issues as the continuing influence of English common law and government support for economic growth. This urban political in-fighting brought Simon Snyder of the Pennsylvania backcountry into early national politics. The Snyderites, Shankman contends, brought practicality to Pennsylvania politics, as Snyder, a former mechanic, farmer, and merchant, could claim direct involvement in the developing economy. Since he helped produce Pennsylvania's riches, should he not have a say in how it was governed? Many rural Pennsylvanians agreed with Snyder's logic and propelled him to the center of state government. Yet just as the Jeffersonians had split, so too did the Snyderites. The bedrock issue of how to secure liberty and popular rule confronted backcountry and urban residents alike. The Snyderites, like the factions debating the role of newspapers in politics, encountered myriad challenges in solidifying the American republic.

INTRODUCTION

Industrialization and De-Industrialization in the Countryside

At the end of the eighteenth century, as Stephen Cutcliffe and Karen Huetter have concluded, the Moravian industrial district in Bethlehem lost steam, eclipsed by the Brandywine River mills near Wilmington, Delaware, and other sites in the northeastern United States. The Moravian Church's tight economic regulation brought temporary stagnation to Bethlehem proper. Conditions changed in the larger Lehigh Valley, however, with increasing shipment of anthracite coal from northeastern Pennsylvania along the Lehigh River. The region expanded from supplier of iron goods, flour, and other agricultural products, to provide fuel for the nation's cities and growing manufacturing base. With its advantageous mix of lush countryside, mineral resources, industrious immigrant and resident workers, and entrepreneurial talent (also including both immigrants and previous residents), the Lehigh Valley rode each wave of industrial development. Coal pushed the region into the canal and then the railroad age. Bethlehem Steel Corporation, which ranked second in the U.S. steel industry by 1930, was founded initially to supply iron rails. With the decline of coal and steel in the middle to late twentieth century, Lehigh Valley entrepreneurs turned to high technology.

The final essays in the collection tell part of this story. Another volume is necessary to include the work of other scholars already exploring the region's nineteenth- and twentieth-century history, and the additional research we hope this book will inspire. Augustine Nigro analyzes efforts to tame the Lehigh River, to make it "an integral part of the industrial process." The Philadelphia manufacturers Josiah White and Erskine Hazard needed coal for their Schuylkill River nail factory. Founding the Lehigh Coal and Navigation Company, they hired hundreds of immigrant laborers to reconfigure the river with an intricate system of locks and dams. The LCNC's high tolls stimulated complaints against its monopoly of the river; by 1855 investors built the Lehigh Valley Railroad to compete. As Nigro poignantly details, however, nature and ill-conceived technology defeated the canal, as the flood of 1862 sent water and lumber crashing through Mauch Chunk, Allentown, and Bethlehem, taking more than one hundred lives.

Extractive industries – coal, zinc, cement, and iron – continued in the region, primarily with rail transportation to market. John K. Smith's essay, "The Improbable Success of Bethlehem Steel," looks at the company's rise from a tiny supplier of iron rails for Lehigh Valley entrepreneur Asa Packer's railroads, to produce more than a billion pounds of steel for armaments during World War I, build ships and submarines, and supply I-beams for many of New York City's skyscrapers. Smith demonstrates that several factors outside Bethlehem Steel's control – Charles Schwab's takeover and the outbreak of World War I – as well as its dominance in the steel market east of the Appalachians and several canny mergers were most significant in the company's early phenomenal growth.

Roger D. Simon's essay, "Bethlehem Social Elites, 'The Steel,' and the Saucon Valley Country Club," parallels Smith's paper in showing the impact of Bethlehem Steel's growth on the Lehigh Valley's upper class. The company's management succeeded the earlier Moravian and railroad elites, building expensive homes and the Saucon Valley Country Club with huge bonuses from company profits. The country club, then and now one of the finest golf courses in the United States, became part of the region's cultural scene. Sufficiently distant from Philadelphia and New York City, with Bethlehem Steel's profits and other resources, Lehigh Valley elites created an independent, provincial society. As Simon quotes from a 1941 *Fortune* article, "Bethlehem [Steel]'s management lives in Bethlehem. By day it works together, and by night it strolls across the street to visit itself."

These two articles on Bethlehem Steel and its management focus on its heyday during the first third of the twentieth century. After World War II, the company declined as U.S. steel manufacturers failed to compete against rising imports. By 2001, only its corporate headquarters remained in the Lehigh Valley, with plans to turn the manufacturing site – encompassing an enormous machine shop and blast furnaces – into a museum and entertainment complex.

De-industrialization ravaged the anthracite coal mines of the northern Lehigh Valley earlier than steel, as Thomas Dublin and Walter Licht discuss in "Gender and Economic Decline: The Pennsylvania Anthracite Region, 1920-1970." Using evidence from some ninety oral history interviews of men and women of coal mining families, Dublin and Licht recount the impact of the mine closings on family relationships. Before the collapse of anthracite, when men garnered a dependable family wage, they ruled the home. When times got tougher, many still resisted their wives' working in local garment factories and other paid employment, but then had to adjust. As women provided wages, their household authority grew in subtle and more obvious ways. In several respects this chapter brings us back to the volume's initial essays, which explored the intersection of gender and ethnic attitudes, migration, and economic change. Over the centuries, the Lehigh Valley has faced economic challenges in both upturns and declines, and has received generation upon generation of new immigrants. Its history is distinct and significant beyond its bounds, emblematic of economically viable and autonomous regions outside the seaboard cities.

These fourteen essays originated in a series of symposia and lectures sponsored by the Lawrence Henry Gipson Institute for Eighteenth-Century Studies, the Bitting Family Gift, and the Department of History at Lehigh University. We thank Richard and JoAnn Bitting for their generosity in supporting the conference, "Historical Perspectives on the Lehigh Valley Region," and for promoting regional history more generally. We also recognize the foresight of Lawrence Henry Gipson, Pulitzer Prize-winning chair and professor of history at Lehigh, who endowed the Gipson Institute. Complementing his broad interest in the Anglo-American world of the eighteenth century, Gipson more specifically explored the history of Pennsylvania and its people.

We thank the participants in the lecture and symposia series, including the contributors to this volume and Leslie Patrick of Bucknell University, William Pencak of Pennsylvania State University, and Steven Lubar of the Smithsonian Institution, who chaired sessions and provided comments. Janet Walters and Susan Hoffman contributed unparalleled energy and dedication to the success of the

INTRODUCTION 19

"Historical Perspectives" conference. Michael Baylor, Gail Cooper, Stephen Cutcliffe, James Saeger, William Shade, and Roger Simon of the Lehigh Department of History generously lent their expertise and long experience to planning the Lehigh Valley series and shaping this volume. Thomas Saxton assisted with the illustrations and Michele Baer, Tim Hayburn, Holly Kent, and Judith Mayer helped to prepare the manuscript for publication. We are particularly indebted to our husbands, Michael Parzynski and Rudy Soderlund, for their support of all of our professional endeavors, including this book.

Notes

1. A important book that makes this point even in its title is John B. Frantz and William Pencak, eds., *Beyond Philadelphia: The American Revolution in the Pennsylvania Hinterland* (University Park: Pennsylvania State University Press, 1998).

2. Many scholars have published local studies of the rural mid-Atlantic region, particularly during the colonial and early national periods. Michael W. Zuckerman, in *Friends and Neighbors: Group Life in America's First Plural Society* (Philadelphia: Temple University Press, 1982), provided a broad comparative perspective with urban and rural studies for the colonial period. Wayne Bodle offered a comprehensive overview of the mid-Atlantic literature in "Themes and Directions in Middle Colonies Historiography, 1980-1994," *William and Mary Quarterly* 3d ser., 51 (1994): 355-88.

3. Steven Craig Harper, *Promised Land: Penn's Holy Experiment, The Walking Purchase, and the Dispossession of Delawares, 1600-1763* (Bethlehem, Pa.: Lehigh University Press, 2006).

4. Jean R. Soderlund et al., eds., *William Penn and the Founding of Pennsylvania: A Documentary History, 1680-1684* (Philadelphia: University of Pennsylvania Press, 1983), 144-45.

5. Evarts B. Greene and Virginia D. Harrington, *American Population Before the Federal Census of 1790* (New York: Columbia University Press, 1932), 117-20; Stella H. Sutherland, *Population Distribution in Colonial America* (New York: Columbia University Press, 1936), 130-31.

6. Jane T. Merritt, "Dreaming of the Savior's Blood: Moravians and the Indian Great Awakening in Pennsylvania," *William and Mary Quarterly* 3d ser., 54 (1997): 723-46; Merritt, "Cultural Encounters along a Gender Frontier: Mahican, Delaware, and German Women in Eighteenth-Century Pennsylvania," *Pennsylvania History* 62 (2000, revised): 503-32; Rachel Wheeler, "Women and Christian Practice in a Mahican Village," *Religion and American Culture* 13 (2003): 27-67.

Backcountry Crucibles

I

The Transatlantic Context of European Settlement

Immigrant Kin and Indentured Servants: Fuel for Economic Growth in Colonial Pennsylvania

Marianne S. Wokeck

THE CONNECTION BETWEEN ECONOMIC GROWTH and immigration seems straightforward. In most cases, migrants are attracted to countries, regions, and localities like the eighteenth-century Lehigh Valley, and Pennsylvania more generally, because they appear to offer better opportunities than are available at home. Thus, if immigration is an indicator of economic growth, colonial Pennsylvania enjoyed significant economic expansion. James Logan called it the "best poor man's country" – a phrase that captures the attraction of the Delaware Valley to a steady, and at times spectacular, stream of immigrants.[1] The phrase also simplifies – albeit nicely – the complexities that underlie the relationship between economic growth and immigration in colonial Pennsylvania. To explore that linkage in some of its details is the focus here: first with a brief overview of immigration to Pennsylvania before the Revolution; second, by outlining the critical role the first generation played in creating and capitalizing on conditions for growth that lured more newcomers across the Atlantic; and third, by tracing the impact of a flexible modified system of bound servitude in expanding the regional economy.

Immigration through Philadelphia was not just a short-term phenomenon but a sustained feature that contributed significantly to economic growth in the middle colonies, especially Pennsylvania. The influx of people from German-speaking territories and Ireland, who provided labor and capital to fuel an economic boom that lasted through much of the colonial period, resulted from a process by which immigrants who successfully made the transition from newcomer to resident in turn attracted the next generation of immigrants by purchasing their labor or otherwise assisting their relocation across the Atlantic. Farmers, artisans, and merchants were crucial to immigration because reports of their achievement drew more of their kin and former neighbors to colonial America and because they sponsored the indentured servants and redemptioners whose labor was critical to Pennsylvania's growing economy. The colony's success depended in large part on the obligation that well-established residents felt toward kin, coreligionists, friends, and even strangers of similar ethnic background who arrived later and with limited resources. The willingness of Pennsylvania's diverse ethnic population, from the earliest years, to take risks and extend opportunities to new immigrants provided the plentiful labor supply and more general demographic growth that fostered rapid economic development in colonial Pennsylvania.

Irish and German Immigration

In the eighteenth century, Philadelphia was an exceptional magnet for voluntary immigration from all parts of Great Britain and also from Ireland and the German-speaking lands along the Rhine River on the continent.[2] German colonists formed the largest stream of immigrants who landed on the Delaware River – about 111,000 from the founding of Penn's colony until the American Revolution. Migrants who left from Irish ports made up about half the number of German arrivals, but, since Irish immigration continued strong in the new Republic, the numerical differences between German and Irish immigrants evened out somewhat by the end of the eighteenth century.[3]

Immigration to Pennsylvania increased from the 1680s to the 1770s in waves that crested and waned unevenly, not in one or several steadily rising streams. After the initial group of founding colonists arrived in the early years of the province, migration of Irish and German colonists first peaked significantly in the late 1720s, then surged around 1740 for Irish newcomers and around mid-century for German arrivals, and then swelled again, mostly with Irish settlers and less so with Germans, in the 1760s and 1770s. Over the course of the eighteenth century the tide of German immigration reached its height in the early 1750s while the influx of Irish migrants climaxed later, in the 1780s. The strong waves of immigration developed when ships could sail safely across the Atlantic. In times of war, migration to the American colonies declined, often significantly. More generally, occasional record-setting surges reflected a complex interplay among opportunities that lured colonists to relocate to Pennsylvania and diminished prospects at home.[4]

The waves of German and Irish immigrants to the Delaware Valley demonstrated two distinct patterns in the eighteenth century: a fairly steady flow of boys and young men; and a substantial segment of families.[5] Most of the single youths from Irish ports were indentured servants who came in parcels of one or two dozen bound laborers that merchants and sea captains loaded as ancillary cargo and sold upon arrival in the American colonies to the highest bidder. Other Irish immigrants traveled as members of relocating households.[6] Like the indentured servants, such families – kith and kin and their servants – filled up space on ships that would otherwise go unused and thus increased the merchants' profits. Among German immigrants a similar distinction between passengers and servants existed, although the difference between those who bound themselves to masters in the colonies and those who needed no help in financing their relocation across the Atlantic usually became apparent only after landing in Philadelphia, when the newcomers had to settle their fare debts.[7] Those who could not pay for their pas-

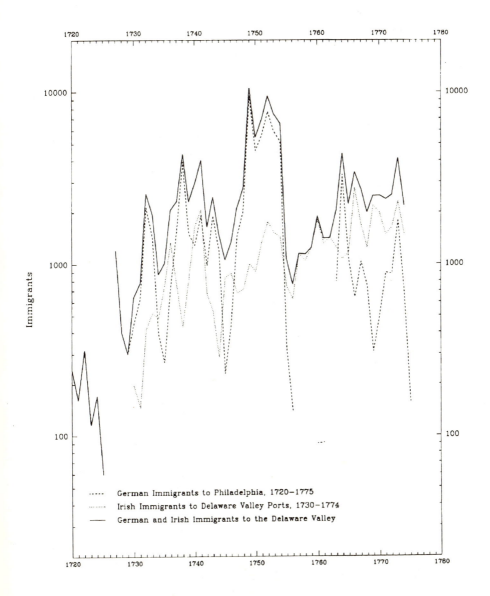

German and Irish Immigration to the Delaware Valley, 1720-1774.

Source: Marianne S. Wokeck, *Trade in Strangers: The Beginning of Mass Migration to North America* (University Park: Pennsylvania State University Press, 1999), 45-46, 172-73.

sage most often became bound servants, so-called redemptioners, pledging their future labor in return for payment of their outstanding fares by their masters.

The process by which Irish and Germans migrated to Pennsylvania was quite different. Most of the Irish servants originated from the city of Dublin and its hinterland in southern Ireland, while the majority of emigrating Irish families set out from rural areas in Ulster and sailed from Belfast and other northern ports.[8] In the case of the Germans, almost all emigrants boarded ships apparently quite indiscriminately in the same port, Rotterdam, the endpoint of a lengthy, arduous, and expensive journey down the Rhine. Along the way were several major collection points of predominantly Protestant travelers, jumbling and obscuring the precise geographic origins of the emigrants.[9] Clearly kin, coreligionists, and neighbors made the journey together and some localities in the Rhine lands sent significant numbers of migrants once or more often to the American colonies, but German networks cannot be mapped in the manner possible for the migration flows from English and Irish ports in the second half of the eighteenth century.[10] In general terms, links of communication and trade channeled individuals or families from particular localities in Europe to certain areas of the Mid-Atlantic region.

Trade connections linking merchants and captains in particular European ports with their partners who had settled in Delaware and Pennsylvania created lasting networks[11] that facilitated emigration of groups such as servants from Dublin and southern Irish ports to New Castle and Philadelphia, Mennonite farm families from the Rhine lands to Lancaster County, and Moravians to the Lehigh Valley.[12] Pennsylvania lured different kinds of immigrants from a variety of European backgrounds throughout the colonial period – an attraction that complemented the diverse and unevenly distributed expansion of farming, manufacturing, and trading in the province and its vast backcountry.

Differences in the flow and character of the German and Irish immigrations occurred as a consequence of the variations in the transportation business that enabled migrants to relocate across the Atlantic. Colonists who started their voyage to the New World in Irish ports faced very different circumstances and odds than those who set out from Rotterdam because Ireland was fully integrated in the British North Atlantic trade, with especially well developed roles in the shipping of victuals, flaxseed, and linen overseas, while most German principalities along the Rhine were landlocked and had few transatlantic interests. This meant that migrants from Ireland could respond promptly and quite flexibly to the various pulls and pushes that made moving to colonial Pennsylvania appear advantageous and desirable. Once Irish emigrants had decided to leave, they could count on readily available transatlantic transportation at reasonable prices.

In other words, relocation costs were relatively low for potential Irish migrants and therefore presented much less of a barrier to following through with settlement plans in the Delaware Valley than was the case for Germans lured by prospects of making a decent living in Penn's province.[13] German-speaking lands were obviously not an integral part of the British empire that forged North Atlantic trade connections. German emigrants not only had greater difficulties in

Rotterdam van de Maas te zien, by Gerrit Groenewegen.
Most German immigrants to American boarded ships at Rotterdam for the transatlantic voyage.

Rijksmuseum Amsterdam, The Netherlands.

reaching a seaport but also faced considerable constraints when making arrangements for overseas transportation. As foreigners they were unfamiliar with the various British mercantile interests that determined the supply and demand of shipping across the Atlantic and also with the navigation acts that circumscribed the routes, cargoes, and management of English vessels bound for North America.

Role of Founding Generation

Consequently, the threshold for choosing to relocate to Pennsylvania was high and the difficulties and costs for acting on that option substantial. Moreover, movement over long distances was restricted for most residents of the many Rhine territories because territorial lords exercised tight control over their subjects through strict population policies. Only emigrants with some means or those who could obtain financing for their move overseas could undertake such a venture.[14] More Irish emigrants could move across the Atlantic more readily, more easily, more often, and more cheaply than German emigrants – differences that had an influence on who came, when, where they settled, and how successful newcomers were in making their lives in America.

Sustained immigration to the Delaware Valley throughout the eighteenth century resulted partly from trading patterns that made the transportation of passengers and servants profitable for merchants and affordable for large numbers of emigrants of limited means, and partly from ongoing opportunities for settlement and work – real or perceived – in Philadelphia and its hinterland. The founding generation of colonists played a crucial role in setting these dynamics into motion. The pioneers transformed William Penn's vision of a "holy experiment" to suit their own experience in the New World. Their success in making a decent living for themselves and their children promoted the expansion, trade, prosperity, and reputation of the colony. This vanguard attracted others through their economic success and also by purchasing the immigrant servants to improve their farms and operate trades. Thus, the first generation afforded subsequent settlers a chance to succeed in their new environment. In due course the second generation of colonists also prospered sufficiently to invest in land and employ immigrant labor on farms and in households and shops, thereby luring still more immigrants to Philadelphia and the Pennsylvania backcountry.

As a group the settlers who arrived in 1683 and the decade thereafter shared characteristics that made Penn's province a magnet for newcomers.[15] Although the story of Pennsylvania's beginning is well known, the nature of this pioneering cohort bears repeating. Many of the original investors in Penn's lands were Quakers drawn from a wide range of localities in England, Wales, Ireland, and the continent,[16] who left kin, coreligionists, and neighbors behind. This founding generation differed in wealth from most who followed in that many of the early settlers had sufficient resources to finance the move across the Atlantic and pay the start-up costs in Pennsylvania. Families, more often households that included extended kin and servants, were common among the early settlers; their occupational structure was diverse, including farmers, artisans, and merchants.[17] In short, the first colonists in Pennsylvania were well positioned to organize their lives within the framework of Penn's government, with freedom to practice their religious beliefs and work for economic success, employing the human and capital resources they brought with them and ties with trading partners elsewhere in the colonies and in Europe.

For Pennsylvanians the hardships of the early years were relatively brief, soon followed by stability and even booming conditions. In very general terms, Pennsylvania was poised early on for economic expansion because it could capitalize on assets transferred and activated by immigrants, gain from the structure and security forged early and reliably through ties of kinship and religious convictions among its citizens, and benefit from a "quiet" government and the peaceful acquisition of land from the indigenous peoples. While the high cost of relocation from Europe restricted the influx of immigrants, and the availability of other sources of labor – especially enslaved Africans and free laborers – moderated the demand for indentured servants, each wave of newcomers who came to colonial Pennsylvania fueled economic growth by building more houses, clearing more land, planting more crops, and consuming more goods.

Kin and coreligionists who had stayed in Europe took a keen interest in the fate of the pioneering settlers, as did business partners who invested in Pennsylvania by outfitting ships or speculating in land. Transatlantic networks of communication expanded and became denser as the colony thrived. The links between relatives and coreligionists on both sides of the Atlantic attracted more settlers to Penn's holy experiment, as the positive experience of the founding generation gave the province a good reputation. Perhaps even more important, though, new immigrants often chose Pennsylvania over other colonies because of the willingness of already well established colonists to sponsor compatriots bound for a new life in North America. Successful first-generation Pennsylvania colonists quickly experienced labor scarcity, as indentured servants served their terms and became free. Two solutions for augmenting the number of laborers were to import indentured servants and to invite less venturesome relatives, friends, and coreligionists who had delayed moving overseas until they could count on familiar people there for assistance.[18]

Lending a helping hand to newcomers served diverse interests, of course, and took many different forms. In the context of immigration as fuel for economic development, however, it had a self-generating effect on the German and Irish migration streams that made Pennsylvania distinctive among colonies in need of labor for economic growth. The pioneering generation from Ireland and Germany was instrumental in transforming a culturally based – and biased – custom of private outlays for immigrant labor into a more generalized system of bound labor. The willingness of early settlers in Pennsylvania to assume the risk when purchasing immigrant labor stimulated merchants to expand the occasional trade in servants and emigrants of the early eighteenth century into a regular business, which, in turn, broadened the pool of European colonists attracted to the mid-Atlantic region.[19]

Servitude and Economic Growth

The trade in servants was central to this transformation from augmenting provisions cargoes with small numbers of emigrants to a regular transatlantic business in Irish and German passengers. Long before the founding of Pennsylvania, merchants and captains had transported servants from England and Ireland to the English colonies in America, most often as ancillary cargo on ships that sailed between Europe and the West Indies and North America. By the beginning of the eighteenth century, transportation and sale of servants was embedded in the transatlantic trade.[20] Expanding the destinations for servants to include ports of the middle colonies required no fundamental shift in business operations except to add the Philadelphia link. As ties between Pennsylvania and Ireland intensified, trade developed increasingly around the shipping of flaxseed from the middle colonies and linen and victuals from Irish ports, and included readily available shipping for servants.[21] The transportation of servants was an attractive supplementary cargo for Philadelphia merchants who could profit from the steady demand for servant labor, the short credit lines that were customary when transporting servants, and the use of otherwise underutilized cargo space on vessels making the return voyage to Philadelphia.

Had servants been the only kind of European immigrant labor shipped to the Delaware Valley, the influx of new colonists would have been fairly steady but relatively light in overall volume. The flow of families made the critical difference in swelling the migration streams from Ireland and Germany. Providing migrants with transportation on ships to Philadelphia suited German and Irish families who had decided to relocate to the middle colonies and merchants who profited both from using empty space on Pennsylvania-bound vessels and from financing the migrants' transatlantic move. Many of the immigrants who traveled in families lacked sufficient funds to pay all of the fares they owed captains, freighters, or merchants for the voyage. They redeemed these debts upon arrival in Pennsylvania by binding out themselves or members of their families to serve masters in the Delaware Valley. These redemptioners became part of the population of bound laborers only after they landed in Delaware River ports.[22]

By extending credit to families through the redemptioner system, merchants gained greater profits. The higher the number of passengers on board, the larger the returns from transatlantic fares. Freighters who offered emigrants the opportunity to pay for their transportation by contracting their labor upon landing in the Delaware Valley effectively extended those passengers a form of credit for which the promise of future labor served as collateral. This innovative modification of the traditional form of indentured servitude broadened the pool of emigrants.[23] Families who could not afford to pay the fare in advance, as custom otherwise required, could now venture overseas. In theory, it was a win-win situation for merchants and emigrants because it allowed shippers to pack more passengers per ship and it enabled prospective colonists of limited means to follow up on their desire for a better life in the Delaware Valley and beyond. In practice, circumstances were more complicated as ships filled variably with emigrants and as passengers and servants experienced the harsh realities of the voyage and the difficulties of starting life anew in a strange place.[24] In effect, however, the flexibility in financing transatlantic transportation was crucial for expanding settlement in Pennsylvania and developing frontier regions such as the Lehigh Valley.

The Pennsylvania model of modified indentured servitude contributed to the growth of the colony in three major ways. It was effective as a labor system; it created intricate and far-flung networks of credit; and in its cultural – mostly ethnic – dimension it shaped the character of families, households, and local communities. In Pennsylvania bound servants competed successfully with family, wage, and enslaved labor; contract (or bound) labor provided the economic benefits and other significant trade-offs that made it a viable option throughout the eighteenth century. The employment of contract labor was widespread among urban as well as rural residents of Pennsylvania and, conversely, a significant proportion of European immigrants – especially teenagers and young men and women – served some time as indentured servants.[25]

In addition to the readily calculable economic returns on bound labor, the use of servants in households, on farms, and in the trades, and the conditions for such service had to be sufficiently tolerable for contract laborers not to run away, and for employers the laborers' work had to be reasonably satisfactory in terms of quality and performance. Extreme expectations, undue exploitation, and unjustifiable behavior by masters or servants strained the system. Yet as long as most participants gained from it, occasional difficulties and abuses had little lasting effect.[26]

Flexibility in labor contracts contributed to the success of servant labor in Pennsylvania. The early settlers imported boys and single young men from England and Ireland whose labor contracts, or indentures, had been made in the ports of departure with the intent of selling those agreements to interested American colonists. This source of labor continued throughout the colonial period, but it diminished in relative importance when increasing numbers of immigrants, especially German-speaking newcomers, became redemptioners. In Pennsylvania, there were no differences in legal terms between servants who were imported with binding contracts and those who negotiated their indentures in Philadelphia.

Conventional indentures covered the cost of the voyage for mostly boys and young men from England and Ireland who migrated to the colonies to serve for a set number of years – traditionally four or until reaching the age of maturity.[27] Servants were generally familiar with this kind of arrangement from practices common in their homelands.[28]

Employers, too, acted according to their understanding and experience in the system, assuming the added cost of freedom dues at the end of the servant's term. The masters put a premium on matching an immigrant's characteristics and skills with their particular labor needs. Trained and competent artisans whose trades were in demand cost more than unskilled, ill-suited, or inept laborers. Making good choices was difficult for masters because they were constrained by what they required and how much they could spend, and also by lack of reliable, independent information about the immigrants. The servants were strangers and usually came without recommendation; merchants and captains, of course, had vested interests of their own. Resales of indentures and running away can be viewed as reactions to bad matches between masters and servants.[29]

In the case of redemptioners, whose labor contracts were negotiated upon arrival in Philadelphia, the situation for both masters and servants was different. First of all, redemptioners were more varied as a group than traditional indentured servants. They included male and female immigrants of various ages, family status, backgrounds, and skills, and they sought agreements for terms of service that allowed for payment of their unpaid fares.[30] The specifics of individual indentures showed many permutations, most often balancing the lengths of service to adjust for the fare owed as well as special qualifications or additional provisions.

Second, redemptioners were part of very specific immigration flows in that they boarded ships from Rotterdam or from diverse ports in Ireland, especially Ulster. Among them were immigrants who came upon explicit invitation and others who, following the lead of others more generally, expected somehow to link up with and be assisted by earlier immigrants from the Rhine lands or the North of Ireland. The Irish and German migration streams were distinct in terms of their routes, of course, but also in terms of the time of year they landed most of their immigrants in Philadelphia. German newcomers usually arrived in the fall (August through October) while debarkation of Irish immigrants in Delaware River ports was tied to the seasonal rhythms of the flaxseed fleet and the export trade of linen and victuals to the colonies, which meant Irish arrivals swelled several times each year – in spring, early summer, and late fall.[31] As a result of such differing sailing cycles, Pennsylvania colonists could count on immigrant arrivals almost year-round, but, if prospective masters had special labor needs or preferences, they were likely to discriminate among the various newcomers.

Third, in the case of redemptioners, the variability in agreements did not occur as a consequence of auctioning contracts by which the middlemen (merchants and captains) profited under favorable market conditions but more often it was a reflection of direct negotiations between prospective masters and newly arrived immigrants. Whether such face-to-face dealings resulted in better matches is difficult to gauge, but they undoubtedly offered more choices to masters as well as servants, which had an impact on the specific terms of the labor contracts.[32]

What marked the basis of all indentures for service was a widespread belief in the usefulness, if not advantages, of investing in immigrant labor.[33] Those who procured, traded, employed, and provided such labor did so primarily out of self-interest but the economy of the province gained from the infusion of labor and capital, both important ingredients for expansion and development. In pursuing interest and profit individually, the various participants in the system clearly differed in how they defined their concerns and calculated their gains, although on balance their selfish motivation and behavior combined favorably to attract immigrant labor over the long term.

Tracing the investment in immigrants along the lines of vested interests and credit from Europe to Pennsylvania reveals the intricacy of the prevailing pattern. Merchants in English and Irish ports and in Rotterdam intent on expanding and intensifying trade with the Delaware Valley sought to fill underutilized cargo space on ships with emigrants and their belongings. In order to increase such loads beyond the limited numbers of passengers who could afford the transatlantic relocation costs and indentured servants, merchants offered credit to emigrants of limited means.

This fare policy attracted families, who as redemptioners, postponed final decisions about financing their move across the Atlantic until they landed in Pennsylvania. Shippers could expect additional profits provided they could collect outstanding fares with interest from the indebted immigrants upon arrival in Philadelphia.[34] Under favorable conditions, when newcomers found relatives or friends to assume their debts, sold imported goods to advantage, or made satisfactory agreements for service, balancing the account for a ship's run with migrants was timely, simple, and profitable. When there had been problems during the voyage and when demand for immigrant goods and labor was low, trading partners and factors in Delaware River ports encountered delays, difficulties, and extra costs in closing the books on ill-fated, ill-timed, or badly managed ventures.

For example, additional expenses accrued when passengers became sick and payment of fare debts had to be eased or even dropped in order to attract prospective employers.[35] For merchants, their captains, and partners, voyages were successful when they carried migrants to capacity, when fares paid in advance covered all necessary expenses of the ship's run, and when passengers traveling on credit paid their debts promptly, in full, and in cash according to the fare contract they had signed. As protection against losses on their investment shippers implemented elaborate, sometimes fraudulent, requirements and contract provisions, often at considerable cost and invariably to the detriment of the immigrants.[36] Merchants relied heavily on settlers already established in the Delaware Valley to assume the risk of paying the relocation costs of new arrivals whose only asset was their labor – a form of capital investment that paid off only in the future and that was uninsured. In short, Pennsylvania masters underwrote the credit policies that enabled merchants to develop a profitable business for transporting passengers and servants.

For those who purchased contract labor, the threat of losing the servants' time was counterbalanced by their promised service. How prospective masters weighed potential risks and benefits is difficult to measure, but indications are that the supply of immigrant labor, their variety of skills, the flexibility of terms, and the familiarity with this kind of working arrangement all contributed to its relative competitiveness compared to wage and enslaved labor. In the tight labor market of early Pennsylvania, bound-servant labor was especially attractive to employers with special needs for limited periods of time and those unwilling or unable to pay wages or afford the initial capital outlays for enslaved Africans.

After the founding decades many households in the Delaware Valley included indentured servants, the ranks of those imported in conventional fashion from England and Ireland swelled by redemptioners, first primarily from Germany and then also from Ulster. By the 1730s, when sailing patterns had become routinized and when newspapers reported regularly on incoming and outgoing vessels and their cargoes and carried advertisements for goods and services, prospective masters could count on reliable information about the availability of servants and they could make use of extensive networks of communication for arranging to negotiate contracts with immigrants on board. The more plentiful and diverse the supply of indentured servants and redemptioners, the larger the pool of potential employers and the more common the role of informal and formal brokers in this particular labor market.[37]

When immigration surged in the 1740s and 1750s and over one thousand redemptioners sought employers annually, colonists from farther away and of more limited means became masters of bound servants. As merchants relied more heavily on Pennsylvanians to redeem the fare debts of immigrants, they accepted promissory notes, thus extending their credit lines farther into the province and over longer periods of time, to the advantage of capital-poor settlers who – with the labor of servants – counted on good returns from their farm operations and trades to make the required payments.[38]

Prospective employers had many options when they selected among the increasingly large number of redemptioners (in absolute and proportionate terms). In general, masters in the Delaware Valley preferred German over Irish servants, skilled young men over unskilled men and boys, teenagers over young children or mature adults, single men and women over married couples, healthy arrivals over sickly ones, moderately indebted newcomers over those with heavy debt burdens, and immigrants with connections to familiar places in Europe over those from foreign parts.[39] Moreover, masters who could negotiate agreements on board ship with cash in hand had better choices than those who came late, had to rely on a broker, or had to obtain credit before the transaction could be completed. Whatever decisions Pennsylvania masters made, on balance their returns proved sufficiently satisfactory for them to employ that kind of labor again or to motivate others to assume similar risks.

Much of the evidence for the benefits – and, conversely, losses – masters derived from employing servants is indirect, based on administrative and financial records rather than personal accounts. The picture that emerges from those limited sources underscores the many ways in which Pennsylvanians employed their servants. Forge, mill, and glass works owners, for example, needed the labor of significant numbers of unskilled men to fell timber to clear land and provide fuel. In addition, they also had a critical interest in skilled men to build, manage, and staff their operations.

Typically, such masters drew from sources of traditionally indentured servants for timbering and similar tasks but sought to fill the specialists' slots with properly trained and sufficiently experienced men. The latter were scarce among immigrants and this shortage created circumstances from which unsatisfactory matches between masters and servants resulted and that led to specially targeted recruitment efforts.[40] By contrast, large land speculators intent on clearing and improving their real estate holdings were best served by sizable groups of redemptioners, most often young men and their wives from the Rhine lands, who had experience in farming and could work independently without supervision.[41] Ordinary farmers, however, required but one or two servants to supplement their labor needs temporarily, usually until the homesteaders' children were old enough to carry their weight in operating the farms. Teenaged boys commonly filled those slots because they could help in the fields and with the livestock, while teenaged girls and sometimes young women assisted with household chores and child care.[42]

If farmers needed that kind of help, they chose usually from among indentured servants or redemptioners who came from places in Europe that the prospective masters knew firsthand or to which they had other close connections.[43] Such familiarity with the background of the immigrant provided a sound basis for judging the character of the servant under contract as well as a shared knowledge of language and Old World customs that facilitated communication and understanding of the traditional roles of master and servant. For artisans and others with highly specialized needs, skills and training figured prominently in their choices. Undoubtedly craftsmen had ways of evaluating expertise and experience in fellow artisans by drawing on the conventions that governed the trades all over Europe, but differentiating between true competence and mere claims of qualification called for contract negotiations in person – giving a competitive edge to tradesmen with ready access to vessels that landed with immigrant servants or redemptioners.[44]

Urban households represent yet another example of the wide variety of employment for servants. Since much of the household management was the responsibility of the mistress and many of the chores that had to be done were women's work, it is not surprising that the proportion of girls and women among servants bound to urban residents was high. Some of the servants had mistresses of the same European background as themselves; others received contracts seemingly without regard to ethnicity. Most of the female servants were redemptioners because merchants and captains imported very few female indentured servants.[45]

The widespread use of servitude among Pennsylvania settlers and their choices when negotiating with immigrants for service should not detract from the difficulties employers encountered that complicated and strained the system. Masters incurred considerable losses when their servants died, became sick, or ran away – adversities over which they had only limited control. They sometimes chose the wrong servants for their needs, so traded disappointing servants to other masters and acquired new ones in their stead.[46] Other problems occurred when masters' circumstances changed and forced renegotiation of outstanding terms of the labor contracts, or when masters abused their servants.[47] Yet the continued demand for bound labor in Pennsylvania and steady supply of servants and redemptioners willing to make contracts suggest that the advantages of the labor system outweighed these complications.

How dependent colonists in the Delaware Valley were on the use of formally indentured servants is evident from the substantial number of runaway advertisements and from the intense negotiations the Pennsylvania Assembly conducted with British military commanders during the French and Indian War in order to find ways for compensating masters for the loss of time they suffered when their servants enlisted.[48] The notices masters placed in the newspapers attest to the considerable trouble and expense employers were willing to incur to recapture their servants; they also bear witness to the often harsh and exploitative nature of indentured servitude. From the claims for compensation for servants who had become soldiers it is also clear that a considerable proportion of immigrant boys and young men considered participation in war a better opportunity than completing their terms of service and that their masters experienced not only disruption in their various age and gender-specific work routines and operations but also additional labor shortages because hostilities curtailed the flow of new immigrants and increased competition for a severely restricted labor pool.

Another indicator of the dependence on immigrant indentured servitude is the unwillingness of the resident colonists' children to agree to contract labor past the age of maturity, excepting arrangements for apprenticeships and binding out orphans.[49] Put differently, recruitment of indentured servants was primarily from among immigrants – an interdependent relationship that offered employers an additional, varied source of labor and that provided immigrants with options to finance their move across the Atlantic.

Whether immigrants gained from serving Pennsylvania masters depends also largely on indirect testimony. Ideally, the expectations indentured servants traditionally brought with them were fulfilled when they completed their service and struck out on their own. Very generally, servants who came early had better chances for advancing their lot in Pennsylvania than those who arrived later when competition for land and work cut into the chances of settlers to set up their own households, farms, and shops in the Delaware Valley and even well beyond.[50] For redemptioners the situation was different and more complex. Immigrants who negotiated for service contracts in order to pay off their transatlantic fare debts had options for including provisions that fit their particular circumstances better than newcomers with indentures agreed upon in European ports.

Skillful and healthy single young men and women could try to win short terms, or specific work-related concessions, or additional training, or generous freedom dues packages. Families with large outstanding fare accounts were in different bargaining positions and seem to have had two major objectives when discussing contract terms. They bound out teenagers and sometimes even younger children until they reached maturity in efforts to balance the relatively high prices those fairly lengthy contracts could fetch under favorable circumstances against the debts still owed.[51] Put differently, the strategy of letting children of immigrant families in effect pay for most, if not all, relocation costs enabled their parents to pursue opportunities of making a living unencumbered by debts and obligations to provide for their sons and daughters in this critical phase of starting out and adjusting to life in the New World. Under favorable circumstances parents could amend the customary basic terms of indentures to include special training or schooling for their children. In other cases the terms stipulated in indentures were without advantage to the immigrants – usually a reflection of negative factors that ranged from ill health to a weak labor market.

Normally, however, and irrespective of the particular deals immigrants struck when they bound themselves to Pennsylvania masters, contract laborers accepted the customary terms of service and often benefited from them. As members of their masters' households they were fed, housed, clothed, and generally cared for like other dependents of the heads of household. Although different from apprentices, servants also learned from their masters – sometimes formally, more often informally. Even servants whose contracts did not entitle them to receive special instruction could gain from their experiences. For teenagers, in particular, service away from home also represented a rite of passage into adulthood and toward independence; for immigrants it provided opportunities for learning the ways of their new country.

What use their service was to young men and women after the completion of their terms depended in part on their skills, experience, and connections, in part on how realistically they set their goals for making a living, and in part also on whether they could capitalize on factors conducive to fulfilling their dreams such as reasonable prices to rent or purchase farms or whether adverse conditions like war or recession quashed their hopes. Former servants who met with success were likely to imitate the strategies they had observed in their masters' households, which meant that they would use bound labor when they themselves needed additional help. They contributed thereby to the renewal of the cycle that sustained servitude as a generally acceptable and often attractive labor option.[52]

Significance of Ethnicity

What stands out from the perspectives of masters and servants alike, and what served well the interests of merchants involved in the business of importing immigrants, was the flexibility and fit with which the demand for bound labor and the supply of indentured servants and redemptioners matched over a long period of time. The overall attractiveness of this labor system for Pennsylvanians was in large part a result of the ethnic diversity of the Delaware Valley and the early growth and continued prosperity of Penn's province and its hinterland. The employment of redemptioners could only catch on and become widespread because most settlers from Ireland and especially German-speaking lands, who had no easy or legitimate access to banking services for transferring funds across the Atlantic, were able to finance the transatlantic relocation of their kin, friends, and compatriots once landed in Delaware River ports. At first, when settlers knew the newcomers, arrangements for repayment of their transportation debts were largely informal.[53]

As the ties between well established settlers and newly arrived immigrants became more tenuous, more formal agreements for this kind of credit arrangement seemed warranted, which assured the colonists they would receive some return on their patronage and gave them an option to decline such sponsorship altogether.[54] Immigrants thus "disappointed in their friends" appealed to others among their countrymen and coreligionists for help, pledging their labor in return for redemption of the fares they owed to merchants.[55] The increasing number of such incidents led to the legal and bureaucratic squaring of outstanding accounts, in effect adjusting the already well-known and efficient ways of indentured servitude to fit circumstances in Pennsylvania. Informal individual sponsorship did not cease but was eclipsed by the redemptioner system which opened up opportunities for colonists generally to obtain much needed additional labor and allowed immigrants the kind of flexibility in paying for their relocation to the New World.

Most of the time Irish colonists redeemed Irish passengers and German-speaking settlers contracted for bound labor with German-speaking immigrants. Such distinctively ethnic preferences suggest that Pennsylvanians were more comfortable with, or better at, weighing the relative risks and potential of prospective servants from among people with similar backgrounds. In the German case, the issue of language highlights that point. First, prospective masters could more likely negotiate the terms of service effectively with immigrants in their native tongues than if they had to rely on the judgment of interpreters or brokers; second, employers could more easily obtain acceptable labor from servants who spoke their own dialects and were familiar with Old World ways of husbandry or housewifery. Conversely, immigrants probably figured that their chances for making a satisfactory transition to their new lives in the Delaware Valley were better with masters who had made that adjustment successfully and whose knowledge and connections could be useful when striking out independently upon completion of their terms. Moreover, first- and second-generation German and Irish settlers who were only beginning to establish themselves firmly in the New World seem to have recognized that they could stretch their limited resources farthest when they selected bound labor from among their newly arrived compatriots. Since the prices of redemptioners covered a wide range they suited variable needs and budgets.

Bound service, then, was not only an arrangement that capitalized on labor needs in Pennsylvania and on investment strategies that provided financing of transatlantic relocation costs but also a persuasive mechanism by which newcomers gained familiarity with American ways. For the effectiveness of the process of adaptation the large proportions of teenagers among German and Irish redemptioners were critical. Immigrant youths who came with limited life experi-

IMMIGRANT KIN AND INDENTURED SERVANTS 41

ence in Europe had little reason to resist or shun New World customs as they reached maturity and gained independence because their initiation into adult life took place in Pennsylvania and its hinterland; they established themselves according to local rules. Put differently, the characteristic flow of German and Irish families into the Delaware Valley, many of whose children became redemptioners, contributed to the ethnic mix that became typical for Pennsylvania and that presaged the cultural diversity of later immigration to the United States.

Conclusion

In summary, the dynamics that made immigration through Philadelphia not just a short-term phenomenon but a sustained feature that formed an important component in the economic growth of the middle colonies, especially Pennsylvania, involved two key characteristics. The first was an initial promise of opportunities for making a decent living without undue governmental restrictions or persecution that attracted groups of pioneers from diverse backgrounds – geographically, in terms of religious convictions, and ethnically – colonists who made up a demographically balanced group and among whom was a good mix of people who brought a variety of skills, experiences, and resources for starting life anew in the Delaware Valley. In short, the founding generation was well positioned to overcome the hardships common to all such new beginnings and to succeed in fashioning a better life for themselves than at home.

The second key ingredient for attracting streams of immigrants over the course of the eighteenth century was a spirit of entrepreneurship, or risk-taking, combined with a commitment to lend assistance – often at a price – to kin, co-religionists, and compatriots willing or pressed to follow in the footsteps of the pioneers. It was the reputation of opportunity in Pennsylvania (as modeled by the path-breaking founding generation) and the recognition of the value of the labor and capital that immigrants brought that made investment in their relocation costs worthwhile and desirable as a way to build and strengthen communities of people of similar origins or beliefs.

This strategy worked for different kinds of investors: it benefitted individual households that needed additional help in order to improve their wealth and status; it alleviated the labor shortages that land speculators and developers, owners of mill, forge, and other large-scale and labor-intensive operations faced in the mid-Atlantic region; and it suited merchants in the business of shipping emigrants whose profits depended on large numbers of passengers and lucrative services for them. Although in each case gains were tied to particular circumstances, taken together the infusion of economic resources that immigrants brought in terms of goods, labor, and skills, and the capital residents were willing to risk on their behalf, contributed to the expansion of Pennsylvania as its population grew and the line of European settlements moved westward. Immigration and the trade in strangers also fostered development of Philadelphia's regional market as the connections that linked people, goods, and services became more numerous, denser, and more complex and reached farther within the Delaware Valley and beyond.[56]

If individual Pennsylvanians and the region more generally gained from the investment in immigrants, passengers and servants who landed in Delaware ports, too, could find personal advantage in making Penn's province the starting point of their lives in America and thereby also participate in the economic development of the colony. For indentured servants and redemptioners, contract labor provided affordable credit for making the transatlantic move, room and board over an extended period of time, a base from which to make necessary adjustments to life in the New World, and a springboard for launching careers as free laborers, householders, farmers, and artisans. Immigrants who made the transition from newcomer to resident successfully were crucial in keeping the cycle of immigration going because reports of their achievement drew more of their kin and former neighbors to colonial America and because their ability and willingness to sponsor yet another cohort of strangers assured that economic development continued and that bound servitude remained a viable labor source in Pennsylvania.

The dynamics that set Pennsylvania apart from other colonies because they drew immigration through Philadelphia throughout the eighteenth century lay in the interaction of various forces. The process was fueled in part by the successful example of the pioneers and the continued positive experience of subsequent generations – native-born settlers as well as immigrants. It depended also on the obligation that well-established residents felt toward kin, coreligionists, and friends who arrived later, often with limited resources. Eventually the process relied on the willingness of sufficiently prosperous colonists to assume the risks inherent in employing indentured servants and redemptioners they did not know.

The diversity of the overall migration flow into the Delaware Valley satisfied a wide variety of specific needs and labor requirements, thus broadening the market for immigrant labor across the region and extending opportunities for settlement throughout the colonial period and beyond.

Notes

1. For example, James T. Lemon made it the title of his book on colonial Pennsylvania: *The Best Poor Man's Country: A Geographical Study of Early Southeastern Pennsylvania* (Baltimore: Johns Hopkins University Press, 1972).

2. Since the area of origin of German-speaking colonists had no political cohesion and was geographically and culturally diverse, it is impossible to define it simply and accurately. For convenience, these areas are sometimes termed Germany below and the more accurate "German-speaking" is simplified to "German."

3. For particulars on the flow and character of the German and Irish migrations into Delaware River ports, see Marianne S. Wokeck, *Trade in Strangers: The Beginnings of Mass Migration to North America* (University Park: Pennsylvania State University Press, 1999), chaps. 2 and 5. The following summary is based on those chapters and on Marianne S.

Wokeck, "Irish and German Migration to Eighteenth-Century North American," in *Coerced and Free Migration: Global Perspectives*, ed. David Eltis (Stanford: Stanford University Press, 2002), 152-75.

For a recent summary that draws on the literature of the past fifteen years, see Lorena S. Walsh, "Peopling, Producing, and Consuming in Early British America," in *The Economy of Early America: Historical Perspectives & New Directions*, ed. Cathy D. Matson (University Park: Pennsylvania State University Press, 2006), 124-45. For a more global perspective, see David Eltis, "Introduction: Migration and Agency in Global History" (1-31), and "Free and Coerced Migrations from the Old World to the New" (33-74), in *Coerced and Free Migration*.

4. Historians and policy makers have been interested in analyzing the migration process in order to better understand—and influence—the movements of people. For transatlantic migrations in the eighteenth century, especially of Irish and German migrants, see Bernard Bailyn, *The Peopling of British North America: An Introduction* (New York: Knopf, 1986); Bailyn, *Voyagers to the West: A Passage in the Peopling of America on the Eve of the Revolution* (New York: Knopf, 1986); Barbara DeWolfe, ed., *Discoveries of America: Personal Accounts of British Emigrants to North America during the Revolutionary Era* (New York: Cambridge University Press, 1997); Maurice Bric, "Ireland, Irishmen, and the Broadening of the Late Eighteenth-Century Philadelphia Polity" (PhD diss., Johns Hopkins University, 1990); Louis M. Cullen, "The Irish Diaspora in the Seventeenth and Eighteenth Centuries," in *Europeans on the Move: Studies on European Migration, 1500-1800*, ed. Nicholas P. Canny (Oxford: Clarendon Press, 1994); Robert J. Dickson, *Ulster Emigration to Colonial America, 1718-1775* (London: Routledge and Kegan Paul, 1966); David N. Doyle, *Ireland, Irishmen, and Revolutionary America, 1760-1820* (Dublin: Mercier Press, 1981); Patrick Griffin, *The People with No Name: Ireland's Ulster Scots, America's Scots Irish, and the Creation of a British Atlantic World, 1689-1764* (Princeton: Princeton University Press, 2001); Griffin, "The People with no Name: Ulster's Migrants and Identity Formation in Eighteenth-Century Pennsylvania," *William and Mary Quarterly* 58 (2001): 587-614; Audrey Lockhart, *Some Aspects of Emigration from Ireland to the North American Colonies Between 1660 and 1775* (New York: Arno Press, 1976); Kerby A. Miller, *Emigrants and Exiles: Ireland and the Irish Exodus to North America* (New York: Oxford University Press, 1985); Miller, ed., *Irish Immigrants in the Land of Canaan: Letters and Memoirs from Colonial and Revolutionary America, 1675-1815* (New York: Oxford University Press, 2003); Thomas M. Truxes, *Irish-American Trade, 1660-1783* (Cambridge: Cambridge University Press, 1988); Andreas Blocher, *Die Eigenart der Zürcher Auswanderer nach Amerika* (Zurich: Atlantis-Verlag, 1976); Georg Fertig, "Transatlantic Migration from the German-Speaking Parts of Central Europe, 1600-1800: Proportions, Structures, and Explanations," in *Europeans on the Move*, ed. Canny; Aaron Spencer Fogleman, *Hopeful Journeys: German Immigration, Settlement, and Political Culture in Colonial America, 1717-1775* (Philadelphia: University of Pennsylvania Press, 1996); Fogleman, "Migration to the Thirteen British North American Colonies, 1700-1775: New Estimates," *Journal of Interdisciplinary History* 12 (1992): 691-709; Frley Grubb, "German Immigration to Pennsylvania, 1709-1820," *Journal of Interdisciplinary History* 20 (1990): 417-36; Grubb, "Does Bound Labour Have to be Coerced Labour? The Case of Colonial Immigrant Servitude versus Craft-Apprenticeship and Life-Cycle Servitude-in-Husbandry," *Itinerario* 20 (1997): 28-51; Mark Häberlein, "German Migrants in Colonial Pennsylvania: Resources, Opportunities, and Experience," *William and Mary Quarterly* 3d ser., 50 (1991): 555-74; Häberlein, *Vom Oberrhein zum Susquehanna: Studien zur badischen*

Auswanderung nach Pennsylvania im 18. Jahrhundert (Stuttgart: Kolhammer, 1993); Hartmut Lehmann, Hermann Wellenreuther, Renate Wilson, eds., *In Search of Peace and Prosperity: New German Settlements in Eighteenth-Century Europe and America* (University Park: Pennsylvania State University Press, 2000); Hans Ulrich Pfister, *Die Auswanderung aus dem Knonauer Amt, 1648-1750* (Zurich: H. Rohr, 1987); A. G. Roeber, *Palatines, Liberty, and Property: German Lutherans in British Colonial America* (Baltimore: Johns Hopkins University Press, 1993); Roeber, "In German Ways? Problems and Potentials of Eighteenth-Century German Social and Emigration History," *William and Mary Quarterly* 3d ser., 44 (1987): 750-74.

5. This is evident in the work of Cullen, Dickson, Fertig, Fogleman, Grubb, Häberlein, Lockhart, and Truxes.

6. "Passenger List, with Duties, 29 August 1768-13 August 1772," Historical Society of Pennsylvania, Philadelphia, Pa., hereafter HSP.

7. William John Hinke's compilation of the "ship lists" (Ralph B. Strassburger, *Pennsylvania German Pioneers: A Publication of the Original Lists of Arrivals in the Port of Philadelphia from 1727 to 1808*, ed. by William John Hinke, 3 vols. [Norristown, Pa.: Pennsylvania German Society, 1934; reprint ed. Baltimore, Md., 1966]) form the basis for tracing the character of the German immigration to Philadelphia. Lists of indentures registered in Philadelphia and various merchants' accounts complement that database (for particular references, see Wokeck, *Trade in Strangers*, Appendix and Selected Bibliography).

8. Wokeck, *Trade in Strangers*, Table 4, Figure 3.

9. *Ibid.*, chap. 3, which describes the transportation of emigrants from the merchants' perspective, and chap. 4, which traces the journey from the viewpoint of the migrants.

10. Blocher, *Zürcher Auswanderer*; Fogleman, *Hopeful Journeys*; Häberlein, *Vom Oberrhein*; Pfister, *Auswanderung*; and Roeber, *Palatines*, present good evidence about such migration networks but their research covers only parts of the area from which German migration to the American colonies flowed.

11. For examples of such networks, see Louis M. Cullen, "Economic Development, 1691-1750" and "Economic Development, 1750-1800," in *A New History of Ireland*, ed. T. W. Moody, et al., vol. 4: *Eighteenth-Century Ireland* (Oxford: Clarendon Press, 1986); Doyle, *Ireland*, 22, 39-40, 57, 77; Doerflinger, *A Vigorous Spirit of Enterprise: Merchants and Economic Development in Revolutionary Philadelphia* (Chapel Hill: University of North Carolina Press, 1986), 12, 14, 15, 20, 44, 55-57, 59, 73, 76, 101, 104, 107, 121, 148-49, 152, 155-57, 173, 185-88, 219, 237, 240-41, 253-55, 261, 277-78, 335, 337; Truxes, *Irish-American Trade*, 38, 61, 73, 76-78, 86-87, 106-8, 117-21. See also Joseph S. Foster, *The Pursuit of Equal Liberty: George Bryan and the Revolution in Philadelphia* (University Park: Pennsylvania State University Press, 1994), where the focus is on one prominent Presbyterian Irish merchant in Philadelphia; for Quaker connections, see Audrey Lockhart, "The Quakers and Emigration from Ireland to the North American Colonies," *Quaker History* 77 (1988): 67-92.

12. For trade connections between Irish and Delaware River ports, see Dickson, *Ulster Emigration*; Doerflinger, *Vigorous Spirit*; Lockhart, *Some Aspects of Emigration*; Truxes, *Irish-American Trade*; for an account of the Mennonite migration network, see Richard K. MacMaster, *Land, Piety, Peoplehood: The Establishment of Mennonite Communities in America* (Scottdale, Pa.: Herald Press, 1985), chap. 2; and for a recent overview of the Moravian migration, see Fogleman, *Hopeful Journeys*, chap. 4.

13. For details, see Wokeck, *Trade in Strangers*, chap. 5.

14. For particulars on the relocation from the perspective of the emigrants, see Wokeck, *Trade in Strangers*, chap. 4.

15. Richard S. Dunn and Mary Maples Dunn, et al., eds., *The Papers of William Penn*, vols. 2 and 3 (Philadelphia: University of Pennsylvania Press, 1982, 1986); Jean R. Soderlund, et al., eds., *William Penn and the Founding of Pennsylvania, 1680–1684: A Documentary History* (Philadelphia: University of Pennsylvania Press, 1983); and Craig W. Horle and Marianne S. Wokeck, eds., *Lawmaking and Legislators in Pennsylvania: A Biographical Dictionary*, vol. 1:1682-1709 (Philadelphia: University of Pennsylvania Press, 1991) provide much information about Pennsylvania's pioneering cohort of settlers.

16. Dunn and Dunn, et al., eds., *Papers of William Penn*, 2:630-64.

17. This is evident from the listing of passengers and cargo on the first ships that arrived with settlers for Pennsylvania, foremost among them William Penn's flagship, the *Welcome*. Marion Balderston, "Pennsylvania's 1683 Ships and Some of Their Passengers," *Pennsylvania Genealogical Magazine* 24 (1965): 69-114; George E. McCracken, *The Welcome Claimants Proved, Disproved, and Doubtful* (Baltimore: Genealogical Pub, Co., 1970).

18. The patterns of such chain migration have fascinated historians interested in delineating transatlantic networks; genealogists have traced many of those complex linkages over time. The studies of Roeber (*Palatines*), Fogleman (*Hopeful Journeys*), Häberlein (*Auswanderung*), Miller, ed., (*Irish Immigrants*) and Rosalind J. Beiler ("The Transatlantic World of Caspar Wistar: From Germany to America in the Eighteenth Century" [PhD diss.: University of Pennsylvania, 1994]) reveal the complicated layering of such connections in terms of kinship, religion, and geography. The work of Annette Kunselman Burgert is another vivid testimony of the familial, religious, and regional ties among established settlers, newcomers, and potential emigrants (for example, *Eighteenth-Century Emigrants*, vol. 1: *Northern Kraichgau* and vol. 2: *The Western Palatinate* [Breinigsville, Pa.: The Pennsylvania German Society, 1983 and Birdsboro, Pa., 1985]). By comparison, DeWolfe, *Discoveries*, traces extensive and complex bonds caught in the wave of mostly English-speaking migrants described in Bailyn's *Voyagers*.

19. Indentured servants, including convicts, made up a significant proportion of the laborers imported into the Chesapeake Bay and southern colonies, especially in the early years of establishing plantation societies. With increasing reliance on slave labor, however, servants from Europe became relatively less important. As opportunities for freedmen declined, European emigrants dependent on indentured service for relocating to America chose other colonies, thus limiting the market for merchants and captains with interests

in importing servants. Russell R. Menard, "British Migration to the Chesapeake Colonies in the Seventeenth Century," in *Colonial Chesapeake Society*, ed. Lois Green Carr et al. (Chapel Hill: University of North Carolina Press, 1988), 99-132; see also Menard, "Migration, Ethnicity, and the Rise of an Atlantic Economy: The Re-Peopling of British America, 1600-1790," in *A Century of European Migrations, 1830-1930*, ed. Rudolph J. Vecoli and Suzanne M. Sinke (Urbana: University of Illinois Press, 1991), 58-77; Menard, *Migrants, Servants, and Slaves: Unfree Labor in Colonial British America* (Aldershot, England: Ashgate, 2001).

20. See, for example, David W. Galenson, *White Servitude in Colonial America* (Cambridge: Cambridge University Press, 1981); Menard, *Migrants, Servants, and Slaves*; Kenneth Morgan, *Slavery and Servitude in Colonial North America: A Short History* (Washington Square, N.Y.: New York University Press, 2001); Christopher Tomlins, "Reconsidering Indentured Servitude: European Migration and the Early American Labor Force, 1600-1775," *Labor History* 42 (2001): 5-43; Christopher Tomlins, "Indentured Servitude in Perspective: European Migration into North America and the Composition of the Early American Labor Force, 1600-1775," in Matson, ed., *Economy of Early America*, 146-82.

21. Truxes, *Irish-American Trade*, chaps. 8 and 10; Wokeck, *Trade in Strangers*, chap. 5.

22. Legally there was no difference between indentures made before embarkation in European ports or after debarkation in Delaware Valley ports. In terms of negotiating such customary labor contracts, redemptioners had relatively more flexibility than servants bound in Europe.

23. English merchants involved in the transportation of German migrants from Rotterdam to Philadelphia developed those business practices first – drawing on customs and experiences that prevailed in the trades of shipping servants, troops, and convicts; in turn, merchants engaged in the business of relocating Irish passengers made use of those specialized routines later, when the flow of Irish migration accelerated. For details of those business practices, see Wokeck, *Trade in Strangers*, chap. 3.

24. Marilyn C. Baseler, *"Asylum for Mankind": America 1607-1800* (Ithaca: Cornell University Press, 1998) focuses primarily on immigration in the revolutionary and early national periods and the theme of discriminating selectiveness with which Americans deemed immigrants acceptable and welcome to share in developing American society.

25. Tomlins, "Indentured Servitude in Perspective," reminds readers that in the eighteenth century the proportion of indentured servants among the respective populations of the three major regions of the British North American mainland was small – irrespective of the level and intensity of discussion among Americans about the impact and characteristics of immigrants who could not afford relocation from Europe to America (see Tables A-1 and A-2). For the Mid-Atlantic region, he also points to the relative importance of Philadelphia, where indentured servants were concentrated even though their proportion among all kinds of laborers was small there, too (see Tables 7-11; Tomlin's figures for immigrants and servants in the revolutionary and early national periods should be carefully compared with those presented by Hans-Jürgen Grabbe, *Vor der grossen flut. Die europäische Migration*

IMMIGRANT KIN AND INDENTURED SERVANTS 47

in die Vereinigten Staaten von Amerika, 1783-1820 [Stuttgart: Franz Steiner Verlag. 2001], 24-25, 33-39, 58, 66, 73, 97, 101).

It bears remembering, however, that Philadelphia was the entrepôt for the large majority of immigrants and that the extant recording of formal labor contracts reflect the first arrangement masters and servants made. Neither the frequency nor the distribution among indentures, let alone the occurrence of informal arrangements, with first or subsequent urban and rural masters has been studied systematically. Yet a careful reading of scattered, quantifiable data of all ethnic groups drawn to the Delaware Valley and beyond through the port of Philadelphia in conjunction with qualitative information from the city and the regional hinterland, including the Lehigh Valley, suggests strongly that indentured servitude as well as comparable informal arrangements were forms of labor that occurred in urban as well as rural contexts. The records capturing the procedures and practices concerning bound labor are more concentrated in Philadelphia and hence more often studied than those in the three original counties surrounding the port city and those counties that form the second tier of westward settlement.

26. Few masters and fewer servants commented directly and personally about their experiences with bound labor in letters, diaries, or memoirs. Much of what is known about the practices of indentured servitude comes from various kinds of administrative or financial records that reveal indirectly how masters and servants fared in their respective arrangements. The advertisements in newspapers for runaway servants speak to a particular subset of indentured servants and the court records that detail breaches of those contracts provide insights into the breakdown of this system – a baseline of extremes that allows for some extrapolation of what reasonable and customary practices must have been. Susan E. Klepp, Farley Grubb, and Anne Pfaelzer de Ortiz, eds., *Souls for Sale: Two German Redemptioners Come to Revolutionary America. The Life Stories of John Frederick Whitehead and Johann Carl Büttner* (University Park: Pennsylvania State University Press, 2006), contain rare first-person accounts of the experiences of two German-speaking immigrant men who served masters in Berks County, Pennsylvania, and in New Jersey, respectively, as servants for a set period of time.

27. Galenson, *White Servitude*; James Horn, "Servant Emigration to the Chesapeake in the Seventeenth Century," in *The Chesapeake in the Seventeenth Century: Essays in Anglo-American Society*, ed. Thad W. Tate and David L. Ammerman (Chapel Hill: University of North Carolina Press, 1979).

28. Servitude in a variety of legal and customary forms was common in Britain, Ireland, and in German-speaking lands on the continent. The constant flow of servants to colonial America suggests that at least for a certain proportion of those laborers the prospect of freedom after service in America outweighed the harsh realities of dependence on a master in Europe or America. There is little comparative literature about servitude in Europe and America that would allow clear judgement about the relative aspects – negative or positive – of the respective systems of contract labor on both sides of the Atlantic.

29. Much of the evidence about how well or poorly the system worked is indirect and sporadic, based on impersonal administrative records such as lists of indentures, advertisements for runaway servants, court proceedings concerning disputed terms of indentures, and merchants' accounts rather than personal accounts like the tale of *The*

Infortunate: The Voyage and Adventures of William Moraley, an Indentured Servant, ed. Susan E. Klepp and Billy G. Smith (University Park: Pennsylvania State University Press, 1992) and Klepp, et al., eds., *Souls for Sale.* Sharon V. Salinger, *"To Serve Well and Faithfully": Labor and Indentured Servants in Pennsylvania, 1682-1800* (Cambridge: Cambridge University Press, 1987); Billy G. Smith, *The "Lower Sort": Philadelphia's Laboring People, 1750-1800* (Ithaca: Cornell University Press, 1990); and Richard Schlecht's portfolio of portraits of runaway indentured servants in Bailyn, *Voyagers,* 352-55, are three very different attempts to depict the life of indentured servants in colonial America. See also Michael V. Kennedy, "The Consequences of Cruelty: The Escalation of Servant and Slave Abuse, 1750-1780," *Essays in Economic and Business History* 22 (2004): 127-41.

30. Redemptioners are difficult to profile comprehensively and systematically from the surviving records, which are scattered, sparse, and incomplete. Information from Philadelphia ship lists, registers of indentures, and merchants' accounts form the basis for the following discussion.

31. Strassburger and Hinke, *Pennsylvania German Pioneers,* vol. 1: *Customhouse Notices in the Pennsylvania Gazette.*

32. Ran Abramitzky and Fabio Braggion, "Migration and Human Capital: Self-Selection of Indentured Servants to the Americas," *The Journal of Economic History* 66 (2006): 882-905, present a strictly economic argument for measuring how differences in the characteristics of indentured servants – as evident in the negotiated time of service and overseas destination – could impact development in particular colonies. This kind of argument is very narrowly defined and does not explore whether the thesis can be supported by evidence from additional sources. The nature of particular communication and trade networks, for example, may well affect the choices of overseas destinations, in addition to age, health, occupation, and so on. A very special case of the importance of those networks has recently been made for the migration from the North of Ireland in the last third of the eighteenth century, Stephen R. Royle and Caitríona Ní Laoire, "'Dare the boist'rous main': The Role of the *Belfast News Letter* in the Process of Emigration from Ulster to North America, 1760-1800," *The Canadian Geographer/Le Géograph Canadien* 50:1 (2006): 56-73.

33. There were numerous complaints about indentured servitude, but they were always about particular abuses or situations and not about the system as such. Henry Melchior Mühlenberg is a good example: he condemned the circumstances that forced parents to bind out their children to strangers and that pressed German immigrants into service with Englishmen, but he made use of the system and employed indentured servants in his own household. Kurt Aland, ed., *Die Korrespondenz Heinrich Melchior Mühlenbergs aus der Anfangszeit des deutschen Luthertums in Nordamerika,* 5 vols. (Berlin: Walter de Gruyter, 1986-96), 1:486, 3:334-36, 646, 410; W. J. Mann, B. M. Schmucker, and Wilhelm German, eds., *Nachrichten von den vereinigten Deutschen Evangelisch-Lutherischen Gemeinen in Nord-Amerika, absonderlich in Pennsylvanien,* 2 vols. (1787; reprint ed., Allentown, Pa., 1886; Philadelphia, 1895) [*Hallesche Nachrichten*], 416; see also Gottlieb Mittelberger, *Journey to Pennsylvania,* ed. and trans. Oscar Handlin and John Clive (Cambridge, Mass.: Harvard University Press, 1960), 18. By contrast, Baseler, *"Asylum for Mankind,"* makes the argument that opposition to immigrants deemed unsuitable for integration into American society was general and widespread in revolutionary America.

34. For details, see Wokeck, *Trade in Strangers*, 137-65.

35. See, for example, the accounts kept by Thomas Penrose in his cashbooks (Thomas Penrose Journals, 1738-51, HSP).

36. The well-known account of a German immigrant voyage by Gottlieb Mittelberger cast a negative image of the shippers of human cargo at the peak of German immigration to the American colonies. The discussions about the regulation of the German immigrant trade in the Pennsylvania Assembly present another, more complex view of the interests of the merchants involved in that business. Mittelberger, *Journey*; Sally Schwartz, *"A Mixed Multitude": The Struggle for Toleration in Colonial Pennsylvania* (New York: New York University Press, 1987), 101-3, 193-96; Craig W. Horle, Joseph S. Foster, and Jeffrey L. Scheib, eds., *Lawmaking and Legislators in Pennsylvania: A Biographical Dictionary*, vol. 2: 1710-1756 (Philadelphia: University of Pennsylvania Press, 1997), 50-51.

37. Of the names of masters who appear repeatedly in the surviving lists of indentures, some acquired indentured servants for their own use such as the operation of forges; others, who had smaller businesses – taverns, for instance – acted as middlemen for prospective masters among their regular clients. "Record of Indentures of Individuals Bound Out as Apprentices, Servants etc., and of Germans and Other Redemptioners in the Office of the City of Philadelphia, 1 Oct. 1771 to 5 Oct. 1773," City Archives of Philadelphia; "Record of Indentures of Individuals Bound Out as Apprentices, Servants etc. in Philadelphia, Penna., by Mayor John Gibson, 5 Dec. 1772-21 May 1772, and Mayor William Fisher, 1773," HSP; "Servants and Apprentices Bound and Assigned Before James Hamilton Mayor of Philadelphia, 1745 and 1746," HSP.

38. This is evident from merchants' accounts which list the form of payment they received for squaring the accounts of indebted immigrants. The best example is the "Munster [sic] Book" of the ship *Britannia* [1773], HSP.

39. This hierarchy of preferences by Delaware Valley masters emerges from comparing ship lists with lists of indentures.

40. The strategies for meeting the necessary labor demands for forges are detailed in John Bezis-Selfa, "Forming a New Order: Slavery, Free Labor, and Sectional Differentiation in the Mid-Atlantic Charcoal Iron Industry, 1715-1840" (PhD diss., University of Pennsylvania, 1995); for Caspar Wistar's solutions for staffing his glassworks, see Beiler, "Caspar Wistar," chap. 6.

41. When George Washington tried to improve his western landholdings, he inquired into the feasibility of obtaining German settlers. "James Tilghman Jr. to George Washington, Philadelphia, 7 Apr. 1774," Washington Papers, Library of Congress Manuscript Division (microfilm).

42. For the brief period of time in the early 1770s, when ship lists and lists of indentures provide sufficient information, the ease with which immigrant boys and girls found masters – and mistresses – underscores the general need for teenaged help for the highly sex-segregated tasks common in the households of farmers and artisans.

43. From the diverse lists of indentures it is evident that more often than not German-speaking masters employed German immigrants; similarly, masters with Irish connections usually acquired newcomers from Ireland.

44. There is some evidence that immigrant journeymen carried certificates from their European master. Some such reports of former employment have survived (Society Miscellaneous Collection: Redemptioners, HSP).

45. For details, see Marianne S. Wokeck, "Servant Migration and the Transfer of Culture from the Old World to the New," *International Seminar of the History of the Atlantic World*, Harvard University, Cambridge, Mass., 1996.

46. Advertisements for runaway servants provide the broadest insight into the strains of the system. See, for example, Bailyn, "Voyagers in Flight: A Sketchbook of Runaway Servants, 1774-1775," in *Voyagers*, 352-53; Daniel Meaders, *Eighteenth-Century White Slaves: Fugitive Notices*, vol. 1: *Pennsylvania, 1729-1760* (Westport, Conn.: Greenwood Press, 1993); Farley Ward Grubb, *Runaway Servants, Convicts, and Apprentices Advertised in the Pennsylvania Gazette, 1728-1796* (Baltimore: Genealogical Pub. Co., 1992).

47. No systematic account exists of complaints that masters and servants pursued in Pennsylvania courts.

48. "List of Servants Belonging to the Inhabitants of Pennsylvania and Taken in to His Majesty's Service, for Whom Satisfaction Has not Been Made by the Officers According to the Act of Parliament" (21 Apr. 1757), HSP.

49. There is little evidence of indentured servitude among second-generation immigrants.

50. Billy G. Smith, *"Lower Sort,"* and Sharon V. Salinger, *"To Serve Well,"* demonstrate the difficulties poorer residents faced as the eighteenth century progressed.

51. This practice is evident from comparing ship lists, merchants' accounts, and lists of indentures. For details, see Wokeck, *Trade in Strangers*, chap. 4; also, Bailyn, *Voyagers*, chap. 10.

52. Historians generally agree that conditions of servitude were often harsh and difficult and that servants had only limited prospects for upward mobility. From a perspective informed by late-twentieth-century sensibilities it is especially easy to see the hardships commonly linked with bound labor; yet the resiliency of the system suggests that immigrants and settlers in the Delaware Valley were willing to accept those problems.

53. Some colonists instructed their emigrating friends about the resale value of particular household goods, which suggests one way in which established settlers could assist newcomers in squaring their accounts with the merchant who provided them with transatlantic passage: the proceeds from the sale of knives and cloth – imported duty-free as part of the immigrants' baggage – went toward the payment of fare debts. For details, see Wokeck, *Trade in Strangers*, chap. 4.

54. Anecdotal evidence from immigrants' letters home suggests that newcomers expected assistance from compatriots. Leo Schelbert and Hedwig Rappolt, eds., *Alles ist ganz anders hier: Auswandererschicksale in Briefen aus zwei Jahrhunderten* (Freiburg i. Br.: Walter-Verlag, 1977).

55. This phrasing occurred in the earliest advertisements about German redemptioners in the *American Weekly Mercury* (1718) and often thereafter in other newspapers (see especially the *Pennsylvania Gazette*).

56. Walsh, "Peopling, Producing, and Consuming," 142-44, points to the important relationship between issues of demography and migration and patterns of consumption and demand.

Pennsylvania: "Hell for Preachers"?: Religion and the German Colonists

Michael G. Baylor

GERMAN SETTLERS IN COLONIAL PENNSYLVANIA were what Peter Burke calls "cultural amphibians" – people capable of operating in several different cultural environments.[1] Residents of a frontier region, they were in contact with Native Americans and Amerindian culture, and at least some early German observers noticed the baleful effect that contact with Europeans had on Indian culture.[2] For many legal and commercial purposes Germans also entered a British and Anglophone cultural world. English was the language of courts and markets in Pennsylvania, and Germans had to come to terms with this. Yet they also staunchly maintained their own German cultural identity, especially with respect to their domestic life, education, and churches.[3] These linked dimensions of their lives make it meaningful to examine the European origins of a specifically German religious culture in colonial Pennsylvania. For the most part, German immigrants transferred to the new world a complex religious culture formed in Europe. They transferred it, however, to a very different ecclesiastical environment.

The title of this paper comes from Gottlieb Mittelberger, a Lutheran schoolteacher and church organist from the small Swabian town of Enzweihingen in the duchy of Württemberg, who between 1750 and 1754 traveled to and lived in Pennsylvania. Mittelberger subsequently wrote an extensive report about his stay in the colony. He recognized the cultural intermixing that was occurring there and described Pennsylvania as "a peculiar mixture of the European and the American environment, of the customs of the Old and the New World."[4] Mittelberger wrote specifically to warn fellow Germans *against* emigrating to Pennsylvania and joining this multicultural world. On his title page Mittelberger announced that this book was an account "of the sad and unfortunate circumstances of most of the Germans who have moved to that country or are about to do so."[5] Such a move, he admonished, "will mean for most who undertake it the loss of all they possess, of freedom and peace, and for some the loss of their very lives, and I can even go so far as to say, of the salvation of their souls."[6] Despite his gloomy purpose, Mittelberger's account provides us with one of our most detailed descriptions of the life of German colonists in mid-eighteenth-century Pennsylvania.

PENNSYLVANIA: "HELL FOR PREACHERS"?

In his report, Mittelberger tells us that the following saying was current when he lived in the colony: "Pennsylvania is heaven for farmers, paradise for mechanics [i.e., artisans], and hell for officials and preachers" (*Pennsylvania ist der Bauern ihr Himmel, der Handwerksleute ihr Paradies, der Beamten und Prediger ihre Hölle*).[7] Only the final part of this piece of folk wisdom will be examined here – was colonial Pennsylvania really a hellish place for preachers? As we will see, from Mittelberger's standpoint, officials and preachers were not fully distinct from one another. But what could this "hell for preachers" mean, especially given the common image of the Pennsylvania Germans as embracing almost every variety of religion? One might imagine the place as presenting preachers with a rich field of opportunity.

Before taking up this question, the broader theme of the extent, tempo, and character of the migration of German-speaking colonists to Pennsylvania will be briefly considered. Then the paper examines the European background of the religious life of these colonists, especially as it manifested itself in both irreligion and a profusion of churches and sects. The general contention of this study is that at least in relation to the European religious context from which the German colonists came, there was good reason indeed for viewing the situation in Penn's Woods as a kind of clerical inferno.

The key to Mittelberger's negative assessment of clerical opportunities in Pennsylvania is to be found in the state-supported and politically privileged position enjoyed by the clergy in the princely states of Germany. The paper analyzes the difficult situation that the clergy in Pennsylvania faced in comparison to the Holy Roman Empire. However, for certain religious groups – those commonly described as sectarians – the situation in America clearly provided a new, positive opportunity. The final part of the paper briefly examines the comparative development of four key German religious groups who broke away from the European state churches – the Mennonites, the Schwenckfelders, the Brethren, and the Moravians.

The German Immigrants to Pennsylvania

Mittelberger described both the Germans who came over with him on the *Osgood* in 1750 and those who arrived while he was living in Pennsylvania as Palatines, Württembergers, Durlachers, and Swiss.[8] Modern studies confirm that the great majority of German colonists came from the southwestern part of the Holy Roman Empire, especially the upper Rhine and Neckar valleys, and the adjacent German-speaking cantons of Switzerland.[9] This region was both politically fragmented and religiously diverse. The largest principalities were the electorate of the Rhenish Palatinate, the duchy of Württemberg, and the margravate of Baden-Durlach, but there were numerous other smaller principalities and free imperial cities in the region as well. In this part of the empire, the religious environment was especially complex; in close proximity to one another were Roman Catholics, Lutherans (or Evangelicals), and Calvinists (or Reformed), as well as a variety of dissenting groups.

Gottlieb Mittelbergers
Reise
nach
Pennsylvanien
im Jahr 1750.
und
Rükreise nach Teutschland
im Jahr 1754.
Enthaltend
nicht nur eine Beschreibung des Landes nach seinem gegenwärtigen Zustande, sondern auch eine ausführliche Nachricht von den unglükseligen und betrübten Umständen der meisten Teutschen, die in dieses Land gezogen sind, und dahin ziehen.

Stuttgard,
gedrukt bey Gottlieb Friderich Jenisch. 1756.

Title page of Gottlieb Mittelberger's *Journey to Pennsylvania in the Year 1750 and Return to Germany in the Year 1754*.

Rare Books Division, The New York Public Library,
Astor, Lenox and Tilden Foundations.

Germans began to move into Pennsylvania in the late seventeenth century, but their number rose rapidly only from the 1730s, and reached a high point in the 1750s, after which the numbers fluctuate considerably, with other high points in the mid-1760s and early 1770s.[10] Modern studies suggest that somewhere around 100,000 Germans came to the British colonies during the colonial period.[11]

In fact, Germans constituted the largest group of non-British, European immigrants who arrived in North America during the eighteenth century.[12] In Pennsylvania, Germans constituted an especially impressive portion of the total population. Pennsylvanians of German ancestry accounted for 50 to 60 percent of the colony's European population in 1760, and a third of the population in 1790.[13] In the Lehigh Valley, during the first third of the eighteenth century, individual German settler families moved into the region after scattered Dutch, English, and Scots-Irish pioneers opened it to European habitation. They established farms, mills, shops, and stores. In the 1730s, especially after the 1737 "Walking Purchase," German settlers came in larger numbers. After the failure of their mission in Georgia, Moravians moved to Nazareth in 1740 and to Bethlehem in 1741.

From 1727 on, passenger lists of Germans arriving at Philadelphia have survived, and these provide the basis for some analysis of the social composition of the immigrants.[14] When compared with those arriving from England, several important differences gave the Germans a distinctive social profile. In the first place, German immigration was significantly more family oriented than was English. Single adults comprised about 90 percent of English immigrants in the 1770s, nearly twice the German percentage (47 percent). Not surprisingly, Germans also tended to be older – over 30 percent were above the age of 30, twice the rate among English immigrants. German colonists were also more literate. From 1727 to 1775, male immigrants above the age of 15 were required to sign loyalty oaths. Despite many methodological problems, historians commonly use signatures to derive literacy rates. Doing so suggests that the literacy rate of German immigrants rose over the eighteenth century from 60 percent in the 1730s, to 70 percent in the early 1750s, to 80 percent after 1760. These rates largely explain the proliferation of German-language printers and printed materials in colonial Pennsylvania; in terms of readership, the demand was there.

Roughly half of all German immigrants entered servitude on their arrival in Pennsylvania.[15] Gottlieb Mittelberger was especially appalled by the working of an immigration system in which recruiting agents called Newlanders (*Neuländer*) traveled the Rhine and Neckar valleys recruiting potential colonists, then passed them on to Dutch merchants in Rotterdam. These merchants convinced immigrants to pay the price of their passage by working for those who redeemed the cost of their voyage once they arrived in the New World. The upshot was that German colonists commonly lacked the specific terms of the indenture contract that was common for English immigrants. Instead, the labor of German colonists was auctioned off to whoever would pay the cost of their redemption, and the redemptioners themselves were helpless in fixing the terms of their service.[16] Mittelberger announced that "what really drove me to write this book was the sad and miserable condition" of the German colonists and "the irresponsible and merciless proceedings of the Dutch traders in human beings and their man-stealing emissaries – I mean the so-called Newlanders."[17] He was particularly appalled that families were sometimes split up as they entered servitude in America.[18]

Churches and the Clergy in the Holy Roman Empire – and in Pennsylvania

The question of the immigrants' motives is one that has much exercised historians, and it permits no easy resolution. The classic question has been that of motivational "push" vs. "pull" – that is, were colonists motivated by factors constraining subsistence that pressured them to leave Germany, especially the considerable demographic growth of the early eighteenth century and its resulting economic difficulties, or were they lured by the opportunities for a better life in the new world?[19] There is no evident way of resolving the question as to whether these were "subsistence" or "betterment" migrations. Similarly incapable of clear resolution is the issue of whether colonists came for so-called "religious" or "secular" motives. In some cases, of course, religious groups came to Pennsylvania for reasons we can readily identify as religious. But it is too simple to ascribe to all others, especially the many families who arrived independently of a religious group, simply secular motives. This point becomes evident when one considers the nature of religious and ecclesiastical life in the Holy Roman Empire and why, by contrast, Gottlieb Mittelberger regarded Pennsylvania as a "hell for preachers."

The basic framework of religious life in the empire was complicated. Its defining parameters were the result of a series of wars, both confessional and political, that were waged in the sixteenth and seventeenth centuries and the terms of the compromise peace agreements that settled these conflicts. The most important of these agreements was the Peace of Westphalia (1648), which ended the Thirty Years' War. Under the terms of this treaty only three Christian denominations had legal status in the Empire; these were the Evangelical (or Lutheran) church, the Reformed (or Calvinist) church, and the Roman Catholic church.[20] More specifically, the treaty gave to each of the roughly 300 territorial princes of the empire the so-called "right of reformation" (*jus reformandi*), that is, the right to regulate all manifestations of religion in the public life of the community. In effect, the princes of Germany had the right to choose one of the three denominations as the confession of their principality's established church. The notion was that there would be limited religious pluralism in the empire as a whole – but not within an individual principality, where one and only one of the three would function as the established church.

The Peace of Westphalia thus gave the princes control of public religious life, a situation sometimes expressed by the maxim *cuius regio, eius religio*, that is, the religion of the ruler is the religion of the state. But the treaty also recognized the principles of "freedom of conscience" and the right to "private" religious practice.[21] In theory, worship at home and such domestic devotions as family prayers, bible reading, and perhaps hiring a private tutor, were outside the control of the princely state and the established church; freedom of conscience was defined as the right to live according to one's faith and not to be compelled to participate in the devotions of another church. But such guarantees frequently proved difficult to enforce. Above all, the state churches remained deeply suspicious of any form of organized religiosity that escaped their control.

In practice, the religious life of the empire was a strange blend of toleration and intolerance. Many of the free imperial cities, especially, tolerated religious diversity and some were required by imperial law to maintain it. Some princes also had a reputation for religious tolerance. The problem was that minority religious groups – Protestants in Catholic states, Catholics in Protestant states, Jews and various Christian sectarian groupings anywhere – had no protection in imperial law. Individual cities or princes might informally tolerate them, even issue charters that formally granted privileges and rights. But what was granted could also be withdrawn or curtailed at the personal whim of a ruler, or through a dynastic change or a shift in the balance of an elected town council. The general insecurity faced by all religious minorities in the empire has an important implication: it is impossible to confine the religious motivation of German colonists simply to those who came in organized sectarian groups. Individual dissenters of all types also had reason to leave for a more tolerant environment.

Another aspect of religious motivation takes us back to Gottlieb Mittelberger. Recently, historians of early modern Germany have been much interested in the phenomenon of "confessionalization," a cumbersome term for a process that transformed German society between the middle of the sixteenth and the middle of the eighteenth century.[22] There are basically three interrelated components to confessionalization. In the first place, it meant the formation of subjects who had a clear sense of confessional identity and denominational loyalty – whether as Lutherans, Calvinists, or Roman Catholics. It was the task of the official church of the principality to impart this sense of confessional identity. It did so by recruiting, training, ordaining, and supervising a clergy who ministered to the population; by formulating a creed that defined the confession and that was taught to the populace; and by establishing and operating ecclesiastical institutions whose rituals, schools, sermons, and cultural activities would produce Christians with a strong sense of denominational identity. Secondly, confessionalization was closely bound up with a new social discipline that early modern states and churches imposed on their subjects. This social discipline concerned especially marital and sexual matters – outlawing marriages that lacked parental consent or ecclesiastical ceremony and punishing fornication – but it also included such issues as appropriate recreational activities and the imposition of a new work ethic and systems of poor relief. Thirdly, both social discipline and confessional identity were components of an underlying political process that is central to confessionalization – the consolidation of power by the territorial state in Germany. The churches were, in the last analysis, branches of the state and they worked to enhance the power of the princes.

The negative side of all this, from the standpoint of many subjects, were three official churches which, despite the conflicts of the Reformation, resembled each other in fundamental ways. Above all they all lacked spiritual vitality – they were consumed in stultifying dogmatic definitions and wrangles (this is the so-called "age of orthodoxy" in Protestant theology); they engaged in repressive and coercive activities of various kinds; and their social teachings stressed obedience, conformity, and political passivity. The clergy of these churches constituted a privileged strata of state servants, and it is no wonder that anticlericalism is an important theme in early modern German popular culture. The Pennsylvania immigrants whose dislike of this religious environment contributed to their decision to leave Germany, like the sectarians or dissenters who faced persecution in their homeland, were migrating for religious motives.

And, on the other side of the Atlantic, it is no wonder that Gottlieb Mittelberger, writing from a state-church standpoint, should bemoan the life of the Pennsylvania clergy as a kind of hell. Like Dante's inferno, there were in fact several "circles" to Mittelberger's hell. In the first place, of course, preachers in the colony did not have the backing of a state church and they themselves could not function as ministers who were simultaneously agents of the state. From the outset of his plans for Pennsylvania, William Penn envisioned, in the famous phrase, a "holy experiment," a society that would attain Christian moral and devotional perfection but without the coercive apparatus of an established church. Although the Pennsylvania oath for political office required a commitment to Christianity, the colony had no official church.[23] Hence preachers lacked the political authority they possessed in Germany. "Throughout Pennsylvania," Mittelberger wrote, "the preachers do not have the power to punish anyone, or to force anyone to go to church."[24] How radically different from the situation in most parts of Germany! There the clergy had the authority, backed by the state, to tell people what to believe, to compel attendance at religious services, and to punish the recalcitrant.

After the clergy's political impotence, the second level of Mittelberger's hell was its economic insecurity, the consequence of the clergy in Pennsylvania lacking the guaranteed economic support they had in Germany as salaried officials of a state church, one which was financed by tithe payments that were as legally compulsory as any other form of taxation. The result, as Mittelberger put it, was this: "In Pennsylvania preachers receive no salary or tithes.... Most preachers are engaged for the year, like cowherds in Germany; and when anyone fails to please his congregation, he is given notice and must put up with it."[25] The notion that the minister should be economically dependent on the will of the congregation was alien and disheartening. Mittelberger's conclusion was stark: "I myself would therefore rather be the humblest cowherd at home than be a preacher in Pennsylvania."[26]

A third level to Mittelberger's hell concerned the clergy's own lack of internal organization, discipline, and strength. As he put it, "Nor can they [clerics] give orders to each other, there being no consistory to impose discipline among them."[27] That is, the clergy in Pennsylvania lacked an authoritative institution to regulate their affairs. Down to the 1740s, the Protestant state churches of the Holy Roman Empire saw no reason to invest anything substantial in the development of ecclesiastical institutions in Pennsylvania. The result was that literally a handful of preachers, without institutional support, attempted to minister to a widely scattered and rapidly growing population. As late as 1741 there were in the Middle Colonies only four effective, ordained ministers of the Reformed church serving over fifteen thousand settlers, and only three capable Lutheran pastors.[28] To make matters worse – and, again, radically different from Germany – there was nothing to prevent a variety of what the ordained clergy viewed as clerical rascals and imposters from freely operating in the colony.

Just at the time Mittelberger was complaining about the miserable situation of the clergy, however, an important transformation was taking place. From the 1740s on, both the Lutheran and Reformed churches embarked on major campaigns to establish themselves in Pennsylvania. An important motive was Lutheran and Calvinist churches' fear that the German settlers would fall prey to the sectarian groups that were establishing themselves at the same time. In 1742, the Lutheran church, through its Halle Missionary Society, dispatched Heinrich Melchior Muhlenberg to Pennsylvania.[29] He was an extremely talented minister and ecclesiastical organizer. A few years later, in 1746, the Reformed church in Amsterdam sent a Swiss pastor, Michael Schlatter, to minister to German Calvinists. Schlatter, too, worked zealously to build up an effective ecclesiastical organization. Muhlenberg and Schlatter are usually credited as the effective founders, respectively, of the German Lutheran and German Reformed churches in Pennsylvania. Both built on the sense of confessional identity that many colonists brought with them to Pennsylvania. In the Lehigh Valley, already by 1739 a Reformed service was held on Saucon Creek.

Mittelberger, however, remained doubtful about the prospects for churches in the colony. For there was a fourth circle to his clerical hell, the deepest *bolgia* at the center of the inferno: the character of the laity to whom the clergy ministered. Mittelberger described the German settlers, generally, as filled with crude anticlericalism, materialistic irreligion, and divisive sectarianism. He wrote that many colonists were uninterested in the most fundamental beliefs of Christianity and given over to a primitive naturalism: "there are many hundreds of adult persons who not only are unbaptized, but who do not even want baptism ....Many others pay no attention to the sacraments and to the Holy Bible, or even to God and His Word. Some...think that everything visible is of merely natural origin."[30] Mittelberger was not alone in voicing dismay at the lack of interest in religion among many German colonists. According to the Moravian bishop, Augustus Gottlieb Spangenberg, many thousands of the settlers farming the Perkiomen Valley cared little about religion. As Spangenberg put it, "it has become proverbial to say of a man who does not care about God and his Word: he had the Pennsylvania religion."[31] Or Muhlenberg himself, to take another example, reported that when a poor preacher attempted to borrow money from a rich farmer in Oley Township, the farmer pointed to his manure pile and said, "There is my God; he gives me wheat and everything I need."[32]

Of course, when clerics appealed for support, it was in their own interest to magnify the need for their work and the challenges they confronted. And it certainly served Mittelberger's literary purpose to present a picture in which the primitive conditions of the wilderness led many German settlers to lose their faith. For him, the excessive freedom of the frontier corrupted refined spirituality. "Such outrageous coarseness and rudeness," he wrote about the irreligion he observed, "result from the excessive freedom in the country.... Liberty in Pennsylvania does more harm than good to many people, both in soul and in body."[33]

What Mittelberger and the others seem not to have considered is the extent to which the apparent irreligion of many German colonists was simply a reaction to the ecclesiastical situation in the Holy Roman Empire with its confessionalizing state churches. Given the oppressive religious environment from which they came, many colonists did not want to have anything to do with churches. They took advantage of an environment in which they had the liberty to repudiate their confessional identity and to express their distaste for a clergy that attempted to reestablish it. Spangenberg's "Pennsylvania religion" and Mittelberger's "hell for preachers" may have been less the result of religious decay and breakdown in a frontier environment than it was the result of emigrants fleeing the state churches of the Empire.[34]

The Sectarians

For other Germans, the religious motivation for journeying to Pennsylvania, while it might include a negative desire to avoid the state churches, was also much more positive. This was the case for the many sectarians who came for a variety of motives. For some, penalization by state churches was coupled with a positive desire to lead a perfect Christian life on different social foundations than existed in Germany. For others, the move was linked to eschatological beliefs about the coming end of the old European world and the dawn of the millennium in the New World. And for still others, the move was part of an evangelical missionary program. Because these sects were often opposed to any government that claimed power over them and at odds with the society which surrounded them, they have made an important contribution both to the social diversity of America and to its tradition of political radicalism.

The migration process that brought the German sectarians to Pennsylvania was different from that of the majority of German settlers. In the first place, the sectarians came earlier than most of the other colonists. As a result of William Penn's missionary trip to the empire in 1677 and his advertising campaign there to promote his colony, Mennonites were the first to arrive in 1683.[35] By 1718 a small group of "Mennonite Baptists" had settled in Saucon Valley. Other groups continued to come throughout the colonial period, but the principal German sectarians were all established by the early 1740s. Secondly, except at the very beginning, the sectarians remained a small minority among the German colonists. If something like a hundred thousand Germans came to the colonies in the eighteenth century, the total of the sectarians was perhaps between three and five-and-a-half thousand, in any case well less than ten percent of the total.[36] Thirdly, the sectarians came not just in individual families but in larger groups and collectives. This meant that they normally had at their disposal the economic resources of a much larger support network than most Germans could call upon, thus avoiding the redemptioner system. At various times during the eighteenth century, for example, the Moravians operated four different ships bringing colonists from Europe to Pennsylvania.[37] And because they settled near one another in distinct enclaves, the sectarians often exerted an influence greater than their numbers alone might suggest.[38] In less than a decade after 1740, the Moravians had established five settlements in the Barony of Nazareth.

Of Pennsylvania, Mittelberger wrote, "it offers people more freedom than the other English colonies, inasmuch as all religious sects are tolerated there." He attempted to enumerate the religious groupings one might encounter in the colony as follows: "Lutherans, members of the Reformed Church, Catholics, Quakers, Mennonites or Anabaptists, Herrnhuters or Moravian Brothers, Pietists, Seventh-Day Adventists, Dunkers, Presbyterians, Newborn, Freemasons, Separatists, Freethinkers, Jews, Mohammedans, Pagans, Negroes and Indians."[39] The trajectory of his list was perhaps predictable. It moved from the state churches of the Holy Roman Empire, through a variety of German and English sectarian groupings, to non-Christian religious and ethnic groups. There were still other specifically German sects that Mittelberger completely omitted – Amish, Labadists, Boehmists, Schwenckfelders, and so on. What emerges is a picture of bewildering diversity and complexity. How are we to make any sense at all of this welter of contending groups?

The history of sect formation in the Holy Roman Empire during the early modern period is complex, extended over time, and precludes such sweeping interpretations of sectarianism as those that ascribe it either to a generic pietism or to the effect of endemic poverty.[40] The larger and more stable sects, accounting for the vast majority of German immigrants who came as members of a religious group, were the product of two specific and quite different periods in the history of German Protestantism. That is, some of the sects, notably the Mennonites (including the Amish Mennonites) and the Schwenckfelders, stemmed from the early years of the Reformation in the sixteenth century and from the radical Protestant tradition usually described as Anabaptism. Others, by contrast, especially the Dunkers (or Brethren) and the Moravians, did grow out of the pietist movement of the late seventeenth century, and may accurately be described as "radical Pietists." These four, taken together, constituted well over ninety percent of the German sectarians who came to Pennsylvania.[41]

How did both the Anabaptism of the early Reformation and the pietism of the late seventeenth century come to generate the major sectarian groups? These two religious movements bracket the age of confessionalization. Anabaptism presented a radical alternative to the set of political and ecclesiastical arrangements that, in fact, developed in the Holy Roman Empire. Pietism was an effort to reform the religious life that resulted from these arrangements.

Recent studies of the early Reformation in Germany emphasize both its religious diversity and its social breadth. In the 1520s a powerful wave of popular evangelicalism swept German society and rapidly absorbed secular complaints as communities large and small sought to transform their lives according to the

Word of God. The central event of this social upheaval was the great Peasants' War of 1525, a popular insurrection that because of both its size and its failure may truly be described as "titanic." The Peasants' War was, in effect, the social and political expression of a massive popular reformation – and ultimately the turning point on which this reformation failed.[42]

The most burning issue of the early Reformation was this: having overthrown traditional papal and episcopal authority, who had the right to regulate religious and ecclesiastical affairs? Over this issue, various "radical" reformers separated from "magisterial" reformers, such as Martin Luther and Huldrych Zwingli, who insisted that only magistrates (i.e., the existing secular authorities) had the right to regulate religious life. The most common feature of the radical reformers was their rejection of the subordination of the Christian life to the existing secular authorities. They insisted that any Christian congregation or community had the right to regulate itself. Further, they held that, should rulers command something that violated Christian principles, it should be ignored. In the face of repression, some radicals adopted a strategy of passive resistance, others argued that rulers who behaved in un-Christian and tyrannical ways should be overthrown, violently if necessary.[43]

The issue of the legitimacy of violence in resisting oppressive secular authority was central to divisions within the radical Reformation. In the aftermath of the failed Peasants' War, the victorious princes and urban magistrates labeled the radicals "Anabaptists," rebaptizers, and began a ferocious persecution of those charged with this offense, a capital crime which was simultaneously civil and ecclesiastical. In the face of this persecution, the strategy of the surviving radical groups shifted. Most either went underground, organizing themselves into secret and quietistic "conventicles" or hidden groupings, or they attached themselves to a protector, a tolerant city or prince, who would allow them a public existence.

The Mennonites and the Schwenckfelders were the crystalized remnant of the early radical Reformation. In both cases, the price of survival was metamorphosis to more moderate forms. The Mennonites were named after Menno Simons, originally a priest from Friesland, who picked up the pieces of the Anabaptist movement in the lower Rhine valley and the Netherlands after the final major episode of Anabapist revolutionary violence in 1535.[44] Later, his variety of pacifistic Anabaptism spread from the Netherlands and Lower Rhine across the north German plains, and up the Rhine valley to the German-speaking cantons of Switzerland. Mennonites and their later derivatives, the Amish, were the first German sectarians to arrive in Pennsylvania.

The Schwenckfelders were the followers of the Silesian nobleman and mystical spiritualist Caspar Schwenckfeld von Ossig, an educated layman and onetime follower of Luther.[45] In the early 1520s Schwenckfeld broke with Luther. The odd thing about Schwenckfeld is that, as a consistent spiritualist, he laid little emphasis on the sacraments and was little interested in organizing a church of any kind. Circles of his followers nevertheless developed as a series of congregations in both Silesia and Württemberg. A combination of severe persecution and loose organization depleted their numbers. In 1734 practically the whole Schwenckfelder group, numbering only 250, came to Pennsylvania.[46]

Despite their differences, both the Mennonites and the Schwenckfelders had their origins in the turmoil and upheaval of the early Reformation. Certain of their beliefs reflected the Anabaptist view that the secular authorities and their churches were a perversion of true Christian society. Nowhere was this more evident than in Mennonite and Schwenckfelder teachings about violence. For sixteenth-century Christians, the state was defined in terms of coercive power, and "the sword" was a synonym for the state itself. The pacifism of both Mennonites and Schwenckfelders was a symbol of their absolute rejection of the prevailing political order.[47] By the late seventeenth century, however, both groups sought little more than to be left alone – that is, to be allowed to practice the Christian life as they understood it, without interference from the political authorities. In this sense, although the oldest and originally most radical of German Protestant sects, these Anabaptists had become quiescent and accommodating, respectable nonconformists.

At their outset, Mennonite and Schwenckfelders had not wanted to form separate gathered churches. They adopted the ideal of a gathered church, because they were persecuted.[48] The same is true of the sectarians who derived from the pietist movement of the late seventeenth century – the Dunkers (or Brethren) and the Moravians. Both were reluctant, unwilling separatists, who were finally forced out of official state churches of the Holy Roman Empire – the Reformed church in the case of the Brethren, and the Lutheran church in the case of the Moravians. Indeed, the Moravians remained formally identified with the Lutheran confession in the Empire and only emerged as a separate denomination elsewhere. Because they were also the products of a much more recent and vital wave of revivalism, the pietistic sects were also much more dynamic and innovative than the Anabaptist groups. Radical pietists were animated by apocalyptic fears, by ecumenical and missionary energies, and by an interest in experimenting with new forms of social organization. For the Anabaptist groups, all this lay in the past.

The broader revival movement of German pietism that generated both the Brethren and the Moravians is – like English Puritanism – one that historians have endlessly debated.[49] Like Puritanism, pietism's pervasive influence makes it difficult to interpret. But whatever else it was, pietism was a reaction against what had happened to the territorial churches in the age of confessionalization. Pietism was generally more politically conservative than Anabaptism, without its revolutionary beginnings. Instead, most German pietists accepted the existing state churches and sought to revitalize them. In their view, the churches had lost contact with important dimensions of Christian experience. From their approach to this experience, one can gather where they found fault.

Two features of pietism stand out. First, pietists called for moral and social reform. They were disappointed by what they saw as a lack of moral seriousness in the state churches. They were especially discontent with the way that the territorial churches carried out their charitable function in society. Probably the single most influential pietist institution was the large orphanage and school established in the 1690s at Halle, one of pietism's key centers. Second, pietism was uninterested in formal theology or doctrinal precision. Indeed, pietism was a reaction against the sterile theological bickering that had gone on within the state churches for a hundred years. Instead of the rational side of faith, pietists stressed its emotional side – faith as a sentimental experience (using "sentiment" here in its eighteenth-century sense, referring to the whole affective and voluntary dimension of human nature). For pietists, the emotional experience of a "new birth" or an "awakening" became an initiation rite and an identification badge.[50]

The strategy of pietism was to work for change from within. This meant developing what pietists commonly referred to as an *ecclesiola in ecclesia*, a little church inside the state church. Devout activists and the morally earnest would come together within the fold of the official church and organize themselves as a new agency to transform the larger whole. By tradition, the birth of pietism is ascribed to Philipp Jakob Spener, a Lutheran minister at Frankfurt, who in 1670 organized what he called a *collegium pietatis*, a "school of piety," a discussion and devotional circle within the city's Lutheran church. The practice of establishing similar pietistic groupings quickly spread to other cities and other churches, Reformed as well as Lutheran. Rulers reacted to pietism in various ways. Some princes accepted it and incorporated pietist reforms into their state churches (e.g., Prussia).[51] Other princes saw the "little church" as a dangerous challenge to their authority and a violation of their exclusive right to organize public religious life. Both the Brethren and the Moravians sprang from state churches that refused to accept the activities of pietist groups.

The Brethren began in the early eighteenth century in the Palatinate of the Rhine as a result of the preaching of an odd noble evangelist, Hochmann von Hochenau. Hochenau experienced an awakening while studying at Halle and thereafter devoted himself to a life of wandering evangelical preaching. In 1706, a group of his followers in the Palatinate found themselves in growing difficulty with the authorities of the electorate as they sought to spread the evangelical message. The Reformed consistory quickly condemned them and called in the secular authorities. The elector's council sentenced the pietists to hard labor on a diet of bread and water. "They will be kept at it," the decree sentencing them stated, "until they have learned better and again professed one of the three churches tolerated in the empire. This decree is to be distributed in the whole county [of the Palatinate] to the end that we may be rid of them."[52] A distinct sectarian group emerged only slowly, after repeated punishments. As was the case with the sixteenth-century Anabaptists who influenced them, the Brethren came to reject infant baptism and to practice adult or believer's baptism. This both severed their ties with the state churches and brought down further persecution.[53] By 1719, after a series of imprisonments, banishments, and separations, the Brethren had had enough of Europe and sought asylum in Pennsylvania. Their migration continued into the 1730s, and at the end of it, the Brethren, like the Schwenckfelders, had so completely migrated from Germany that not a single congregation remained. In America, as the Brethren grew and changed in the eighteenth and nineteenth centuries, they generated a series of utopian communities in Pennsylvania, Ohio, and Indiana.[54]

By contrast with the Brethren, the Moravians remained a presence in Europe as well as the founders of a far-flung missionary system that included settlements in Pennsylvania. The origins of the Moravian church go back to Count Nicholas Zinzendorf's decision in 1722 to open his estate at Berthelsdorf in Upper Silesia to groups of refugee pietists, sectarians, and other dissenters, including Schwenckfelders from Silesia and Protestants from Habsburg lands in Bohemia and Moravia. Zinzendorf himself was the offspring of a noble family strongly influenced by pietism and, like Hochenau, he studied at Halle – although Zinzendorf later had a falling out with the Halle pietists.[55] The dissenters and refugees on his estate founded a community, Herrnhut, which by 1727 had a population of three hundred.

In 1727 Herrnhut also reached a turning point. Political difficulties arose between Zinzendorf and the governments of both electoral Saxony and the Holy Roman Empire, especially over the issue of his accepting refugees from Habsburg territories. Initially, Zinzendorf had sought to keep the diverse and divided community at Herrnhut within the Lutheran church. But as political problems mounted, a rationale was worked out to justify a break. The historical justification was the notion of the so-called "hidden seed" – that among the refugees at Herrnhut were members of the Bohemian Brethren, the moderates among the followers of the late medieval Czech reformer, Jan Hus. Hence, the separation from the Lutheran church was actually the restoration of a still older church – a church that could in fact claim to be the Ur-Protestant church of Europe. Nor is it clear that what occurred was exactly a break – Zinzendorf continued to regard himself as an adherent of the Augsburg Confession and he came to Pennsylvania in 1741 as the pastor of a Lutheran church in Philadelphia. And the Renewed Unity of the Brethren, as the Moravians called their church, turned out in fact to be a strange amalgam of what the sociologist Ernst Troeltsch too simplistically divided into "church" and "sect" forms of ecclesiastical organization.[56]

Given the political threat the Moravians came under from both the Saxon and imperial governments, it was almost unavoidable that they would become a missionary church. At several times the survival of the group at Herrnhut was in doubt. By 1732, tensions between Zinzendorf and Saxony had escalated to the point where the Saxon government issued an edict ordering Zinzendorf's exile and the sale of his property. In that year a Saxon ecclesiastical commission also began formally investigating whether those at Herrnhut were practicing one of the three tolerated religions of the empire.[57] In the face of such threats, the Moravians adopted a twofold strategy: some would remain at Herrnhut, prepared to migrate if necessary; others would embark on a global campaign of missionary activity that would establish colonies in places like Pennsylvania, where greater tolerance prevailed.

When Zinzendorf came to Pennsylvania in 1741, he was interested in more than establishing Moravian communities oriented toward missionary work among Native Americans. He was also captivated by a Philadelphian dream of human harmony that, in retrospect, seems naive almost to the point of delusion. He was convinced he could overcome the multiplicity of religious divisions and create a single, unified ecclesiastical organization. Beginning in January 1742, Zinzendorf organized a series of synods to which he invited leaders of various religious groups. He hoped their differences could be resolved and they could all be united in what Zinzendorf called the "Pennsylvania Congregation of God in the Spirit."[58] As might be expected, in Pennsylvania this ecumenical project was a non-starter. Zinzendorf's dream foundered on the depth of the sense of confessional identity that prevailed among the diverse religious groups of Pennsylvania Germans.

Conclusion

By way of conclusion, let us return again briefly to Gottlieb Mittelberger. Naturally, Mittelberger was little interested in reporting accurately about the religious life of the sectarians. From his standpoint, they all illustrated the dangerous consequences of religious fanaticism. Of the sects, his narrative offers a brief description of only the Brethren spin-offs, the Seventh-Day Adventists at Ephrata, whom Mittelberger confused with the Moravians at Bethlehem.[59]

Like the irreligion that he felt characterized many German colonists, Mittelberger thought that their sectarianism, too, contributed to the "hell for preachers" in Pennsylvania. The sects generally reviled the learned and ordained clergy of the state churches. "In this country," Mittelberger wrote, "it is no rarity to find many totally unlearned men preaching in the open fields, for the sectarians say and believe that today's scholars are no longer apostles and have turned their learning into a trade."[60] The sectarians' charge that the ordained preachers were "false prophets" and "hireling parsons" was an old one, and Mittelberger wrote "it is difficult to be a conscientious minister, especially since one has to tolerate and suffer a great deal from so many hostile, and to some extent vile, sects."[61]

The odd thing about Mittelberger is that he collapsed into a single entity two features of the religious life of the German colonists that, from a modern perspective, seem sharply opposed – irreligion and sectarianism. For us, these stand at the opposite structural poles of secular materialism and pious credulity. But for Mittelberger they were almost synonymous. He wrote, for example, "Many [German colonists] pray neither in the morning nor in the evening, nor before or after meals. In the homes of such people are not to be found any devotional books, much less a Bible. It is possible to meet in one house, among one family, members of four or five or six different sects."[62] How odd is this linking of religious indifference and sectarianism! And Mittelberger was not alone in collapsing together irreligion and sectarianism as the two distinguishing features of the German colonists. A half-century before Mittelberger, Justus Falckner, another Lutheran observer, wrote of Pennsylvania: "there are Germans here, and perhaps the majority, who despise God's Word and all outward public order...(for the spirit of errors and sects has here erected for itself an asylum: *Spiritus einim errorum et Sectarum Asylum sibi hic constituit*)."[63]

Of course, the vast majority of Germans were neither materialists nor sectarians. What explains Mittelberger's and Falckner's peculiar melding is that, from the perspective of the state churches of the Holy Roman Empire, the twin evils of irreligion and sectarianism were the natural and evident products of an environment lacking a coercive state church.

Notes

1. Peter Burke, *Popular Culture in Early Modern Europe* (New York: Temple Smith, 1978), 28. Burke speaks of Europe's educated elites as culturally amphibious in that they both had access to literate culture, yet could participate in the oral culture of the illiterate.

2. Daniel Francis Pastorius, for example, who came to Pennsylvania in 1683, distinguished between Indians who had little contact with Europeans and those who were becoming corrupted by such contact. He also reported the following belief among Amerindians: "as many Indians must die each year as the number of Europeans that newly arrive." See Jean R. Soderlund, et al., eds., *William Penn and the Founding of Pennsylvania, 1680-1684: A Documentary History* (Philadelphia: University of Pennsylvania Press, 1983), 357, 360.

3. A. G. Roeber, "'The Origin of Whatever is Not English Among Us': The Dutch-speaking and German-speaking Peoples of Colonial British American," in *Strangers within the Realm: Cultural Margins of the First British Empire*, ed. Bernard Bailyn and Philip D. Morgan (Chapel Hill: University of North Carolina Press, 1991), 220-83, here at 257-59. See also, A. G. Roeber, "In German Ways? Problems and Potentials of Eighteenth-Century German Social and Emigration History," *William and Mary Quarterly*, 3d ser., 44 (1987): 750-74.

4. Gottlieb Mittelberger, *Reise nach Pennsylvanien im Jahr 1750 und Rückreise nach Deutschland im Jahr 1754*, ed. Jürgen Charnitzky, *Fremden Kulturen in alten Berichten*, vol. 6 (Sigmaringen: J. Thorbeck, 1997), 67. Mittelberger's "Foreword" (Vorrede) makes it clear that he deliberately cast his account as a geographic and ethnographic description. Mittelberger's work has been twice translated into English: (1) *Gottlieb Mittelberger's Journey to Pennsylvania in the Year 1750 and Return to Germany in the Year 1754*, translated by Carl Theodore Eben (Philadelphia: Private printing for J. Y. Jeanes, 1898) and (2) *Journey to Pennsylvania*, ed. and trans. Oscar Handlin and John Clive (Cambridge, Mass.: Harvard University Press, 1960). The passage quoted here is at p. 3 of the Handlin and Clive edition. Hereafter Mittelberger's account will be cited simply as "Mittelberger" followed by page references to the Handlin and Clive edition. Occasionally, when Mittelberger's German is cited, page references will also be given to the Charnitzky edition; this edition is much the best available as it is lavishly illustrated and contains a valuable introduction, a detailed commentary, and a full bibliography.

5. Mittelberger, 1. See also Charnitzky, ed. *Reise*, 58, where the original title page is reproduced.

6. Mittelberger, 10.

7. Mittelberger, 48; Charnitzky, ed. *Reise*, 124.

8. Mittelberger, 7 and 26.

9. Some observers referred to German colonists simply as "Palatines" because of the large number who came from the Rhenish Palatinate. It is, of course, anachronistic to speak of "Germany" in any political sense in the eighteenth century, but the term may also be used to refer to German-speaking parts of the Holy Roman Empire; it is in this sense that Mittelberger evidently used the term "Deutschland" in the title of his work.

10. See the graph of legal emigration of families from several regions of the southwestern part of the Holy Roman Empire in Aaron S. Fogleman, *Hopeful Journeys: German Immigration, Settlement, and Political Culture in Colonial America, 1717-1775* (Philadelphia: University of Pennsylvania Press, 1996), 26.

11. This is to take a mean of estimates that generally range between 85,000 and 115,000. For the low end, see Fogleman, *Hopeful Journeys*, 2, and for the high, Hans Fenske, "International Migration: Germany in the Eighteenth Century," *Central European History* 13 (1980): 332-47, here at 344. Fenske's estimate of 115,000 excludes the Swiss. Fenske also makes the point that as the aim of international German immigration in the eighteenth century, America held a distant second place to Hungary, which received at least 350,000 German immigrants.

12. Farley Grubb, "German Immigration to Pennsylvania, 1709-1820," *Journal of Interdisciplinary History* 20 (1990): 417-36, here at 417. The "European" qualifier is important since the number of Germans who arrived in the eighteenth century was dwarfed by the number of Africans (c. 278,000) who arrived as slaves. See Fogleman, *Hopeful Journeys*, 2.

13. Grubb, "German Immigration," 417.

14. The following quantitative comparisons are drawn from Grubb, "German Immigration," 420-30.

15. Ibid., 436.

16. Handlin and Clive describe the working of the redemptioner system at Mittelberger, x-xi.

17. Mittelberger, 9.

18. Mittelberger, 18. In a comment that reveals something of eighteenth-century attitudes toward children, Mittelberger bemoaned both the fate of young children who were separated from their parents and the inability of parents to realize any financial value from their children: immigrants "who have children under the age of five," he wrote, "cannot settle their debts by selling them. They must give away these children for nothing to be brought up by strangers; and in return these children must stay in service until they are twenty-one years old."

19. This debate about the prime motivating cause is discussed in Roeber, "In German Ways?", 760-63.

20. The terms of the treaty actually recognized just two parties, Catholics and Protestants, with Protestants being defined as adherents of the Augsburg Confession of 1530; but various editions of this confession, among which the Westphalian agreement drew no distinction, made it possible to include German Calvinists as well as Lutherans among the Protestants recognized by the treaty. Hajo Holborn, *A History of Modern Germany*, vol. 1, *The Reformation* (New York: Knopf, 1964), 370. Holborn's work remains the best English-language account of German political history in this period.

21. Holborn, *History of Modern Germany*, 1:369.

22. The literature on confessionalization in English remains somewhat sparse, but the essential survey of the whole process is R. Po-Chia Hsia, *Social Discipline in the Reformation: Central Europe, 1550-1750* (London: Routledge, 1989). An overview of the subject that also examines its implications for German state building in the nineteenth century is Joel F. Harrington and Helmut Walser Smith, "Confessionalization, Community, and State Building in Germany, 1555-1870," *Journal of Modern History* 69 (1997): 77-101. The work of Heinz Schilling has been especially influential in the development of confessionalization as a historiographical tool. See also Schilling, *Religion, Political Culture and the Emergence of Early Modern Society: Essays in German and Dutch History* (Leiden: E.J. Brill, 1992); Susan R. Boettcher, "Confessionalization: Reformation, Religion, Absolutism, and Modernity," *History Compass* 2 (2004), 1-10; John M. Headley, Hans J. Hillerbrand, and Anthony J. Papalas, eds., *Confessionalization in Europe, 1555-1700: Essays in Honor of Bodo Nischan* (Burlington, Vt.: Ashgate, 2004).

23. In Penn's original Frame of Government (1682), Law 34 required all voters and office-holders to be professing Christians, but Law 35 guaranteed religious freedom to all who believed in monotheism. Soderlund, et al., eds., *William Penn and the Founding of Pennsylvania*, 132.

24. Mittelberger, 47.

25. Ibid., 46-47.

26. Ibid., 48.

27. Ibid., 47.

28. John Franz, "The Awakening of Religion among the German Settlers in the Middle Colonies," *William and Mary Quarterly* 3d ser., 33 (1976): 266-88, here at 270. For Pennsylvania in particular, according to Martin E. Lodge, the situation was especially stark – in 1740 there were just three Reformed pastors for twenty-six congregations and only one Lutheran cleric for twenty-seven congregations. Martin E. Lodge, "The Crisis of the Churches in the Middle Colonies, 1720-1750," *Pennsylvania Magazine of History and Biography* 95 (1971): 202-28, here at 199.

29. Franz, "Awakening of Religion," 280-81.

30. Mittelberger, 22.

31. John Joseph Stoudt, "Pennsylvania and the Oecumenical Ideal," *Bulletin of the Seminary of the Reformed Church in the United States* 12 (1941): 171-97, here at 180.

32. Henry Melchior Muhlenberg, *The Journals of Henry Melchior Muhlenberg*, ed. and trans. Theodore G. Tappert and John W. Doberstein, 3 vols. (Philadelphia: Evangelical Lutheran Ministerium of Pennsylvania and Adjacent States and Muhlenberg Press, 1942-58), 1:138.

33. Mittelberger, 48.

34. Lodge, "The Crisis of the Churches," 197-98, argues that the essential precondition of the German Awakening of the 1740s was a "breakdown" of church religion in which the laity abandoned its inherited faith. But the issue may be rather more complicated than this.

35. Oswald Seidensticker, "William Penn's Travels in Holland and Germany in 1677," *Pennsylvania Magazine of History and Biography* 2 (1878), 237-82. On the English political context for the founding of Pennsylvania, see Mary Geiter, "The Restoration Crisis and the Launching of Pennsylvania, 1679-81," *English Historical Review* 112 (1997): 300-318.

36. Fogleman, *Hopeful Journeys*, 102-5. Fogleman estimates that the sectarians account for only 3.6 to 6.5 percent of all German immigrants, 103.

37. John W. Jordan, "Moravian Immigration to Pennsylvania, 1734-1765," *Pennsylvania Magazine of History and Biography* 3 (1909): 228-48, provides details on the use and fate of these ships.

38. Fogleman, *Hopeful Journeys*, 105-7. The map on sectarian congregations in southeastern Pennsylvania on 106 is especially helpful.

39. Mittelberger, 41.

40. In his study of German immigration and settlement, Aaron S. Fogleman describes the German sects that came to Pennsylvania simply as "radical Pietists." Fogleman, *Hopeful Journeys*, chap. 4 "The Radical Pietist Alternative," esp. 101-2. But this all-inclusive categorization is clearly inaccurate. The growth of German pietism (*Pietismus*) in the late seventeenth century can account for some of the groups, but not others – Mennonites and Schwenckfelders were much older, dating from the early sixteenth century. These groups were scarcely influenced by pietism; their basic identity was fixed much earlier. The second hypothesis is presented by Mittelberger's most recent translators and editors, Oscar Handlin and John Clive; they shift the issue from religious to socioeconomic terms and attempt to explain German sectarianism as a product of the endemic suffering of the lower classes. Handlin and Clive write: "Perhaps as a result of the misery of their lot in the world, the peasants and artisans of the Rhineland were subject to recurrent religious revivals. A multitude of mystical sects flourished in the area, holding forth to true believers the promise of future redemption as compensation for the trials of the present." Mittelberger, viii. But of course the state churches offered future redemption, too, and on the face of it endemic poverty fails as an explanation of recurrent revivalism.

41. Fogleman, *Hopeful Journeys*, 105. Useful studies of some of the more marginal hermits and groups are Elizabeth W. Fisher, "'Prophecies and Revelations': German Cabbalists in

Early Pennsylvania," *Pennsylvania Magazine of History and Biography* 109 (1985): 299-333; Klaus Deppermann, "Pennsylvanien als Asyl der frühen deutschen Pietismus," *Pietismus und Neuzeit* 10 (1982): 190-212; and the older studies of Julius F. Sachse, *The German Pietists of Provincial Pennsylvania, 1694-1708* (Philadelphia: Printed for the author, 1895) and *The German Sectarians of Pennsylvania* (Philadelphia: Printed for the author, 1899).

42. On the connections between the early, communal Reformation and the upheaval of the Peasants' War, the work of Peter Blickle has been especially influential. See his collection of essays *From the Communal Reformation to the Revolution of the Common Man* (Leiden: Brill, 1998), and Blickle, *Die Revolution von 1525*, 4th ed. (Munich: R. Oldenbourg, 2004).

43. My collection of sources in translation, Michael G. Baylor, ed. and trans., *The Radical Reformation* (Cambridge: Cambridge University Press, 1991), illustrates the various camps of radical thought as well as the strategies for survival that various sects developed after the defeat of the Peasants' War.

44. James Stayer has argued that 1535 may be the best date for the end of the radical phase of the Reformation and the onset of a more accommodating posture among the surviving groups of Anabapists. J. Stayer, "The Passing of the Radical Moment in the Radical Reformation," *Mennonite Quarterly Review* 71 (1997): 147-52. For Menno Simons, see the recent study by Abraham Friesen, "Present at the Inception: Menno Simons and the Beginnings of Dutch Anabaptism," *Mennonite Quarterly Review* 72 (1998): 351-88.

45. An excellent biographical sketch of Schwenckfeld and a rich bibliography are provided by Ulrich Bubenheimer in *Biographisch-Bibliographisches Kirchenlexikon* (Herzberg: Traugott Bautz, 1995), vol. 9, cols. 1215-35. An excellent if incomplete English biography is R. Emmet McLaughlin, *Caspar Schwenckfeld, Reluctant Radical* (New Haven: Yale University Press, 1986). Also useful is the study by Peter C. Erb, *Schwenckfeld in His Reformation Setting* (Valley Forge, Pa: Judson Press, 1978).

46. Developments within the Schwenckfelder movement between the Reformation and the decision to leave for Pennsylvania are narrated in the chronicles of Martin John, Jr., and Balthazar Hoffmann, *The Tumultuous Years: Schwenckfelder Chronicles 1580-1750*, trans. L. Allen Viehmeyer (Pennsburg, Pa: Schwenckfelder Library, 1980).

47. The older study of Wilbur J. Bender, "Pacifism Among the Mennonites, Amish Mennonites, and Schwenckfelders of Pennsylvania to 1783," *Mennonite Quarterly Review* 1 (1927), 3:23-40 and 4:21-48, is much better on the moral dimension of Anabaptist pacifism than the political.

48. This point is made in Geoffrey Dipple, "'Yet, from time to time there were men who protested against these evils': Anabaptism and Medieval Heresy," *Protestant History and Identity in the Sixteenth Century*, vol. 1, *The Medieval Inheritance*, ed. Bruce Gordon (Aldershot, Eng.: Scolar Press, 1996), 123-37.

49. Indeed one of the more comprehensive histories of pietism traces its origins to seventeenth-century "moral Puritanism" in England. While some Puritan influence on early pietists is possible, this is to cast a very wide net in the search for origins. See F. Ernest Stoeffler, *The Rise of Evangelical Pietism* (Leiden: Brill, 1971). This work and its

sequel, *German Pietism during the Eighteenth Century* (Leiden: Brill, 1973), provide perhaps the fullest study of German pietism in English. Useful for their discussions of the meaning of German pietism are the essays in Martin Greschat, ed., *Zur neueren Pietismusforschung* (Darmstadt: Wissenschaftliche Buchgesellschaft, 1977), especially the essays of Johannes Wallmann, "Pietismus und Orthodoxie," 53-81, and Hartmut Lehmann, "Zur Definition des 'Pietismus,'" 82-90; Johannes Wallman, *Der Pietismus* (Göttingen: Vandenhoeck & Ruprecht, 2005); Jonathan Strom, "Problems and Promises of Pietism Research," *Church History* 71 (2002): 536-54.

50. For a detailed discussion of this point, see W. R. Ward, *The Protestant Evangelical Awakening* (Cambridge: Cambridge University Press, 1992).

51. In Prussia, King Frederick William I especially used pietism against the independence of both the ecclesiastical hierarchy and the Prussian nobility. The Hohenzollern family in Prussia found itself in an odd position in that the dynasty itself was Calvinist and yet the state church was Lutheran. Hence the monarchy promoted pietism as a vehicle for curtailing the independent power of the Lutheran church.

52. Donald F. Durnbaugh, ed. and trans., *European Origins of the Brethren* (Elgin, Ill.: Brethren Press, 1958), 42.

53. See the letter of Hochmann von Hochenau to George Grebe and Alexander Mack, written from the prison at Nuremberg, 24 July 1708, in Durnbaugh, ed. *European Origins*, 111.

54. Donald F. Durnbaugh, "Work and Hope: The Spirituality of the Radical Pietist Communitarians," *Church History* 39 (1970): 72-90.

55. I would like to express my gratitude to Arthur J. Freeman, who provided me with valuable material about Zinzendorf prior to the publication of his study, *An Ecumenical Theology of the Heart: The Theology of Count Nicholas Ludwig von Zinzendorf* (Bethlehem, Pa.: Moravian Church in America, 1998). Also useful for Zinzendorf's religious ideas is Leiv Aalen, "Die Theologie des Grafen Zinzendorf," in Martin Greschat, ed., *Zur Neueren Pietismusforschung*, 319-53.

56. Troeltsch himself recognized the extreme difficulty of trying to situate the Moravian church, which he saw as the zenith of pietist mysticism, within his sociology. Zinzendorf's mysticism Troeltsch regarded as "in extremely bad taste," and he argued that, despite Zinzendorf's claim to be in agreement with Lutheran theology, he broke with Lutheran ecclesiology and sociology. Troeltsch also held that Zinzendorf used the Moravians to form a sectarian organization, yet the sectarianism was repeatedly contradicted by the Count's Christological mysticism. See Ernst Troeltsch, *The Social Teaching of the Christian Churches* (New York: Macmillan, 1949) 2:789.

57. Ward, *The Protestant Evangelical Awakening*, 128-36.

58. John Joseph Stoudt, "Count Zinzendorf and the Pennsylvania Congregation of God in the Spirit," *Church History* 9 (1940): 366-80. See also Stoudt, "Pennsylvania and the Ecumenical Ideal."

59. Mittelberger, 94-95, where in describing the roads out of Philadelphia into the inhabited regions of eastern Pennsylvania, he asserted "the third road runs to the left toward Lancaster and Bethlehem, where there is a monastery and convent full of Dunker Brethren and Sisters." For the German text at this point, see Charnitzky, 183: "*die dritte Strasse geht linker Hand Lancaster und Bethlehem zu, welches ein Kloster und voller Dümpler mit Brüdern und Schwestern bewohnt ist.*"

60. Ibid., 44.

61. Ibid., 47-48.

62. Ibid., 55.

63. Julius Friedrich Sachse, "The Missive of Justus Falckner, of Germantown, Concerning the Religious Condition of Pennsylvania in the Year 1701," *Pennsylvania Magazine of History and Biography* 21 (1898): 216-23, here at 220.

Gender Prescriptions in Eighteenth-Century Bethlehem

BEVERLY PRIOR SMABY

IN 1741 AT BETHLEHEM, PENNSYLVANIA, the recently formed pietistic Moravian Church established a settlement that was highly unusual in the eighteenth-century world. Not only did the members live in "Choir" groups organized by age, gender, and marital status, but women leaders of the female Choirs held clerical and governing responsibilities that were rarely enjoyed by women in other eighteenth-century religious groups in America. This study explores gender concepts underlying women's leadership in Bethlehem – concepts formulated not in Bethlehem itself, but across the Atlantic by Count Nicolaus Ludwig von Zinzendorf. As the charismatic leader of the tightly controlled Moravian Church from the late 1720s to 1760, Zinzendorf developed a set of constructs about women. The outlines of these constructs remained constant, and the majority of them were positive.

However, Zinzendorf's tone and emphasis changed over time in response to events in Moravian Church history, and he always maintained an ambivalence about the nature and abilities of women. His ambivalence cut two ways. On the one hand, it gave him room to experiment and loosen the boundaries around the roles of Moravian women without completely abandoning his culture. On the other hand, it allowed Moravian leadership after Zinzendorf to tighten those boundaries again and bring them into line with those in most other eighteenth-century Protestant churches without seeming to completely contradict him.

The *Gemeine*, as the Moravian Church was known among its own members, was devoted to saving souls, their own and as many others' as possible. Bethlehem was conceived as a special "Pilgrim" *Gemeine* to carry out this mission in America. The residents were divided into two groups. One was composed of the missionaries who traveled and ministered to African slaves in the Caribbean, as well as Native Americans and European settlers on the mainland. The other group was set up to support the missionaries by staying in Bethlehem or one of its satellite settlements to construct buildings, raise food, and manufacture various material goods. The entire community operated under a communal system known as the General Economy. For religious reasons, the community was further divided into its separate "Choirs": children in the Nursery, Little Boys, Little Girls, Older Boys, Older Girls, Single Brothers, Single Sisters, Married Sisters, Married Brothers, Widows, and Widowers.[1]

Visitors to Bethlehem were always struck by these divisions, and they were fond of commenting on the arrangements necessary to support them. But had they stayed long enough to understand more deeply the inner workings of the Choirs and the community-wide governing boards, they would have been even more amazed to witness the activities of the leading women in Bethlehem. Women like Anna Rosel Anders, Anna Maria Lawatsch, Juliana Nitschmann, and Maria Spangenberg served the community in ways usually reserved for male ministers among other Protestant groups – they led worship services, gave short sermons, evaluated members' spiritual state through "Speakings" during the few days before Communion, and decided who would be allowed to participate in Communion and who not. They also ordained deaconesses, consecrated acolytes, wrote monthly reports to Moravian leaders in Europe, and served as delegates to general (international) synods of the Moravian Church, usually held in Europe.[2]

Others, like Margarethe Jungmann traveled out from Bethlehem to evangelize among Indian women beyond the Pennsylvania frontier. Anna Ramsberg traveled tirelessly and extensively in eastern Pennsylvania ministering among European women in non-Moravian settlements. As a result of her efforts, fifty women joined the Single Sisters Choir in Bethlehem during the eight-and-a-half years preceding her death in 1757. (This represented well over half the total number of Single Sisters in Bethlehem at the time.) Anna Rosel Anders frequently walked the ten miles to Nazareth to minister to the Single Sisters housed there, who served as caretakers and teachers for Bethlehem's young children.[3]

There *were* limits to women's ministerial activity that did not apply to male ministers. Though women might well help serve Communion, they were not allowed to consecrate the elements. And their spiritual work was confined almost exclusively to women. They were not, for instance, allowed to lead services attended by both men and women, nor were they allowed in general to give sermons before groups that included men.[4]

When women leaders of the worldwide Moravian Church traveled to Bethlehem, they were welcomed as visiting dignitaries and treated with the utmost respect. Anna Johanna Piesch was one such Moravian dignitary – among women in the *Gemeine*, second only to Anna Nitschmann. Piesch was a General Eldress and the leader of all Single Sisters Choirs in the entire church. During the 1740s and 1750s, she frequently lived and traveled with the *Jüngerhaus* (the Moravians' top governing body) along with Zinzendorf, Anna Nitschmann, and other Moravian leaders. In 1752, she led a migration of seventeen Single Sisters to Bethlehem. Because of Piesch's high status, Anna Rosel Anders met her a few miles outside of town and accompanied her for the last part of the journey. When they arrived together in Bethlehem, the Single Sisters lined the walkway and the whole community rejoiced, while the trombone choir sounded its welcome.[5] During her two-month stay Piesch visited extensively among outlying congregations, including

Count Nicolaus Ludwig von Zinzendorf,
leader of the Moravian Church from the late 1720s to 1760.

Unity Archives, Herrnhut, Germany.

the Indian mission at Gnadenhütten. She also talked with many individual Sisters and attended meetings of the local governing boards. Upon her return to Europe, she was expected to report frankly about the condition of the settlement at Bethlehem.

Women also served in ways that we would call "secular." Maria Spangenberg governed the entire settlement when her husband was absent.[6] Leaders of the women's Choirs served on Bethlehem's governing boards, and minutes of the meetings show that they participated very actively and that others sought their opinions. In addition, they managed the large Choir houses for children in the Nursery, Older Girls, Single Sisters, and Widows, and they ran their communal economic enterprises.

Judging from autobiographical accounts of women in Bethlehem, the leading women embraced their important roles in spiritual and secular matters, but they clearly had not conceived the system that gave them those roles. From letter exchanges and meeting minutes, it is also obvious that male leaders in Bethlehem hadn't either. Rather, international leaders in Europe developed Moravian Church policy and created multiple systems for making sure that it held sway in all Moravian settlements.

Leaders were transferred frequently – they moved back and forth constantly between headquarters in Europe and other settlements through-out the world and brought freshly established policies with them. Leaders of Moravian settlements and of Choirs around the world had to send handwritten copies of the diaries they kept, along with monthly reports, to the international leaders in Europe. Specific international leaders in Europe held responsibility for maintaining communications with specific Moravian settlements. The *Jüngerhaus Diary* (or later the *Gemeinnachrichten*) was kept at Moravian headquarters and issued regularly as a Moravian journal. Scribes made copies of the *Jüngerhaus Diary* by hand and sent them to Moravian settlements around the world. They distributed synod records in a similar manner. In these ways, Moravian leaders in Europe monitored outlying congregations, including the one in Bethlehem, and kept them apprised of any new policies established in Europe.

More than anyone else in the *Gemeine*, Count Nicolaus Ludwig von Zinzendorf set Moravian policies in both Europe and America and conceived the ideas behind them. During the early 1720s he had offered a place on his Silesian estate to refugees from the beleaguered Ancient Unitas Fratrum, a Protestant church in Moravia that predated Luther by half a century. By 1730 he was not only their manor lord, but also the unchallenged spiritual leader of their renewed church. In this role, Zinzendorf kept the *Jüngerhaus Diary* until he died and attached to it hundreds of his sermons. Many of these sermons spelled out Zinzendorf's understanding of gender in great detail, and in that regard, they are highly unusual sources.

During the eighteenth century, distinctions based on gender were fundamental to social organization in European societies on both sides of the Atlantic. For the most part, they were taken for granted. They appeared in literature, in laws, in social organization, in economic structures, and in paintings as reflections of existing norms, but they were discussed or explored as separate subjects primarily when challenged. Zinzendorf's sermons represented a radical departure from this general rule. They explicitly explored differences between the genders in order to establish how the Church could best serve women and men as distinct groups and how each could best serve the Church. In the process they formed the basis of roles for Moravian women that often pushed beyond the boundaries of women's roles in other churches.

Having said this, we must be careful not to make Zinzendorf into a modern-day egalitarian. It is important to accept that his understandings of the roles of men and women remained characteristic of the eighteenth century in many ways: he believed that hierarchy was good. In the world he constructed, an elite ruling class maintained its authority over rank-and-file members, and men maintained their authority over women. However, he went far enough in encouraging untraditional roles for women to cause discomfort inside the Church and bitter criticism outside of it. These competing strains in Zinzendorf's thinking produced a portrait of women that was highly ambiguous. He was apt to take a position in one paragraph and contradict it in the next. Quoted out of context, he can be interpreted as misogynist or feminist.[7]

Zinzendorf started from the premise that the souls of all human beings could be saved if they could be awakened to the depths of their own corruption and converted to absolute dependence on Christ. A theology claiming that anyone could gain salvation, if given the chance, required a program giving such a chance to as many people as possible. As a result, Zinzendorf felt a responsibility to develop a program within the Moravian fold that made salvation more likely among all its members, no matter which station in life they occupied. In the 1720s and 1730s he observed that people of like circumstance quite naturally encouraged awakening and conversion in each other. It was in this context that Zinzendorf developed the Choir system of social organization.

A key ingredient in these groupings was the separation of sexes after age four. One reason Zinzendorf separated men and women was to prevent them from confusing religious enthusiasm with sexuality. But, more important to the subject of this essay, he also believed that the nature of the two genders was different and that Christian nurture should be tailored to each of them. The Choirs provided an efficient structure for delivering the nurture, but to be effective, Zinzendorf believed he had to be clear about the different natures of the genders.

Such emphasis on gender distinctions in religious experience represented a major contrast with other Protestant groups of the seventeenth and eighteenth century. Recent studies of gender and spirituality have established that among early Puritans, Quakers, and Evangelicals, the conversion process resulted in a suspension of self and the gender identity that went along with it. In those groups to varying degrees, women's roles were expanded for a time by rejecting gender as relevant to a relationship with God.[8] In stark contrast, among early Moravians, gender was not suspended but emphasized by conversion. For them, the conversion process was based on an understanding of gender differences and it resulted in a celebration of each gender's special relationship to Christ.[9]

To support conversion as Moravians understood it, Zinzendorf felt a need to define the differences between men and women. At first he used hymns to outline traits of different Choirs. Beginning in the early 1740s, Zinzendorf began to analyze gender roles and sort them out in sermon after sermon for Older Boys, Older Girls, Single Sisters, Single Brothers, and Married People. These sermons served as socialization devices for the entire Moravian Church. Distributed along with the *Jüngerhaus Diary*, they were read in worship services over and over again by leaders in Moravian settlements around the world.

The emphases that Zinzendorf gave to particular views about women changed over time, but all the themes were present in his first sermons on the subject and they remained important to his conception of women throughout his life. To appreciate the changes, it is important to understand the underlying consistencies in Zinzendorf's thinking. From beginning to end, Zinzendorf developed both negative and positive views of women as reverse images of each other. Using a philosophical viewpoint, we see that these polar opposites helped to illuminate each other: beginning with his first sermon on women in 1742, Zinzendorf used Old Testament women as illustrative foils for those in the New Testament. Taking a psychological perspective, we conclude that Zinzendorf was ambivalent toward women: although he identified in general with the positive views he found about women in the New Testament, he never dissociated himself entirely from the negative ones he saw in the Old Testament.

That Zinzendorf would turn to the Bible for information and authority in his early explorations of gender differences is hardly surprising. What is surprising is that Zinzendorf did not accept biblical evidence without question. Noting the contrasts between Old and New Testament accounts of women, he took the Bible to be not only the Word of God, but a record of cultures that had changed and progressed under God's guidance. The Old Testament, Zinzendorf said, reflected values of the Jewish world. In that world, women were to be used "for service, for work" but other than that, they had earned "no respect, no consideration and no deference." They were therefore "pushed into the background on every occasion." Zinzendorf did not mean by this that women were treated unfairly.

Their treatment in Old Testament times was, in fact, "a wise providence of God, a certain discipline...for the unhappiness that was brought into the world by them." In case his listeners missed the point, he elaborated that "they allowed themselves to be deceived and, through their Fall, brought themselves and others into ruin."[10] Note that Zinzendorf did not use the singular pronoun here as a reference to Eve; he used the plural. Apparently, the Fall was caused not just by Eve as an individual. Rather Eve served as a symbol for womankind. The weakness of allowing oneself to be deceived was a flaw shared by women in general, and therefore all women needed to be disciplined so they would not continue to harm themselves and others. As will become clear, deception was a continuing theme in Zinzendorf's conception of women.

Zinzendorf also used the Bible to provide positive examples for Moravian Sisters, examples which came from the New Testament. Moravian women should strive "to become warmhearted [*herzliche*] Mary Magdalenes, Salomes, Annas, and Marys."[11] In several sermons Zinzendorf also presented Mary Magdalene, Salome, Anna, and Mary as examples of loyalty and simplicity.

Zinzendorf conjoined his biblical examples with others from his own experience and culture that agreed with those in the New Testament but extended well beyond them. From all these examples, Zinzendorf formulated ideals for women in his early studies of gender that he repeated again and again until his last sermons on the subject shortly before his death. Through the years, he developed a cluster of synonyms and associated concepts for the five ideals he repeated most often.

Love was an important goal for women that grew out of the female attributes of warmheartedness and loyalty. Zinzendorf said, "The Single Sisters Choir was created to love."[12] Because of its importance, he found numerous synonyms for love as it should be expressed by women and various aspects of female love to explore. Ideal women were friendly, tender, and intimate, and they tended toward connection with others. Loyalty reflected another side of friendship and connection, that of "complete dependability," and "iron-like" solidity.[13]

Simplicity was understood as the opposite of the deceptive character that Zinzendorf saw in Old Testament women. In his descriptions of women in the New Testament as well as his independent descriptions, he grouped simplicity with the "openness" and "straightforwardness" that was thought to be "characteristic of children." In his view children were exactly what they seemed to be and that kind of honesty was what women should strive for.

Purity was another ideal that Zinzendorf identified as female and associated with "chastity," "virginity," and "cleanliness." The white dresses that Moravian women wore on Festival days were meant as a symbol of purity.

Quietude was the frame from which the ideal woman revealed her piety. Zinzendorf sometimes argued that Paul's admonition for women to keep silent in the churches was directed only to the women in Corinth, but Zinzendorf also often urged women to strive for a "quiet essence." A woman's conduct was to be still, gentle, soft, and withdrawn. Her conduct by itself would speak to her faith. It would "win people without words."[14] "In the New Testament," claimed Zinzendorf, "the jewelry of the virgins is hidden in the heart."[15]

Sensitivity was, in Zinzendorf's view, a natural trait for women. He carried out the metaphor by referring to individual senses – feeling and taste. Women were supposed to "feel the love of Christ" and "savour his cause." In the same context, Zinzendorf repeatedly claimed that women had a special ability to "enjoy" the services and sacraments of the Moravian Church. Zinzendorf repeatedly connected enjoying with feeling and savouring: "[The ability] to enjoy, feel, and savour is a special privilege of the Sisters, which no one can deny them."[16] Joy was an especially important feeling that constituted the crowning relationship to Christ. Because of its importance, Zinzendorf outdid himself in finding related words. Joyful or *freudig* was associated with *fröhlich, licht, heiter, munter, vergnügt, selig,* and *spielerhaft.* When he ran out of German words he used an English one – "cheerfull." (That series can be translated as: happy, bright, gay, cheerful, delighted, blissful, and playful.)

Moravian love feast in Herrnhut, Germany, with females seated on one side and males seated on the other. Moravians in Bethlehem and elsewhere held similar gatherings.

Moravian Archives, Bethlehem, Pennsylvania.

The ability to love Christ completely, to believe in him with childlike simplicity and purity, to wear one's faith quietly, and to sense it deeply and joyfully were all actually goals for every Christian, not women only. The fact that Zinzendorf believed these ideals were natural for women, explains why he considered women an "edifying" force for everyone in the community.[17]

Although Zinzendorf revisited these negative and positive themes from the early 1740s until his death in 1760, Table 1 suggests that we can group his sermons into three distinct periods.

Table 1:
Zinzendorf's Positive and Negative Emphasis – in percentages
(total number of references in sample = 295)[18]

	Positive Traits	Negative Traits	Total %
1740s	92	8	100
Early 1750s	58	42	100
Late 1750s	74	26	100
All periods	69	31	100

Table 1 shows that Zinzendorf's sermons from the 1740s focused almost entirely on a positive view of women. In sermons from 1750 to 1755 Zinzendorf continued to discuss positive characteristics of women, but over 40 percent of his emphasis was on negative traits he found in women. Sermons from 1756 to 1759 reflected a continuing and substantial concern with women's negative traits, but they clearly also showed a revived interest in the positive characteristics of women. In spite of the different emphases, however, it is important to stress that the great majority of references in all three periods were positive.

The 1740s

During the 1740s Zinzendorf used the notion of women acting like Eves (who had been deceived) as well as the notion of women acting like other Old Testament women (who in his view were themselves deceivers). He used their stories to demonstrate the kind of behavior good Christian women should avoid and admonished women not to:

> enter into the genus of the holy snakes, like Rachel and Rebekah. For the greatest holy women in the Bible have carried out the most desperate, snakelike schemes such as one sees in the examples of Deborah, Judith, and Esther in the story with Haman.[19]

The Old Testament heroines could also be described as intensely loyal – loyal to their family and their people, but Zinzendorf chose to focus instead on their propensity to play the part of snakes. These women were not merely deceived by a snake as Eve was. In Zinzendorf's language, they *were* snakes. This is clearest in the cases of Rebekah, Rachel, and Judith. Rebekah connived to convince her blind husband Isaac that Jacob was Esau, so that Jacob would receive the blessing that Isaac intended for Esau. Rachel, the wife of Jacob, stole images from her father upon leaving her father's place, and when her father later searched for the stolen images, she sat upon them and pretended that she had her monthly period and could not rise. Judith lured the general of the invading Assyrian army into her tent by persuading him that she could be seduced, but she cut off his head instead.

The snakelike characteristics of Deborah and Esther are not as easy to discern. Although Deborah did not deceive directly, perhaps Zinzendorf blamed her for setting the stage for Jael who killed the defeated Canaanite general, after assuring him he could find protection in her tent. It is hard, however, to understand why Zinzendorf would consider Esther deceptive. She was remarkably forthright in her efforts to foil Haman's plot against her people. She confronted Haman with his evil plan and in front of Haman beseeched her husband, the king, to protect her people against Haman. When the king decided to kill Haman, she unambiguously ignored Haman's pleas to intercede for him and later encouraged the king to kill Haman's family and his supporters. One might accuse Esther of careful strategizing and acting with grim determination, but not of deceiving anyone. Perhaps in Zinzendorf's eyes, a snakelike woman was not merely a deceiver, but a clever and resolute foe.

Although Zinzendorf used these Old Testament examples in his early sermons to warn women about the character and behavior they should avoid, his primary emphasis during the 1740s was on positive views about women, as Table 1 makes clear. In fact, Zinzendorf's negative examples from the Old Testament served primarily to place in relief Christ's revolutionary, positive conception of women in the New Testament. Christ was born and reared a Jew, but his perception and treatment of women, according to Zinzendorf, broke suddenly and cleanly with traditional Jewish practice. Zinzendorf's words were designed to make clear that Christ had made this break consciously:

> Because the Savior had made good again...the harm one woman brought into the world by [his] being born and made human through another woman, so he intended to give them back their respect.[20]

Zinzendorf interpreted this gift of respect first of all as *self*-respect: just as womankind had had to share the disgrace for Eve's disservice, womankind could share the honor of Mary's service. And just as all women were disciplined for causing the Fall, Mary's deed was reason for all women "to find joy in their station, especially in the great honor that was done to them...[when] the Savior became human through one of their sex."[21] Women, who in Old Testament times had been taught to despise their womanhood, could now rejoice in it.

But according to Zinzendorf, Christ's behavior also required that women be respected by others. Since Christians should follow Christ's lead in everything, they should develop a positive perception of women and treat them with respect because *he* did. Zinzendorf cited several cases where Christ demonstrated his high regard for women, including among others, Mary (who gave him human life and whom he loved deeply), Anna (who spread the message of his coming after his childhood visit to the temple), Mary and Martha in Bethany (the sisters of Lazarus, whom Jesus loved deeply), and Mary Magdalene (who was the first to see the resurrected Jesus).[22] Zinzendorf was claiming that, in these cases, Christ not only modeled loving respect for women, but in the Gospel, he gave them important roles that demanded respect.

Within the *Gemeine*, Zinzendorf also argued, women deserved respect because of the good example they could provide:

> Natural circumstances bring many more distractions and tests to men than to [women], and therefore it can happen that we get more dust on our feet and that our manner [Gestalt], our character, our testimony among people can appear not as impressive, as edifying, as devout, as [women's] can be without any effort, if they just stay true to the grace [of God].... We intend therefore to present the examples of the godly women in future services.[23]

From other sermons we know that Zinzendorf thought the "natural circumstances" causing men to gather "more dust on [their] feet" were their responsibilities to govern and carry authority. Because women usually did not carry such burdens, they could reach Christian ideals much more easily than men. Because of this, one of their most important roles in the *Gemeine* was to serve as models for the rest of the community – men and women alike.

During this early period, Zinzendorf emphasized especially women's ability to feel the joy that was the pinnacle of a relationship with the Savior and a goal for every believer. In 1747 he told the Single Sisters that their Choir:

> must have a kind of quality of soul (the soft and steady feeling of his love and all the enjoyment of the graces of the *Gemeine*, something unforced and playful…[and] sort of sensitive) that not everyone has….When you celebrate your festival, one feels something special in you, something happy, bright, something gay and blissful, and that is what one should be aware of in you, every day and every hour.[24] [parentheses mine]

The fact that Zinzendorf began discussing women's character in detail in the early 1740s is intriguing. The Choir system developed gradually in the 1730s, beginning with the Single Sisters and Single Brothers Choirs. During the same period, the concept of "marriage militant" encouraged many married Moravian men and women to serve the Savior as partners with their spouses, either in the work of saving souls or supporting those who saved souls. Both the leaders of female Choirs and the female partners in a "marriage militant" were being asked to play roles that were unusual in the eighteenth century. In addition, Zinzendorf named Anna Nitschmann as Mother of the Church in 1746, and together that year they ordained twelve women as Presbyters, the Moravian office above Deacon(ess) and below Bishop. It is natural that Zinzendorf would feel the need to buttress all these new roles with conceptions of women that suggested they were capable of playing them well. In this way, perhaps Zinzendorf's studies of gender prepared the way for innovation with respect to women's roles.

It is important to remember, however, that alongside this early emphasis on the positive influence of Christian women, Zinzendorf revealed some ambivalence toward them by espousing the commonly held view that they had inherited deceptive characteristics from Eve and other Old Testament women. It may well be that this ambivalence provided additional support for Zinzendorf's innovations. If he had discussed only women's virtues, male leaders around him would likely not have accepted new responsibilities for women because such changes would have appeared too threatening to the widely accepted view that men should hold the predominant authority in society. In 1740, Zinzendorf spoke directly to limitations on women's governing roles as if to reassure others (and himself) that his innovations would not give women too much authority:

> It is highly necessary that a Brother from the *Gemeine* be deputized to direct the female gender, albeit through...separate female Elders and Helpers,[25] for the male sex must maintain the direction in the *Gemeine* and the female Choirs must stand under him, according to God's plan. If the Sisters reigned supreme, then there would be a confusion in the *Gemeine*.[26]

Zinzendorf's caveat, however, should not detract from his main point about women during this early period: that they provided a positive influence on the Moravian community and that they should be respected and depended upon as examples of ideal Christian behavior for all Moravians, men and women alike. Furthermore, despite his protestations, women did in fact share considerable responsibility in matters of governance and spirituality.

The Early 1750s

During the second period from 1750 through 1755, Zinzendorf rather suddenly switched from a positive emphasis on women's positive traits to a detailed exploration of their negative traits, and he did so with vengeance. In the 1740s Zinzendorf had confined his negative examples of women to those in the Old Testament. In 1750 he began to draw negative examples from his own experience with women inside and outside the Moravian Church. His tone also changed, betraying at times even bitterness and frustration toward women. During this period he characterized them as having "underhanded natures" and "leftovers of snakelike deceit."[27] At times Zinzendorf seemed to have particular women in mind. He described one instance, for example, when a "deceitful snake" began a rumor that a teacher held an "unconsecrated service" because he didn't use an expression that was thought to be particularly important in worship, thereby causing the downfall of that teacher in the eyes of some.[28]

During this period, Zinzendorf outlined in great detail three major problems he saw in the nature of women. First, the possible exemplary Christian character among women was compromised by their tendency to deceive – they might feign it. For this reason, he warned Moravian Sisters against the dangers of hypocrisy. In a 1755 sermon for Single Sisters, for instance, he claimed that "the way of single women, before they were blessed by the Savior, was to compose themselves in such a way, that one would not notice what was going on in their soul."²⁹ At the international synod for Single Sisters during that same year, he again addressed the issue of hypocrisy: "all worldly single women are thought guilty of dissembling and...they hypocritically present themselves as chaste and saintly, even though they are not."³⁰ In these sermons, Zinzendorf made clear that he thought the snakelike character of Old Testament women was alive and well among eighteenth-century women of his acquaintance.

Second, although Zinzendorf continued to believe that God also wanted women to focus their lives on love, he seemed now to think that they would have a hard time practicing on other women. He said on one occasion:

> If womenfolk seem hard against menfolk, under the surface they are soft and dependent, while among themselves, they can't stand each other very well.... a society of women who heartily love each other is a great rarity in the world.³¹

Zinzendorf claimed that women's lack of love for each other was caused by envy and quarrelsomeness, which he seemed to think was characteristic of women:

> no one doubts that among women folk, [each] is envied by her neighbor and all the nice things [the neighbor] says to her are not true.... love and respect among the Sisters is something rare, for jealousy and disagreement creep in easily among you.³²

Third, Zinzendorf thought women had to struggle to maintain the state of joy and happiness which was expected of them. Zinzendorf repeatedly warned Moravian Sisters against despondency, anger, discontent, and aggravation, emotions that Zinzendorf thought were unbecoming, but common enough in the women he knew. "You must never be despondent," he told the Sisters, "for that doesn't suit you, even when it is linked with the same measure of pretended saintliness."³³ Reaching and maintaining the ideal of joy was especially hard for single women in Zinzendorf's view:

> In the world outside, an old maid is mocked and scorned; that makes them disgruntled.... In the *Gemeine*, we are not in the habit of mocking disgruntled Single Sisters, but they depress us, because we know a secret which they seem to ignore, namely that if such a person enters into [the married estate] with her disgruntled heart, she becomes even more disgruntled and unhappy, and she tortures herself and others.³⁴

During the early 1750s Zinzendorf often portrayed the characteristics of one gender by comparing them with those of the other. In doing so, he revealed very different standards for men and for women. In his view, women had the potential for being much better than men, as well as much worse. For the most part, men occupied a more innocuous middle ground. On the one hand Zinzendorf felt that Moravian Brothers were more likely than the Sisters to be "dry" or spiritually barren. "Enjoyment, feeling, and taste is a special privilege of the Sisters, which nobody can deny them. A dry Sister should be ashamed of herself three times over, [in the same circumstance] when a dry Brother is ashamed of himself once."³⁵ Zinzendorf also continued to suggest that Sisters had greater childlike sensitivity to Christ.³⁶ For these reasons, even during the early 1750s when he was most concerned about women's negative tendencies, Zinzendorf continued to point to the Sisters as good examples of Christian behavior.

But if women could be better followers of Christ than men could be, they could also be more evil. According to Zinzendorf, men were more prone to fall into evil than women were, but the roots of evil did not grow as "firmly" in men as in women. So if a woman did fall into evil, it was "much harder to drive it out [of her]."³⁷ During the early 1750s, there were numerous indications in Zinzendorf's discussion of women, that he thought their negative traits were more firmly entrenched than their positive ones. He presented the positive traits as something women should strive for, whereas he treated their negative traits as part of their fundamental character. In fact Zinzendorf connected women's negative traits with the concept of original sin:

> [In girls,] I place the expression of original sin...in their snakelike ways.... In girls one must work [against] craftiness, artifice, and envy.... For them, the simplicity of Mary must be compared with the snakelike manner of Eve.³⁸

It follows that the only way females could get rid of their deceptive character was the same way that they could get rid of all original sin – through the intervention of Christ.

In contrast, the original sin of men – the animal-like, the lustful – was apparently less harmful than the snakelike, deceitful original sin of women. In fact, men's original sin could encourage their conversion, whereas women's could hinder theirs. The first step toward conversion was to become aware of the depth of one's sin – or in eighteenth-century parlance to "become a sinner." In Zinzendorf's view, this first step was easier for men than for women:

> Inside the Brothers themselves, there already lies great assistance for becoming a sinner, one doesn't have to flatter them half as much as the Sisters to persuade them and to make becoming a sinner important to them.³⁹

Men were, in other words, more comfortable with their sinful natures than women were, so men could admit their failings more easily. The problem for women was that their tendency toward deception could extend to self-deception as well – they could think of themselves as better than they were.

Some of Zinzendorf's comparisons between men and women seem contradictory, but underneath the surface was a consistent logic that placed boundaries around the roles of women. Zinzendorf considered women more active and stronger when he wanted to say that they made the best nurses for the sick and the best housekeepers – typically female roles.⁴⁰ On the other hand, Zinzendorf claimed women were weaker when he was protecting men's predominance in governing roles. Using 1 Peter 3:7 (which the Luther Bible renders as "you men ...should honor the female [sex] as the weakest worktool"),⁴¹ Zinzendorf declared:

> When the scripture calls women a weak worktool, what it means is that you can't think as broadly, as deeply, or as persistently as the Brothers, therefore one finds fewer among you than among us, who have the gift to govern.[42]

Zinzendorf's assertion is interesting in several ways. First, he did not state that women *never* had the gift to govern. If he had taken that position, he would likely have heard a word or two from leading Moravian Sisters! Instead he claimed only that fewer women were capable of governing than men. In doing so, he was avoiding the Sisters' wrath and making room for some of them to play a substantial part in church governance. But he was also limiting their authority and influence by suggesting that women with such abilities were not typical of their gender. The reason Zinzendorf gave for limiting female authority was particularly damning – he described their weakness as intellectual, not physical: "you can't think as broadly, as deeply, or as persistently as the Brothers."

The timing of Zinzendorf's intensive exploration of women's negative side and his insistent comparison of men and women is suggestive. It followed closely upon his discovery of serious problems with the "Sifting" (a time of passionate religious enthusiasm and sensuality that grew out of the Moravian focus on the blood and wounds of Christ). Although Zinzendorf originated this blood and wounds theology among Moravians, he repudiated its Sifting expression in 1749 with a strongly written reprimand.[43] The reprimand was directed toward all Moravians, not just women, but it is reasonable to ask if there might have been a connection between his repudiation of Sifting and his in-depth exploration of the negative side of women. His attack on the woman who caused the downfall of a particular teacher was a pointed rejection of the zealousness typical of the Sifting, and it came in the year after he wrote his reprimand. Perhaps Zinzendorf felt that female participation had somehow intensified the Sifting. Historians of religion have uncovered other cases in which periods of fervent religious activity were later devalued by associating them with the influence of women.[44]

The Late 1750s

As Table 1 shows, Zinzendorf's emphasis on women's negative characteristics subsided in the late 1750s. But the change in emphasis was reflected not only in the numbers: Zinzendorf's purpose also seemed to change. Although he still might from time to time characterize women in highly negative terms, these negative characterizations did not stand on their own. They were coupled with contrasting positive traits: "being artificial, crafty, and secretive, saying the truth after a half a year, and in the meantime beating around the bush, that is not the right character of the Sisters.... God made the Sisters honest, God created them true."[45] Clearly, Zinzendorf's exasperation still showed through, but he had begun again to use negative examples as foils for the good behavior he expected of women.

In 1756 Zinzendorf also found a mitigating circumstance for the disgruntlement he had previously found inexcusable in Single Sisters. That circumstance was office holding. As Zinzendorf knew from his own experience, leadership responsibilities were apt to make a person cross. Although the ordinary Single

Sister didn't earn the right, she might be allowed some leeway if she carried responsibilities that were heavier than usual. "If a Single Sister is disgruntled," he said, "and she doesn't have an office which excuses the disgruntlement,...then it doesn't suit her.[46] On the other hand, Zinzendorf was quite explicit that some behavior associated with public service would be objectionable in women but allowable or even praiseworthy in men.

> What one considers advantageous in ordinary men: intrigue, focus on method, a fierce nature, a kind of coarseness, that is very shocking in a woman.... It is against the tenor of their creation, they stretch beyond their species. Menfolk ...have much to bear in mind and take care of, must mingle with hundreds of things, with hundreds of kinds of creatures, and may look after things in whatever way works.[47]

Table 1 also demonstrates that the percentage of positive references in Zinzendorf's sermons grew markedly during the third period, but the positive emphasis in the third period was not just a repeat of that in the first period. It is true that Zinzendorf continued during this last period to describe women's good behavior in terms of the five characteristics he had used from the beginning: love, simplicity, purity, quietude, and sensitivity. However, the degree to which Zinzendorf stressed each of these ideals suggests a general change in Zinzendorf's attitude toward women. As Table 2 shows, his emphasis on love and simplicity increased greatly during the three periods under consideration, whereas his focus on sensitivity (feeling) and purity decreased just as strongly.

Table 2:
Zinzendorf's Emphasis on Desirable Traits for Women – in percentages
(total number of references in sample = 132)

	Love	Simplicity	Purity	Quietude	Sensitivity	Total %
1740s	18	9	14	14	45	100
Early 1750s	33	8	17	19	23	100
Late 1750s	52	21	6	10	11	100
All periods	39	14	11	14	22	100

In a 1757 sermon Zinzendorf connected the concept of love (friendship, connection) and simplicity (innocence, childlikeness) with each other:

> you know how lovingly...and kindly the Savior treated people...how beautiful he made it with his friends [Mary and Martha] in Bethany, what a friend he is of innocence and the simple being.

> Show now your simplicity and childlikeness. Inquisitiveness, cleverness, and reasoning are not sisterly, but childlikeness and simplicity are.... [The Savior] is a very special object for the Sisters, and he finds true joy in that, because the temperament and the acquired tendency of the Sisters always goes toward

friendship and connection with someone, because they like to put their trust in someone else and to pour their concerns into someone else's laps.[48]

This description suggests that Zinzendorf viewed women as relational beings, but dependent ones – like simple children who trust so completely as to put their fate entirely in the hands of others. This rendition sounds negative to our modern ears, but Zinzendorf meant it positively. The relational quality in women was ideally directed first and foremost toward the Savior. A boundless love and sense of complete dependence was in fact the foundation of any Christian's relationship to the Savior. So again, women as loving, dependent beings were natural guides to all Moravians about how to relate to the Savior.

But this conception also served to underscore the subordinate role that women, according to Zinzendorf, should play vis-à-vis men in their families, in the *Gemeine*, and in eighteenth-century European society. "Menfolk [were] created as the guardian angel of the female sex," he said in 1756. The protective role of men made it possible for women to lead a life in which they had "nothing to take care of and [nothing] to fear." Women's part was to give men "dependable loyalty and be ready to serve without reproach."[49] The relationship between genders outlined by Zinzendorf neatly fit the relationships commonly assigned to members of the family in early modern Europe. Protection and governance was expected of husbands toward wives, parents toward children, and masters toward servants. And in return, wives, children, and servants were required to obey and serve.

Zinzendorf's descriptions of gender relationships do not sound as if he thought in terms of gender equality, and yet that is exactly what he claimed Christ required. He believed this in spite of Peter's and Paul's admonitions to the contrary. Zinzendorf resolved this New Testament inconsistency by noting that Paul and Peter had been raised as Jews, implying that they were not able to overcome the prejudices against women which were institutionalized among Jews, but that as Christians, the Moravians must "act exactly like the Savior." "Mimicking him," Zinzendorf continued, "one must strive for equality of Brothers and Sisters."[50]

But Zinzendorf's conception of equality was different than ours. He began an extended discussion of equality by outlining two extreme cases of *inequality* between men and women. One extreme was found in the Old Testament, in which women were treated as if they were a "lesser species."[51] "The difference between men and women," Zinzendorf said, "was driven to the greatest extreme.... It was, as if the whole worship service was directed only to the Brothers."[52] And "only the male sex had the privilege to draw near to God."[53] Since the Apostles were still influenced by the "principles" of the Old Testament, their position on women was, in Zinzendorf's eyes, almost as extreme:

> [Paul] even forbid them [to engage in] spiritual discussions and flatly directed them to their husbands, if they wanted to know or research something about spiritual things.... Peter said of men that they should raise their holy hands and attend to the priesthood, wherever they were.... The Sisters, however, should...

GENDER PRESCRIPTIONS

relate to [God] in seclusion and let nothing of their connection with God appear outwardly.[54]

The opposite extreme was represented by Satan who "placed the female sex so high, that he would have freedom to do evil in almost all of the lands of the earth."[55] Zinzendorf thought that women in high positions would be weaker than men against the forces of evil.

If it was the will of Satan that women should hold positions of power, it was, according to Zinzendorf, the will of Christ that men should serve as governors and priests. Zinzendorf's rationale for male control over females was that men shared the trait of maleness with Christ and that he had given them the appropriate gifts for leadership. "Our souls are, to be sure, just as much his maids as those of the Sisters," he said,

> but because of the similarity with his human person, he gave [us] a certain spirit that is suitable to [our] work of being public teachers, for example, creators of order, of providing for, attending to, and furthering the best for society, and so forth.[56]

But in contrast to writers of the Old Testament and the Apostles, Christ placed limits on men's leadership, in Zinzendorf's view. Men must rule "through kindness, not through fierceness, not through anything that resembles superiority, which is often tyranny."[57] Furthermore, men no longer had the right to deny women equal access to worship services and to Christ:

> As far as the grace [of God], liturgies and sacraments, [and] intimacy with the eternal Bridegroom are concerned, [the Sisters] are made just like us Brothers, and everything...in the church principles that applies to the Brothers is also the concern of the Sisters.[58]

In addition, men must overcome the traditional Old Testament scorn they felt for Eve's descendants and treat them with respect. Interestingly, Zinzendorf felt that the traditional lack of respect for women was tied to men's sexual desire for women. After Eve's fall, he claimed, "the evil spirit entered into men," and instead of rejoicing in their soul...they made them only into an object of their lusts and their fleshly desires, which do not contribute to love."[59] To cancel this curse, Christ

> had to give to everyone who had received his spirit, the ability to not need the opposite sex.... First the blessed, pure whole had to become apparent, [the whole] that for both sexes lies in Christ, so that the words "Brothers and Sisters" would become valid through the mutual [and] chaste love, respect, and tenderness that each has for the other.[60]

Zinzendorf was not encouraging celibacy for Moravians. Rather, this was "just a temporary arrangement, for the purpose of overcoming the old sin."[61]

Zinzendorf's depiction of Christ's way was clearly not as extreme as either Satan's rule by women or the Old Testament's unlimited rule by men, but it wasn't in the middle either. Zinzendorf never considered the idea that authority might be shared by men and women. Such a stance would have been completely out of character with eighteenth-century ideas about authority. Instead he just underscored his belief that God ordained men to maintain ultimate authority over women.[62]

It is clear, then, that Zinzendorf did not believe that equality of the sexes meant women should exercise civil and religious authority. What he did mean was that women should be respected, that men and women were equal before God, and that women should have direct and equal access to God. This is clearly the position espoused by Luther and other early Reformation leaders, but as Lyndal Roper has shown, the Reformation eventually bound women within the confines of marriage, putting them under the social control of husbands. As time went on, this social control subsumed spiritual control as well, in the sense that wives' religious duties became synonymous with their domestic service to their families. This meant that in practical terms, women did not have equal access to God. They were not encouraged to engage in the "independent study of God's word" as men were.[63] Support for this stance came from the Bible itself in the Books of the Apostles, which seemed to require that women turn to their husbands for information and guidance in spiritual matters.

The existence of the Single Sisters and Widows Choirs among Moravians shaped Zinzendorf's thinking about women's relationship to God and encouraged him to develop a position that contrasted with the stance of both the Apostles and the majority of eighteenth-century Protestant churches. The Apostles' stance could possibly apply to women who were married, but what about all the Moravian women who had never had husbands or who had lost them? Obviously they must learn to approach the Lord on their own. And once they were used to that, what happened to their relationship to the Savior if and when they married? Zinzendorf spelled out the consequences of sticking too closely to the edicts of the Apostles:

> when we think about…our Single Sisters…after many of them have had…a relationship to the Savior and done spiritual work [in their Choir] for ten to twenty years, it would appear ludicrous if they would lose [all that] when they got married. They would say "No, thank you" to the change and there would be few new marriages.[64]

The obvious conclusion according to Zinzendorf was that

> we no longer want to hear from our Sisters: "You men, you talk with God; we will do everything you tell us, just put yourselves between God and us, so that we don't get too close to him." Instead they are all there to hear him and his word themselves, and we might well see to it, that we [Brothers] conduct ourselves, so that the word which he gives to them and our words and actions always agree.[65]

Clearly the usual Protestant position that wives must be spiritually dependent on their husbands could work only in a society where marriage was the primary option for adult women. Among the Moravians this practice was not sustainable because many women stayed single for their entire lives or at least a major portion of it. It may well be that Zinzendorf had not originally intended that Moravian Sisters would attain such spiritual independence when he first instituted the Choir system – he certainly never justified it in that way. It was likely the experience of actually living with this innovation that forced Moravians to adjust their values and accept more spiritual independence even among Sisters who were married.

The situation was tricky, however, because Zinzendorf did not want it to appear as if Moravians allowed married women the upper hand. Zinzendorf reassured his followers and the public that "the rule of wives in marriage is not an arrangement of the [Moravian] Brethren,"[66] but while maintaining the required standing of husband over wife, the husband had to make sure he did not disturb the relationship of his wife to the Savior. This required a careful balance between the husband regarding his wife "as his partner, who is on the way to the [eternal] bridegroom, who assists him in certain things" and the wife "showing her companion every deference and willingness along the way."[67]

After several years during the early 1750s of berating women for negative traits he saw, Zinzendorf had turned in 1756 to exploring in depth the notion that women were equal to men in their spiritual relations with the Savior and were, if anything, in a better position to serve as good examples to other would-be Christians. What can explain this shift? Zinzendorf did not say, but it is noteworthy that the revived focus on women's positive traits came shortly before he reintroduced the practice of ordaining women as Presbyters in 1758 after a twelve-year hiatus. Whether done consciously or unconsciously, this shift toward emphasizing the positive would have prepared the way for that remarkable step.

As an introduction on the day of the first public ordination, Zinzendorf defended his decision:

> now after 12 years, we begin again to confer this office as a rank among the Sisters, [and to do it] publicly in front of the *Gemeine*. The Sisters, after all, also have a right to the priesthood; they have among themselves and in their capacity, the [same] first 3 ranks of church offices as the Brothers do. The rank of Elder in the Church is an honor which comes with the years; the priesthood, however, is motivated by a certain requirement of [religious] office. It is of course understood that no person will receive this honor for whom it would not be suitable in that person's society.[68]

Zinzendorf made the point that the priesthood is a "requirement of [religious] office," suggesting that the Sisters, who that day received the Presbyter ordination, already carried responsibilities of office that made this step necessary. So, the act of ordination served partly to lend credibility to the ministerial activity women already engaged in. A year later, Zinzendorf spoke even more plainly, expressing the idea that women, like men, could develop traits that made them worthy servants of Christ.

> We have proof that our Sisters, [who] witness [and] bear the message on land and sea are just as valued as we are,...that they have carried them out with just as much steadfastness as we and in that regard are not beneath the Brothers.... Therefore, in that way there is no difference.[69]

Zinzendorf did not speak hypothetically here. His conclusions were based on observations of work that women had done already to spread the message of the Church.

If women were so effectively carrying out their ministerial roles, why would Zinzendorf still think it necessary to emphasize their subordinate position and their state of dependency on men, as he continued to do in the late 1750s? One reason may well have been that Zinzendorf faced many criticisms outside the Moravian world. At least one anonymous critic complained that Zinzendorf was encouraging a "Weiber-Religion," or female religion, by which he did not necessarily mean a religion in which women dominated, but one in which traditional feminine values, like kindness, were encouraged in men. "They often put aside their masculine language," he wrote, "they can laugh and cry in one breath, and everything they do must be heartfelt, pleasant, and beautiful."[70] A number of Zinzendorf's critics were also appalled at the unorthodox roles assumed by some leading Moravian women.[71] We know that Zinzendorf responded to his critics, both by writing answers and by changing Moravian practices. In a discussion about whether women should preach, Zinzendorf said,

> It is well known that in most Christian religions the sentence, "May the women keep silent in the church," is generalized, although it is not even clear that the Apostle said it about the female gender. Rather he said it only to one nation: "Let *your* women be silent in the church." [Zinzendorf's emphasis].... Among the Quakers it so happens that their women preach more than the men.... We have followed the other [non-Quaker] religions and have thrown the baby out with the bathwater, so that we could rid ourselves of the constant quarreling with others.[72]

Zinzendorf implied that Moravian women *had* been engaged in preaching, until Church leaders stopped the practice in order to avoid disputes with the majority of other Christian churches. He also expressed regret about having made this decision: "We...have thrown the baby out with the bathwater." If he was willing to change women's level of participation as a response to outside criticism, he would surely have been willing to reassure outsiders by underscoring women's subordinate position and their dependent status in Moravian society.

In addition, Zinzendorf continued to be genuinely ambivalent about the nature of women. He thought that some women had the ability to govern, but made clear that most women were too weak to do it well and that governing often caused (and even required) ill humor, intrigue, anger, and fierceness – behavior that he considered unsuitable for women but acceptable or even commendable in men. Quite possibly this mixed message gave him some room to maneuver in this later period, as it had earlier. While his dismissive views could reassure his non-Moravian critics that he shared their basic understanding about gender differences and especially about the limits of women's abilities, his positive views opened the way for him to expand the role of women within the Moravian Church.

After Zinzendorf

It appears, however, that Zinzendorf may have had critics inside the *Gemeine* as well. Certainly his successors lost little time in attempting to dismantle his innovations after his death in 1760, and in doing so, they made use of the very ambivalence which had supported new roles for women: as their authority, they could point to Zinzendorf's own more negative and more limiting words about women.[73] Beginning in the mid-1760s, they set out to institutionalize the leadership that Zinzendorf had held through his status as manor lord and his considerable charisma. In four general (international) synods (sometimes known as "The" Four Synods) held between 1764 and 1782, they completely redesigned the governing structure of the church. In the process, women were deprived of more and more roles they had played before his death.

The General Synod of 1764 decided that "the Brothers must always hold the Directorate…the Sisters, however, are their helpers and advisors…. The general offices previously [held by] the Sisters, were found to be not good." (The Directorate was the chief governing body, and the general offices were those with authority over the entire Moravian Church.) This same synod decided that women's Choirs needed male oversight in secular matters and established the office of Curator for that purpose.[74] The General Synod of 1769 demoted the Sisters even further. Instead of acting as advisors to the Directorate (now called the Unity Elders Conference), they would serve only as advisors to the Helpers Conference, a subdivision of the Unity Elders Conference.[75] The General Synod of 1775 held that only Bishops could ordain women as deaconesses and that women could not even assist in ordinations.[76] At the General Synod of 1789 (the first one following The Four Synods), male delegates were astonished by the large number of women attending (46 percent of 119 attendees) and discussed whether any women should be allowed to attend general synods in the future. After submitting the question to the Lot several times, the synod finally decided that the Unity Elders Conference would decide which Sisters could attend synods in the future.[77]

The synod minutes as distilled for Moravian settlements around the world tell us what decisions were made, but they do not reveal much about women's reactions to the new boundaries around their roles. However, other records from the 1764 synod demonstrate that they were not happy with the changes. First, the Moravian custom at synods was to discuss important decisions in plenary sessions, but this issue was debated in a special session that excluded Sisters, on the grounds that Brothers could speak more freely and openly if they were alone.[78] Surely this would not have been necessary unless the Brothers expected opposition from the Sisters. Second, after the Brothers reached their original conclusions, they consulted with a committee of Sisters to get their perspective before making a final decision. During the joint session, Sisters argued for some responsibilities that would be theirs alone and expressed concern that the proposed limitations "just wouldn't be extended too far."[79]

It is also telling how the men made the decision to remove women from the Directorate. Usually they consulted the Lot for such an important change in order to learn the will of the Savior.[80] This time they did not. They simply decided on their own to remove women.[81] Later they cast the Lot only to ask if women could serve the Directorate as advisors and which women could act as the advisors. Surely this second decision was less important than the first. Were members of the synod afraid the Savior might decide against female exclusion from the Directorate, if the proposal were submitted to the Lot?[82] Significantly, when the 1769 synod began to consider whether women should continue to serve as advisors to the Directorate (Unity Elders Conference), the Sisters strongly urged the Brothers not to discuss the issue in a separate session, but to submit it immediately to the Lot. They were obviously not pleased with the outcome of the separate session in 1764 and wanted explicit input from the Savior this time.[83]

In addition, women's anxiety about changes in their roles is reflected in the figures of female attendance at synods from 1764 to 1789. (See Table 3)

Table 3:
Attendance at General Synods

	Sisters	Brothers	Ratio of Sisters to Brothers
1764	21	69	0.30
1769	34	82	0.41
1775	28	52	0.54
1782	29	50	0.58
1789	55	64	0.86

The steady and remarkable rise in ratios shown in Table 3 (from .30 to .86) may well by itself indicate that the Sisters were concerned about the continuing constriction of their participation and responsibilities in governance. They likely wanted to be there to defend themselves, which is exactly what they did in 1789. As that synod moved towards excluding them from synods altogether, they organized themselves and submitted an unusually pointed memorandum directed to the Brothers. Calling the move "degrading" (*demüthigend*), they stressed the importance of the separation of sexes and then continued:

> We readily admit that it is,...everywhere outside of the Moravian Church, an entirely unusual circumstance, that people of our sex are included in such gatherings; it is however [part of] our whole system and the way of His *Gemeine*-folk,...found in no other place, and included in that [system] is certainly this: that the Savior has given our sex the grace, to be willingly guided and directed by him, which, especially in spiritual matters, is not usual anywhere else in the whole world.

> To uphold this plan and to legitimate the service of the Sisters in the *Gemeine*, it is necessary that the servants of Jesus value them with respect and trust. The opposite can have none other than bad consequences and, without fail, our concern will fall into confusion, if the maids of the Savior are more and more pushed into the background.[84]

The Sisters were arguing that the unusual circumstance of their attendance at synods was made necessary by the equally unusual organization of the *Gemeine* (the separation of the sexes), which required the separate oversight of the female sex. But they ventured much further and also emphasized that they were graced not only with immediate access to the Savior but with his direct guidance of their spiritual work (read: independently of mediation by Brothers). Such heavy responsibility required that they receive respect and trust from the Brothers. This strong and eloquent plea was successful to some degree. As shown above, the Brothers backed off of completely excluding Sisters' attendance at synods and settled instead for strict control of the numbers by the Unity Elders Conference.

The record of individual women's reactions to the diminution of Sisters' central roles is thin, but it does exist in one poignant record, if we read between the lines. Anna Johanna Piesch (the same leading Sister who was welcomed to Bethlehem in 1752 by the celebratory trombone Choir) described her response to the General Synod in 1769 in her autobiographical life story. In 1761, she had been called to marry Nathanael Seidel, move with him to Bethlehem, and help him dissolve the communal economy there. Because of the overwhelming challenges in Bethlehem at the time, they had not attended the General Synod of 1764, but they were delegates to the one in 1769. She recounted the experience with characteristic forthrightness:

> In the year '69 I traveled with my dear husband to Europe for the general synod. We left our beloved Bethlehem the last of March,...arrived safely in London on the 29th of May, and traveled after a few days' stay...toward Marienborn, where we arrived safely on the 28th of June. I rejoiced greatly to see and embrace many of my dearly loved, old acquaintances. And that was all, too, for I had no joy otherwise, but sorrow only, and [I] cried many, many tears. We hurried back, as soon as the Synod was over.[85]

Not only was this the first general synod after 1764, when women were excluded from active participation in the Directorate, but this new general synod was the one to downgrade them even further by making them advisors of the less authoritative Helpers Conference. It is not unlikely that her sorrow and tears were a reaction to experiencing, for the first time, how changed was her role and that of other leading Sisters. When she left Europe in 1761, she and other women had been part of the innermost circle of Moravian leadership. Now suddenly in 1769 she discovered a very different world. Gone was the time when the top Moravian leadership sought her intelligent, clearly thoughout, and refreshingly frank participation. As she said, she and her husband hurried away. After returning to Bethlehem, she never traveled back to Europe. Perhaps she hoped that her talents might still used and better appreciated in her beloved Bethlehem for a time and that she could adjust to these profound changes more gradually in that place.

But even in Bethlehem, she soon must have felt excluded. Along with Moravian settlements all over the world, Bethlehem moved quite swiftly to implement the decisions of The Four Synods, including those that limited women's roles. The numbers of newly received deaconesses and women acolytes declined drastically during the next decades. By 1780 Eldresses no longer ordained deaconesses. Only male bishops, acting alone, played that role.[86] Although women did continue to act as heads of the Single Sisters House and the Widows House, male "Curators" had been named to oversee their financial and legal matters. The ambiguity of Zinzendorf's language about women could easily support either the contraction or the expansion of their public roles in the Moravian Church. Zinzendorf had chosen the former, but his successors chose the latter.

Notes

1. For general descriptions of early Bethlehem, see Hellmuth Erbe, *Bethlehem, Pa.: Eine kommunistische Herrnhuter Kolonie des 18. Jahrhunderts* (Stuttgart: Ausland- und Heimat-Verlagsaktiengesellschaft, 1929); Gillian Gollin, *Moravians in Two Worlds: A Study of Changing Communities* (New York: Columbia University Press, 1967); and Beverly Prior Smaby, *The Transformation of Moravian Bethlehem: From Communal Mission to Family Economy* (Philadelphia: University of Pennsylvania Press, 1988).

2. For accounts of these activities, see Erbe, *Bethlehem*, as well as the *Single Sisters Diary* (bound manuscript in the Moravian Archives in Bethlehem).

3. See *Single Sisters Diary*.

4. For a detailed account of the preaching activities of Moravian women, see Peter Vogt, "Herrnhuter Schwestern der Zinzendorfzeit als Predigerinnen," *Unitas Fratrum* 45/46 (1999): 29-60, esp. 42-60. An earlier English version of this article is: Peter Vogt, "A Voice for Themselves: Women as Participants in Congregational Discourse in the Eighteenth Century Moravian Movement," in *Women Preachers and Prophets through Two Millennia of Christianity*, ed. Beverly M. Kienzle and Pamela J. Walker (Berkeley: University of California Press, 1998), 227-47.

5. *Single Sisters Diary*, 25 Nov. 1752.

6. Erbe, *Bethlehem*, 33.

7. For an account of the positive side of Zinzendorf's portrait of women, see Peter Zimmerling, "Zinzendorfs Bild der Frau," *Unitas Fratrum* 45/46 (1999): 9-28.

8. See Amanda Porterfield, *Female Piety in Puritan New England: The Emergence of Religious Humanism* (New York: Oxford University Press, 1992); Phyllis Mack, *Visionary Women: Ecstatic Prophecy in Seventeenth-Century England* (Berkeley: University of California Press, 1992); and Susan Juster, *Disorderly Women: Sexual Politics and Evangelicalism in Revolutionary New England* (Ithaca: Cornell University Press, 1994).

9. Beverly Prior Smaby, "Female Piety Among Eighteenth-Century Moravians," *Pennsylvania History* 64 (1997): 151-67.

10. "Reden vor die Frauenspersonen, gehalten in Philadelphia in 1742," Erste Rede, Moravian Archives in Herrnhut (MAH), R 14 A 38, 1a, quoted in Otto Uttendörfer, *Zinzendorf und die Frauen: Kirchliche Frauenrechte vor 200 Jahren* (Herrnhut: Verlag der Missionsbuchhandlung, 1919), 6.

11. "Reden vor die Frauenspersonen," 1742, quoted in ibid., 6.

12. From a sermon dated 28 Dec. 1758, quoted in ibid., 12.

13. From a sermon dated 8 Apr. 1757, quoted in ibid., 15.

14. "Reden vor die Frauenspersonen," 1742, quoted in ibid., 6.

15. From a sermon given 15 Jul. 1755, quoted in ibid., 16.

16. From a sermon given 6 Apr. 1755, quoted in ibid., 16.

17. Zinzendorf especially emphasized the importance of the Single Sisters Choir, which he believed "is an especially important one for the *Gemeine*. It should always stand as an example ... and as an answer to the question why the Scriptures say virgin [as a symbol] for pure heart." From a sermon given 17 Oct. 1750, quoted in Uttendörfer, 16.

18. The sample of sermons are those included in Uttendörfer's book *Zinzendorf und die Frauen*. The 295 references were those I collected in a painstaking analysis of all the sermons included in Uttendörfer's first chapter on "The Character of the Sisters." Uttendörfer presented his book as a monograph on the subject of Zinzendorf and women, but it is in fact a collection of Zinzendorf's sermons and other documents on the subject of women, glued together with transitions of one or two sentences. Uttendörfer engaged in very little analysis of his own on the subject.

19. "Reden vor die Frauenspersonen," 1742, quoted in Uttendörfer, 6.

20. Ibid.

21. Ibid.

22. Specifically, he caused Anna to "come forth and witness about him [after having] waited...for the Messiah for a long time" (Luke 2:36-38), second, he "bequeathed his mother to his most beloved disciple" (John 19: 26-27), third, he "caused an important account of himself to be written [in which] he showed an especially heartfelt love for the two sisters at Bethany [Mary and Martha]" (John 11:1-57), fourth, he "first appeared [after the crucifixion] to Mary Magdalene, a great sinner" (Matthew 27:54-66), and fifth, he publicly defended the sinful woman who bathed his feet with her tears (Luke 7:36-50). "Reden vor die Frauenspersonen," 1742, quoted in Uttendörfer, 6.

23. "Reden vor die Frauenspersonen," 1742, quoted in ibid., 7.

24. From a sermon given 14 May 1747, quoted in ibid., 15.

25. Helpers were spiritual leaders in the various Moravian settlements.

26. From a 1740 quote included in Zinzendorf's *Barbyshe Samlungen: Alter und Neuer Lehr-Principia, Sitten-Lehren, und den vorigen itzigen Gang der Oeconomie Gottes und ihrer Diener illlustrirender Stükke...* (Barby, 1760), 118.

27. From a sermon given on 22 Aug. 1755, Jüngerhaus Diarium, Beilage 30, quoted in Uttendörfer, 11.

28. From remarks given 9 Sept. 1750 at a synod in Barby, quoted in ibid., 13.

29. From a sermon given 15 May 1755, as quoted in ibid., 12.

30. From a sermon given 3 Sept. 1755, as quoted in ibid., 12.

31. From a sermon given 7 Nov. 1753, as quoted in ibid., 17.

32. The first two quotes are from a sermon given 7 Nov. 1753, and the third is from one given 25 June 1755, as quoted in ibid., 16-18.

33. From a sermon given 26 Oct. 1750, quoted in ibid., 9.

34. From a sermon given 17 July 1755, quoted in ibid., 12.

35. From a sermon given 17 Oct. 1750, quoted in ibid., 18.

36. From a sermon given 23 June 1755, quoted in ibid., 16.

37. From a sermon given 11 Aug. 1755, quoted in ibid., 10.

38. From a sermon given at a Synod for Single Brothers on 29 Dec. 1752 (MAH, R2 A32 B, pp. 200f.) quoted in Uttendörfer, 10-11.

39. From a sermon given at a Synod for Single Brothers on 29 Dec. 1752, quoted in Uttendörfer, 8.

40. "You are also much stronger than the Brothers, and therefore the Sisters can endure much more. They are much more loyal, more active, and stronger. That is why people prefer to trust women in various concerns, and [why] one gives them the sick to look after; [why] one entrusts them with the household; [why] one gets advice from them in perplexities about the body, [and] yes, [why] one often trusts their cure[s] more than that of the greatest physicians and surgeons." From a sermon given 26 Oct. 1750, quoted in ibid., 9.

41. The King James version translates this passage "ye husbands dwell with them ... giving honour unto the wife, as unto the weaker vessel."

42. From the same sermon given 26 Oct. 1750, quoted in Uttendörfer, 9-10.

43. For a careful analysis of it and a redefinition of what the Sifting meant in Moravian history, see Craig D. Atwood, "Zinzendorf's 1749 Reprimand to the Brüdergemeine," *Transactions of the Moravian Historical Society* 29 (1996).

44. See especially Susan Juster, *Disorderly Women*, and Phyllis Mack, *Visionary Women*.

45. From a sermon given 19 Apr. 1756, as quoted in Uttendörfer, 13.

46. From a sermon given 17 May 1756, as quoted by ibid., 15.

47. From a sermon given 6 Apr. 1757, as quoted by ibid., 10-11.

48. From a sermon given 8 Apr. 1757, as quoted by ibid., 15.

49. From a sermon given 6 Apr. 1757, as quoted by ibid., 10-11.

50. From a sermon delivered to the Married People's Choir on 22 Aug. 1756, quoted in ibid., 45.

51. From a sermon delivered to Married Sisters on 26 Dec. 1758, quoted by ibid., 43.

52. From a sermon given 2 Dec. 1756 to Married People, quoted in ibid., 44.

53. From a sermon given 22 Aug. 1756, quoted in ibid.

54. From a sermon given 22 Aug. 1756 to Married People, quoted in ibid., 45.

55. From a sermon given 2 Dec. 1756 to Married People, quoted in ibid., 44.

56. From a sermon given 22 June 1759, quoted in ibid., 48.

57. Ibid.

58. From a sermon given 2 Dec. 1756 to Married People, quoted in ibid., 44.

59. From a sermon given 26 Dec. 1758, quoted in ibid., 43.

60. From a sermon given 22 June 1759, quoted in ibid., 47-48.

61. From a sermon given 22 June 1759, quoted in ibid., 47.

62. From a 1740 quote in Barbysche Sammlungen, 118, included in Hans-Christoph Hahn und Hellmut Reichel, eds., *Zinzendorf und die Hernnhuter Brüder: Quellen zur Geschichte der Brüder-Unität von 1722 bis 1760* (Hamburg: Wittig, 1977), 295.

63. Lyndal Roper, *The Holy Household: Women and Morals in Reformation Augsburg* (Oxford: Clarendon Press, 1989), chaps. 3, 6, and 7.

64. From a sermon given on 22 Aug. 1756, quoted by Uttendörfer, 46.

65. From a sermon given 22 June 1759, quoted in ibid., 46-47.

66. From a sermon given 2 Dec. 1756, quoted in ibid., 44.

67. From a sermon given 22 Aug. 1756, quoted in ibid., 46.

68. *Jüngerhaus Diary*, 12 May 1758, MAH.

69. From a sermon given 22 June 1759, quoted in Uttendörfer, 48.

70. Anonymous, "Ausführlich Historische und Theologische Nachricht von der Herrenhuthischen Brüderschafft" (1743), in Erich Beyreuther, *Materialien und Documente*, ser. 2, vol. 14, *Antizinzendorfiana aus der Anfangzeit, 1729-1735* (Hildesheim: Olms, 1976), 96.

71. Peter Vogt, "Herrnhuter Schwestern," 42-45.

72. *Jüngerhaus Diarium* 1757, Beilage I, Vierte Rede (also quoted in Hahn und Reichel, 293-94).

73. Paul Peucker, "'Gegen ein Regiment von Schwestern': Die Stellung der Frau in der Brüdergemeine nach Zinzendorfs Tod," *Unitas Fratrum* 45/46 (1999): 61-72. See pp. 65-66 for one example of using Zinzendorf as the authority for limiting women's control.

74. Verlass des General Synodi in Marienborn Mense Julii & Augusti 1764 (bound ms. in the Moravian Archives Bethlehem), 28, 90.

75. Peucker, "Gegen ein Regiment," 68.

76. Verlass der im Jahr 1775 zu Barby gehaltenen Synodi der Evangelischen Brüder-Unität (bound ms. in the Moravian Archives Bethlehem), XIV, 24.

77. Peucker, "Gegen ein Regiment," 68-71.

78. Ibid., 63-64. At least one Brother argued for the continued participation in the Directorate by Sisters on the grounds that the Savior was born of a woman, thereby demonstrating that women should be involved in important religious matters.

79. Ibid., 65.

80. Moravians' usual practice for important decisions was to write a proposal on one slip of paper, put a statement against it on a second, and leave a third one blank. They then inserted the three slips of paper into separate tubes, mixed the tubes, and drew one to open and read. The result, they believed, revealed the will of the Savior. If the blank slip was drawn, the Savior was thought not to favor or disfavor the proposal for the time being. For a detailed discussion of the history and function of the Lot among Moravians, see Elisabeth Sommer, *Serving Two Masters: Moravian Brethren in Germany and North Carolina, 1727-1801* (Lexington: University Press of Kentucky, 2000), chap. 4 ("Gambling with God"), 86-109. See also my briefer discussion in *Transformation of Moravian Bethlehem*, 23-24. Because of

the importance Moravians attached to decisions by Lot, they were very careful to indicate the ones that were decided this way by marking them with an asterisk.

81. 1764 General Synod Minutes, Moravian Archives Herrnhut, R. 2. B. 44. l. c. 2., August 14, 1764, p. 1394.

82. Sommer shows that some Moravians had begun by this time to question the efficacy of the Lot or at least to bridle under too strict an adherence to it. She quotes August Gottlieb Spangenberg (Zinzendorf's successor as the head of the Moravian Church) as saying, "Many indeed would gladly have the lot consulted in matters in which they had no desire of their own: however, if they would rather do this or not do that and feared that the lot might fall against their inclination, they would rather not have asked the lot." Sommer, *Serving Two Masters*, 96.

83. Peucker, "Gegen ein Regiment," 68.

84. Quoted in ibid., 69-70.

85. Lebenslauf of Anna Johanna Seidel, nee Piesch, MEM Box 4, Moravian Archives Bethlehem.

86. Catalog of Ordinations, Church Register, Bethlehem, Vol. II, Moravian Archives Bethlehem.

Religion, Expansion, and Migration: The Cultural Background to Scottish and Irish Settlement in the Lehigh Valley

NED C. LANDSMAN

THERE MAY BE NO BETTER PLACE to begin a discussion of the cultural backgrounds of the Scottish and Irish settlers who settled in the Lehigh Valley during the eighteenth century than with William Allen, the prominent Philadelphia lawyer and political figure, for whose son James the town of Allentown was named. William Allen, the son of an Irish Presbyterian emigrant of Scottish parentage, was born in Philadelphia in 1704 and baptized in the city's first Presbyterian Church. The young man rose quickly in Philadelphia as a practitioner of the law, probably studying at the Inns of Court in London, which was closed to religious dissenters, as Presbyterians in England were. That does not seem to have been a problem for Allen in spite of his ancestry, for by that time he had apparently established ties to some powerful Philadelphia families and to the Church of England, a communion increasingly associated with elite famlies in the province.

In 1733 Allen married Margaret Hamilton, daughter of the Scottish native Andrew Hamilton, speaker of the assembly of Pennsylvania, in Philadelphia's Anglican Christ Church; his in-laws included such prominent families as the Penns. Allen's marriage did not sever his connections to the Presbyterian communion, and in 1735 he began to sponsor the settlement of families from Ulster, predominantly Presbyterians, at the Forks of the Delaware, the junction of the Lehigh and Delaware Rivers, in a vicinity that would be variously known as "Craig's settlement" and the "Irish settlement," the principal Presbyterian habitation within what would become Allen Township.[1]

The church that served that settlement apparently started as an offshoot of several other congregations, especially the Presbyterian church at Neshaminy, thirty or so miles to the south. The minister there was the renowned William Tennent Sr., who, like William Allen, traced his parentage to a family that had left Scotland for Ulster during the Restoration years. Unlike the elder Allen, who departed Ireland as a Presbyterian, Tennent took orders in the Irish Episcopal Church. Tennent's religious progress from there was seemingly the opposite of the younger Allen's, for upon his arrival in Pennsylvania in 1718 he forsook the Episcopal for the Presbyterian communion, citing the "anti-scriptural discipline" and the "ceremonial way of worship" of the former church. In Neshaminy he established the celebrated "Log College," where students studied for the ministry and the professions in a training that incorporated both divinity and the classics.[2]

Tennent was succeeded at Neshaminy by one of those pupils, Charles Beatty, still another Ulster emigrant of Scottish ancestry, who had received a classical education in Ireland. Beatty established close ties to the settlement in Allen Township, preaching there frequently, and lecturing often also at the nearby Indian mission, which had been established by the famous Presbyterian missionary David Brainerd, funded by the Society in Scotland for Propagating Christian Knowledge.[3] Beatty maintained his missionary efforts throughout his career, even though relations between Presbyterians and Indians in the vicinity – as elsewhere in rural Pennsylvania – were seriously marred by outbreaks of violence, including one that took place in the neighborhood of Stenton's Tavern near the Forks of the Delaware in 1763, resulting in the deaths of perhaps twenty settlers, many of them Scots or Irish Presbyterians. That incident was an important episode in the progression of events that led to what would be known as the Paxton uprising in central Pennsylvania, carried on principally by Irish Presbyterian settlers there; the Paxton rebels would cite the massacre near the Forks as one of their principal justifications for attacking supposedly friendly Christian Indians in both vicinities.[4]

For all of the diversity of their experiences, there were some common themes. Most prominent among those was mobility – from province to province, region to region, across the Atlantic, or back and forth across the Irish Sea; the very frequency of movement contributed to the seemingly amorphous quality of their experiences. Another, related theme was their frequent participation in imperial expansion. A third was a common Presbyterianism that affected settlers at all levels, including elite migrants such as William Allen, who established ties to other communions as well.

There was also a considerable diversity of behavior among Scots and Irish settlers, as the very different religious journeys of William Allen and William Tennent surely attest. We are all by now well beyond the point of debating whether or not cultural backgrounds were an important influence on the behavior of various groups in early America: the question is how and when they mattered.[5] Shared backgrounds certainly seem to have produced markedly different outcomes for the mission-minded Charles Beatty, of Ulster Presbyterian origin, for example, and the murderous Scots-Irish Presbyterian settlers who sought to attack the very mission where he preached.

What remains to be explored, then, is not simply the nature of the different cultural backgrounds found among various early American groups, but also the *salience* of those backgrounds for American identities and experiences. For while cultural backgrounds certainly played an important role in shaping the kinds of questions that various groups addressed, and consistently brought specific kinds of issues to the fore, they often left participants an array of choices and alternatives. This essay will explore the cultural backgrounds of Scottish and Irish settlers who came to the Lehigh Valley and the Delaware Valley in general during the eighteenth century and will attempt to say something about what gave their traditions significance.[6]

To discuss Scots and Irish together itself poses something of a problem, since they came from different backgrounds and circumstances and did not share a common nationality, although there is still much ambiguity about the precise identities of Irish Presbyterians, as we shall see. Nor was emigration from either place restricted to Presbyterians: Scots migrants included adherents of the Scottish Episcopal Church along with some Quakers, while those from Ulster incorporated some members of the Church of Ireland and the Catholic Church.

Yet trying to separate emigrants from Scotland and Ulster may pose even greater problems than does lumping them together, for both their histories and many of the settlements they created were inextricably linked. The Irish settlers who migrated to Pennsylvania were predominantly Presbyterians from the north, mostly of Scottish origin or descent. While it is often assumed that those Ulster Scots were primarily the descendants of participants in the Ulster plantations of the first decades of the seventeenth century, who had experienced a hundred years of separate development before they began the move to America, that was not in fact the case. The movement of Scots to Ireland was not confined to the plantation period of the early years but took place in repeated waves. Of perhaps a hundred thousand Scots migrants to Ulster over the course of the seventeenth century, certainly less than twenty percent arrived during the plantation years, while as many as two-thirds migrated during the second half of the century. A third or more embarked for Ireland during the 1690s alone.[7] Emigration from Ulster to America began in earnest only a few decades later. Thus many of those emigrants were not far removed from their days in Scotland. Indeed, of those emigrants from Ireland at the Forks of the Delaware whose origins have been traced, virtually all had either lived in Scotland themselves or had come from families that had departed Scotland not long before.[8]

Recent accounts of the divergence of Scotland and Ulster focus on the eighteenth century; the century before provided less opportunity for separate development. Instead, the records suggest frequent movement to and fro over the course of the seventeenth century, which is hardly surprising given the scant twenty miles that separates the north of Ireland from Galloway in Scotland's extreme southwest. Moreover, during certain periods, such as the civil war years of mid-century, there was considerable return migration to Scotland; the resident Scottish population in Ulster apparently declined by anywhere from a third to a half during the years of protracted warfare. Some of those return migrants would depart again for Ireland during the 1660s in the face of the persecution of Presbyterians in Restoration Scotland. Scattered references in the record indicate frequent movements thereafter as well, as the migratory backgrounds of William Allen and William Tennent, among a great many others, both illustrate.[9]

The two areas maintained other kinds of links as well. There were many commercial connections, for example, that were often closely linked to the emigrant trade. While commerce with Ireland never represented more than a small portion of Scottish trade measured by volume, more ships departed Scottish ports for Ireland than for any other destination.[10] Moreover, while the names attached to northern Irish emigrants varied, from "Irish" to "Ulster Scots" to "Scots-Irish" – the latter used principally in America – most emigrants from both Scotland and Ulster identified themselves as Presbyterian and shared memories of persecution and resistance; that common identity had been responsible for much of the movement between those places during the seventeenth century.[11]

Thus it is not surprising that the various communities labeled as "Irish," "Scots," or "Ulster Scots" in early America, including the "Irish settlement" near Allentown, often contained a mixture of persons who had migrated from Scotland and Ireland. Thus one of the pamphlets published in defense of the Paxton rebels referred to the inhabitants of the region as "Scotch and Irish." Scottish and Ulster merchants involved in the emigrant trade regularly advertised for settlers both in Ireland and Scotland, and emigrant vessels from the west of Scotland might stop in Ulster to pick up passengers. Conversely, especially before 1760, when emigration from Ulster far exceeded that from Scotland, passengers from Scotland sometimes traveled to Ireland to depart.[12]

Perhaps most important among the things these groups shared was a history of movement – back and forth across the Irish Sea, across the Atlantic to Pennsylvania, and to various places within the colony. A second, growing out of the first, was their common participation in empire and expansion, in the form of transatlantic migration, western settlement, and other activities that facilitated expansion, including missions, diplomacy, commerce, warfare, and imperial administration, in all of which persons identified as Scots or Scots-Irish were particularly active. A third was the establishment of religious identifications, of the sort that even a William Allen, in moving beyond the church to which most of his countrymen belonged, acknowledged through his continuing support for the Presbyterian Church, in Allentown and elsewhere. Presbyterianism offered those settlers a very particular kind of cultural background, incorporating an assertive lay culture and an active evangelical spirit with a marked interest in literacy, education, and secular learning, and a strong sense of identity. Together those traditions shaped, if they did not always determine, the nature of Scots and Irish settlement in the Lehigh Valley and throughout the mid-Atlantic region.

We will begin with migration, a persistent theme for Scots and Irish of all social levels – within Europe, in the transatlantic crossing, and in North America. Historians have more often considered a high frequency of migration as an indicator of poverty and social insecurity within the society from which migrants departed than as an inherent characteristic of the culture, but in the case of Scots and Irish that may be too narrow a perspective. Over time, different cultures have often exhibited distinct patterns of migration, apparently reflecting deep-seated social and cultural imperatives as much as short-term economic needs. Traditionally, Scots and their Irish Presbyterian counterparts were among the most mobile and least settled of European populations; that, as we have seen, was one of the principal difficulties in rigidly separating the two. They lived within what might be called cultures of migration, in which the common people had very little attachment to the land or to fixed abodes. In Scotland, only a small percentage of the population had any formal security in the possession of their lands, and at least within the Lowland zone, there was little rootedness among the bulk of the population.[13]

That movement took Scots and Irish not only to nearby places but overseas. For centuries, Scotland was a persistent exporter of population and, because few Europeans had much interest in that remote and generally unproductive land, was perhaps the most consistent net exporter of people in Europe. While emigration from Scotland certainly varied from year to year on the basis of changing economic and demographic conditions, there was almost always some out-migration from Scotland, and very few in-migrants other than Scots from the Continent returning home.[14]

That pattern of movement may have originated in economic necessity, but it came to serve essential functions within the Scottish social order. Mobility became embedded within the structure of Scottish communities, for example. While the regular short-term movement from farm to farm and parish to parish was partly attributable to the general lack of stability in the tenures of the tenantry, few of whom had leases or any other permanent claim upon their lands, that mobility, in turn, allowed an otherwise powerless common people a measure of independence from their landlords, to whom their attachments rarely went beyond the superficial. These were not the hallowed villages of mutual dependency that have shaped our romantic images of past times, but rather places where people knew precisely what they owed their social superiors, and what they did not. Scottish commoners created a form of extended neighborhoods, or regional communities, within which people regularly circulated, in which mobility was less a barrier to community than an essential ingredient.[15]

Movement overseas was also firmly embedded within the social order, providing an economic safety valve during frequent moments of overpopulation and dearth, as occurred during the famine years of the 1690s, when parishes in some parts of Scotland lost as much as half of their population to starvation or emigration, most of it to the north of Ireland. Moreover, the opportunity to travel or migrate to overseas communities provided many middling Scots a greater range of opportunities than the limited domestic economy could offer. The fact that some overseas communities maintained close connections to Scotland, to which people could migrate and then return, allowed for the maintenance of a larger Scottish population overall than the impoverished countryside would otherwise have permitted; "Scotsmen" were never simply those who lived in

Scotland.[16] Migration was also essential to the character of Ulster society and its relationship to Scotland, where virtually all of its Presbyterian leadership was educated or trained.

The migration cultures of Scotland and the north of Ireland were closely linked to empire and expansion. While Scots and Scots-Irish certainly lived up to their reputation as a nation of emigrants during the eighteenth century, the level of transatlantic migration the century before was in fact rather meager. Potential migrants from Scotland simply had better places to go.[17] The result was that when Scots and Ulster Scots did begin to move to the New World in significant numbers in the early decades of the eighteenth century, much of the coastal land was already occupied, and they were compelled to move rather quickly into the backcountry.

The mobile traditions of emigrants from Scotland and Ulster help to make sense of their willingness to participate in the establishment of frontier settlements, which they did so often not only in the Lehigh Valley but throughout the long backcountry region that stretched from central Pennsylvania south to the western portion of the Carolinas, which has been dubbed "Greater Pennsylvania."[18] Scots and Irish Presbyterians became the predominant settlers of some western regions. The point here is not that those groups were in some sense natural frontiersmen who would willingly forsake the ties of civilization for isolation on the frontier, as has sometimes been suggested, but rather that they did not have to break those ties when moving west. Scottish community life was structured in a way that allowed settlers to join new settlements while still maintaining ties of kinship and friendship to older neighborhoods. From the earliest Scottish settlements in East New Jersey to their migrations across West Jersey and into eastern Pennsylvania and south into Delaware, Scots established groups of interlocking settlements and extended family networks in which the movements of neighbors and kin among the different locales served as an important foundation of community.[19]

An important factor in establishing ties between older communities and those on the frontiers was the involvement of Scottish and Irish merchants, landowners, and clergymen. In Pennsylvania and throughout the backcountry, prominent men such as William Allen, James Logan, and Hugh Henry Brackenridge were instrumental in sponsoring settlements, establishing backcountry trade networks, and creating communication links to cosmopolitan centers. Throughout North America, Scottish merchants were renowned for their aggressive activity on the peripheries, while Presbyterian clergymen devoted unparalleled efforts to establishing schools as well as churches on the frontiers.[20]

None of the links those overseas Scottish communities established was more important than the church. While some of the most prominent families in the Lehigh Valley attached themselves to the elite Episcopal communion, the vast majority of settlers adhered to the Presbyterian Church, including some who, like William Tennent, had not been Presbyterian before their arrival. Thus unlike other national groups in Pennsylvania, who dispersed into an ever more varied set of sects, Scots and Irish settlers moved towards uniformity in denominational form. Most of those who separated from the Presbyterian Church in colonial Pennsylvania joined Presbyterian offshoots such as the several varieties of "seceder" churches or the Reformed Presbyterian Church, all of which claimed to be more firmly presbyterian in doctrine and discipline than the Presbyterian Church.[21]

Presbyterian church life was itself well suited to extended settlements and mobile communities. In form, Presbyterianism constituted something of a middle way in eighteenth-century American religion. Lacking the formal hierarchy of the Episcopal Church, Presbyterians did not require metropolitan involvement to establish new congregations, as Anglicans did. Yet unlike New England Congregationalists or other voluntarist groups, whose congregations were essentially independent of one another, Presbyterian congregations were linked together in regional presbyteries. And as members of an inclusive church rather than a gathered congregation, Presbyterians could move easily from one meeting to another. Because the Allentown church grew out of older congregations in Philadelphia, Neshaminy, and Easton, members had little difficulty crossing from one to the other or, subsequently, to any of the congregations to the west. Moreover, the meetings of the presbytery, composed of ministers and elders from each congregation, and the larger synods to which each Presbytery sent representatives, linked dispersed congregations across the region.

The Presbyterianism they supported had distinct Scottish roots, with a particular concern for issues of doctrine and the importance of secular learning. Elizabeth I. Nybakken has suggested that Presbyterianism in Ireland acquired a character distinct from that found in Scotland, one that was more liberal and tolerant in doctrine and policy than its Scottish counterpart.[22] Yet the difference may well have been more a matter of situation than of religious sentiment; in fact, doctrine and learning remained important for Presbyterians everywhere. Their circumstances differed, however; Irish Presbyterians were not restrained by membership in a national church, as their Scottish colleagues were. The liberal Irish "New Lights" always had close correspondents among the Scottish ministry; one of their principal teachers was John Simson of Glasgow, who twice faced ecclesiastical trials for heterodoxy, while Ireland had its share of orthodox evangelicals. The fact that Irish Presbyterians have been cited by Nybakken for liberal sentiments and by Marilyn J. Westerkamp for opposite tendencies towards evangelicalism and orthodoxy suggests that Presbyterianism in Ulster manifested almost the full range of positions along the religious spectrum. Even the seceders, who clung tenaciously to Scottish traditions, had a substantial presence in Ireland and among Irish Pennsylvanians as well. William Marshall, later of Philadelphia, and among the most prominent seceders in America, had his first pulpit at the Forks of the Delaware.[23]

Presbyterianism represented a middle way in American church life in another way also. Out of their concerns for orthodoxy and learning, Presbyterians were unusually successful at merging the seemingly opposite forces of evangelicalism and the Enlightenment. On the one hand, they maintained a consistent fidelity to doctrinal orthodoxy. Even when the Presbyterian Church divided over the intercolonial religious revival known as the Great Awakening during the 1740s, both sides in that dispute maintained a firm adherence to a basic Calvinistic creed.[24] That sharply contrasted with the avowed Arminianism that emerged among some Congregationalist opponents of the Awakening in New England. On the other hand, even Presbyterian proponents of the religious revival sought to temper the emotional fervor of evangelicalism with the reasoned moderation of the Enlightenment.[25]

In the aftermath of the Awakening, Presbyterians of all factions moved increasingly toward agreement upon a broader kind of evangelicalism that was more concerned with the revival of religion in common life than with loud and demonstrative religious revivals. To do so, they focused on the cultivation of religious character. Unlike earlier generations of Puritans and Presbyterians, who decried an excessive emphasis upon moral virtue, eighteenth-century Presbyterians portrayed the avoidance of sin as fundamental to creating the proper temper for receiving grace. Thus they employed new Enlightenment understandings of the role of the passions in human psychology and an increased emphasis upon secular learning within Presbyterian education, including history, the new natural and moral philosophies, and even belles lettres.[26]

As the church extended its reach into the backcountry, Presbyterian ministers of all affiliations began to establish academies wherever they settled, through the backcountries and into the frontier regions. Charles Beatty, a member of the evangelical or New Side faction, took over William Tennent's academy in Neshaminy. James Latta, an Ulster emigrant of Old Side affiliation, established another in the vicinity at Chestnut Level, on land donated by William Allen. By the 1770s, Presbyterians established a line of academies across the Pennsylvania backcountry and into the backcountries of Maryland, Virginia, and the Carolinas. By the following decade those schools extended into Kentucky and Tennessee as well. Those academies trained not only clergymen but aspiring lawyers, physicians, and political leaders, disseminating both evangelical fervor and an enlightened interest in the principles of society and morals.[27]

To their critics, Presbyterians ranked as unbridled opponents of established authority. In Pennsylvania, critics of the Paxton rebels equated Presbyterianism with rebellion and opposition to "kingly government." Presbyterianism and rebellion were "twin-sisters," a link they traced backwards to the revolutions of mid-seventeenth-century Britain. Presbyterianism was identified with a blunt resistance to authority.[28] After 1776, it became common among Loyalists to blame the American Revolution upon Presbyterians, under which they included not only members of the Presbyterian Church, headed by the Whig and member of the Continental Congress, John Witherspoon, but also New Englanders, whose independency made them an equally ungovernable people. Both groups favored government of the church not by bishops but ministers or presbyters without

Paxton Expedition, 1764.

In this cartoon, Henry Dawkins mocked Philadelphians who prepared to defend the city against the Paxton boys. The fourth verse below the cartoon reads:

> There was Lawyers & Doctors, & Children in Swarms.
> Who had more need of Nurses, than to carry Arms
> The Q[uaker]s so peaceable as you will Find:
> Who never before to Arms were Inclined.

The Library Company of Philadelphia.

higher authority. In short, Presbyterian churches insisted upon the right of governing themselves.

What linked the political outlook of Scottish and Irish Presbyterians was a shared history and mythology. Presbyterianism was associated with the Scottish National Covenant of 1638, in which signers pledged to uphold the true religion against external imposition, and the Solemn League and Covenant of 1643, in which the signers committed themselves to work to install a uniform religion, on the model of the best Reformed churches, in all three British kingdoms. With the Restoration of the monarchy in 1660, the commitment to the covenants placed radical Presbyterians in opposition to the new religious establishment, and those who refused to renounce the covenants were fined, imprisoned, exiled, or even executed for their resistance. Some of the most ardent Presbyterians traversed the Irish Sea in both directions in order to avoid the hand of authority. Presbyterianism was henceforth associated with whiggery – that is, with opponents of the royal prerogative and the established order; the term "whig" itself originated in Scottish politics of the period. Out of that experience grew legends of martyrdom and resistance both in Scotland and in Ireland, which migrants from both places carried to America.[29]

In Scotland, the Presbyterian Church was the church of the west, the only part of the Scottish lowlands containing a class of small landowners who were able to maintain a degree of cultural independence from the authority of the wealthy heritors. Presbyterianism was largely the religion of small owners, tenants, and artisans, along with some of the merchants. That made it suitable to conditions in Ulster as well, which also had a class of small landowners, along with substantial groups of artisans and merchants. The congregation, moreover, was often the only public realm in which such groups were able to participate, as the suffrage in Scotland was restricted to only a handful of voters in most districts, while Presbyterians in Ireland suffered legal disabilities. Within the churches, lesser folk were able to assert their will in such matters as the calling of ministers, which they often did in an active and aggressive manner.[30]

Presbyterianism was well suited to the situation of Scottish and Irish settlers in Pennsylvania also, where most were either small landowners or tenants. While Presbyterians initially lacked a substantial political role in Pennsylvania, from the beginning they were able to participate actively in ecclesiastical politics, which they began to do in earnest from the 1720s.[31] Moreover, the Church and its ministers functioned as an important political voice for Pennsylvania Presbyterians during the repeated partisan battles of the mid-eighteenth century. And during the Paxton uprising of the 1760s, as a largely Presbyterian group of armed men first attacked and killed the Christian Indians housed at Conestoga and then marched on the city of Philadelphia, demanding the removal of all of the Christian Indians from the province, critics laid the blame for fomenting the riots squarely upon Presbyterian ministers.[32]

Presbyterian activism did not necessarily imply overt political radicalism, although it did take that form on occasion. Adept Scottish and Irish politicians such as William Allen were often able to secure the support of Presbyterian congregations through relationships of patronage, by serving the essential needs of the church and the community and demanding little in the way of deference other than political support. Allen was careful to provide for churches and schools in the vicinity. Throughout Pennsylvania, he and other such men were often able to maintain the loyalty of Presbyterian settlers even in times of extreme turbulence, such as the Paxton uprising or the political conflicts of the 1780s and 1790s.[33]

More famously, Presbyterian communities in North America were politically contentious when they believed officials in the colony or the state were attempting to impose their authority upon the community without responding to its needs. Thus Scots and Irish Presbyterians were known for their active participation in the Paxton uprising, in the Regulator movements in the backcountry of the Carolinas during the 1770s, and in the Whiskey Rebellion in western Pennsylvania during the 1790s.[34] The victims of that contentiousness were often Native Americans and the authorities who defended them, as in the case of the Paxton massacres, and those settlers have developed reputations as Indian-haters *par excellence.* That was partly because their relatively late arrival in the colonies and their willingness to migrate to the frontiers made Scots-Irish settlers more likely than others to come into conflict with their Indian neighbors. By the 1750s, Scottish and Irish colonists faced the consequences not only of their own aggressive settlement but of imperial disputes and of high-handed diplomacy in the colony over the previous several decades.

More than just their situation accounts for the propensity of Presbyterian settlers to enter into frontier conflicts, in which they engaged much more aggressively than other national groups. The events that took place in and around Stenton's Tavern near the Forks of the Delaware in 1763 are revealing. In that incident, a group of Delawares from the neighborhood, apparently responding to an earlier altercation that had taken place at the tavern, attacked several houses, killing John Stenton and numerous others, including several residents of the Irish settlement. Stenton's widow later alleged that an Indian named Renatus, a member of the "friendly" Moravian Indians living in nearby Bethlehem, was a member of the party. The Paxton rebels, residing far to the southwest, cited Renatus's alleged involvement as one of the justifications for their own attack on the peaceful Christian Indians living in Conestoga, whom they also accused of collaboration in attacks upon the settlers. Renatus was later tried and released.[35]

Several aspects of the story stand out. One was the importance of the links of religion and communication that tied those Presbyterian communities together in extended neighborhoods. Had these been isolated settlements without significant identification or communication, the frontiersmen would have been far less likely to have viewed themselves as targets of coordinated attacks. Paxton was located some eighty miles southwest of the Forks, but the Paxton marchers considered the settlers at the Forks to be part of a common community of frontiersmen and Presbyterians and quickly learned of the allegations against Renatus by Stenton's widow. The ministers were a likely source of communication; Paxton's

John Elder, a Scottish native, was alleged to be an instigator of Paxton protests, if not the violence. In communities such as these, numerous other possible links existed as well. For example, John Roan, another Ulster native and New Side minister of Paxton and Derry, was probably a contemporary of Charles Beatty at the Log College and had stayed on in Neshaminy as a schoolmaster while Beatty served as minister there.[36]

Another important aspect of the story is suggested by the voice that the Paxton men chose to employ in their defense, as the "distressed and bleeding frontier inhabitants" of Pennsylvania, as they called themselves in one of the most important publications.[37] The language itself almost certainly derives from that used by Scottish and Irish Presbyterians during the persecutions of the seventeenth century, where they referred to themselves as a "poor, wasted, misrepresented remnant" of the "suffering...true Presbyterian Church," and other similar expressions.[38] Because the phrases and the perspective they implied originated in persecutions and warfare in a border setting, they were highly adaptable to the situation of Presbyterians in the North American backcountry and became firmly embedded within Presbyterian popular culture on both sides of the Atlantic.[39]

The language of martyrdom and resistance implied something else for backcountry Presbyterians that had important ramifications for their dealings with their Indian neighbors: a marked sense of moral certainty. These were godly people who believed that they were suffering grievous trials on behalf of divine truth. On both sides of the Atlantic, the agents who imposed that suffering were identified as markedly un-Christian. Those included the native Irish during the Civil War years of the 1640s and again during the pitched battles between Protestants and Catholics that followed an anything but peaceful "Glorious Revolution" of 1688 in Ireland; the Scottish dragoons, many of them Highlanders, who pursued and punished recalcitrant Presbyterians during the "Killing Times" of the 1680s; and Indians on the Pennsylvania frontiers, many allied with Catholic France before the surrender of New France in 1763, which made them especially feared by Scots and Irish Presbyterians.

One of the defenders of the Paxton men referred to them as "descendants of the Noble Eniskillers," referring to a place in Ireland where Ulster Protestants had bravely defended their town against a Catholic army in 1688 in order to uphold the Protestant succession.[40] Behind those "un-Christian" agents were persecuting authorities: the Restoration monarchy of the Stuarts and their Jacobite adherents who were more interested in establishing arbitrary rule than in protecting their subjects; and in Pennsylvania, a Quaker government that denied fair representation to the back settlements, ignored their requests for security and assistance, and acted more affectionately and protectively toward native inhabitants than Christian subjects.[41]

Like many other religious groups, Scottish and Irish Presbyterians were firmly wedded to the notion of an unvarying religious truth, but the manner in which that truth was defended by Presbyterians in Scotland and Ireland gave it an unusual rigidity. Those groups traditionally defended their faith through public testimony, such as signing the National Covenant, affirming the status of Presbyterianism as a providentially ordained religion, or subscribing to articles of faith. During the Restoration years, Presbyterians were fined, imprisoned, or banished from their homelands for refusing to subscribe to a test oath renouncing the obligations of the Presbyterian covenants. In succeeding years, orthodox Presbyterians repeatedly testified against what they viewed as the failure of the Scottish Church to adhere to its public testimonies.[42]

During the eighteenth century, most groups who dissented from the Presbyterian Church in Scotland or Ulster joined either the Reformed Presbyterian Church or one or another variety of "seceder" churches, who had broken away from the Presbyterian Church largely because of its abandonment of the national covenants and its perceived departures from traditional confessions and testimonies. The new churches justified their secessions on the basis of fidelity to the traditional Reformation principles of the Scottish Church, and their adherence to the Confession of Faith on the basis of "Proofs From Scripture." All of the seceding churches attracted adherents in Pennsylvania.[43]

Presbyterians in Pennsylvania maintained their concern with the issue of an unvarying religious truth. They did not voice a single position on the matter. In 1727, a minister from Ireland named John Thomson presented the Synod with a measure requiring that all ministers formally subscribe to the Confession of Faith, derived from a similar proposal that had racked the Presbyterian community in Ireland a few years before. In Ireland, a group of younger ministers known as New Lights opposed that effort, and the "subscription controversy" almost fractured the American Synod as well. It was finally settled through a compromise plan known as the Adopting Act, which nearly all were willing to support."[44]

A culture that disseminates legends of martyrdom and of divine deliverance for the adherence to scriptural truth, and which codifies faith through subscription and public profession, is likely to possess a high degree of confidence in its place within the divine scheme, and that was certainly true of Scots and Irish Presbyterians. Compared to either the Quaker doctrine of the inner light or the pietist faith of some of their German neighbors, both of which allowed at least an occasional voicing of the call of conscience against the consensus of the community,[45] Presbyterian orthodoxy left little ethical space for questioning prevailing moral certainties.

Thus one finds few pronouncements among the public statements of orthodox Scots or Irish Presbyterians suggesting that they ever doubted the justice of defending and extending their own Christian civilization against what they considered the barbarism or savagery of Highlanders, native Irish, or Indians. Ironically, even the spread of Presbyterian educational institutions into the backcountry, which advanced Scottish Enlightenment ideas about the progress of civilization, only reinforced their belief that they were bringing moral progress with them in their march into the wilderness.[46]

By itself, Presbyterianism did not lead to inveterate Indian hating. In other circumstances, Scots and Irish settlers displayed the more tolerant side of their enlightened educations. Thus Charles Beatty and other clergymen connected with the Society in Scotland for the Propagation of Christian Knowledge (S.S.P.C.K.) devoted themselves to mission work. Cadwallader Colden, another Scot born in Ireland and the son of a Presbyterian minister, became one of the most attentive provincial scholars of Indian culture, which was evident in his *History of the Five Indian Nations Depending on the Province of New-York* (1727-44), a work that was read by many among the Scots literati in their attempts to develop an understanding of the stages of civilization. And everywhere, members of the Scots and Scots-Irish imperial elites were among those especially committed to developing strategic alliances with their Indian neighbors as a means of securing the interests of both the provinces and the empire – alliances that were often opposed by Scots-Irish settlers on the frontiers.[47]

The involvement of those many officials in the search for Indian alliances represents the opposite side of Scottish and Irish involvement in imperial affairs from the expansive settlements of the backcountry. It can tell us something about the *resonance* of cultural traditions in the Lehigh Valley and elsewhere. If the Scottish and Irish backgrounds provided Presbyterian settlers with some common traditions upon which to draw, they did not necessarily determine how those traditions would function in the New World. Their backgrounds established some of the parameters within which settlers could adapt, but they did not necessarily limit those adaptations to a single pattern. Rather, in different situations and for different individuals, those traditions provoked alternative responses.

All of these settlers derived from a mobile culture, which provided an impetus to migration and participation in imperial expansion through settlement, administration, and trade. For some, this meant an immersion in the world of trade, while others moved far enough on the frontiers to push trade to its limits. Their backgrounds also provided a common Presbyterianism, one that combined personal piety with a taste for education and letters, and a common imagery of martyrdom and resistance. From that grew a strong emphasis upon holding fast the truth, and a marked degree of moral certainty about the status of their communities.

That shared background led to some common features of those societies. Those included an unusual degree of participation on the provincial frontiers – whether as settlers, officials, or as traders. Another common feature was the widespread adoption of Presbyterianism as a repository of a national or ethnic identity, providing a strong justification, where necessary, for attacking their enemies and resisting authorities that failed to protect them, but also, on occasion, for aggressive missionary efforts. The expansive Presbyterian educational system extended to those frontiers a distinctive synthesis of religion and Enlightenment.

Within that culture there was considerable room for alternatives. A William Allen could move outside the world of common folk and into the world of the gentry. If that sometimes lured him out of the Presbyterian Church, it did not lead him to end his sponsorship of local Presbyterian congregations, upon whom he depended for political support as much as they depended upon his economic patronage. A William Tennent could move in the opposite direction, from Anglican to Presbyterian, establishing an academy to instruct a new generation of evangelical leaders and Enlightened men of medicine, law, and letters. His student and successor, Charles Beatty, could combine an evangelical and tolerant support for missions with the patronage of institutions of learning, even if he might have wished to dissuade his countrymen from undoing his work through their martial resistance to Quaker authorities and their Indian allies. Beatty's classmate, John Roan, could support his belligerent frontier community even as he continued to promote the academy tradition and the dissemination of the Presbyterian Enlightenment.

Notes

1. The details of Allen's life are taken from *Dictionary of American Biography*, vol. 1, ed. Allen Johnson (New York: Scribner's Sons, 1928), 208-209; on Hamilton, see Burton Alva Konkle, *The Life of Andrew Hamilton, 1676-1741: "the Day-Star of the American Revolution"* (Philadelphia: National Pub. Co., 1941). On the Irish settlement near Allentown, see *The Scotch-Irish of Northampton County, Pennsylvania* (Easton, Pa.: Northampton County Historical and Genealogical Society, 1926), 26-27.

2. *Records of the Presbyterian Church in the United States of America, 1706-1788*, ed. Guy S. Klett (Philadelphia: Presbyterian Historical Society, 1976), 34. See also Archibald Alexander, *Biographical Sketches of the Founder, and Principal Alumni of the Log College* (Philadelphia, 1851) and T. C. Pears, Jr., and Guy S. Klett, "Documentary History of William Tennent and the Log College," *Journal of the Presbyterian Historical Society* 28 (1950): 37-64, 105-28, 167-204.

3. *Journals of Charles Beatty: 1762-1769*, ed. Guy Soulliard Klett (University Park: Pennsylvania State University Press, 1962).

4. On the massacre near Lehigh, see Joseph J. Mickley, *Brief Account of the Murders by the Indians and the Cause Thereof, in Northampton County, Pennsylvania* (Philadelphia, 1875); and Charles Rhoads Roberts, *History of Lehigh County, Pennsylvania*, 2 vols. (Allentown, Pa.: Lehigh Valley Publishing Co., 1914), 1:102ff; and see Brooke Hindle, "The March of the Paxton Boys," *William and Mary Quarterly* 3d ser., 3 (1946): 461-86; Jane Merritt, *At the Crossroads: Indians and Empires on a Mid-Atlantic Frontier, 1700-1763* (Chapel Hill: University of North Carolina Press, 2003), 276-94; and Krista Camenzind, "Violence, Race, and the Paxton Boys," in *Friends and Enemies in Penn's Woods: Indians, Colonists, and the Racial Construction of Pennsylvania*, ed. William Pencak and Daniel K. Richter (University Park: Pennsylvania State University Press, 2004), 201-20.

5. Useful illustrations of the very different roles cultural backgrounds can play can be taken from A. G. Roeber, "'The Origin of Whatever is Not English Among Us': The Dutch-speaking and the German-speaking Peoples of Colonial British America," in *Strangers within the Realm: Cultural Margins of the First British Empire*, ed. Bernard Bailyn and Philip D. Morgan (Chapel Hill: University of North Carolina Press, 1991), 220-83; also

compare the role of religion in Huguenot communities, as detailed in Jon Butler, *The Huguenots in America: A Refugee People in a New World Society* (Cambridge, Mass.: Harvard University Press, 1983), with its role among Scots, in Ned C. Landsman, *Scotland and its First American Colony, 1680-1760* (Princeton: Princeton University Press, 1985) and David A. Wilson and Mark G. Spencer, *Ulster Presbyterianism in the Atlantic World: Religion, Politics and Identity* (Dublin: Four Courts, 2006).

6. Such an approach is consistent with the general evolution of the culture concept, which is no longer viewed as a rigid determinant of behavior, but in flexible and symbolic terms. For a recent discussion, see Sherry B. Ortner, *Anthropology and Social Theory: Culture, Power, and the Acting Subject* (Durham, N.C.: Duke University Press, 2006), 11-14.

7. Estimates of the movement from Scotland to Ulster are far from precise, but this paragraph draws upon T. C. Smout, Ned C. Landsman, and T. M. Devine, "Scottish Emigration in the Seventeenth and Eighteenth Centuries," in *Europeans on the Move: Studies on European Migration, 1500-1800*, ed. Nicholas Canny (Oxford: Clarendon Press, 1994), 76-112. See also W. Macafee and V. Morgan, "Population in Ulster, 1660-1760," in *Plantation to Partition: Essays in Ulster History in honour of J. L. McCracken*, ed. Peter Roebuck (Belfast: Blackstaff Press, 1981), 46-63; and Philip S. Robinson, *The Plantation of Ulster: British Settlement in an Irish Landscape 1600-1670* (Dublin: Gill and Macmillan,1984), chap. 4.

8. *Scotch-Irish of Northampton County*; John C. Clyde, *History of the Allen Township Presbyterian Church* (Philadelphia, 1876).

9. Smout, Landsman, and Devine, "Scottish Emigration"; and see Edward M. Furgo, "The Military and Ministers as Agents of Presbyterian Imperialism in England and Ireland, 1640-1648," in *New Perspectives on the Politics and Culture of Early Modern Scotland*, ed. John Dwyer, Roger A. Mason, and Alexander Murdoch (Edinburgh and Atlantic Highlands, N.J.: Distributed by Humanities Press, 1982), 95-115; and Patrick Griffin, *The People with No Name: Ireland's Ulster Scots, America's Scots Irish, and the Creation of a British Atlantic World, 1689-1764* (Princeton: Princeton University Press, 2001). This essay was essentially completed before Griffin's book appeared.

10. L. E. Cochran, *Scottish Trade with Ireland in the Eighteenth Century* (Edinburgh and Atlantic Highlands, N.J.: Distributed by Humanities Press, 1985), 140-41, 158-61.

11. For the designations of Ulster emigrants, see especially discussion at the beginning of Maldwyn A. Jones, "The Scotch-Irish in British America," in *Strangers*, ed. Bailyn and Morgan, 284-85; and Griffin, *People with No Name*.

12. On the problem of delineating Scots from Ulster Scots or Scots-Irish, see Smout, Landsman, and Devine, "Scottish Emigration in the Seventeenth and Eighteenth Centuries," 92-100; T. M. Devine, *Scotland's Empire and the Shaping of the Americas, 1600-1815* (Washington, DC: Smithsonian Books, 2004), chap. 7; Griffin, *People with No Name*; Griffin, "The People with no Name: Ulster's Migrants and Identity Formation in Eighteenth-Century Pennsylvania," *William and Mary Quarterly* 58 (2001): 587-614; David A. Wilson and Mark G. Spencer, *Ulster Presbyterianism in the Atlantic World: Religion, Politics and Identity* (Dublin: Four Courts, 2006). The Paxton pamphlet was "The Cloven-Foot

Discovered" (Philadelphia, 1764), in *The Paxton Papers*, ed. John R. Dunbar (The Hague: M. Nijhoff, 1957), 85-86. Examples of emigration pamphlets printed both in Scotland and Ulster include "A Candid Enquiry into the Late and the Intended Migrations from Scotland" (Glasgow, n.d.); and see *Glasgow Journal*, 11 Feb. 1773; John Stevens to Campbell Stevens, 6 Feb. 1751, Stevens Family Papers, New Jersey Historical Society; and Gregg and Cunningham Letterbook, 1756-57, New-York Historical Society. Usable studies of the Ulster Scots as a group are few and far between, but see M. Perceval Maxwell, *The Scottish Migration to Ulster in the Reign of James I* (London: Routledge and Kegan Paul, 1973); Robinson, *Plantation of Ulster*; Ian Macbride, *Scripture Politics: Ulster Presbyterians and Irish Radicalism in the Late Eighteenth Century* (New York: Oxford University Press, 1998); W. F. Dunaway, *The Scotch-Irish of Colonial Pennsylvania* (Chapel Hill: University of North Carolina Press, 1944); James G. Leyburn, *The Scotch-Irish: A Social History* (Chapel Hill: University of North Carolina Press, 1962); R. J. Dickson, *Ulster Emigration to Colonial America 1718-1775* (London: Routledge and Kegan Paul, 1966); E. Estyn Evans, "The Scotch-Irish: Their Cultural Adaptation and Heritage in the American Old West," in *Essays in Scotch-Irish History*, ed. E. R. R. Green (London: Routledge and Kegan Paul, 1969), 69-86; Jones, "The Scotch-Irish in British America"; and H. Tyler Blethen and Curtis W. Wood, Jr., eds., *Ulster and North America: Transatlantic Perspectives on the Scotch-Irish* (Tuscaloosa: University of Alabama Press, 1997). For examples of Ulster migrants in the Scottish settlement of East New Jersey, see Landsman, *Scotland and its First American Colony*, chaps. 5, 7. On the Irish settlement, see the sources listed in note 8, above.

13. Landsman, *Scotland and its First American Colony*, chap. 1; R. A. Houston, "The Demographic Regime," in *People and Society in Scotland*, vol. 1, 1760-1830, ed. T. M. Devine and Rosalind Mitchison (Edinburgh and Atlantic Highlands, N.J.: Distributed by Humanities Press, 1988), 9-26. Unless otherwise noted, this whole section draws upon Smout, Landsman, and Devine, "Scottish Emigration." A high degree of mobility was common elsewhere in Britain and early modern Europe as well, of course, but the degree of movement in Scotland seems to have been especially high, and there is some evidence that the rate of stability – the ability of families to establish any measure of permanence upon the land – may have been lower than elsewhere also. See, for example, *Migration and Society in Early Modern England*, ed. Peter Clark and David Souden (Totowa, N.J: Barnes & Noble Books, 1987), 32, 316; and compare Houston, "Demographic Regime," esp. 20-23; *Scottish Population History from the Seventeenth Century to the 1930s*, ed. Michael Flinn (Cambridge: Cambridge University Press, 1977).

14. Smout, Landsman, and Devine, "Scottish Immigration"; and see L. M. Cullen, "The Irish Diaspora of the Seventeenth and Eighteenth Centuries," in *Europeans on the Move*, ed. Canny, 113-49.

15. Landsman, *Scotland and its First American Colony*, chap. 1.

16. Ned C. Landsman, "Nation, Migration, and the Province in the First British Empire: Scotland and the Americas 1600-1800," *American Historical Review* 104 (1999): 463-75.

17. Ibid.

18. On "Greater Pennsylvania," see Carl Bridenbaugh, *Myths and Realities: Societies of the Colonial South* (Baton Rouge: Louisiana State University Press, 1952). Still standard as a reference work on Ulster emigration is R. J. Dickson, *Ulster Emigration*, but see also Bernard Bailyn, *Voyagers to the West: A Passage in the Peopling of America on the Eve of the Revolution* (New York: Knopf, 1986), chap. 1; and Marianne S. Wokeck, "German and Irish Immigration to Colonial Philadelphia," Symposium on the Demographic History of the Philadelphia Region, 1600-1860, ed. Susan E. Klepp, *Proceedings of the American Philosophical Society* 133, no. 2 (June, 1989): 128-43; Marianne S. Wokeck, *Trade in Strangers: The Beginnings of Mass Migration to North America* (University Park: Pennsylvania State University Press, 1999).

19. Landsman, *Scotland and its First American Colony*, chap. 5. For Lehigh Valley Scots who came from older settlements, see *Scotch-Irish of Northampton County*. For an extended portrayal of the Scots and Scots-Irish as borderers who willingly settled the farthest frontiers, see David Hackett Fischer, *Albion's Seed: Four English Folkways in America* (New York: Oxford University Press, 1989), 605-782.

20. On the activity of Scottish merchants on the frontiers, there is an extensive literature, including Jacob Price, "The Rise of Glasgow in the Chesapeake Tobacco Trade," *William and Mary Quarterly* 3d ser., 11 (1954): 179-99; Thomas M. Devine, *The Tobacco Lords: A Study of the Tobacco Merchants of Glasgow and Their Trading Activities c. 1740-1790* (Edinburgh: Donald, 1975); and David S. Macmillan, "The 'New Men' in Action: Scottish Mercantile and Shipping Operations in the North American Colonies, 1760-1825," in *Canadian Business History: Selected Studies, 1497-1971*, ed. David S. Macmillan (Toronto: McClelland and Stewart, 1972). On schools and academies see Douglas Sloan, *The Scottish Enlightenment and the American College Ideal* (New York: Teachers College Press, Columbia University, 1971), and Howard Miller, "Evangelical Religion and Colonial Princeton," in *Schooling and Society*, ed. Lawrence Stone (Baltimore: Johns Hopkins University Press, 1976), 115-45.

21. The seceder churches have received little attention from other than denominational historians on either side of the Atlantic. On the seceders in Scotland and Ireland, see John McKerrow, *History of the Secession Church* (Edinburgh, 1854); Robert Small, *History of the Congregations of the United Presbyterian Church From 1733 to 1900* (1904); and Gavin Struthers, *History of the Rise, Progress and Principles of the Relief Church* (1843). For North America, see James B. Scouller, *A Manual of the United Presbyterian Church of North America, 1751-1887* (Pittsburgh, 1887); and William Melancthon Glasgow, *History of the Reformed Presbyterian Church in America* (Baltimore, 1888). Seceder and covenanting principles are well illustrated in Alexander Creaghead, *A Discourse Concerning the Covenants* (Philadelphia, 1742); *Peace and Harmony Restored: Being an Account of the Agreement Which Took Place Amongst the Burgher and Antiburgher Seceders, and Reformed Presbytery in North America* (Glasgow, 1783); *The Constitution of the Associate-Reformed Synod in America Considered, Disowned, and Testifyed Against, as Inconsistent with the Reformation-Constitution of Britain and Ireland* (Glasgow, 1787). On diversity in Pennsylvania, see especially Sally Schwartz, *"A Mixed Multitude": The Struggle for Toleration in Colonial Pennsylvania* (New York: New York University Press, 1987).

22. Elizabeth I. Nybakken, "New Light on the Old Side: Irish Influences on Colonial

Presbyterianism," *Journal of American History* 68 (1982): 813-32; see also Henry Sefton, "'Neu-lights and Preachers Legall': Some Observations on the Beginnings of Moderatism in the Church of Scotland," *Church, Politics and Society: Scotland 1408-1929*, ed. Norman Macdougall (Edinburgh: Donald, 1983), 186-96.

23. *Triumph of the Laity: Scots-Irish Piety and the Great Awakening 1625-1760* (New York: Oxford University Press, 1988). For another view of the growth of Ulster Presbyterianism, see Raymond Gillespie, "The Presbyterian Revolution in Ulster, 1600-1690," in *The Churches, Ireland and the Irish: Papers Read at the 1987 Summer Meeting and the 1988 Winter Meeting of the Ecclesiastical Historical Society*, ed. W.J. Sheils and Diana Wood (Oxford: B. Blackwell, 1989), 159-70. On connections between Irish and Scottish New Lights, see esp. *The Correspondence of the Rev. Robert Wodrow*, ed. Thomas M'Crie, 3 vols. (Edinburgh, 1842-43), vol. 3, where he follows closely the controversy within Irish Presbyterianism and refers to the friends of the New Lights in Scotland. See also William Marshall, *A Vindication of the Associate Presbytery of Pennsylvania, Respecting their Constitution and Principles* (Philadelphia, 1791).

24. Nybakken, "New Light on the Old Side," does find Old Side Presbyterian tendencies toward the liberal and tolerant perspectives of Francis Hutcheson and the Irish "New Lights," few of whom directly disavowed their doctrinal heritage. The principal doctrinal battle concerned the requirement of subscription to the Confession of Faith; there is little evidence that any opponents of Subscription challenged the Confession itself.

25. Ned C. Landsman, *From Colonials to Provincials: American Thought and Culture, 1680-1760* (New York: Twayne Publishers, 1997), chap. 5.

26. Ibid.

27. Sloan, *Scottish Enlightenment and the American College Ideal*, 281-84.

28. On the Paxton rebels, see *A Looking-Glass for Presbyterians. Or a Brief Examination of their Loyalty, Merits, and other Qualifications for Government* (Philadelphia, 1764), in *Paxton Papers*, ed. Dunbar, 243-55.

29. One of the most important figures in the dissemination of those myths was the itinerant bookseller Patrick Walker, a modest figure in the events, who traveled through Scotland and Ireland collecting covenanting legends, which he recounted in his chapbooks. Walker's works have been collected and republished as *Six Saints of the Covenant: Peden: Semple: Welwood: Cameron: Cargill: Smith*, ed. D. Hay Fleming, 2 vols. (London: Hodder and Stoughton, 1901).

30. Callum G. Brown, *The Social History of Religion in Scotland since 1730* (London: Methuen, 1987), chap. 2; Ned C. Landsman, "Liberty, Piety, and Patronage: The Social Context of Contested Clerical Calls in Eighteenth-Century Glasgow," in *The Glasgow Enlightenment*, ed. Andrew Hook and Richard B. Sher (East Linton, Scotland: Tuckwell Press, 1995), 214-26.

31. Patricia U. Bonomi, *Under the Cope of Heaven: Religion, Society, and Politics in Colonial*

America (New York: Oxford University Press, 1986), chaps. 5 and 6.

32. See, for example, *The Paxtoniade. A Poem* (Philadelphia, 1764), in *Paxton Papers*, ed. Dunbar, 165-71.

33. See Hugh Henry Brackenridge, *Incidents of the Insurrection in Western Pennsylvania in the Year 1794* (Philadelphia, 1795) and, on the rebellion generally, Thomas P. Slaughter, *The Whiskey Rebellion: Frontier Epilogue to the American Revolution* (New York: Oxford University Press, 1986).

34. On Scots-Irish in other frontier rebellions, see especially Thomas P. Slaughter, "The Friends of Liberty, the Friends of Order, and the Whiskey Rebellion: A Historiographical Essay," in *The Whiskey Rebellion: Past and Present Perspectives*, ed. Steven R. Boyd (Westport, Conn.: Greenwood Press, 1985), 9-30; Richard Maxwell Brown, *The South Carolina Regulators* (Cambridge, Mass.: Harvard University Press, 1963); Gregory H. Nobles, "Shays's Neighbors: The Context of Rebellion in Pelham, Massachusetts," in *In Debt to Shays: The Bicentennial of an Agrarian Rebellion*, ed. Robert A. Gross (Charlottesville: University Press of Virginia, 1993), 185-204; and William Hogeland, *The Whiskey Rebellion: George Washington, Alexander Hamilton, and the Frontier Rebels who Challenged America's Newfound Sovereignty* (New York: Scribner, 2006).

35. See the sources listed in note 4, as well as those collected in *Paxton Papers*, ed. Dunbar.

36. Richard Webster, *A History of the Presbyterian Church in America* (Philadelphia, 1858), 498-500; William B. Sprague, *Annals of the American Pulpit*, 9 vols. (New York, 1860-69), 3:129-30.

37. *A Declaration and Remonstrance of the Distressed and Bleeding Frontier Inhabitants of the Province of Pennsylvania* (Philadelphia, 1764), in *Paxton Papers*, ed. Dunbar, 99-110.

38. See, for example, James Renwick, *An Informatory Vindication of a Poor, Wasted, Misrepresented, Remnant of the Suffering, anti-Popish, anti-Prelatick, anti-Erastian, anti-Sectarian, True Presbyterian Church in Scotland* (n.p., 1707).

39. An extensive treatment of the backcountry as borderland is David Hackett Fischer's *Albion's Seed*, "Borderlands to the Backcountry: The Flight from North Britain, 1717-1775," 605-782; I have stated my own reservations about Fischer's portrayal in "Border Cultures, the Backcountry, and 'North British' Emigration to America," *William and Mary Quarterly* 3d ser., 48 (1991), 253-59.

40. *An Historical Account, of the Late Disturbances, between the Inhabitants of the Back Settlements; of Pennsylvania, and the Philadelphians* (Philadelphia, n.d.), in *Paxton Papers*, ed. Dunbar, 125-29.

41. For criticism of the lack of protection from the Quaker government during the Paxton affair, see esp. *Declaration and Remonstrance of the Distressed and Bleeding Frontier Inhabitants; and The Conduct of the Paxton-Men, Impartially Represented: with some Remarks on the Narrative* (Philadelphia, 1764), in *Paxton Papers*, ed. Dunbar, 265-98.

42. A good example, which summarizes half a century of such testimonies, is John Willison, *A Fair and Impartial Testimony, Essayed in Name of a Number of Ministers, Elders and Christian People of the Church of Scotland, unto the Laudable Principles, Wrestlings, and Attainments of that Church; and against the Backslidings, Coruptions, Divisions, and prevailing Evils, both of former and Present Times* (1744), in *The Whole Works of the Reverend and Learned Mr. John Willison,* 4 vols. (Edinburgh, 1816), 4:267-414.

43. *Declaration and Testimony, for the Doctrine and Order of the Church of Christ, and Against the Errors of the Present Times. To which is Prefixed, a Narrative, Concerning the Maintainance of the Reformation-Testimony. By the Associate Presbytery of Pennsylvania* (Philadelphia, 1784). In addition to the seceder churches, which broke away during the eighteenth century, the Reformed Presbyterian Church, dating from the Revolution settlement of 1690, also renounced the Church of Scotland and adhered to the covenants. Sprague, *Annals of the American Pulpit,* vol. 9, "Associate" and "Associate Reformed"; and *Constitution of the Associate-Reformed Synod in America, Considered, Disowned, and Testifyed Against, as Inconsistent with the Reformation-Constitution of Britain and Ireland; The confession of Faith, Agreed Upon by the Assembly of Divines at Westminster, with the Assistance of Commissioners from the Church of Scotland, as Received by the Associate-Reformed Church in North-America. With the Proofs From the Scripture* (New York: T. & J. Swords, 1799).

44. The standard account of the subscription controversy remains Leonard J. Trinterud, *The Forming of an American Tradition: A Re-examination of Colonial Presbyterianism* (Philadelphia: Westminster Press, 1949), chap. 2. Elizabeth I. Nybakken emphasizes Irish dissent from subscription in "New Light on the Old Side," 813-32. On the divisions in Ireland, see especially J. S. Reid, *History of the Presbyterian Church in Ireland,* 4 vols. (Belfast, 1867), 3:110-217.

45. That such a call of conscience was difficult even for Quakers to assert is well demonstrated in Jean R. Soderlund, *Quakers and Slavery: A Divided Spirit* (Princeton: Princeton University Press, 1985). Good examples of the myths of martyrdom and divine deliverance that circulated in the popular cultures of both Scots and northern Irish Presbyterians were the popular biographies by Patrick Walker, which have been collected in *Six Saints of the Covenant.*

46. On the spread of academies and colleges, see esp. Sloan, *Scottish Enlightenment and the American College Ideal,* and Howard Miller, *The Revolutionary College: American Presbyterian Higher Education, 1707-1837* (New York: New York University Press, 1976). On the four-stages theory of civilizations, see Ronald L. Meek, *Social Science and the Ignoble Savage* (Cambridge: Harvard University Press, 1976) and Roger L. Emerson, "American Indians, Frenchmen, and Scots Philosophers," *Studies in Eighteenth-Century Culture* 9 (1979): 21-36.

47. I have discussed those officials in "The Legacy of the British Union for the North American Colonies: Provincial Elites and the Problem of Imperial Union," in *A Union for Empire: Political Thought and the British Union of 1707,* ed. John Robertson (Cambridge: Cambridge University Press, 1995), 297-317.

Domestic, Dependent, Nations: The Colonial Origins of a Paradox

GREGORY EVANS DOWD

IF THERE IS ONE PHRASE COMMON to all courses in American Indian history it is "domestic dependent nations," Chief Justice John Marshall's coinage from the landmark Cherokee cases of 1831-32. Much as the phrases "no taxation without representation" or "manifest destiny" embody critical concepts in revolutionary and antebellum United States history, the phrase "domestic dependent nations" stands as a point of departure for a long, if erratically applied, understanding of the legal status of American Indian tribes from Marshall's time to the present.

This essay moves in the opposite chronological direction. It is not about Marshall. It is less interested in resolving the tension between the implications of wardship intended by the words "domestic" and "dependent" and the implications of sovereignty intended by the word "nations," than it is in viewing the status that Marshall established for Indian tribes in the light of both colonial history and comparative law. Each word of Marshall's formulation, considered apart from the history of Indian law, should itself provoke interest among Early Americanists.

The word *domestic* has ramifications in the histories of gender and of the family. The word *dependent* charges both of those histories, and plays additional roles in the histories of colonialism, American republicanism, the market revolution and the transition to capitalism. The word *nation* is closely bound to the last four histories and goes well beyond U.S. history as the basis itself for national histories, transnational histories, and the histories of nationalism. When to *domestic* are added the related words *domesticity* or *household*, when to *dependent* are added the related words *dependency* or *independence*, and when to nation are added the related concepts of *nationalism* or *nationhood*, the loaded character of domestic, dependent nationhood becomes obvious.

Marshall could not have known any of this subsequent historical interpretation. But the concept of domestic, or domiciled nations was older than he was; it was available to eighteenth-century British colonists. So too was the concept of dependent nations.[1] Marshall may have fused both ideas, but the terms did not come to him out of the clear, blue, Jacksonian sky. The question of the status of

Indian peoples had always been with the colonists, but like so many questions of empire and status, it confronted Great Britain and British colonists with a special intensity in the 1760s.[2]

Paying attention to changing British views about the status of both Indians and Indian nations, this essay posits that the era of Pontiac's War saw the British government imagine a new place for Indians within the empire. In order to posit what was new, the essay must describe what had been imagined before. It then suggests that the era of the American Revolution took the United States and Canada in two different directions. Throughout, the essay addresses the comparative history of sovereignty. How is it that a notion of native sovereignty came to be embraced – and an awkward embrace it has been – by the United States, while it has never been so embraced in Canada? When and how did it become possible for one group of former British North American colonies to accept Indian sovereignty, of an admittedly diminished sort, while another rejected it entirely?[3]

The 1760s, again, was the pivotal decade. Pontiac's War demanded imperial attention, and in Pennsylvania especially its violence bred fierce argument about the place of Indians. Before then, and especially in the seventeenth century, the English colonists in Pennsylvania and elsewhere easily saw Indians as either subjects (this was particularly true of the "settlement," "plantation," "domiciled," or "praying" Indians as well as of such important allied Indians as the Iroquois League and, in the early eighteenth century, the Cherokees) or prospective subjects (in the case of still-independent "foreign" Indians), and did not much concern themselves with Indian dominion.[4] By the middle of the eighteenth century, however, the meaning of the term "British subject" had become so charged with notions of privilege and liberty that it was more difficult for either British colonists or metropolitan authorities to fit the term to Indians.

Those who tried to do so in the 1760s met rebuke and rebuttal, and the British empire began to more ambiguously encode Indian peoples (whether "foreign" or "domestic") as dependent nations and tribes that still, somehow, lacked the vital attribute of sovereignty, which belonged to the Crown alone. Later decades would clarify some ambiguities and create new ones. American Revolutionaries and the founders in Philadelphia would so play with the notion of sovereignty that Indians could get a piece of it, while a separate Canadian tradition reeled back from these possibilities to the simpler notion that Indians were Crown subjects.

If the tragedy of Canadian Indian history has been that native sovereignty has been so consistently rejected, the tragedy of American Indian history may be even greater: that the Founding Fathers' own creative revision of the concept of sovereignty – which John Marshall so problematically applied to Indian nations as he insisted that they retained certain inherent powers – has in the course of the Republic's history been so often ignored.[5]

DOMESTIC, DEPENDENT, NATIONS

Sovereign Indian Nations

Pontiac's War (1763-1766) helped to focus imperial minds. A major cause of Pontiac's War was the British assumption that the conquest of New France automatically entailed the conquest of Indians. Pontiac and his allies rejected that claim, none more eloquently than the Ojibwa leader Minweweh (or Minavavana) in 1761, and we can mark his position as that of most of the still self-governing Indians of the period: "Although you have conquered the French, you have not conquered us. We are not your slaves."[6]

It would be accurate to say that Minweweh was claiming that Indians were sovereign – that is, independent, unconquered, self-governing, and in full political control of their lands and of their external relations. There are difficulties here: the meaning of sovereignty and the meaning of nationhood have changed a great deal in Western history – the terms are historically as well as culturally conditioned. Nonetheless, since Indian peoples did have laws, systems of government, and protocols of diplomacy, it is obvious to most of us today, and to our courts, that Indian nations[7] were, once, fully sovereign. Moreover, since European powers were themselves unable to wield much power over the Indians in the Great Lakes Region, the Ohio Valley, and even portions of the Susquehanna Valley, in 1763, since they could not enact laws and enforce them, since Pontiac and his allies were able to throw out most of the British garrisons in their territories and to confine the remaining soldiers largely to within the garrison walls, it seems safe to say that neither Great Britain in 1763 nor France in prior years could claim sovereignty legitimately (though claim it they vastly did).

Minweweh and Pontiac stood against British officers who soon discovered that they were unable to wield full power over the Indians in the Great Lakes region, the Ohio Valley, and even the Susquehanna Valley. These officers never admitted that their inability to wield the attributes of sovereignty, to enact laws and enforce them, diminished their King's claim to sovereign power, but they did have to look more closely into the empire's relationship with Indian nations.

Audacious British claims to large American territories over which they had no effective rule had long provoked Indian complaints. Laurence Sagouarrab, a Penobscot Indian, denied English claims to sovereignty when he disputed a treaty made at Casco Bay in 1727:

> Much less...did I become [the English King's] subject, or give him my land.... This I never did.... I recognize him King of all his lands; but...do not hence infer that I acknowledge thy King as...King of my lands. Here lies my distinction my Indian distinction. God hath willed that I have no King, and that I be master of my lands in common.[8]

Rarely did Europeans acknowledge Indian sovereignty in the sixteenth and seventeenth centuries, more rarely still did governing Englishmen. Jean O'Brien finds one of those exceptions that proves the rule, a Massachusetts land claims case between the Natick Indians and the town of Dedham in which the court in 1662 found that "native right" to lands "cannot, in strict justice, be utterly extinct." But nevertheless, the court in this case settled the matter with an English grant of Indian land to the Indians, leaving Indians with the land but England, according to the colony's interested view, with the sovereignty.[9]

Some scholars – they are not usually professional historians – argue that the Europeans who colonized North America accepted a position akin to that which Minweweh espoused in 1761, and saw Indian peoples as, in today's terms, fully sovereign. To quote one, a UN Human Rights Subcommission *Special Rapporteur*: "in establishing formal legal relationships with indigenous North Americans, the European parties were absolutely clear...that they were...entering into contractual relations with sovereign nations."[10]

Actually, they were not at all clear. Though there were figures in the history of international law – notably one of the founders of that field, Francisco de Vitoria – who saw Indians as possessing full title to land as well as other attributes of sovereignty, in practice Europeans did not much worry about the justice of Indian claims to land and self-rule. Vitoria is indeed the exception that proves the rule, for he would justify the Spanish conquest of sovereign Indians for a number of reasons including the protection of Spanish travelers and traders in Indian lands, the Spanish use of unused or communal lands, and the protection of missionaries or their Christian converts. He suggested, too, though he did not "dare either to affirm or condemn it out of hand," that if it turned out to be the case, as some of his contemporaries were then speculating, that Indians were incapable of "setting up or administering a commonwealth both legitimate and ordered in human and civil terms," Spain might, "for their own benefit...take over their administration." This last presages nicely the argument for the Indians' status as "wards." While Vitoria, as many have recognized, left Indian dominion considerably up for grabs,[11] he and his fellow Thomists at least seriously considered it. Most other European thinkers preferred not to think about it. English scholars who read and plagiarized Vitoria's arguments about the Indians tended to be more interested in his justifications of conquest in America than in his interest in the rights of Indian nations.[12]

Scholars who credit European powers with taking seriously the sovereignty of North American Indian tribes point to treaties as evidence. Treaties, the argument goes, would only be made with autonomous peoples; they were, by their nature, international documents.[13] Rebecca L. Robbins declares that by the time of the American Revolution many "Indian nations...had already been formally recognized through treaties as legitimate sovereignties." Markku Henriksson states that "From the very beginning, with the first European colonies, treaties were an essential part of Indian-White relations. From early on, the central government maintained the right to make treaties with the Native Americans."[14] The argument would be convincing only if Europeans gave Indian treaties the same status as treaties among Christian princes or European nation-states. Such equality was beyond most early-modern Europeans.[15] A note in the British Public

DOMESTIC, DEPENDENT, NATIONS

Record Office explicitly points this out. Making a treaty with Cherokees at Whitehall in 1730 the British Board of Trade opined that, because "this Treaty is to be only with Savages," His Majesty need only send a letter to the board empowering it to treat, and could ignore other formalities. Parliament did not deliberate about Indian treaties. The Crown did not seal Indian treaties.[16] Even in treaties, imperial powers belittled Indian sovereignty.

Rarely did any European central government directly make such a treaty, and, more surprising, rarely did seventeenth-century colonial governments bestow the word "treaty" upon the signed agreements that they made with Indians. Many of the documents that our histories blithely call treaties were not referred to as such at the time. A recent collection of early "treaties" and "laws" in Pennsylvania and Delaware actually contains no seventeenth-century English or Dutch document that carries the word "treaty" anywhere in its original text. Thirty-four are called "indentures," "grants," "patents," or, most commonly, "deeds."[17] An additional four, three Dutch and one English, are each called "treaty" in its heading, but this reflects the phrasing of a modern editor, not a seventeenth-century participant.

Finally, there is the modern translation of a Swedish document of 1638, styled, not a treaty, but an "Affadavit." This document does in fact convey a full and clear sense of Indian sovereignty. In that, it is unique. In early Pennsylvania and Delaware, Europeans only rarely wrote of their transactions with Indian nations as treaties with fully sovereign peoples.[18]

It is mistaken, then, to credit Europeans with making frequent international treaties with Indians in the seventeenth century. Seventeenth-century treaties are often the products of later imaginations. The best example is William Penn's famous treaty with the Delaware Indians under the great spreading elm in 1682 – or was it 1683 – at Shackamaxon – or was it Burlington Island? The image has been immortalized by Benjamin West in 1771 and by Edward Hicks (about 60 times) later on, and most ironically by Nicholas Gevelot, where, at the United States Capitol Rotunda, Penn and his Indian diplomats stand in stone and where, having been completed in 1827, they soon witnessed the passage of the Indian Removal Act (1830). No written agreement that can be certainly connected with this image survives.

We can indeed follow Voltaire in calling this "the only treaty that was never sworn to and never broken," though we might be adding an irony even he did not intend. Several early land cessions from the Delawares to Penn do survive in the record. The first was not called a treaty, but an indenture. Others were called deeds or conveyances. Penn occasionally offhandedly referred to them as treaties, but he used the same term to refer to instruments that he negotiated with the neighboring province of West New Jersey, which he hardly considered to be an independent nation.[19]

Until the eighteenth century the word "treaty" meant both more and less than it means today. It covered a wider range of senses, yet that very breadth thinned it, denying it force. *Treaty* was once synonymous with *treatise*, for example. It was also used to refer to just about any discussion that led to an agreement, even to those between ordinary individuals and not confirmed in writing.[20] The point is simply that neither existence of written instruments confirming negotiations between Indians and colonists nor the odd seventeenth-century use of the word treaty can imply a European acknowledgment of Indian sovereignty. Such an acknowledgment would, to be sure, have been just; that is no argument that it was made.

English colonies often deployed their written agreements with Indians in efforts to advance their claims against those of rival English colonies, but for the most part they agreed that Indian "pretensions" to fundamental title to land could not stand against the Crown. As early as 1622, at a court held in London for the Virginia Company, English lords and gentlemen ruled that land could not be directly purchased by individuals from Indians, even from an Indian King, lest a "sovereignty in that heathen Infidel [be] acknowledged, and the companies [sic] Title thereby be infringed."[21] Only the company, in other words, as the patented representative of the Crown, could negotiate for land with Indian occupants of what were, somehow, already Crown lands.

In the eighteenth century, the term "treaty" became increasingly common in Indian affairs. Pennsylvania authorities wrote regularly of their meetings and agreements with Indians as "treaties," especially after 1715. But even then the term should not be overrated; it was still highly ambiguous. When Lieutenant Governor Charles Gookin met with Delaware and Schuylkill Indians in June 1715, he had no trouble referring to his meeting as a "Treaty" while at the same time calling these Indians subjects of King George I: "under him as well they as we his other subjects may live in the same peace." Gookin said the Indians and the English "should be Joyned as one,...that they might better be as the same" and "grow up in the same Union." Gookin's was less an image of legitimately independent people agreeing to come under British authority than of savages without legitimacy submitting to the benefits of British lordship.[22]

Gookin's use of the term "treaty" reflected a change, a bifurcation, in the word's meaning. In formal international diplomacy, the word "treaty" came in late seventeenth-century England to denote, and to only denote, the formal, written agreements made between sovereign princes. This is how most modern scholars – especially diplomatic historians – understand the word. But the term also retained, especially in America and especially when applied to Indian affairs, an older meaning, which the *Oxford English Dictionary* (*OED*) defines as rare: "The treating of matters with a view to settlement; discussion of terms, conferences, negotiations."

The *OED* notes that this meaning lives on in the phrase "in treaty," yet when it lists several quotations to illustrate this practically obsolete usage, two are from colonial Pennsylvania and one of those two is the solitary example of the use of "treaty" to denote the *process of negotiations* rather than the *written document* itself. That example is from Benjamin Franklin's *Autobiography*, and it refers to the Treaty of Carlisle of 1753. Franklin recalls that the Indians promised that they would remain "sober during the Treaty." He writes that "Treaty was conducted very orderly, and concluded to a mutual satisfaction." This Pennsylvanian's usage lifts the word from the confines of a written document and diffuses it into the process of negotiations between Indians and Britons, so that the word can refer to the negotiations themselves. This usage is not, contrary to the *OED*, uncommon in Indian history today.

William Fenton, the late "dean" of Iroquois studies writes, for example: "the large conferences leading to a definite result – extending the Chain, fixing boundaries, land cessions, and formal alliances for peace and war – which are documented by deed or written proceedings afterward published – are what we know as Indian treaties." The treaty is not only the written agreement, but the conference, too.[23] Since Indians, according to their own diplomatic protocols, paid more attention to the conduct and content of both the formal proceedings and the informal "talks in the bushes" than to the paper that resulted, the persistence of this meaning is an example of Indian influence on American English.[24]

We might celebrate that Indian influence and we might in justice to Indians insist that our courts pay attention not only to documented treaties, but to the broader expectations generated in the course of negotiations. At the same time, we might reflect on the double-edged convenience of the colonial understanding of the word "treaty." Colonists could, Janus-like, smile on treaties held with Indians in American clearings or council-chambers, while frowning on Indian participation at treaty councils among sovereigns in the European corridors of power. The former admitted of no sovereignty, the latter expressly had sovereignty at stake. That this was both a deception and a unilateral viewpoint prejudicial to Indian rights is precisely the point.[25]

Scholars may claim that "All of the colonial powers...recognized the sovereignty of Indian nations by entering into...treaties with Indians," but doing so, such scholars confer upon early modern European statesmen the values of openness, tolerance, and equanimity that such empire-builders did not and could not possess. Legal historian Robert Williams has put it starkly and well: "the nation-states of Europe and their subjects asserted the right" to exploit the New World "without any limitation except that imposed by a rival's superior forces. As for the indigenous inhabitants,...as heathens and infidels they were regarded...as fit subjects for conquest."[26] In June, 1771, the legal counsel for Connecticut in the case before the Privy Council of *Mohegan v. Connecticut*, William Samuel Johnson (no relation to Sir William Johnson) said much the same thing. It was not just that the Mohegans had settled under colonial guardians that led Johnson to dismiss their sovereignty; he insisted that they had never possessed it.

He argued that "the Idea of the Mohegans being a separate or a sovereign state, in America, where the state and condition of Indians is known to everybody[,] might expose Majesty and Sovereignty to Ridicule." To speak of Indian sovereignty, in other words, would be to ridicule sovereignty itself. He went on: "When the English treated with them it was not with Independent States ...but as with savages, whom they were to quiet and manage as well as they could."[27] If it would be wrong, then, for historians to credit early-modern European colonizers

The Indians giving a Talk to Colonel Bouquet in a Conference at a Council Fire, near his Camp on the Banks of Muskingum in North America, in Oct.r 1764.

This engraving of a sketch by Benjamin West of negotiations in the Ohio Valley during Pontiac's War depicts a typical treaty scene – with a Native leader speaking from a wampum belt and a British scribe taking minutes.

Rare Books Division, The New York Public Library, Astor, Lenox, and Tilden Foundations.

with the liberal understanding that their agreements with Indians were made among equals, it would be equally wrong for western nations today to deny their accountability for agreements they made with Native Americans who knew that they lived under no foreign prince.[28]

Sovereignty, after all, was taken seriously by such Indians as Minweweh, who understood that his Ojibwa were entirely free of British authority and possessed the fundamental right to lands he described as "our inheritance." Europeans easily understood such Indian declarations, and they fill the record.[29] So let us list formal independence and full dominion as the first position that would fix the place of Indians during the crisis that followed the English conquest of Canada.

His Majesty's Subjects

A second position, which has a long history in the colonies, would define the Indians inhabiting lands claimed by the crown as crown subjects. This was a logical extension of long-standing English practices. Nicholas Canny has examined the carefully scripted ceremonies through which the English hoped to make vassals and subjects out of both seventeenth-century Indian "Kings" such as Powhatan and sixteenth-century "Gaelic Lords" in Ireland. Through these rites, says Canny, both Indian and Irish leaders were to be "recognized as subjects and granted titles of nobility and legal claim over their lordships, as a reward for the surrender of their estates and political authority to the Crown." Canny points out that Powhatan himself refused to fit into this secondhand Irish suit. Still, the English persisted in their efforts with others.

In 1614 the Chickahominies of the Chesapeake, Ralph Hamor remembered, called themselves "King James his subjects." Governor Thomas Dale gave eight Chickahominy men coats and medallions by which they became known as "King James his noble Men" and as "English men."[30] Seventeenth-century New Englanders often assumed that local Indians were subjects, who even had a certain access to law. A document of 1644 even has Narragansett Indians petitioning to become "humble, loving, and obedient subjects of His Majesty," with the proviso that they be protected by the King and that they "have our matters and causes heard and tried according to his just and equal laws."[31]

At the end of King Philip's War, some English colonists reflected on the status of Indian captives and saw them as English subjects, however rebellious. Daniel Gookin complained of his fellow English that "Some men were so violent that they would have these Indians put to death by martial law, and not tried by a jury, though they were subjects under the English protection."[32] And when Massachusetts sent many of the captives – even women and children – into slavery in the West Indies, it could send with the ship's captain a certificate claiming that they had followed a rebel, Philip, and that they had rejected "their obedience unto the Government [of] our Sovereign Lord his Majesty...unto which they had willingly Subjected themselves & have been protected by and enjoyed the privilege of English Laws."

English laws could not prevent their sale into slavery, but somehow, access to those laws was a privilege they had as subjects.[33] Indeed, access to law was a defining characteristic of the English subject, which the Narragansetts in 1644 had understood. As late as 1703, three Indians acted as justices of the peace on Martha's Vineyard, something that had occurred but was by then anachronistic elsewhere in Massachusetts.[34]

As the metropolitan English government paid increasing attention to the colonies following the Restoration of the Crown in 1660, it too came to style Indians as subjects. The Royal Commissioners sent to Virginia in the wake of Bacon's Rebellion (1676) made peace with the local peoples, who acknowledged that they "have their immediate Dependency on, and owe all Subjection to the Great King of England, our now Dread Sovereign." At the same time, the articles of peace distinguished between, first, "the said Indian Kings and Queens and their Subjects" and, second, "others His Majesties [sic] Subjects." It promised both King Charles II's Indian subjects and his other subjects the secure enjoyment of their possessions. The Board of Trade in January 1699/1700 confirmed this agreement and ordered that a "Patent be granted to the Indians for the lands Reserved to them...in the same manner as Patents are usually granted for lands to other his Majesties [sic] Subjects." In other words, Indian subjects, like colonial subjects, held the land at the pleasure of the Crown. To be sure, Indian lands, unlike colonists' patented lands, were not to be sold to any but Crown officials, but this does not imply that the Crown lacked sovereignty. Far from it, in the English scheme of things, the Crown (however preposterously) held the fundamental title. The idea that Indians "under the allegiance of the crown" were Crown subjects with "the same privilege of other English Subjects," including, especially, rights to trial by jury, persisted in Virginia well into the eighteenth century.[35]

If we can trust the record, New York's Governor Thomas Dongan called the Five Nations Iroquois "Subjects" to their faces in 1687. And they, perhaps not grasping the English implications of the term, concurred; the Mohawk, Rode, even called King James II "our King," and his delegation of Five Nations diplomats said that they considered themselves to be the governor's "subjects in whose land we live." The Oneida, Cheda (also Oheda), asked in 1692 for the New Yorkers' more active support against Canada: "How can they and we be subjects of the same great King, and not be engaged in the same War?" Article 15 of the Treaty of Utrecht, 1713, is usually translated from the French into English as describing the Iroquois League as "subject to" Great Britain, though the original French, "*soumis à*" might more ambiguously mean "under the sway of" Great Britain.

In 1727 the British protested the French building of Fort Niagara in part on the grounds that the land was held by British subjects – that is, by the members of the Iroquois League. In the previously mentioned Cherokee Treaty of 1730, the Cherokees are called the king's "good children and subjects." This list of references to Indians as British subjects could be extended. Far from treating Indians as sovereign, in other words, the British generally treated allied Indians as under

Crown subjection throughout the seventeenth and well into the eighteenth centuries.[36]

This pattern changed over the course of the early eighteenth century. Britons spoke less commonly, and in more subdued and cautious tones, of Indian subjection. Colonial diplomats gradually stopped calling the Iroquois "subjects" to their faces. In 1733, New York's Governor William Cosby, calling members of the Six Nations League "Brethren and Children," insisted only on an acknowledgment that the Nations of the League see the king as their Father, and that they submit to "the protection of the King of Great Britain." He asked that they renew the Covenant Chain between them and the King's subjects, making it clear that they were not themselves subjects. He did not use the phrase "others His Majesty's subjects" which we have seen earlier in Pennsylvania.

Throughout the first part of the century, the League protested to the French that it was not under British subjection, and by the end of the Seven Years' War, Britons had stopped making the claim, even among themselves. The language of subjection had largely been abandoned. The League, fully understanding British conceptions of subjection by the middle of the eighteenth century, fully rejected them.[37] British officials like the superintendent of Indian affairs for the Northern Department, Sir William Johnson, understood the Iroquois position and avoided the term "subject" at all costs.

If by the 1760s the British no longer *generally* viewed the Indians as Crown subjects, they had little problem incorporating conquered Europeans under that rubric.[38] In the conquest of Canada (1760) and in the subsequent efforts to take over the Illinois territory, the British made it clear that the French inhabitants would "become subjects of His Majesty" and "shall enjoy the same rights and privileges, the same security for their persons and effects, and the liberty of trade, as the old subjects of their [new] King." Such promises were not made, could not be made, to Indians. Not only had Indians come to resist the label of British subject, but Britons by the 1760s had taken much of the sting out of what the label meant, and they were unwilling to affix it to Indians. Indians were to be allies under the King's protection and within the King's dominion, or they would be enemies. Rarely did the king's men call them subjects as Pontiac's War approached and still less after; those who did were, from the imperial perspective, in error.[39]

There were a few. Col. John Bradstreet, commander of a large relief expedition to Detroit in 1764, made several treaties with Indians. He demanded that the Indians acknowledge themselves as "Subjects and Children" of the King. When Indians hesitated and referred to the English as "brothers," Bradstreet insisted on his usage, and Wapacomagat of the Missisaugas of Ontario acknowledged that his peoples were "Subjects and Children of the King of England, which they should always in the future call themselves."[40] Exactly how Bradstreet or Wapacomagat understood the term "subject" is difficult to know, but British officialdom was against them both.

Sir William Johnson waxed apoplectic about Bradstreet's treaties. On the term "subject," he wrote, "The very word would have startled" the Indians; its very meaning is "repugnant to their Principles;...no Nation of Indians have any word which can express, or convey, the Idea of Subjection."[41] Even Bradstreet's loyal subordinate and ally, Thomas Mante, took a more accurate view of Detroit's peoples when he wrote, "No people on the face of the earth, are fuller of the idea of liberty, than the North-American Indians."[42]

"Nations or Tribes who live under Our Protection"

Most of Pontiac's allies avoided Bradstreet and made it clear that they remained independent of British rule: they were unconquered, they were not subjects, they were formally independent. This was equally intolerable to the British. But what status did the Indians have, if not conquered, if not subjects, if not independent? Pontiac's War forced Britons, colonist and imperialist alike, to reconsider the issue. The Royal Proclamation of 1763 embodied the newly emerging imperial understanding. Issued in response to the crisis by King George III on October 7, 1763, the proclamation promised to regulate trade with Indians, to ban colonial settlement west of the famous if vague boundary line, and to forbid the purchase of Indian land without Crown approval through its Indian superintendents.[43]

For all its vagueness, inadequacy, and ineffectiveness, the proclamation remains a testament to Whitehall's understanding of the Indians' status in the empire. In drawing up the proclamation, the Board of Trade sought to regulate relations between the British and the Indian "Tribes and *Nations*," a remarkable but common usage, "which are now under His Majesty's immediate protection." The Proclamation itself expressly concerned "the several Nations or Tribes with whom We are connected, and who live under our Protection." It placed Indians and their lands under the Crown's "Sovereignty, Protection, and Dominion." It promoted the idea, which influenced a key feature of American Federal Indian law, that Indian *nations* and *tribes* existed as entities, within the empire, and apart from the British.[44]

This was the *third position*, neither the independence of Minweweh and Sagouarrab nor the subjection of Hamor and Bradstreet: though *not subjects*, though *nations*, these were *dependent nations within the King's dominion*.[45] When one notes an etymological relationship between the words dominion and domestic, one sees the roots of John Marshall's formulation of tribes as domestic, dependent nations. Organized in tribes with a high degree of internal independence, not subjects of the Crown nor of the colonies, yet under the pseudo-control and pseudo-protection of a Crown that was, paradoxically, making war on many of them, the Indian nations were already a puzzle and an anomaly.[46]

Sixty years later, John Marshall, in *Johnson and Graham, Lessee v. William McIntosh* (1823) would write that conquered peoples "most usually...are incorporated with the victorious nation and become subjects or citizens.... But the tribes of Indians inhabiting this country were fierce savages."[47] This is precisely how most British had come to see Indians by the 1760s: not ready for incorporation as subjects, and therefore separate, in a measure autonomous, and yet dependent.

The British did not concede that Minweweh's people and their neighbors had sovereignty (nor has Canada yet done so, nor has, say, New Zealand yet acknowledged as much of its indigenous peoples). The British had not reached the point that Marshall would reach when he conceded in 1823 that sovereignty, in a more "diminished" sense, remained with the tribes. The Board of Trade approached this point in 1768, when it referred to King George III as "Lord of the Soil of ungranted Lands which the Indians may be inclined to give up." The Board was nicely ambiguous: while it defined the King as Sovereign over some lands still in Indian possession, it said nothing about lands that the Indians might *not* be inclined to give up. It did, in the same document, call Indian lands "their lands," but it did not definitively state (however it might be reasonably inferred) that Indians were the ultimate lords of that soil.[48] The precise status of Indian Nations and the nature of their title were left vague – Indian sovereignty was not openly asserted.

If the British continued to deny Indian sovereignty in 1763, they nonetheless were then approaching the idea that tribes were domestic (within the King's dominion), dependent (at least for trade and protection), nations (at least in terms of separateness and internal governance). This is not a concept of Indian sovereignty, not at all. It could just as easily tend toward the concept of colonial mandate or trust territory that flourished during Europe's later era of imperialism, a concept that also expressly denied native sovereignty.[49] Still, it is a concept of domestic, dependent, nations.

Delawares, Conestogas, and Pennsylvania

The protectorate status that the British were envisioning was far from simple, for if the British no longer held Indians to be the conquered subjects of the Crown, they still held some Indians to be conquered subjects, not of the Crown, but of other Indians under the Crown's protection. Among Indians who held such a complicated status in British eyes were the Delawares, whose ancestors had supposedly negotiated that legendary treaty with Penn.

Delawares had come under Iroquois League influence as English colonial strength grew.[50] A remarkable thing happened, for those interested in what is now called the "gendered discourse of politics." Some time in the early eighteenth century, Delawares gained the status of fictive "women," a term that defined their place in the Covenant Chain of friendship that bound the Iroquois League and its Indian allies to the British colonies. By calling the Delawares "women," the Iroquois League, some scholars suggest, recognized Delawares as having a special role among the varied Indian peoples settling the Susquehanna Valley. Delawares came to mediate relations between the Iroquois League and other migrants – especially Algonquian speakers – to the valley. "Women," initially, was no clear designation of subjection. Closely examining Iroquois-British treaty council records, Nancy Shoemaker has recently argued otherwise. Indian speakers in those councils often honored women, but they frequently hurled female terms as epithets. Like British men, they could disparage women. As the British also called the Delawares "women," they did so with the understanding that Delawares were dependent subjects under League dominion. As women, Delawares held what was for the British the perfect designation of dependency: here, if ever there was one, was a *domestic*, dependent nation.[51]

As the idea of womanhood infused the Delawares' political status, they sloughed it off and picked up their weapons. Ohio Delawares began to fight in 1755, Susquehanna Valley Delawares joined them the next year, and the Lieutenant Governor of Pennsylvania declared them to be "Enemies, Rebels, and Traitors," for having broken the commands of "the Six Nations, to whom they owe Obedience and Subjection." In 1764, the same logic allowed Governor John Penn to declare the Delawares "Enemies, Rebels and Traitors." Sir William Johnson even suggested that Delawares should be tortured when captured. Torture was, after all, proper for traitors.[52]

Enemies, rebels, and traitors: this triple indictment charged an unusual explosion of Delaware Indian hating in 1763 and 1764. The correspondence of British officers in those years is littered with imaginative methods for killing Delawares. Colonel Henry Bouquet sought to use bloodhounds; Captain Simeon Ecuyer proposed bear traps and "crow-feet traps...pointed enough for their moccasins." General Jeffery Amherst ordered several times that there be "*No Prisoners*" taken among any Indians, an order later repeated by Sir William Johnson as he sent Iroquois allies out against Delawares. Amherst's regulars for the most part obeyed the order, giving all prisoners, as one of them termed it, their "quietus," while Sir William's warriors for the most part ignored the order and dispersed captives among their nations.[53] At Fort Pitt during the first summer of fighting, Captain Ecuyer thought Delawares should be exterminated at "one stroke."

On June 24, 1763, when two Delaware leaders visited him for talks, he made them a present of two blankets and two handkerchiefs from the fort's smallpox hospital. A receipt notes that the purpose was "to Convey the Smallpox to the Indians." Smallpox did break out among the Indians, and though the disease could have come to the Delawares and Shawnees through other vectors, it is plain that the British considered the Delawares well beyond Europe's laws of war, which, Grotius tells us, had it "from old times...that it is not permissible to kill an enemy by poison."[54]

Given this kind of official loathing for Delawares, it is hardly surprising that the Royal Proclamation's insistence on the protection of Indians failed to impress the colonial populus. The notion that Indian nations should be protected by the Crown was, for many settlers, a bad joke. They saw little good for them in the imperial vision for an orderly procession of the frontier. They knew that imperial officials were no more ready than they were themselves to see the western lands remain in Indian hands forever, and they determined to take local action against Indians in their midst. Doing so, they too, questioned the status of Indians.

The most famous action was taken against a group of so-called settlement Indians – Indians living within the colonies – in this case the Indians of Conestoga Manor, Pennsylvania. This community of twenty-two "Conestogas," composed of Susquehannocks, Senecas, Delawares, and others, had occupied about four hundred acres with the governor's blessing since 1717. In the first few months of Pontiac's War, the inhabitants of the town of Paxtang, commonly called Paxton, in Lancaster County, formally petitioned for the "immediate removal" of all Indians in the colony, including the Conestogas. John Penn, the newly arrived governor and a proprietor of the colony, saw these Indians as his dependents and himself as their guardian, and he refused the recommendation on the grounds that the "faith of this Government is pledged for their protection."[55]

After violence leapt from the Susquehanna Valley to the Lehigh, Penn began to reverse course. On August 20, 1763, militiamen killed four Moravian Indians, one Zachary, his wife, their child, and another woman who had come to Fort Allen to trade. The killers announced their intention to kill all Indians who crossed their path; instead, an Indian party returned the favor.[56] Less than three weeks later, Indians attacked the militia at John Stenton's house, killing Stenton and six others, including the militia captain, and wounding several others, before ranging through the region, leaving some twenty people dead, homes plundered, survivors grieving and panicked.[57]

To the west, leading settlers called for the removal of all Indians from the province. Penn ordered the Moravian Indian missions to remove from the Lehigh and Susquehanna regions to Philadelphia, where he promised to shelter them. As one band made its way to the city in November, a mob put its village to the torch.[58] When Renatus, an Indian convert to the Moravian faith, was formally accused of complicity in the October attacks, the Assembly, at the request of the lawyer, Lewis Weiss, arranged to have Renatus tried in Philadelphia, where, much to the outrage of many, he was acquitted.[59]

Still, amid the reality of frontier violence, the Conestogas remained unmoved on the lower Susquehanna, while rumors circulated in the town of Paxton that the Conestogas had harbored enemy spies. On December 14, more than fifty mounted Paxtonians burst upon the Indian hamlet, killing the six people they found there. Fourteen other Conestogas, as they returned from their chores and discovered what had happened, fled to the protection of the Lancaster Work House. At least fifty mounted Paxtonians killed them all on December 27, in little more than ten minutes.[60]

Penn issued fruitless proclamations calling for both the arrest of the killers and the protection of the Indians who remained at peace in the colony.[61] Furious and threatened, the Paxtonians gathered a force of three hundred, advanced on Philadelphia, and advertised their intentions to kill the protected Indians, to demand greater representation in the legislature, to gain greater protection for the frontier. The story of their march has been told before – they never entered the city but negotiated with Benjamin Franklin and other prominent men in Germantown. Facing not only armed Philadelphians but the King's Highlanders and Royal Americans, the Paxtonians agreed to submit a petition to the governor and assembly, and they went home.[62]

The Paxtonians' murders and march resulted, not in civil war among the colonists, but in a pamphlet war in which writers argued a host of issues that had little to do directly with the shooting, bludgeoning, and dismembering of unarmed innocents. But when the pamphleteers did broach the murders themselves, they confronted the vexing issue of the Conestoga and Moravian Indians' place in colonial society.[63] How were colonists to view these people? Pro-Paxtonians called them enemies. Anti-Paxtonians called them, variously, fellow subjects of the King, friends, neighbors, sojourners, allies, and strangers; each term suggested a different relationship to the colony and to the empire.

Charles Read, chief justice of the New Jersey Supreme Court, took what was by now an archaic position. Despite their "yellow" skin, the Conestogas had become "subjects," and therefore deserved the same treatment "as other subjects in like Circumstances." Read, interestingly, would in 1766 preside over capital trials that actually convicted four colonial men of killing Indians in New Jersey, and he hanged three of them. Read, who stood as an embodiment of the position that Indians were subjects and should have access to the law, was unusual, if not unique. Another anonymous pamphleteer was less systematic, and almost casually called the Conestogas subjects, neighbors, and Christians deserving of protection.

For the most part, however, there was confusion as to the Indians' place. One anti-Paxtonian author implied that the Conestogas had the status of a separate, friendly, nation, yet also suggested that they had agreed by treaty in 1701 to live with the colonists "as one People." Benjamin Franklin and another writer took a more narrow tack, and called them "strangers" or "sojourners," who, while without the liberties of British subjects and without any sovereignty of their own, deserved what Franklin called the "Sacred Rites of Hospitality," and, at least, protection.[64]

The murders seemed a personal affront to John Penn. While he never called them "subjects," he did say they "were as much under the Protection of the Government, and its Laws, as any others amongst us."[65] Still others argued that the Conestogas had assimilated enough, "had in Manner...become white People, and expected the same Protection from us."[66] All anti-Paxtonian writers argued for the colony's duty to protect the refugee Moravian Indians in Philadelphia and to bring the Conestogas' killers to justice, but together they failed to fix clearly the place of "domestic Indians."

In this, they were outclassed by the pro-Paxtonians. These claimed consistently, if unconvincingly, that the domestic Indians had become enemies – either by virtue, as some writers alleged, of individual misdeeds and bad character, or by virtue, as others alleged, of simply being Indian. One went so far as to advocate the killing of Indian children, anticipating nineteenth-century advocates of genocide on the High Plains, when he declared that "out of a SERPENT'S EGG, there should come...a fiery flying SERPENT." All agreed with high consistency that Indians had no place in the British nation and were undeserving of the government's protection. They said it was not in the power of government to shelter its own enemies, and it was an indignity for "Free-Men and English Subjects" to become tributary to such Indians as were then being supported by taxes in Philadelphia.

One seized directly on the autonomous character of Indian communities as a reason for their elimination: To permit these "independent Commonwealths," who "never came under our laws nor acknowledged Subjection to our King and Government" to "live in a Time of War in our Bounds" was "contrary to the Maxims of good Polity." Anticipating Andrew Jackson, this writer argued that states within a state were dangerous.[67] Pro-Paxtonians advanced the case, which for generations would gain power in America, that Indians could not be permitted to live among the colonists as separate communities. The best policy was their expulsion to the west of a hardening frontier line. So the debates of the Removal period were here anticipated.

Even in the short term, the Paxtonians won the debate. None faced charges for the Conestoga and Lancaster murders. The Paxtonians' desire to kill the confined Moravian and other Indians in Philadelphia was also met, part way, for smallpox broke out in the barracks, and 56 of the 140 died by September. The government acceded to the demands that it both reimburse ad hoc locally organized frontier patrols and place a bounty on enemy Indian scalps. The bounty, which included premiums for the scalps of women and children above ten years of age, ensured that Pennsylvania would remain a dangerous place for any Indian, friend or enemy, for the duration of the war.

Rendering Pennsylvania unsafe with the bounty, Penn and his government also tried to remove the Indians who had sought its protection from the province, attempting to send them north to live among the Six Nations. New York would not have them, but it is clear that the Paxtonians' desire for the removal of Indians had struck a chord with John Penn.[68]

Pontiac's War, then, saw an imperial discussion of the Indians' place, replete with pamphleteering, armed demonstrations, murders, and warfare. In a sense, it complemented the imperial crises that followed, for at stake were real constitutional issues. It was also, of course, vastly different than the imperial crises, because Pontiac's allies never wanted to be a part of the empire. They were not "reluctant revolutionaries," indeed they were not revolutionaries at all, for Great Britain had not yet established its rule over them.[69]

Rejecting British sovereignty, many Indians tried to remove the British from the West in 1763. They failed to remove the British entirely, but neither did British armies march as planned through Indian villages, putting them to the torch. The war's ending was negotiated, and one of its results had been to stir up, among British colonists and officials, a discussion of the Indians' place in the empire. The discussion took place in Whitehall, which drew up both the Proclamation of 1763 and the Plan of Indian Regulation in 1764. It took place in the pamphlet debate over the Paxton murders and march of the same years. And it took place in the dreadful language of war.

Revolutionary Departures

The American Revolution swept that discussion to the margins, but there it continued. Americans during the Revolution negotiated their first official treaty with an Indian tribe. Fittingly, it was with Delawares, at Fort Pitt in 1778. As a document, it is bizarre. On the one hand, the treaty calls the Delawares a nation, calls itself a treaty, and provides for mutual peace and mutual alliance against enemy nations. On the other hand, its last article – for which there is no corresponding council evidence – offered to allow the Delawares and any other local Indians friendly to the United States "to form a state whereof the Delaware nation shall be the head, and have a representation in Congress."[70] Since states were then the seats of sovereignty, this is truly extraordinary. There is no evidence that Congress ever discussed or ratified this treaty. Nor would many American citizens have taken the last proposal very seriously in 1778, but there the proposal stands, in print, and it does suggest that the revolution permitted a new opening in the concept of Indian sovereignty, even if that opening went unexplored.

The Philadelphia Convention of 1787 created another opening, by suggesting to some that sovereignty could be "diminished" without ceasing to be sovereignty. In 1787 Alexander Hamilton spoke of diminishing the states' sovereignty. As *Publius* he also broached the idea in the *Federalist Papers*. By the late 1790s, some Americans – interested in federal-state relations – interpreted the United States Constitution as providing for a compound republic with a divided sovereignty. James Madison and Thomas Jefferson advanced this concept in the Virginia and Kentucky Resolves in 1798.[71] If sovereignty could be diminished it could also be divided, and Indians could get a piece of it.

Such toying with sovereign power was less possible in Canada or elsewhere in the British Empire. British North Americans recoiled from such tinkering, leaving sovereignty fully with the King-in-Parliament. In Blackstonian interpretations it was unitary, and the Indians within the realm had none of it – though it might be exercised for their benefit. Canadian courts continue to hold to this view: sovereignty begins with the Treaty of Paris, 1763, to which Indians were not parties.[72] Under terrific pressure in recent years, Canadian courts have recognized Indians as possessing such liberties as "aboriginal title," a liberty the overall sovereignty is bound to protect.[73] The tendency in recent years may resemble that of the United States in its effect, but the premises of the two legal systems are quite different.

The Revolutionary and Confederation eras, generally seen as disastrous for Indians in the United States, left a conceptual legacy that would become highly important in our time, once skilled lawyers and leaders, many of the Indians, discovered it.[74] Even in the 1880s, during a long period in which the tribes were under strong state and federal assault, there was an odd glimmer of hope in the Crow Dog Cases, which culminated in a Supreme Court decision that recognized a measure of Brule Lakota sovereignty. Crow Dog had killed a tribesman on the reservation, the case had been settled according to Lakota law, but had then been taken up by the state and federal courts.

Crow Dog's attorney, arguing for the persistence and legitimacy of Lakota law, directly linked his client's struggle with the American Revolution: to rule against Crow Dog would be to "take away his local laws and customs," and to "place him upon trial under laws in the making of which he has no voice." It was, he argued, "upon the transcending of this God-given right that our forefathers made war upon the mother country."[75]

As the British Empire continued to spread and to displace indigenous peoples after the American Revolution, it claimed vast territories for the Crown. In Canada, like the United States, the empire's pretension to sovereignty over vast lands long antedated its actual jurisdiction within them. Unlike the United States, it was unthinkable for the empire that Native Americans possessed some residual sovereignty. In 1852 a Canadian judge ruled that "It can never be pretended," that the Six Nations "were recognized as a separate and independent nation;...but yet as British subjects, and under the control of, and subject to the general law of England."[76]

The legal status of Indians in Canada and the United States has been different ever since the revolution.[77] The decade of the 1760s was the common point of departure for the American and Canadian, indeed Commonwealth traditions.[78] In the 1760s, Indians from Pennsylvania to the westward demonstrated that they were capable of challenging Great Britain's armies. In the 1760s, too, the liberties of British subjects became matters of high importance to Britons from the Philadelphia taverns to the King's own chambers. It is not surprising, then, that during that decade British Imperial authorities largely discarded the idea that Indians were either British subjects or conquered nobodies. Instead they adopted the position that tribes were separate nations under the empire's protection. Indians were, to use phrases that would not have startled imperial authorities, domestic nations and dependent nations. Neither subjected nor sovereign, these were puzzling entities, and they still are, throughout North America, as discussions of Indian sovereignty, tribal status, and federal recognition regularly grace our newspapers, legislatures, councils, and courts. The colonial question is alive.

Notes

This essay was presented to the history departments of the University of Notre Dame, the University of Connecticut, and Michigan State University. It was delivered as well to the Kerry Scholars Seminar at Davidson College, the Omohundro Institute for Early American History and Culture Conference, and, of course, to the Lawrence Henry Gipson Institute at Lehigh University. A portion of it, in very different form, was presented to the Newberry Library, New Jersey Historical Commission's Annual Conference and another at the University of Michigan. I offer thanks to all participants in these sessions, in particular, to commentators George Abram and Jean O'Brien, whose criticisms have given shape to the piece. Portions of this essay appear in chapter 6 of my book, *War Under*

Heaven: Pontiac, the Indian Nations, and the British Empire (Baltimore: Johns Hopkins University Press, 2002).

1. For the concept of domiciled Indian nations and dependent Indian nations on the same eighteenth-century page see the reference to the Catawbas as a "domiciliated" nation and the Iroquois as having "Dependants" in the "Representation of the Lords of Trade on Indian Affairs, March 7, 1768, in Clarence Walworth Alvord and Clarence Edwin Carter, eds., *Collections of the Illinois State Historical Library* (hereafter *CISHL*) *vol. 16, British Series vol. 3., Trade and Politics* (Springfield: The Trustees of the Illinois State Historical Library, 1921), 194. For "domestic": Gage to Halifax, June 7, 1764, in Clarence Carter, ed., *The Correspondence of General Thomas Gage* (New Haven: Yale University Press, 1931), 1:8; "Domestick," Daniel Claus to Johnson, 30 Aug. 1764, abstracted in *The Papers of Sir William Johnson*, 14 vols., ed. James Sullivan, et al. (Albany: University of the State of New York, 1921-65), 4:516 (hereafter *WJP*); "domesticated," William Johnson to Roger Morris, 26 Aug. 1765, *WJP* 11:912.

2. P. J. Marshall, "Empire and Authority in the Late 18th Century," *Journal of Imperial and Commonwealth History* 15 (1987): 114.

3. W. J. Eccles, "Sovereignty – Association, 1500-1583," in *Essays on New France*, ed. Eccles (Toronto: Oxford University Press, 1987), 158.

4. W. Stitt Robinson, "The Legal Status of the Indians in Colonial Virginia," *Virginia Magazine of History and Biography* 61 (1953): 247-59 and Yasuhide Kawashima, "Jurisdiction of the Colonial Courts over the Indians in Massachusetts, 1689-1763," *New England Quarterly*, 62 (1969): 532-50, both note the colonists' readiness to distinguish among Indians who had first, effectively assimilated into colonial society, and whose legal status (in colonial terms) was therefore indistinguishable from that of the slaves or freemen who made up colonial society; second, formed separate but surrounded communities of Crown subjects under regular colonial authority; and third, remained free of regular imperial rule but might someday become subjects. In no case were Indian peoples seen to be sovereign. It is a contention of this paper that in the 1760s the British colonists and imperial authorities had, especially southwest of New England, for the most part abandoned the idea of Indians as Crown subjects.

5. Sidney L. Harring, *Crow Dog's Case: American Indian Sovereignty, Tribal Law, and United States Law in the Nineteenth Century* (Cambridge: Cambridge University Press, 1994), emphasizes the limits of John Marshall's decisions in actual practice. For most of the nineteenth century, state courts rejected tribal sovereignty, he finds, as the Worcester case became "largely irrelevant to Indians confronted with" state power. Marshall's doctrines were too often "hollow and abstract in practice" (52-53). See also Charlotte Coté, "Historical Foundations of Indian Sovereignty in Canada and the United States: a Brief Overview," *American Review of Canadian Studies* 31 (2001), 15-23.

6. Alexander Henry, *Travels and Adventures in Canada: March of America Facsimile Series*, no. 43 (Ann Arbor: University Microfilms, 1966), 44.

7. By "nation" I do not mean nation-state, but instead the indigenous social formations antecedent to the modern Indian nations. That these varied and changed tremendously over time and space before, during, and after the colonial period is only to say that they had history. For a work that deeply troubles the term "nation," see Michael J. Witgen, "An Infinity of Nations: How Indians, Empires, and Western Migration Shaped National Identity in North America" (PhD diss., University of Washington, 2004).

8. E. B. O'Callaghan, et al., eds., *Documents Relative to the Colonial History of the State of New York* (hereafter *NYCD*), 15 vols. (Albany: Parsons, Weed, 1853-87) 9:966-67. Colin Calloway, an expert on British Indian relations and Eastern Indians in general, includes this remarkable document in his collection, *The World Turned Upside Down: Indian Voices from Early America* (Boston: St. Martin's Press, 1994), 93. For a treatment of Indian, and especially Longhouse Iroquois, conceptions of sovereignty as exercised and understood in the context of diplomacy, see Robert A. Williams, Jr., *Linking Arms Together: American Indian Treaty Visions of Law and Peace, 1600-1800* (New York: Oxford University Press, 1997) and Taiaiake Alfred, "Sovereignty," in *A Companion to American Indian History*, eds. Philip J. Deloria and Neal Salisbury (Malden, Mass: Blackwell Publishing, 2002), 460-74.

9. Jean M. O'Brien, *Dispossession by Degrees: Indian Land and Identity in Natick, Massachusetts, 1650-1790* (Cambridge: Cambridge University Press, 1997), 38-41. It is possible that Daniel Gookin, who gave the Court's reasoning and who had had extensive experience in Ireland, was hearkening back to the English tradition of demanding grants from Irish lords and then regranting them to the Irish under English sovereignty. See the discussion of Nicholas Canny's findings, below.

10. Miguel Alfonso Martinez, "Discrimination against Indigenous Peoples: Study on Treaties, Agreements and Other Constructive Arrangements Between States and Indigenous Populations," *First Progress Report, United Nations, Commission on Human Rights, Subcommission on Prevention of Discrimination and Protection of Minorities,* Forty-fourth session, Item 15, August 25, 1992, Fourth World Documentation Project Archives, [pp. 23-24]. This document was accessed at: http://www.cwis.org/fwdp/International/untrtstd.txt. An example of this dubious assertion can be found in Carole Goldberg's otherwise excellent "Review Essay: A Law of their Own: Native Challenges to American Law," *Law and Social Inquiry* 25 (2000): 264. Frederic Gleach comes close to this position regarding the English in the Chesapeake in the seventeenth century, *Powhatan's World and Colonial Virginia: A Conflict of Cultures* (Lincoln: University of Nebraska Press, 1997), 136-37, 183. I find his arguments unpersuasive. While scholars can properly discover sovereignty in the Indians of the Chesapeake, the English never saw it. Nowhere do the articles of peace that he cites (178-81) recognize the Powhatans' or the Chickahominys' sovereignty.

11. Francisco de Vitoria, *Political Writings*, ed. Anthony Pagden and Jeremy Lawrence (Cambridge: Cambridge University Press, 1991), 278-79, 284-87, 290. Robert A. Williams, Jr., *The American Indian in Western Legal Thought: The Discourses of Conquest* (New York: Oxford University Press, 1990), 96-108, has it that, precisely because Vitoria believed that Indians had full access to natural law, the foundational jurist also justified the Spanish conquest on the ground that Indian violations of that law—their idolatry and their cannibalism—called for the very conquest that would have been sinful, had Indians had better manners. This kind of thinking is indirectly challenged by Mauricio Beuchot, "The

Philosophical Discussion of the Legitimacy of Conquest of Mexico in the Sixteenth Century," trans. Concepción Abellán, in *Hispanic Philosophy in the Age of Discovery: Studies in the History of Philosophy*, ed. Kevin White, vol. 29 (Washington, DC: Catholic University of America, 1997), 31-44. Thanks to Ivan Jaksić for this reference.

12. The best example here is George Peckham, whose writing is treated in Williams, *American Indian in Western Legal Thought*, 165-72. John T. Juricek sees "lingering" English "doubts about Indian rights" to North American territory as vanishing in the reign of James I. See Juricek, "English Territorial Claims in North America under Elizabeth and the Early Stuarts," *Terra Incognitae* 7 (1975): 7, 18n45, 19, 22.

13. Martinez, pointing to the fact that treaties formalized relations between Indians and colonizers for some 250 years, says, "Such a pervasive utilization of this particular modality offers solid proof of extensive European recognition of both the international (not internal) nature of the relations between both parties, and of the inherent international personality and legal capacity of the indigenous part." Martinez, "Discrimination," 23 of 71. Vine Deloria, Jr., and Clifford M. Lytle, following Felix Cohen, make the same point in *American Indians, American Justice* (Austin: University of Texas Press, 1983), 3.

14. Rebecca L. Robbins, "Self-Determination and Subordination: The Past, Present, and Future of American Indian Governance," in *Native American Sovereignty*, ed. John R. Wunder (New York: Garland, 1996), 289 and Markku Henriksson, "Treaty Legislation," in *Native American Sovereignty*, 66.

15. Olive P. Dickason, *Canada's First Nations: A History of Founding Peoples from Earliest Times* (Norman: University of Oklahoma Press, 1992), states: "So far as is known, none of these treaties were put through the procedure in the British Parliament that would have been necessary for such a status [equal to European Nations] to be recognized," 177. In "Concepts of Sovereignty at the Time of First Contacts," in *The Law of Nations and the New World*, ed. L. C. Green and Olive P. Dickason (Edmonton: University of Alberta Press, 1989), 239, Dickason writes "In the English way of doing things, a treaty had to have the royal seal in to order possess international significance. In any event, in view of their stand that America was terra nullis, it is not clear what status the English accorded these treaties at any level from a legal standpoint." She echoes Max Savelle, *The Origins of American Diplomacy: The International History of Angloamerica, 1492-1763* (New York: Macmillan, 1967), 205: "The 'treaties,' themselves, were generally oral, written down only in the reports made by the interpreters. Based heavily upon expediency, they were considered binding only so long as it suited the interests of the contracting parties to observe them. They were, in fact, ephemeral agreements made by representatives of two widely disparate cultures.... No Indian treaty ever had the status, either in law or in diplomacy, that any treaty between two European powers was recognized as having."

16. Indeed the whole point of that treaty, as with most that the British made, was to strengthen British claims to North America by formalizing Crown sovereignty. As the Board informed the Secretary of State: The Cherokees "acknowledging their Dependence upon the Crown of Great Britain, which Agreement remaining upon Record in our Office, would upon future Disputes with any European Nation, greatly Strengthen our Title in those Parts, even to all the Lands which these People now Possess." Board of Trade...to

Duke of Newcastle, 20 Aug. 1730, Colonial Office Papers, ser. 5, vol. 4: fol. 19, British Public Record Office, Kew, England, (hereafter as, for example, C.O. 5/4: 19).

17. Donald H. Kent, ed., *Early American Indian Documents: Treaties and Laws, 1607-1789*, vol. 1, *Pennsylvania and Delaware Treaties, 1629-1737*, gen. ed. Alden T. Vaughan (Washington, DC: University Publications of America, 1979), chap. 1, docs. 1, 2, 4, 8, 12, 13, 16; chap. 2, docs. 1, 4, 6, 8, 9, 10, 11, 12; chap. 3, docs. 6, 7, 10, 11, 12, 13, 15, 22, 23, 25, 28, 29, 32, 38, 58, 73; chap. 4, doc. 8.

18. Kent, ed., *Pennsylvania and Delaware Treaties*, chap. 1, docs. 5, 10, 12, 14; chap. 2, doc. 3.

19. For examples of indentures, deeds, and conveyances see Richard S. Dunn and Mary Maples Dunn, et al., eds., *The Papers of William Penn* (Philadelphia: University of Pennsylvania Press,1982) 2:261-69, 392, 404. Benjamin West's painting is reproduced in black-and-white on 453. See also a reproduction of one of Edward Hicks's 60-odd images of the event in Jean R. Soderlund et al., eds., *William Penn and the Founding of Pennsylvania, 1680-1684: A Documentary History* (Philadelphia: University of Pennsylvania Press, 1983), cover. Both appear and are discussed in James H. Merrell, *Into the American Woods: Negotiators on the Pennsylvania Frontier* (New York: Norton, 1999), 28-30. The Capitol Rotunda image is discussed (and Voltaire is quoted) in Vivien Green Fryd, "Imaging the Indians in the United States Capitol during the Early Republic," in *Native Americans and the Early Republic*, eds. Frederick E. Hoxie, Ronald Hoffman, and Peter J. Albert (Charlottesville: University Press of Virginia, 1999). For scholarly discussions of the legendary treaty see Frederick D. Stone, "Penn's Treaty with the Indians: Did it take place in 1682 or 1683?" *Pennsylvania Magazine of History and Biography* 6 (1882): 217-18; Francis Jennings (also quotes Voltaire), "Brother Miquon: Good Lord!," in *The World of William Penn*, eds. Richard S. Dunn and Mary Maples Dunn (Philadelphia: University of Pennsylvania Press,1986), 198; Donald H. Kent (also quotes Voltaire), "Introduction" to chap. 3 in Kent, ed., *Pennsylvania and Delaware Treaties*, 52; Harry Emerson Wildes, *William Penn* (New York: Macmillan, 1974), 180; James O'Neil Spady, "Colonialism and the Discursive Antecedents of *Penn's Treaty with the Indians*," in *Friends and Enemies in Penn's Woods: Indians, Colonists, and the Racial Construction of Pennsylvania*, ed. William Pencak and Daniel K. Richter (University Park: Pennsylvania State University Press, 2004), 18-40.

20. The *Oxford English Dictionary* lists several obsolete, seventeenth-century uses of the word "treaty," each of which carries no implication of sovereignty.

21. W. Stitt Robinson, ed., *Early American Indian Documents, Treaties and Laws, 1607-1789*, vol. 4: *Virginia Treaties, 1607-1722*, gen. ed. Alden T. Vaughan (Frederick, Md.: University Publications of America, 1983), 27-28; Williams, *American Indian in Western Legal Thought*, 215-16.

22. "Council of Gov. Gookin and Council with Chiefs of Delaware and Schuylkil Indians," June 14-15, 1715, and "Minutes of the Provincial Council," June 21-22, 1715, in Kent, ed., *Pennsylvania and Delaware Treaties*, 157, 159.

23. William Fenton, "Structure, Continuity, and Change in the Process of Iroquois Treaty Making," in Francis Jennings, et al., *The History and Culture of Iroquois Diplomacy* (Syracuse: Syracuse University Press, 1985), 27. *Oxford English Dictionary*, s.v. "Treaty." Benjamin Franklin, *The Autobiography of Benjamin Franklin*, ed. Louis Masur (Boston: St. Martin's Press, 1993), 119. James Merrell, for instance, uses the word treaty in this manner in his elegant book, *Into the American Woods*, 256-57 and throughout. Here Indians are "enticed to a treaty." They make a "camp at a treaty." As Merrell describes them, treaties have sounds, and to this American, the word rings true. American Indian treaties were not merely written agreements.

24. Merrell, *Into the American Woods*, 254; Raymond DeMallie, "Touching the Pen: Plains Indian Treaty Councils in Ethnohistorical Perspective," in *Ethnicity on the Great Plains*, ed. Frederick C. Luebke (Lincoln: University of Nebraska Press, 1980), 38-53.

25. The United Kingdom's "Treaty of Waitangi," promulgated unilaterally by Great Britain and then signed by various Maori chieftains over the course of 1840, provides a fascinating illustration of a Janus-faced treaty; perhaps Cybil is a better face than Janus for this one. As a written document, it is in both English and Maori (the singular indigenous language of New Zealand). But on the issue of sovereignty and subjection, the two versions differ widely. There are other "versions" of the treaty, too; see James Belich, *Making Peoples: A History of the New Zealanders from Polynesian Settlement to the End of the Nineteenth Century* (Auckland: Allen Lane, 1996), 193-97.

26. Williams, *American Indian in Western Legal Thought*, 134. W. Stitt Robinson makes the same point in "Legal Status of the Indian in Colonial Virginia," 258, 259. The Crown, in English eyes, had the absolute title (*dominium directum*), Indians possessed only usage rights (*dominium utile*).

27. Quotation: Bruce A. Clark, *Native Liberty, Crown Sovereignty: The Existing Aboriginal Right of Self-Government in Canada* (Montreal: McGill-Queen's University Press, 1990), 28, 43. Clark argues that the Privy Council, which ruled against the Mohegans, accepted the fact of Mohegan sovereignty. His argument is based on jurisdictional technicalities that support his thesis that Canadian Courts must, as a matter of law, accept the idea of native sovereignty. Perhaps this is legally correct. But nowhere does he quote a judgment that is explicit in support of native sovereignty, and it is critical, too, that the Mohegans lost their case. See 28-53.

28. Williams, *Linking Arms Together*, convinced of the insufficiency of Western law in general and United States law in particular to render justice to Indians, suggests that we pay greater attention to the "legal visions of American Indian peoples," to "the Indian legal visions that have sustained the decolonization struggles of Indian tribal peoples in the United States." He embarks upon this project with an examination of such diplomatic rites among Indians as those involving wampum belts, condolence ceremonies, calumet pipes, and mourning rituals. See 7, 44–57.

29. See, for example, James H. Merrell, "Declarations of Independence: Indian-White Relations in the New Nation," in Jack P. Greene, ed., *The American Revolution: Its Character and Limits* (New York: New York University Press, 1987),197.

30. Nicholas Canny, "England's *New World and the Old, 1480s-1630s,*" in *The Oxford History of the British Empire*, vol. 1: *The Origins of Empire*, ed. Canny (Oxford: Clarendon Press, 1998), 157. In the case of Pennsylvania, it is worth recalling that Penn referred to his settlements as "our English Pale." William Penn to the Lords of Trade, 2 July 1701, Kent, ed., *Pennsylvania and Delaware Treaties*, chap. 4, doc. 11. Robinson, ed., *Virginia Treaties*, 11-22; Gleach, *Powhatan's World and Colonial Virginia*, 136-37. Williams, *American Indian in Western Legal Thought*, 136-47, 207, also treats Powhatan's coronation and the Irish precedents; his excellent book is devoted more to the question of the Europeans' justifications for conquest than to the concept of Indian subjection. Liam Séamus O'Mellin, "The Imperial Origins of Federal Indian Law: The Ideology of Colonization in Britain, Ireland, and America," *Arizona State Law Journal* 31 (1999): 1207-75, places recent Supreme Court rulings against the concept of tribal sovereignty within the context of early modern English conceptions of Irish and Indian subjection. Here Indians subject themselves to the English in order to gain release from their own abject condition into a happy state of permanent servitude committed to their civility. O'Mellin emphasizes Indian consent, forgetting that, as Thomas More himself made clear, such consent was unnecessary.

31. Excerpted in Calloway, ed., *World Turned Upside Down*, 81-82. For an analysis of this document see Glenn W. LaFantasie, ed., *The Correspondence of Roger Williams*, 2 vols. (Providence: Brown University Press/University Press of New England, 1988), 1:221. For a fresh treatment of authority and subjection in colonial New England, see Jenny Hall Pulsipher, *Subjects unto the Same King: Indians, English, and the Contest for Authority in Colonial New England* (Philadelphia: University of Pennsylvania Press, 2005).

32. Rhode Island even tried captured Indians on the grounds that they were subjects who had had the gall to "traterously, rebelliously ryotously, and tortously, arm, weapon, and array themselves," against the English, quoted in Jill Lepore, *The Name of War: King Philip's War and the Origins of American Identity* (New York: Knopf, 1998), 137, 155.

33. Lepore, *Name of War*, 163. Lepore rightly points out the ambiguity over whether "King" Philip and his people were sovereign or subjects was embodied in this document. Edmund S. Morgan has pointed out that in the early seventeenth century the House of Commons considered English subjects to have the rights to "freedom from arrest," to "security of property" and to "trial by jury." Edmund S. Morgan, *Inventing the People: The Rise of Popular Sovereignty in England and America* (New York: Norton, 1988), 23. For the disabilities faced by "Friend Indians" in Massachusetts after King Philip's War see O'Brien, *Dispossession by Degrees*, 67. Natick Indians frequently resorted to the General Court.

34. Kawashima, "Jurisdiction of the Colonial Courts," 533, 533 n.52.

35. Robinson, ed., *Virginia Treaties*, chap. 1, doc. 6, 11-22; chap. 3, doc. 5, 82-83, and doc. 25, 117-18; Robinson, "Legal Status of the Indian in Colonial Virginia."

36. On Rode and the delegation see Barbara Graymont, ed., *New York and New Jersey Treaties and Laws 1609-1682*, vol. 8, *Early American Indian Documents*, gen. ed. Alden T. Vaughan (Frederick, Md.: University Publications of America, 1985), 90-91. On Cheda, see Cadwallader Colden, *History of the Five Nations* (London, 1747), 2:126; "Descriptive Treaty Calendar" in Jennings, et al., *The History and Culture of Iroquois Diplomacy*, 161, 169. On the

Treaty of Utrecht and the original French, "soumis à la Grande Bretagne": Max Savelle, *The Origins of American Diplomacy: The International History of Angloamerca, 1492-1763* (New York: Macmillan, 1967), 150n65, 189, 203. For Dongan in 1687: *NYCD*, 3:438-39, 515, 516. Whitehall concurred: *NYCD*, 3:503. The Iroquois denied this the next year: *NYCD*, 9:384-86. Cherokees: "Articles of Friendship and Commerce, proposed by the Lords Commissioners for Trade and Plantations, to the Deputies of the Cherokee Nation in South Carolina.... 7 Sept. 1730," C.O. 5/4:211-14. On Niagara: Savelle, *Origins*, 363-64; Memoir respecting for Niagara, presented to his Eminence, Cardinal de Fleury, 9 May 1727, *NYCD*, 9:997-99.

37. For Cosby and the Iroquois in 1733: *NYCD*, 5:962-69, 970. Cosby's treaty included a disputed provision that the Iroquois had put their lands under the king's protection, see "Descriptive Treaty Calendar," Jennings, et al., *History and Culture of Iroquois Diplomacy*, 177. The Iroquois deny subjection in Jennings, et al., 184.

38. Timothy J. Shannon suggests that British metropolitan reformers generally thought of the Indians as subjects, and he offers several direct references, in *Indians and Colonists at the Crossroads of Empire: The Albany Congress of 1754* (Ithaca, N.Y.: Cornell University Press, 2000), 12, 21, 22, 24, 59. Where he sees the usage as consistently maintained, I see it as in dramatic decline. Meanwhile, the Irish, Scottish, and Welsh were all deemed British subjects. Curiously, but not surprisingly, there are ripples in the pattern. As J. C. D. Clark writes, "William III was only Stadholder in the Netherlands, and George I only Elector in Hanover. It appears that the national status of the Dutch during William's reign was never judicially decided; the status of Hanoverians as subjects "until 1837 was only confirmed by a judgement in 1886": J. C. D. Clark, *The Language of Liberty, 1660-1832: Political Discourse and Social Dynamics in the Anglo-American World* (Cambridge: Cambridge University Press, 1994), 50.

39. Proclamation of Gage to the Inhabitants of the Illinois, 30 Dec. 1764, *CISHL*, 10:395-96; Plan of Forts and Garrisons proposed for North America, Jeffery Amherst, *CISHL* 10:5-7; Message of Gen. Amherst to the Indians, 1761, in Samuel Hazard, ed., *Pennsylvania Archives* (Philadelphia: Joseph Severns, 1854) ser. 1, 4:48-49; Report of Roberts, 8 March 1764, in *CISHL*, 10:218; Morgan, *Inventing the People*, 25.

40. Thomas Mante, *The History of the Late War in North-America, and the Islands of the West Indies, including the campaigns of MDCCLXIII and MDCCLXIV against His Majesty's Indian Enemies* (London, 1772 [reprinted New York: Research Imprints, 1970]), 519; Congress with the Western Nations, Detroit, 7-10 Sept. 1764, *WJP*, 4:528-529, 532-33; John Campbell, 27 Jan. 1765, *WJP* 11:550-551; Thomas Morris to Lt. Mante, Rochebedout Village of the Ottawas, 31 Aug. 1764 in Gage Papers, vol. 24, William Clements Library, Ann Arbor, Michigan (hereafter WCL).

41. Johnson to Lords of Trade, 25 Sept. 1763, *NYCD* 7:561; Johnson to Gage, 31 Oct. 1764, *WJP* 10:395; Johnson to Gage, 6 Dec. 1764, *WJP* 11:493; Johnson to Lords of Trade, 26 Dec. 1764, *CISHL* 10:391.

42. Mante, *History of the Late War in North-America*, 481.

43. Few thought much of the measure. Commander in Chief of British forces in North America Thomas Gage supported it, but wished it had been "fallen upon some years ago." Land speculators were horrified at the effects the proclamation would have on their claims to the West. Squatters, who had been violating official wishes in any case, would go right on squatting once peace was restored. Indians on all sides of the conflict were not well impressed. Even the King conceded that the proclamation was a temporary measure, undertaken only "for the present and until Our further Pleasure be known." Proclamation of 1763, *WJP* 10:982; Gage to Johnson, Dec. 1763, *WJP* 4:290-91; Jack M. Sosin, *The Revolutionary Frontier, 1763-1783* (New York: Holt, Rinehart, and Winston, 1967), 15-19.

44. Lords of Trade to Johnson, 5 Aug. 1763, *CISHL* 10:17-18. This is close to what Grotius had in mind when he wrote of the "unequal alliance." In an unequal alliance, a treaty gives "one of the contracting parties a permanent advantage of the other...that is, to put forth every effort that its sovereignty remain secure and its prestige, which is understood by the word majesty, remain unimpaired. This is what Tacitus called 'the feeling of awe for the empire,' explaining what he had in mind as follows: 'In respect to place of habitation and territories they belong on their own bank, in mind and heart they act with us.'" The Indians, under such an unequal alliance, would have been given the rights of "protection, defense, and patronage." In exchange, they would give "the customary signs of respect, a deferential attitude, undoubtedly, and certain outward marks of honor." Hugo Grotius, *Hugonis Grotii De Jure Belli Ac Pacis, Libre Tres [1625], The Classics of International Law*, ed. James Brown Scott, trans. Francis W. Kelsey, et al. 2 vols. (Washington DC: Carnegie Institution of Washington, 1913-25), vol. 1, book 1, chap. 3:130 (hereafter Grotius, *JB*). Jill Lepore writes that Grotius was influential in colonial New England. Lepore, *The Name of War*, 107-108.

45. "Plan for the Future Management of Indian Affairs, [10 July] 1764" and "Commissioners of Trade to John Stuart, Whitehall, 10 July 1764," *Pennsylvania Archives*, ser. 1, 4:182-83, 189.

46. The Crown, moreover, had no real policy with which to deal with Indians beyond the Proclamation line; after a brief flirtation with imposing tight regulations across the entire colonial-Indian borderlands, it by 1769 gave all such regulation, except over the purchasing of land, back to the colonies.

47. Wheaton (21 U.S.) 543 (1823). It is unfortunate that such language pervades this first of Marshall's three most important decisions on issues relating to American Indians. To be sure, the Federal Government, including its highest court, did not often give tribal sovereignty much weight in the balance against Federal power over Indians or against western expansion, especially in the century that followed Marshall's remarkable rulings. Recently the Court seems to be veering again in the direction of Federal power. See Frank Pommersheim, *Braid of Feathers: American Indian Law and Contemporary Tribal Life* (Berkeley: University of California Press, 1995), 192-93; O'Mellin, "Imperial Origins and Federal Indian Law," 1208; Lindsay Gordon Robertson, *Conquest by Law: How the Discovery of America Dispossessed Indigenous Peoples of Their Lands* (New York: Oxford University Press, 2005). David E. Wilkins reveals the hollowness of sovereignty in American Federal Indian Law in his *American Indian Sovereignty and the U. S. Supreme Court: The Masking of Justice* (Austin: University of Texas Press, 1997).

48. "Representation of the Lords of Trade on the State of Indian Affairs," 7 Mar. 1768, *CISHL* 16:186. For New Zealand, Canada, and Australia, see P. G. McHugh, *Aboriginal Societies and the Common Law: A History of Sovereignty, Status, and Self-Determination* (Oxford: Oxford University Press, 2004), 243, 262, 264, 276-77. I thank Damon Salesa for this reference.

49. At the end of the imperial era, a widely used British introduction to international law reached several conclusions regarding colonial protectorates and states under mandate or trust. First, "the inhabitants of a protectorate do not take on the nationality of the protecting state." Second, "to introduce the concept of sovereignty into any discussion of the nature either of mandates or trust territories is, from the point of view of international law, merely confusing. The notion that we must look for sovereignty in a mandated or a trust territory implies that sovereignty is an indestructible substance which we shall surely find in any area if only we look closely enough. But government under a mandate or trust is surely an alternative to, not a species of, government under sovereignty; and just as English law has two different regimes for the holding of property, namely, private ownership and trusts, so now international law has acquired two regimes for government, that is to say, sovereignty and the mandate or the trust." J. L. Brierly, *The Law of Nations: an Introduction to the International Law of Peace*, 5th ed. (Oxford: Clarendon Press, 1955), 157, 166-67.

50. Minisinks or Munsees, the Northern Delaware speakers, refused to support the Iroquois League militarily when asked to do so during King William's War and Queen Anne's War. League members protested about this to the English, expecting some support from England's good Indian allies, but it is clear that well into the eighteenth century, the Iroquois could not coerce even Munsees, the most proximate of the Lenape people. Robert Grumet, "'We Are Not So Great Fools': Changes in Upper Delawaran Socio-Political Life, 1630-1758" (PhD diss., Rutgers University, 1979), 66, 76.

51. Francis Jennings, *The Ambiguous Iroquois Empire: The Covenant Chain Confederation of Indian Tribes with English Colonies* (New York: Norton, 1984), 159-62. Contrast with the older interpretation in C. A. Weslager, *The Delaware Indians: A History* (New Brunswick, N.J.: Rutgers University Press, 1972), 103, now revised by Nancy Shoemaker, *A Strange Likeness: Becoming Red and White in Eighteenth-Century North America* (New York: Oxford University Press, 2004), 109-14.

52. *Pennsylvania Gazette*, 15 Apr. 1756, item #19413; 12 July 1764, item #33691, Accessible Archives CD-ROM version; John Clarence Webster, ed., *The Journal of Jeffery Amherst: Recording the Military Career of General Amherst in America from 1758 to 1763* (Chicago: University of Chicago Press, 1931), entry for 24 Oct. 1763, 325. For a concise statement of Iroquois authority over the Shawnees in the West, see Gage to Hillsborough, 6 Jan. 1770, C.O.5/88:26.

53. Ecuyer to Bouquet, 16 June 1763, in Mary C. Darlington, ed., *Fort Pitt and Letters from the Frontier* (New York: Arno Press, 1971 [1892]),130-32; Amherst to Bouquet, 29 June 1763, in Agnus Burton, et al., "Bouquet Papers," *Michigan Pioneer and Historical Collections* 19 (1892): 203, hereafter *Michigan Pioneer*; Amherst to Gladwin, 29 June 1763, Jeffery Amherst Papers, American Series, vol. 2, no. 3, WCL; Bouquet to Gage, 7 June 1764,

Michigan Pioneer 19:261; William Johnson to John Penn, 9 Feb. 1764, *Pennsylvania Archives*, ser. 1, 4: 163. For "quietus," see *Pennsylvania Gazette*, 1 Sept. 1763, item #18966, Accessible Archives CD-ROM, and the *OED*, definition 3. Strictly speaking, the killing of captives, even of women and children, was not seen by writers such as Grotius to be outside the law of nations. See Grotius, *JB*, Book III, chap. 4, 649. But it was not in vogue in eighteenth-century Europe. For the Law of Nations, see L.C. Green, "Indian Claims to Territory in Colonial America," in *Law of Nations*, ed. Green and Dickason, 3-127. Green writes, "international law did not recognize the aboriginal inhabitants of such newly discovered territories as having any legal rights that were good as against those who 'discovered' and settled their territories." Here he is correct. But he is wrong when he claims Indians were "subjects," 125-26.

54. Donald H. Kent and Bernard Knollenberg, "Communications," and Bernard Knollenberg, "General Amherst and Germ Warfare," *Mississippi Valley Historical Review* 41 (1954-55): 762-63, 489-64; Albert T. Volwiller, "William Trent's Journal at Fort Pitt, 1763," ibid. 11 (1924): 400; Ecuyer to Bouquet, 16 June 1763, and "Orderly Book," 1 Aug. in Darlington, ed. *Fort Pitt*, 93, 130-32, 182; Bouquet to Amherst, 23 June 1763, *Michigan Pioneer* 19: 195; Howard H. Peckham, *Pontiac and the Indian Uprising* (Chicago: University of Chicago Press, 1961), 226-27. On smallpox in 1764, see: *CISHL* 10:236, 397, *WJP* 4:640, *WJP* 11:537, 618, 660; Col. Lewis to Col. Henry Bouquet, 10 Sept. 1764, Bouquet Papers, British Museum, Add. Mss. 21650 London, England; Examination of Gershom Hicks, 15 Apr. 1764, Gage Papers, vol. 24, WCL; Grotius, *JB*, Book 3, chap. 4, 651-52.

55. John R. Dunbar, "Introduction," in *The Paxton Papers*, ed. Dunbar (The Hague: M. Nijhoff, 1957), 22; "Instructions to Col. Armstrong, 11 July, 1763," and "Recruiting Instructions to Armstrong, Elder &c., 1763," in *Pennsylvania Archives*, ser. 1, 4:114-17.

56. John Heckewelder, *A Narrative of the Mission of the United Brethren among the Delaware and Mohegan Indians* (New York: Arno Press, 1971; reprint of Philadelphia, 1820), 67-70, 76-77; *Pennsylvania Gazette* 11 Aug. 1763, 15 Sept. 1763; "A Conference," 1 Dec. 1763, *Colonial Records of Pennsylvania*, (Harrisburg: T. Fenn, 1852), 9:77-79.

57. *Pennsylvania Gazette*, 13 Oct. 1763, item #31823; 10 Nov. 1763, item #32016; 22 Mar. 1764, item #32891, Accessible Archives CD-ROM.

58. Dunbar, "Introduction," in *Paxton Papers*, ed. Dunbar, 21-22; Rev. John Elder to Gov. Hamilton, 25 Oct. 1763 in *Pennsylvania Archives*, ser. 1, 4:127; Votes of Assembly, 21 Oct. 1763 and 24 Dec. 1763, *Pennsylvania Archives*, ser. 8, 6:5482-83, 5497; Heckewelder, *Narrative of the Mission*, 73; John Penn to Gage, 31 Dec. 1763, Gage Papers, vol. 11, WCL.

59. Petition from Lewis Weiss, 23 Dec. 1763, *Pennsylvania Archives*, ser. 8, 6:5495.

60. Dunbar, ed., *Paxton Papers*, 23, 27; Humbertis M. Cummings, "The Paxton Killings," *Journal of Presbyterian History*, 44 (1966): 219-30; Council Minutes, 21 Dec. 1763, 29 Dec. 1763, in *Colonial Records of Pennsylvania*, 9:93-95, 9:100.

61. *Pennsylvania Gazette*, 29 Dec. 1763, item #32365; 5 Jan. 1764, item #32414; 12 Jan. 1764, item #32449, Accessible Archives CD-ROM; Rev. John Elder to Penn, 16 Dec. 1763, Penn to Elder, 29 Dec. 1763, *Pennsylvania Archives*, ser. 1, 4:148-49, 153.

62. Thomas McKee to Johnson, 15 Feb. 1764, *WJP* 11:56; John Penn to Johnson, 17 Feb. 1764, *WJP* 4:327; *Pennsylvania Gazette*, 9 Feb. 1764, item #32610, Accessible Archives CD-ROM; Heckewelder, *Narrative of the Mission*, 80-86; *Colonial Records of Pennsylvania*, 9:101-32; Gage to Halifax, 12 May 1764, Carter, ed., *Gage Correspondence*, 1:26; Votes of Assembly, 3 Feb. 1764, *Pennsylvania Archives*, ser. 8, 7:5536-37; Instructions of Gov'r to Capt. Schlosser, 4 Feb. 1764, *Pennsylvania Archives*, ser. 1, 4:161.

63. Though my reading differs from hers, Notre Dame graduate student Nicole Gothelf drew my attention to this debate in her paper, "'English Subjects' or 'His Majesty's Perfidious Enemies'; 'Insurrection' or 'Dissent': The Political Significance of the Paxton Massacres Reconsidered," graduate seminar paper, 1995. Gothelf's interpretation now appears in Nicole Mische Gothelf, "Persecution, Identity, and Politics: The English Protestant Martyr Narrative and Oppositional Politics in Early New England and Pennsylvania" (PhD diss., Notre Dame University, 2001).

64. [Benjamin Franklin,] "A Narrative of the Late Massacres, in Lancaster County, of a Number of Indians, Friends of this Province, by Persons unknown;" Charles Read, "Copy of a Letter from Charles Read, Esq: To the Hon: John Ladd, Esq: And his Associates, Justices of the Peace for the County of Gloucester," "A Serious Address, to Such of the Inhabitants of Pennsylvania, As have cannived at, or do approve of, the late Massacre of the Indians at Lancaster; or the Design of Killing those who are now in the Barracks at Philadelphia," "A Dialogue, Containing some Reflections on the late Declaration and Remonstrance, Of the Back-Inhabitants of the Province of Pennsylvania," and "The Quakers Assisting. To Preserve the Lives of the Indians in the Barracks, Vindicated And proved to be consistent with Reason, agreeable to our Law, hath an inseparable Connection with the Law of God, and exactly agreeable with the Principles of the People call'd Quakers," all in *Paxton Papers*, ed. Dunbar, 64, 65, 80, 93-95, 115, 119, 356.

65. Carter, ed., *Gage Correspondence*, 1:8; *Pennsylvania Gazette*, 5 Jan. 1764, item #32414, Accessible Archives CD-ROM.

66. Penn to Assembly, Votes of Assembly, 20 Dec. 1763, *Pennsylvania Archives*. ser. 8, 6:5493; Thomas McKee to Johnson, Lancaster, 15 Feb. 1764, *WJP* 11:56-57.

67. "A Declaration And Remonstrance Of the distressed and bleeding Frontier Inhabitants Of the Province of Pennsylvania, Presented by them to the Honourable the Governor and Assembly of the Province, Shewing the Causes Of their late Discontent and Uneasiness and the Grievances Under which they have laboured, and which they humbly pray to have redress'd," "An Historical Account, of the late Disturbance, between the Inhabitants of the Back Settlements; of Pennsylvania, and the Philadelphians, &., "The Apology of the Paxton Volunteers addressed to the candid & impartial World," [Thomas Barton?] "The Conduct of the Paxton-Men, impartially represented: with some Remarks on the Narrative," all in

DOMESTIC, DEPENDENT, NATIONS 155

Paxton Papers, ed. Dunbar, 101, 102, 105 (quotation); 128, 193 (quotation), 194 (quotation), 202-203, 273-74, 282 (quotation), 293.

68. Votes of Assembly, 29 Feb. 1764, *Pennsylvania Archives*, ser. 8, 7:5559, for earlier rejections of petitions see 6:5437, 5440; Paul A.W. Wallace, ed., *Thirty Thousand Miles with John Heckewelder* (Pittsburgh: University of Pittsburgh Press, 1958), 81; Johnson to Penn, 9 Feb. 1764, *WJP* 4:324; George Croghan to Johnson, 25 Sept. 1767, *WJP* 5:701; *Pennsylvania Gazette*, 12 July 1764, item #33691, Accessible Archives CD-ROM; Johnson to Penn, 18 June 1764, *WJP* 11:241.

69. Copy of letter from M. de St. Ange, Commandant at the Illinois, to M. Dabbadie, Director General, 12 Aug. 1764, *CISHL* 10:294-95; Testimony of Thomas King, Sandusky, 3 Oct. 1764, *WJP* 11:372.

70. Weslager, *Delaware Indians*, 305; Annie H. Abel, "Proposals for an Indian State, 1778-1878," *Annual Report of the American Historical Association for the Year 1907*, 2 vols., (Washington, DC: G.P.O., 1908), 1:89; Francis Paul Prucha, *American Indian Treaties: The History of a Political Anomaly* (Berkeley: University of California Press, 1994), 32-33.

71. Jack N. Rakove, *Original Meanings: Politics and Ideas in the Making of the Constitution* (New York: Knopf, 1996), 105. J. C. D. Clark sees *The Federalist* as prevaricating on the unitary or divisible character or sovereignty. In *Federalist 9*, Hamilton wrote: "The proposed constitution, far from implying an abolition of the State government, makes them constituent parts of the national sovereignty...and leaves in their possession certain exclusive and very important portions of sovereign power." Clark argues that he did not really mean what he said, but there it is, *Language of Liberty*, 135.

72. "English law has long recognized that the sovereignty of the Crown over its territory is exclusive and exhaustive. Once formally declared, the Crown's courts are bound to give effect to the monarch's claims. The Crown's title to territory is indivisible – it shares sovereignty with no one." P. G. McHugh, "Constitutional Questions and Maori Claims," *Waitangi: Maori and Pakeha Perspectives of the Treaty of Waitangi*, ed. I. H. Kawharu, (Auckland: Oxford University Press, 1989), 37; McHugh includes a good brief comparison of how sovereignty is legally understood in the systems of Australia, Canada, and the United States. Coté states that "Native tribes have never been recognized as possessing even a limited degree of internal sovereignty by the Canadian government or by courts." Even cases recognizing aboriginal "rights" to not base these on "sovereignty": Coté, "Historical Foundations," 16, 22.

73. Bruce Clark, *Native Liberty, Crown Sovereignty*, 19. Throughout, Clark argues that Canadian courts should find in favor of Native Sovereignty. On 11 Dec. 1997, the Canadian Supreme Court rendered what may be the most important ruling on Indian issues in all Canadian history: *Delgamuukw v. British Columbia in Right of the Crown*. Here the court overturned an earlier (1991) decision that had scoffed at aboriginal rights, asserting that they existed only at the Crown's pleasure. In *Delgamuukw*, the issue of self-government was sidestepped, and the sovereignty of the Crown was, it appears, fully maintained. For example, the Court uses the phrase, "at sovereignty," which refers to the time at which

Great Britain took over. Sovereignty appears in this line of thinking to begin and end with the Crown, which is a very different approach from that taken by American courts (44). But the Court opened the door to considerable aboriginal control over land, even if ultimate title seems still to lie with the "Crown." I accessed this 64-page ruling at http://www.droit.umontreal.ca/doc/csc-scc/en/pub/1997/vol3/html/1997scr3_1010.html. See also Sidney L. Harring, "Indian Law, Sovereignty, and State Law: Native People and the Law," in *A Companion to American Indian History*, 454-55.

74. Almost no one sees good in the American Revolution for Indians. The literature on its catastrophic effects is enormous. See James H. O'Donnell III, "The World Turned Upside Down: The American Revolution as a Catastrophe for Native Americans," in Francis P. Jennings, ed., *The American Indian and the American Revolution* (Chicago: Newberry Library, 1983), 80-83; Richard White, *The Middle Ground: Indians, Empires, and Republics in the Great Lakes Region, 1650-1815* (Cambridge: Cambridge University Press, 1995); J. Russell Snapp, *John Stuart and the Struggle for Empire on the Southern Frontier* (Baton Rouge: Louisiana State University Press, 1996); Eric Hinderaker, *Elusive Empires: Constructing Colonialism in the Ohio Valley 1673-1800* (Cambridge: Cambridge University Press, 1997). There are many other examples, they cannot all be wrong, and as a war, it was certainly disastrous for Cherokees, Six Nations, and Delawares, among others. The question, however, remains as to whether the British Empire represented, in the long term, an attractive alternative.

75. Harring, *Crow Dog's Case*, 124; Goldberg, "A Law of their Own," 281.

76. Quoted in Bruce Clark, *Native Liberty, Crown Sovereignty*, 19.

77. The history of subjection in the British Empire has yet to be written, though much has been written on British conceptions of sovereignty. J. C. D. Clark, in *Language of Liberty*, 89, 92, presents the "Blackstonian" concept of sovereignty as a clear counterpoint to the notions of popular sovereignty that developed in England among dissenters and, especially, in Revolutionary America. That concept, he argues, lodged sovereignty firmly, and singularly, in the King-in-Parliament. This was a unitary sovereignty. What this implied for subjects who were not "British" is in need of research. India might provide the most fruitful locale, since it came to form the heart of the second British empire. In the mid-eighteenth century, British conceptions of the constitutional status of peoples within the power of the East India Company were vague and confused, but over the course of the latter part of the century British governors struggled to legitimize their despotism by imposing British forms of governance upon conquered peoples, whom they, in a reversion to older forms employed in seventeenth-century America and sixteenth-century Ireland, again viewed as subjects, albeit highly unequal ones. As one Governor-General put it, "Asiatic treachery and falsehood" mandated that "we exclude our native subjects from all participation in the legislative authority." Quoted in Rajat Kanta Ray, "Indian Society and British Supremacy," in P. J. Marshall, ed., *The Oxford History of the British Empire*, vol. 2: *The Eighteenth Century* (Oxford: Clarendon Press, 1998), 525.

78. The role of Crown Sovereignty in Commonwealth countries is treated in the New Zealand context by McHugh, "Constitutional Questions," 37: "by the eve of the American Revolution, the British were becoming too attached to the doctrine of parliamentary

sovereignty to be persuaded there existed a set of natural and common law rights beyond legislative reach." Parliamentary sovereignty and Crown sovereignty, it should be noted, are one and the same. See ibid., 33.

II

Settlement at the Forks:
Economic Development and Religious Conflict

Perfection in the Mechanical Arts: The Development of Moravian Industrial Technology in Bethlehem, Pennsylvania, 1741-1814

STEPHEN H. CUTCLIFFE and KAREN Z. HUETTER

SOME YEARS AGO, historian of technology Norman B. Wilkinson called attention to the fact that despite the rapidly expanding state of American industry in the late eighteenth and early nineteenth centuries, the nation was still largely indebted to Europe for its technology. In an article entitled "Brandywine Borrowings from European Technology," Wilkinson referred to the estimates of the French traveler Duc de la Rochefoucault Liancourt that as early as 1797 some sixty to eighty mills of varied sorts operated along the Brandywine River near Wilmington, Delaware. By 1804, Jedidiah Morse noted in his *American Gazetteer* that "Wilmington and its neighborhood are probably already the greatest seat of manufactures in the United States."[1] Although by 1800 the Brandywine River Valley may have been the greatest seat of manufactures, it was by no means the first or only such early concentration of industrial activity.

When Revolutionary War leader John Adams arrived in Bethlehem, Pennsylvania, in late January 1777, he wrote to his wife Abigail that the Moravians "have carried the mechanical Arts to greater Perfection here than in any Place which I have seen."[2] Although not founded until 1741, within six years the Moravians were practicing more than thirty-five crafts and industrial trades within the community, and by the mid-1750s, the number had grown to approximately fifty. Many of the heavier trades such as grist milling, tanbark crushing, oil milling, and a pumped waterworks depended on an extensive (for the period) waterpower system for their source of energy.

This early concentration of industrial technology occurring along the Monocacy Creek makes Bethlehem an important site in American technological development. The location, design, and early successes of this complex of mills was due to a combination of technological borrowing and community planning. Although often overlooked because of subsequent nineteenth-century industrial activities, this early example of American proto-industrial development is, nonetheless, valuable for what it reveals about technological practice in the latter half of the eighteenth century.

Why Bethlehem developed such a concentration of crafts and trades in one location at such a relatively early date, and why that growth subsequently stagnated, helps us to understand how the economic history of the community evolved and complements much of what historians know generally about early American technological practice.

Religious and Economic Background

The Moravians, a Protestant group with roots in fifteenth-century Bohemia and Moravia in Czechoslovakia (now the Czech Republic), came to Pennsylvania from Herrnhut, Germany, where they lived under the patronage of Count Nicholas von Zinzendorf, a German Lutheran nobleman.[3] Herrnhut became the center of all their subsequent religious endeavors throughout the world. Zinzendorf played an instrumental role in redefining the Moravians' religious experience and thus in developing their worldview regarding everything from the family and marriage, to commerce, industrialism, and agriculture.

For the first twenty years of Bethlehem's existence, religion infused every facet of life. To support their mission activities in North America to the Native Americans[4] and to other German settlers, the Moravian leadership purchased 500 acres of land at the confluence of the Lehigh River and Monocacy Creek, establishing Bethlehem as a Settlement Congregation with two groups of workers. The first group consisted of the pilgrims, or missionaries, whose job was to preach the gospel and convert "souls for the Lamb." During the early years of Bethlehem, the position of missionary was highly sought after by nearly all members of the congregation and was, indeed, available to the majority of residents. The second group of residents were the workers who remained in the town and, through various tasks, trades, and occupations, supported the missionaries. Unlike most colonial communities, Moravians tended toward industrial trades in contrast to agriculture, which tended to tie farmers to the land.

The Moravians instituted a form of economic communism formalized as the General Economy in 1744, which augmented a communal lifestyle. The church in Herrnhut owned all the land and buildings in Bethlehem. Everyone worked for the good of the community under an agreement that was purely voluntary, and in return each member was assigned a share of food and clothing and received education, health care, religious indoctrination, and old age and death benefits. The Moravians also developed a unique social system called the choir system in which the community was divided by age, gender, and marital status. The choirs became self-contained working units in which different members performed various tasks, with the result that there was no unemployment or idleness. This system was particularly useful in the early years when the majority of the population in Bethlehem consisted of single men and women.[5] The Single Sisters took on the roles of nurses, teachers, seamstresses, laundresses, cooks, maids, gardeners, and caretakers of livestock within their own choir. The Single Brethren managed similar tasks within their choir but were also assigned the operation of most of the heavier industries and crafts in the community such as blacksmithing, tanning, and milling. An important goal of the Moravians was self-sufficiency to limit contact between Bethlehem residents and outsiders, thereby protecting their community from worldliness.

For the first decade, the General Economy worked fairly well in Bethlehem with little outside interference. In 1753, the Moravian leadership accepted the need to develop a new branch of the General Economy dealing with trade and commerce because the community's population was growing at a high rate and neighboring individuals and communities demanded Moravian goods and services. Most importantly, Moravians had to trade with "strangers" to obtain goods that they could not make or raise themselves such as iron, gunpowder, glass, and salt. To obtain the cash they needed for these purchases, they sold excess goods such as tanned hides and linseed oil to outsiders. The Moravians participated in the regional commercial network that Michael Kennedy describes hereinafter.

With the establishment of the Strangers Store in 1753, Bethlehem became a center of commerce in which Moravians and non-Moravians took part. The community erected the Crown Inn (1745) and the Sun Inn (1758) as controlled lodging places for non-Moravian tradesmen and others visiting Bethlehem. Church leaders justified these endeavors by requiring the resident traders and innkeepers to turn over all the profits to the central administration for subsequent distribution to the residents. A trades conference fixed all the prices, and outsiders who came to Bethlehem were not allowed to bargain.[6]

Thus, by the late 1750s-early 1760s a new spirit pervaded Bethlehem, a spirit that would eventually lead to a change in the economic system. Wealth and prosperity, in part the result of interaction with the outside world, increased the desire of many craftsmen to create independent businesses of their own. Tradesmen and craftspeople, tired of the economic constraints placed on them by the church, were still willing to support the church but by working for a profit. At the same time, the missionary system began to change. Whereas in the early years of Bethlehem everyone could aspire to be a missionary, as the community grew and prospered, tradesmen and craftsmen occupied a more prominent economic position because the burden of generating revenue rested squarely on their shoulders. They gradually lost the mobility they had enjoyed in the early years to leave their professions, become missionaries, and in time return to the community and pick up where they had left off in their trades.

A class of professional missionaries had developed, and many workers resented supporting people who had attained a station in life to which they could no longer aspire. The choir system gradually became less popular as well, because workers wanted to regroup as nuclear families and provide for their own children and spouses.

The final element in the breakup of the General Economy, however, was Herrnhut's insistence on closer supervision and control of all affairs in Bethlehem.

Herrnhut, after Zinzendorf's death in 1760, found itself in extreme debt and now looked upon its religious "child" on the other side of the Atlantic, with its successful trades, crafts, and industries, as a source of revenue rather than as a missionary center that absorbed money. Herrnhut and Bethlehem's leaders sought to meet these challenges by opting to have Bethlehem operate on its own and to develop plans to transform the community from communism to capitalism.

Thus in 1762, the General Economy was abolished. The church retained ownership of all the land and buildings until 1845, but great changes began to occur in the way the community conducted its everyday life. Some of the original ventures including agriculture, the mills, and the strangers' store remained under community control for the next few years. The church now paid people working in these businesses a small wage. In the individual trades and crafts, some masters now took over their own businesses. Tradesmen such as the blacksmith and the potter could purchase or lease the capital assets needed to ply their trades. These assets might include the workshop or house, the fixtures, and tools. However, those trades under the control of the Single Brethren's Choir, such as the oil mill, remained in their hands until 1814.

These changes did not mean that individual tradesmen were completely free from control of the church, which in 1771 adopted a restrictive economic code. The church had to give its consent to establishing a new industry, expanding an existing one, or developing a subsidiary industry. Similarly, it had to consent to hiring and firing apprentices. The church also had to approve the borrowing or lending of money. No businessman could develop a trade monopoly. A person could own a home, but not the land on which it stood, for the land still belonged to the church. A building could be sold only at a church-approved price. Bethlehem thus remained exclusive until 1845 when the lease system was finally terminated and the town opened to non-Moravians for the first time.[7]

Crafts and Trades

Almost from the beginning, the spectrum of trades practiced in Bethlehem was quite broad. Thomas Pownall, who would later become Governor of Massachusetts but in 1754 was serving in a semi-official capacity as an observer for the British Board of Trade, provided a revealing catalog of trades.

> There were, when I was there, the Following Trades carried on by the Fratres at this Settlement. Saddle-tree maker, Sadler, Glover, Shoemaker, Stocking-weavers,...Button maker, Taylor & Women Taylor, Hatter, Ribband-weavers; Linnen-weavers,...Woollen-weavers,...Wool-comber, Dyer, Fuller, Dresser, Tanner, Currier, Skinner, Butcher, Miller, Chandler, Oil-maker; Baker, Cooper, Joiner, Carpenter, Mason, Glazier, Brick maker, Stone Cutter, Turner, Potter, Stovemaker, Wheelwright, Blacksmith, Gunsmith, Nail-maker, Lock-smith, Pewterer, Tinman, Silver-smith, Clockmaker, Harnessmaker, Hemp dresser, Boat-builder, Surgeon, Apothecary.[8]

Clearly we cannot talk about forty odd trades in an essay of this length, but we can identify and focus on several of the more important industries. Thus, we will discuss industries that were both central to the economic well-being of the community and which, because of their locational concentration and heavy dependence on waterpower, gave Bethlehem, if not a unique history, certainly a special place in the history of early American technological development. The American colonial era has been sometimes characterized as an age of wood and water, for most things were made of wood, although iron was clearly well known and used. Beyond the animate sources of power found in humans and animals, waterpower was the major energy source for operating early manufacturing processes such as saw and grain milling, two of the more important industries found in most colonial communities of even modest size.[9]

In Bethlehem, Moravians performed most of the lighter crafts, such as spinning and linen weaving by the Single Sisters, and tailoring and cobbling by the Single Brethren, in the "upper," residential portion of the town. The Single Brethren conducted many of the heavier crafts such as those found in the pottery and blacksmith complex, or those that required waterpower, along the Monocacy Creek or nearby. We will focus our attention on this latter industrial quarter in terms of technology transfer and community planning.

More specifically, we will briefly examine Moravian efforts at grist milling and more extensively, their oil milling and tanning industries which were particularly important as sources of outside income. Finally, we will look at the waterworks, the first pumped municipal system in the American colonies. A re-lettered 1772 map of Bethlehem shows the early industrial quarter and the location of a number of the mills and artisan shops. (Today this area, known as the Colonial Industrial Quarter, is being restored and interpreted by the Historic Bethlehem Partnership and can be seen in downtown Bethlehem.) Each of these trades and industries played an important role in the development of Bethlehem's religiously based economy; collectively they reveal an interesting picture of early American technological development.

Gristmill

The year 1743 witnessed the construction of several of early Bethlehem's most important mills and craft shops, among the very first of which was the gristmill for grinding various grains into flour, thus testifying to its importance within the new settlement. Prior to the construction of their own mill, Moravians took their grain to a mill owned by Nathaniel Irish located on Saucon Creek near the present-day town of Shimersville. Bethlehem's first gristmill was a log structure erected on a stone foundation. It was built by Gotthard Demuth, a Germantown, Pennsylvania, man with machinery designed by Henry Antes, a miller and millwright from Frederick Township, Montgomery County. Antes had helped the Brethren establish themselves at Bethlehem. He subsequently became a trustee of the Moravian church and has been regarded as Bethlehem's early town planner.[10]

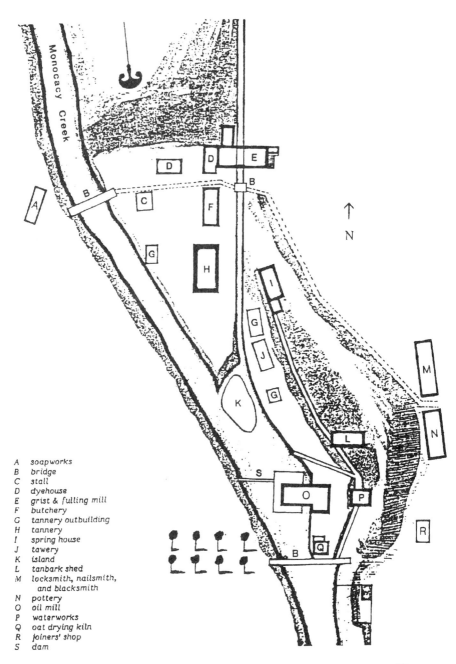

This 1773 map of Bethlehem (relettered) shows many mills, manufacturing buildings, and artisans' shops in the industrial area along Monocacy Creek.

Reprinted from Litchfield, et al., *Bethlehem Oil Mill*, 13, by permission of the authors.

Quickly outgrowing the capacity of this first mill, the Moravians erected a second mill on the same site in 1751. The new two-story structure was built of limestone quarried locally from Nisky Hill. Within two years the community added a second run, or set, of millstones to accommodate the many settlers from the north and west of Bethlehem who brought their grain to this location for grinding.[11]

One, if not two, low breast wheels powered Bethlehem's early grist-fulling mill complex. They utilized water from a small pond created by a low dam located a short distance upstream for the source of power. The master miller controlled the flow of water to his wheel through a sluice and headrace. Although less efficient than an overshot wheel might have been, the relatively shallow drop in water height of the Monocacy dictated the use of either a low breast wheel or an undershot wheel as was utilized downstream in the waterworks and oil mill. The gristmill's tailrace returned the spent water to the Monocacy at a point just above a second dam on the stream which was erected to power the waterworks and adjacent oil mill complex, each of which will be addressed in further detail below. Taken together these dams, raceways, and waterwheels collectively formed a waterpower system, which, even if not unique in its concentration and complexity, certainly pointed to the holistic techno-economic planning of the Moravian community.

The Moravian Congregation controlled and operated the mill through a series of millers who initially lived in the mill building itself. In 1782 the church authorized construction of a separate stone miller's house adjacent to the mill. This building was enlarged in 1834 with a one and a half-story addition, both parts of which still stand today. The church continued to operate the gristmill until 1825 when it was leased to George Henry Woehler. Five years later the church sold the mill to Charles A. Luckenbach who began to modernize the operation. Unfortunately, a devastating fire destroyed the building in 1869. The Luckenbach family promptly erected in its stead a new four-story brick building on the remaining stone foundation, which is the building we see restored today.

This third gristmill on the site remained in operation as a feed and flour mill under various owners until the early 1950s. Although little else is known regarding the specific details of the construction and operation of the two eighteenth-century gristmills, we can be sure that they played a central role in the still heavily agriculture-dependent community.

Oil Mill

In eighteenth-century Bethlehem, linen was a more common fabric than wool, and certainly more so than cotton, which was harder to grow and process. Flax, from which linen is derived, contains seeds, some 30-40 percent of which is linseed oil. However, because the oil can only be extracted under fairly high pressure requiring capital-intensive equipment investments, it was unusual for individuals to attempt to process it at home. Rather, it tended to be a concentrated industrial process which the Moravians established as early as February 1745.[12] Linseed oil was commonly used in paints, printer's ink, and in certain medicines. This first oil mill was a small, 12' x 20' log structure located on the east side of the tailrace of the gristmill.[13] This early mill was shortly replaced in 1752 by a larger, 34' x 46' frame structure that also housed hemp and bark milling machinery. This new mill was designed and built by Hans Christoph Christensen, a thirty-five-year-old Moravian millwright/carpenter from Herrnhut who had emigrated to Bethlehem the preceding year.

Christensen, a Dane by birth, had worked in a royal gristmill for several years before joining the Moravian Brethren in Herrnhut. In Pennsylvania his first assignment was to build an extension to a gristmill in the Moravian community of Friedensthal. While Christensen's millwrighting skills may still have been evolving at this early date, he soon proved himself a master builder and was centrally involved in the construction of a number of mills, not only in Bethlehem, but also in other Moravian communities and for private owners as well.[14] Christensen presumably deepened his knowledge of millwrighting as he traveled and worked throughout Pennsylvania and other colonies, but just as surely he transferred with him technical skills and approaches to his work derived from European, especially Danish and Germanic, practice.

Few records or images of the 1752 mill exist today; however, those that do survive indicate that this was a combination mill that housed oilseed stampers and a press, as well as both tanbark and hemp stampers. In fact, the mill was frequently referred to as the "stamping mill." It was powered by a single undershot waterwheel that drew on water restrained by a new dam erected just above the mill. The new mill produced some 750-1550 gallons of linseed oil annually for the Moravians alone, a figure which does not count extensive sales outside the community. Unfortunately, on November 18, 1763, a fire destroyed most of the mill.[15]

The Brethren quickly began planning to rebuild. Christensen designed the new mill to incorporate not only the linseed oil, hemp, and tanbark processes from the previous mill, but also to house additional machinery for grinding cereal groats and for fulling leather. Later they even added a snuff mill. The multiplicity of operations clearly made it more than an "oil" mill and spoke to the synergy among Moravian industries. It also raised questions and tensions over how best to operate the new mill. Church administrators had determined that the Single Brethren should build and manage the new building. The last supervisor of the previous mill had been Johann Geitner, the tanner, who was not a member of the Single Brethren's Choir. Even though the design of the new mill called for two waterwheels to run all the additional machinery, it was clear that reduced water levels due to extended drought and the recent (1762) construction of a new waterworks (to be discussed below) meant that not all the equipment could be operated at once.

Geitner, concerned for the efficient functioning of the tannery, argued that even if he was not to be allowed to operate the tanbark stamping and leather

This nineteenth-century painting of the Bethlehem industrial area along Monocacy Creek, by Gustav Grunewald, shows the tannery (upper left), waterworks (left center), and oil mill (right center).

Courtesy of Raymond E. Holland and Robin Turner Holland.

fulling components of the mill, he should have ready access to the fulling mill whenever he needed it for processing hides removed from his tanning vats. In the end, it was agreed that the tannery should pay an annual fee of £25 for running the tanbark stamping operation. Leather fulling apparently never became operational in the new oil mill but was conducted in the cloth fulling mill instead.

Christensen drew up plans for the new oil mill at the end of 1764. During that winter the Moravians quarried limestone and prepared the timber for the new building, and in July they laid the cornerstone. By the end of September 1765, the walls of the 33' x 66' mill were two stories high, and the new dam for powering the double waterwheel was almost complete. Bethlehem's diarist noted, "This will be one of the most solid and durable buildings and the only one of its kind to be found in this land."[16] At the same time the building itself was being erected, the Brethren were installing the twin undershot waterwheels, each of which was capable of developing about five horsepower.

On December 27, the hemp mill began operation, with the oil milling machinery becoming operational in mid-February 1766, and the tanbark mill starting in early March. The hemp roller mill was installed in late 1767, but the specialized snuff mill not until 1794. Thus, right from the beginning this was designed as a sophisticated combination mill in contrast to most mills of the colonial era that started out as single-purpose mills and only later added secondary tasks. Rightfully so, Christensen considered the oil mill his greatest engineering achievement.

The oil mill became one of Bethlehem's most lucrative businesses during the next two decades based primarily on the sale of linseed oil, barley groats, and oatmeal, with profits averaging somewhat over £150 per year.[17] A decline in profitability, including a number of years of losses, followed the end of the Revolutionary War, perhaps a result of the general postwar economic downturn. After the turn of the century, modest profitability returned, but other expenses associated with the Single Brethren's Choir led the Church in 1814 to disband this group and lease out its industries to private tenants. At this point the use of the building changed also, with the focus shifting from oil milling to grist milling utilizing the groat mill equipment. Finally, in 1832, the town relocated the waterworks into the building, as the earlier 1762 pumping system had become inadequate to the task.

Returning to the eighteenth century, there are at least two important points that can be made about the oil mill complex that reveal the Moravians' economic planning and technological development. The first, alluded to previously, was the synergistic relationship between the industries contained in the building, as well as their relationship to other needs outside, in particular the tanning industry. Given the relatively small size of each of the industries, it would have been too costly to erect separate mill buildings for each. This restriction was combined with the limitation imposed by a relatively small, two-foot head of water behind the low dam, which could provide little more than a day's supply of water if used constantly, especially as the same dam also supplied the waterworks. As a result, it was not uncommon at times of low water for the oil mill to be idled in order to pump water for the growing town's domestic needs.

Similarly, the tannery depended on the mill for a ready supply of tanbark at a rate of one to two times the weight of each hide. Since the tannery processed several thousand hides annually, this entailed extensive amounts of tanbark. Tanners like Geitner periodically complained about the lack of necessary amounts of tanbark, often due to the limited amount of water available to power the mill. Finally, in the early nineteenth century, tanbark stamping at the mill ceased in favor of a separate horse-driven bark mill, again suggesting the required coordination of the various industrial trades pursued by the Moravians. Thus, it seems quite evident that an operationally flexible system that could be regulated depending on product/process demand and seasonal water availability was required. That Christensen and John Arbo (the overseer of the Single Brethren's choir) recognized this need and were able to achieve it is testimony to both their organizational and technological skills.

The second point that should be emphasized is that technological processes contained within the mill drew heavily on central European and especially Germanic traditions. As they had in their central European homeland, Moravians used hemp as a key fiber in the production of clothing. The Moravians' 1766 advertisement in the *Pennsylvania Gazette* announcing the opening of the new mill for business noted that, "The Hemp is not rubbed with a Pumicestone in the common Way, that being attended with many Dangers; but it is stamped in a particular Manner, and becomes pliabler and fitter than with the Stone." This use of stamps for softening, which can be seen in other Germanic drawings, suggests the transfer of that technological process to Bethlehem, as does the 1767-68 installation of a German-style hemp mill utilizing a stone roller, called in German a *Hanfreibe* or "hemp rubber," to soften the fibers.

Whether or not the latter installation implied the inadequacy of the stamper or not, it nonetheless points to the American adoption of European technological traditions during this period. So too does the Moravian adoption of tanbark stampers utilizing large eighteen-foot stampers with iron heads incorporating cutting knives on the bottom, which resulted in a coarse tanbark powder. In contrast, the more common American bark mills were horse-driven affairs utilizing a cylindrical stone which rolled on a circular bed, thereby crushing the bark. In both cases then (and similar arguments about the technology utilized in the groat and snuff mills can also be made), Moravians clearly drew on European-Germanic practices in designing the technological hardware for the oil mill complex.[18] In many ways this should not come as a surprise, and it is the key argument set forth by Norman Wilkinson in his analysis of Brandywine River industries in the early nineteenth century.[19]

Tannery

Also important to the Moravian economy was the tannery, which Bethlehem's overseer, Bishop John Cammerhof, reported in the 1740s as "one of our most paying [i.e., profitable] and indispensable trades. It supplies all our shoemaking trades…, all our people with leather…, and for horse harnesses and other things in the housekeeping."[20] Bethlehem's industrial quarter was an ideal location for a tannery for several related reasons. First, it had a ready source of water in the Monocacy for the washing of hides and for activating the tannin in the tanbark. Second, the fact that the Moravians ran one of the largest cattle-raising operations in the colony meant that there was an ample supply of hides.[21] Third, extensive forest lands to the north of Bethlehem supplied the large amounts of bark, mostly oak, which the Moravian tanners needed for the tannic acid utilized in the soaking stage. Usually peeled in the spring when the tannin concentration was at its peak, there were frequently over 100 cords of tanbark on hand at any point in time.

Tanning, as J. Leander Bishop, the nineteenth-century historian of American industry, noted, seldom lagged "long behind the first occupants of a new town."[22] Bethlehem erected its first wooden-framed tannery in 1743. The craft knowledge that underlay the tanning process was generally well understood in the mid-eighteenth century and traveled to the colonies firsthand in the heads of tanners or in a number of books fairly readily available at the time.[23] The tanning process was lengthy – taking up to two and a half-years – and laborious, with little but the crushing of the tanbark, as already noted, being mechanized in any way. The craft was strenuous, nasty, and potentially dangerous. It required great strength as the wet hides could weigh several hundred pounds, and not all tanners were up to the task. In 1790, for example, David Gold gave up the job after several years because of what he described as a "weakness in his arms." Most of the tanners in Bethlehem came directly from Germany.

The process began with a day-long washing and soaking of the hides from the freshly slaughtered cattle (salted and dried hides took somewhat longer). To remove the hair, the hides were next usually "limed" in a series of four vats containing increasing concentrations of lime and water, located in the tanyard alongside the Monocacy. The lime from locally quarried limestone destroyed the hair follicles and opened the pores of the skin. After three to six months the tanner could remove the hair and any remaining bits of flesh by "beaming" or scraping the hide with a curved knife as it lay over a partially upturned log or "beaming horse." The hides were then soaked in the tanning liquor solution of tanbark and water. In most American tanneries, the tan vats were located outside the tannery, but in Bethlehem they were inside the building, an advancement that gave the tanner more control over the process than if it were exposed to the external fluctuations of precipitation and temperature.

Inside the tannery were two series of vats – "handler vats" and still vats. Each set was used in a "rising series" as with the liming step, as the hides were moved from weaker to increasingly stronger tanbark solutions. The four "handler vats" were used to begin the process and involved frequent agitation of the hides so that they would begin to absorb the tannic acid, a stage that took about two weeks. The larger "still vats" could each hold about 100 hides alternately layered with tanbark and then flooded with water.[24] Hides might remain in this series of vats for twelve to eighteen months depending on thickness, being frequently rotated because those on the bottom tanned most quickly.

When completely tanned the hides were removed from the vats, washed yet once again, and beaten, or fulled, to compress and strengthen the leather, much as a "fuller" does with woolen cloth. In most American tanneries this latter process was done by hand with mallets on heavy tables. In Bethlehem, however, the gristmill complex, and perhaps the oil mill as noted earlier, was equipped with water powered stampers that performed this task mechanically. After fulling, the hides were returned to the third floor of the tannery for stretching and drying, a step that could entail as much as another six months. Following drying, the thicker sole leather could be used immediately by the shoemaker, but softer leathers for shoe uppers, saddles and harnesses, and clothing required a final step of "currying," which entailed impregnating the leather with oil and performing any coloring required. All told the tanning process took anywhere from eighteen to thirty months. During the course of a year, Bethlehem's tanners normally handled about 3,000 hides, including up to a third in the drying stage and several hundred in storage. During the Revolution this figure jumped to nearly 5,000.

As with many of the industries along the Monocacy, the Moravians utilized two buildings for tanning during the course of the period under study. The first tannery was a small log structure built in 1743 on the east side of the gristmill tailrace. This building may, in fact, have also been a tawry in which craftsmen treated skins with mineral substances such as alum and egg yoke or fish oil to produce finer-quality leathers for gloves, bookbindings, and the like.[25] As the community and tanning operation grew, the community leaders approached the master tanner Johann George Geitner and asked him to design a new larger limestone building. Erected in 1761 on the west side of the gristmill tailrace, the tannery measured 30' x 66' and was four stories tall and is restored today.

The records are scanty as to the specific uses of the tannery's rooms; however, it is clear that the vats were located on the ground floor, while the third floor was utilized for drying. It is also probable that the master tanner and his family lived in rooms within the building. Other rooms were available for "preparing things" and may have housed the currier's operation as well. The tannery remained in the hands of the Moravian congregation until 1829 when it was sold to Joseph Leibert and his son James, the first of a series of private owners to operate the tannery until it finally ceased operation in 1873 due to the high cost of tanbark.

Although not mechanized except for tanbark preparation and leather fulling, the tannery played a vital and synergistic role within the Moravian economy. It supplied Bethlehem with leather for shoes, clothing, saddlery, and harness tack. It used hides that would otherwise have gone to waste from animals slaughtered in large measure for food.[26] In addition, the tannery processed hides from Moravian mission stations in Jamaica and the West Indies, as well as from nearby non-Moravian settlers, thereby enhancing the cash flow of the community. As with many of the other crafts and industries, tanning had to be closely coordinated with processes conducted under the roofs of other mills, most notably in the production of tanbark and at the fulling stage. Even though tanning was a noxious industry, and one that significantly polluted Monocacy Creek, the Moravians recognized its economic centrality well into the nineteenth century.

Waterworks

The waterworks provided an essential service to the community, though not a production industry *per se*.[27] When John Adams visited Bethlehem in 1777, this example of what he called "the mechanical Arts" engendered his most extensive comments. Bethlehem's waterworks was the first pumped municipal system in the American colonies. It replaced the use of horse and wagon to distribute water from the clear spring located at the base of the hill on the Monocacy Creek flood plain to the residential area located several hundred feet away on the crest of the hill where residents used the water for domestic purposes and in case of fire. The "sett of pumps" that Adams witnessed in operation, however, was not the first such endeavor, for the waterworks had also passed through an earlier stages.

Following several earlier unsuccessful attempts to pump water, Hans Christensen, the Danish millwright who had helped design the first oil mill, addressed Bethlehem's water supply problem in early 1754. Christensen worked closely with carpenter John Bohner, who had built a model of a pump, which they tested in June and successfully pumped water some ninety vertical feet to the residential area.

The first pump house was a 14' x 18' frame building situated some 300' south of Bethlehem's main spring to which it was connected initially by an open trench raceway and after 1765 by hollowed-out hemlock logs which served as piping. Inside the pump house was a 5 inch single-cylinder pump constructed of lignum vitae, a tropical hardwood, probably brought from the West Indies where the Moravians maintained missions in which Bohner had served. Utilizing a walking beam, or rocker, type of pump, the system pumped water to the collection tower located on the site of the present-day Central Moravian Church, a distance of somewhat over 300 feet. From the holding tower, the water flowed by gravity through a series of wooden distribution pipes into stone cisterns and from there into the major residential and commercial buildings. Despite its initial success, this first system soon encountered problems including wooden pipes that burst under pressures in excess of 40 psi, the design of the pump itself, and the location of the waterwheel within the wheel pit, all of which contributed to an insufficient supply of water for a rapidly growing town.

As early as 1761, Christensen began collaborating with John Arbo, the overseer of the Single Brethren's Choir, and Frederick von Marschall, the overseer for the community's economic and financial matters, to replace the inadequate 1754 system. Working closely with Christensen was an assistant, Christopher Demuth; together they had substantially completed the pumping machinery by 1762. However, the surrounding building was not completed until 1764. When finished the 24' x 30' limestone building stood two stories high.[28] The machinery consisted of three single-acting force pumps geared to the shaft of an undershot waterwheel. The three piston ends were each attached to a wooden frame or crosshead working in grooves to give them a motion parallel to the pumps.[29]

What is perhaps most revealing about the state of Moravian technology, as revealed by a set of 1766 waterworks machinery drawings (perhaps by John Arbo), is the use of crossheads operating in grooves. By utilizing a connecting rod attached between the oscillating motion of the crankshaft and the top of the crosshead, which was restricted to a vertical motion by the grooves within which it ran up and down, the pump piston could not rock side to side and thereby wear the cylinder. For the time period under discussion, this was a very advanced technological solution to a problem that had long confronted earlier technicians. It suggests that the system was no mere jury-rigged frontier solution, but rather the application of state-of-the-art knowledge, presumably transferred from Europe, although unfortunately the direct pathway cannot be traced.

Another example that further illustrates the important transfer of technological knowledge from Europe to Bethlehem was the design of the waterwheel itself. The undershot wheel, eighteen feet in diameter, utilized a two-foot head of water flowing at about 400 gallons per minute to develop about 3.5 horsepower by turning at a maximum of 7.5 revolutions per minute. In contrast to almost all American-designed waterwheels, such as those described later in 1795 by Oliver Evans in *The Young Mill-Wright & Miller's Guide*, which were of a "compass-arm" design, the Bethlehem waterworks utilized a "clasp arm" design. Whereas the compass-arm design entailed mortising, or pegging, the arms of the waterwheel to the central shaft, the clasp-arm design wedged them to the outside of a square shaft. The significance of this distinction is that the latter was typical of eighteenth-century Danish waterwheels, a design Christensen likely brought from his early experience in the royal Danish gristmill in Haderslev where he worked prior to emigrating. The point is not whether one design was better than the other, but rather to present another example of how European-derived technological knowledge was transferred to America, in this case presumably in the mind of the millwright Christensen.

While the pumping mechanism and the waterwheel were central elements in the waterworks, so too were the raceway and the distribution piping, for this was a technological system in which all the components needed to function interactively. Failure of any one part meant the system as a whole failed. Bursting pipes, whether due to freezing weather or their inability to sustain the pressures involved, were perhaps the most significant early problem. Early experiments with rolled sheet lead, terra-cotta, and wooden pipes all proved problematic. In 1786, it was "decided to lay lead pipe, for the present from the waterworks to water tower, to test their worth."[30] Apparently the experiment was successful, for subsequently all the main pipes were replaced by lead, even though the Moravians understood the associated health dangers. Cast-iron pipes would not be introduced until 1813 because of their cost. The wooden distribution pipes, which remained in use between the water tower and the various buildings, were not subject to the same pressures, although they could freeze.

At the same time the Moravians experienced problems with their piping, they also had to battle fluctuating water levels and increased competition for the limited flow of power available from the Monocacy. In part the problem resulted from silting behind the gristmill dam which affected the flow of the creek, and because several millers competed for power. This was especially problematic for the waterworks which drew on water retained by the same low dam as the oil mill. The situation was so bad that in 1791 the Overseers Conference ordered the sluice gate of the waterworks to stand open at all times to provide a sufficient supply of water for the wheel. In 1799 the wheel itself was adjusted within the pit to take the best advantage of the now-lower water levels, and finally in 1810 the wheel pit and the headrace were rebuilt so that the water entered the pit at less of a sharp angle, thereby increasing the velocity with which the water hit the wheel's paddles. Apparently the rebuild was successful with no further complaints about water supply. Christensen's machinery continued to operate well until 1832 when the waterworks was shifted to the oil mill next door where a new pump had been installed.

Overall the 1762 Bethlehem waterworks was a successful community endeavor serving its citizens well for seven decades. It incorporated the best of European technological understanding coupled with pragmatic on-the-spot adjustments as components subsequently revealed flaws or the system required balancing, as from fluctuating water levels. Bethlehem's waterworks was designed as a technological system within the larger socioeconomic system of Moravian Bethlehem. It was as much a societal endeavor as it was a fascinating technological achievement. In his dedicatory address for the 1976 reconstruction of the waterworks, Brooke Hindle attributed its distinctiveness to two differences between Bethlehem and other American communities.[31]

The first, which was technological, resulted from differences between England, which turned very early to steam power because of limited waterpower sites and denuded forests, and the European homelands of the Moravians, and especially of Christensen, which were more greatly endowed with water power sites and a technological tradition associated with them. Second, Hindle suggested the communal tradition of the Moravians, in contrast to the individualism more typical of English settlers, might go a long way toward explaining the successful development of this early community water system, in contrast to other American towns. Although perhaps simplistic in some ways, by extension, it is this same combination of technological borrowing and community planning that explains the location, design, and early successes of the entire complex of mills along the Monocacy.

Conclusion

The Bethlehem that John Adams described in 1777 was, indeed, a "curious and remarkable Town"; however, its economy reached a high-water mark in the 1780s. Had Adams returned at the turn of the century, he would have found little changed from his earlier visit. Given the seeming promise of the "mechanical Arts" in Bethlehem's early industrial development, one must ask why the community had not become one of, if not "the greatest seat of manufactures in the United States," rather than seeing that accolade attributed to the Brandywine River mills near Wilmington. The reasons were varied, with some resulting from forces external to the community, while others emanated from within. Collectively, however, they took their toll on the growth of the town, leading to a distinct period of stagnation at the end of the century.

During the colonial period, Bethlehem's economic growth must be viewed within the context of British mercantile laws. These laws reflected the British view of the colonies as suppliers of raw materials that could be shipped to England for conversion into finished goods that could, in turn, be exported to the colonies for purchase. Such laws, of course, were designed to protect the British home industries from competition, and cloth manufacture was one of the industries so protected. Many communities chafed under such restrictions, and Bethlehem was no exception. As early as 1752, the Moravians ran into difficulty because British administrators complained to community leaders that the volume of wool and linen cloth produced in Bethlehem surpassed the amounts allowable under mercantile law. Generally what was allowable was the amount of cloth needed to accommodate basic family needs.

Thus Augustus Spangenberg, a Moravian leader, wrote to Count Zinzendorf regarding his fear that, "it might...cause apprehension partly to the local merchants, partly to the House of Commons in Old England, if they would get the wrong news about it,...that could not be reconciled with the laws of England in general and with our Pennsylvania law in special." He went to great pains to assure Zinzendorf, and Parliament, of the "lawfulness" of the Bethlehem "cloth factory" and promised to "evade any trouble as well as is possible."[32] While other colonial artisans at first labored under, then complained, and later agitated to have these laws revoked, the pacifist Moravians yielded to the royal government that had granted them special dispensations on taking oaths and performing military service. After all, the British had legally recognized them as an "Ancient Protestant Episcopal Church" in England and its colonies, thus giving them the same status as the Quakers.

A second more direct influence on the growth of the community was the economic restructuring imposed by the Church following the breakup of the General Economy. The Church continued to maintain strict control over the economy and the community, which remained closed to non-Moravians until 1810. For example, in the late eighteenth century, Church approval was still required to start new businesses and for the hiring and firing of apprentices. The new rules proved too restrictive for many young Moravian men no longer imbued with the earlier missionary zeal. Many left the community and, as a result, the population of Bethlehem began to stagnate. As young men moved away, they took skills required to run the crafts and trades so prominent in early Bethlehem. As a result, many of these industries began to lose money.[33] The Single Brethren's Choir, which had numbered 100 members in 1783, could count but thirty-eight in 1806. In 1814, the choir was formally disbanded and the various trades under its control, including the operation of the oil mill, were leased out to tenant operatives.[34]

Also significant to Bethlehem's economic stagnation were problems limiting technological development including the minimal amount of waterpower available from the Monocacy Creek and a lack of capital investment. Although not all of Bethlehem's crafts required water for power, many of the more significant ones did, and with flows restricted as they were, the opportunity for dramatic expansion was limited. When this limitation was combined with the fact that, except for the initial flurry of building, the Church was in effect using profits from the trades to finance missionaries in the field rather than making capital investments in new mills, equipment, or other possible ventures, it meant there was little likelihood of economic expansion or technological development, despite the earlier transfer of innovative European technical knowledge. The Church apparently felt no overwhelming need for industrial expansion after the Revolutionary War, its immediate needs largely being satisfied by the existing economic and industrial arrangements. This is in contrast to some other areas, such as the Brandywine River Valley at the turn of the nineteenth century, where capital investment was marshaled to underwrite industrial growth.[35]

A final constraint, surely of equal importance, although harder to document concretely, pertained to the density of artisans and tradesmen within the community. For all but the most densely inhabited colonial cities, industrial development had been a very slow process. For most communities the number of craftsmen per capita was too low to encourage the technological exchange that occurs when many similarly skilled people work closely together and collaborate to invent or improve upon products and processes. Coupled with the ready availability of land in colonial America, this meant that the special class of workers needed to run industries was generally slow to develop.

In Moravian Bethlehem, with its early concentration of water-powered mills and where the balance between farmers and artisans was almost reversed from the colonial norm, with less than 20 percent of the labor force engaged in agriculture, one might have anticipated precisely the kind of concentrated artisanal skills that would have led the community to become a "[great] seat of manufactures."

Almost paradoxically, this was not to occur. In large part, this was due to Moravian church policy which forbade more than one craftsperson in most given trades. Despite the number of different mills and trades, and the synergisitic interactions that took place among them, there was still not the concentration of artisanal skills needed for industrialization to take off. Even though the town continued to grow in some ways – for example, the building of new nuclear family housing, the construction of a new Girls Seminary building (1790), the spanning of the Lehigh River with the first bridge (1794), and the erection of Central Moravian Church (1803-1806) – which testified to the town's belief that it would eventually weather the economic downturn, the Moravians' hopes would not be fulfilled. The church's ongoing rigid control of the economy meant, despite many wishes to the contrary, that expansion would be limited within Moravian Bethlehem proper.

Expansion would come to Bethlehem, but it would be in those areas adjacent to the original Moravian community, which are known today as West and especially South Bethlehem, wherein outside forces increasingly played a critical role. The discovery of coal in northeastern Pennsylvania led to the need to ship this product in a more cost-effective way. In 1815 the first coal yard was established along the Lehigh River. In 1822 the Lehigh Coal and Navigation Company was incorporated, and in 1829 the Lehigh Canal opened to carry coal to the Delaware Canal for further shipment to Philadelphia.

The coming of the canal created a new set of economic conditions as non-Moravian entrepreneurs established hotels, stores, and support businesses on property surrounding Moravian Bethlehem because the policy of exclusivism still existed within Bethlehem. The increasing economic activity forced church leaders to rethink the system of exclusivity, which was gradually modified, as restrictions on private enterprise were lifted and finally in 1845, the lease system was terminated. The church sold off its major landholdings, and non-Moravians could own property for the first time, thus opening up the community to outsiders. On August 9, 1845, the voters of Bethlehem approved the reorganization of their community into a borough.

However, it would be the establishment in South Bethlehem in the late 1850s of the Bethlehem Iron Company, the forerunner of the Bethlehem Steel Corporation (1904), that would most dramatically recast the technological image of the community. No longer the quaint and "curious" communal town of Adams's day, Bethlehem was fast becoming one of the region's, if not the nation's, leading "gritty" cities. This industrialization, however, took place outside the original bounds of Moravian Bethlehem.

During this period of transition, the industries that had once thrived in the colonial industrial quarter eventually fell victim to economic change. The oil mill stopped production in 1814, with only the snuff mill and a buckwheat milling operation that would last until 1876 still in operation. In 1832 the water system for Bethlehem was relocated from Christensen's waterworks to his later oil mill building, where in 1868 steam power would be added to power the pumping system until 1912 when the spring, which had served Bethlehem since its founding, was declared contaminated. The tannery stopped production in 1873 due to the high cost of shipping tanbark to the site. Grist milling continued on the site of the original eighteenth-century mills, although after 1869 in a new brick building that replaced the 1752 stone mill destroyed in a fire.

The tawry ceased production at some point during the second quarter of the nineteenth century and was eventually converted into a beer hall, bowling alley, and concert hall. Most of these original buildings became multi-family dwellings and eventually fell into disrepair and disrepute until they were finally torn down for the good of the community.

Thus had this once proud industrial area containing "a fine sett of Mills," which according to Adams were "the best...that are any where to be found," finally fallen. It would not rise again until a new economic development in the 1960s and the final decades of the twentieth century called heritage tourism created opportunities for research and restoration that would enable future generations to learn about the industrial past.

Notes

1. Both the Liancourt and Morse references are quoted in Norman B. Wilkinson, "Brandywine Borrowings from European Technology," *Technology and Culture* 4 (1963): 1-2.

2. John Adams to Abigail Adams, 7 Feb. 1777, in L.H. Butterfield, et al., eds., *The Book of Abigail and John: Selected Letters of the Adams Family, 1762-1784* (Cambridge, Mass.: Harvard University Press, 1975), 167.

3. In what follows we have drawn heavily on the work of several scholars who have narrated and interpreted the Moravians' approach to life by examining the prolific documentation left by them in the form of choir diaries, committee minutes, official church records and correspondence, and personal memoirs. Among the most helpful have been Joseph M. Levering's massive early work, *A History of Bethlehem, Pennsylvania, 1741-1892* (Bethlehem, Pa.: Times Publishing Company, 1903); Helmut Erbe, *Bethlehem, Pa.: Eine kommunistische Herrnhutter Kolonie des 18. Jahrhunderts* (Stuttgart: Ausland- und Heimat-Verlagsaktiengesellschaft, 1929), which was later translated into English as "Bethlehem, Pa., A Communistic Herrnhut Colony of the Eighteenth Century," ms. in Moravian Archives, from which our page citations are drawn; Gillian Lindt Gollin, *Moravians in Two Worlds: A Study of Changing Communities* (New York: Columbia University Press, 1967); Beverly Smaby, *The Transformation of Moravian Bethlehem from Communal Mission to Family Economy* (Philadelphia: University of Pennsylvania Press, 1988); Arthur Freeman, *An Ecumenical Theology of the Heart: The Theology of Count Nicholas Ludwig von Zinzendorf* (Bethlehem, Pa.: The Moravian Church in America, 1998); Craig D. Atwood and Peter Vogt, eds., *The Distinctiveness of Moravian Culture* (Bethlehem, Pa.: Moravian Historical Society, 2003); Craig D. Atwood, *Community of the Cross: Moravian Piety in Colonial Bethlehem* (University Park: Pennsylvania State University Press, 2004).

4. On Moravian missionary activities with the Indians, see Jane Merritt, "Dreaming of the Savior's Blood: Moravians and the Indian Great Awakening in Pennsylvania," *William and Mary Quarterly* 3d ser., 54 (1997): 723-46.

5. Beverly Smaby divides the demography of Bethlehem into three phases. During the first twenty years, there were more men than women, and most people were in the 20-59

year age bracket. Marriages, births, and deaths were frequent. In the early 1760s to 1818, the population stopped growing and began to decline. During this period, the majority of adults were either single or widowed, and there were more people over 60 years. Around 1818, the marriage rate went up, and people married at a much younger age than they had fifty years earlier. Women were predominant. The population subsequently became slightly younger with women continuing in the majority in 1843. These changes in population statistics correlate with the way Moravian leaders implemented policies to focus on or cope with changing economic forces affecting the town. The overall population of Bethlehem was 500 in 1756; 535 in 1771; 470 in 1800; and 865 in 1843. Smaby, *Transformation of Moravian Bethlehem*, 53-59.

6. When the first store opened in 1753, community Brethren had produced 180 out of the 200 items for sale, suggesting on the one hand the level of self-sufficiency that had been attained in little more than a decade's time, but also reflecting the need for importing certain strategic goods that could not be produced locally. Gollin, *Moravians in Two Worlds*, 139, 163-64, 179; Carter Litchfield, et al., *The Bethlehem Oil Mill, 1745-1934: German Technology in Early Pennsylvania* (Kemblesville, Pa.: Olearius Editions, 1984), 12. In his history of the Bethlehem oil mill, Litchfield notes numerous ledger accounts pertaining to outside trade, including one for "Brother Leschinsky" who "came back from Philadelphia where he sold 3 wagonloads of linseed oil for a good price" (107n14).

7. Gollin, *Moravians in Two Worlds*, 203-11.

8. Pownall's description is quoted in Litchfield, et al., *Bethlehem Oil Mill*, 11-12.

9. In an age largely dependent on wood, sawmills, along with gristmills, were often among the first buildings to be erected. Bethlehem, despite the large number of limestone buildings, was no exception. The town appears to have constructed an early saw mill on Sand Island near the end of the present-day Fahy Bridge, although little is known about the details. The town's primary sawmill, however, was located to the north in the more rural and forested community of Gnadenhuetten near present-day Lehighton. Saw timber was utilized in a variety of applications including roofs, joists and flooring, window frames, sashes, and sills, and for the many small outbuildings not constructed of stone. Until Indians burned it down in 1755 during the French and Indian War, most of Bethlehem's building timber was cut to length at the sawmill in Gnadenhuetten and then floated down the Lehigh River on rafts. Following the fire, Bethlehem constructed a new sawmill on the Sand Island site. This mill utilized an undershot waterwheel operating on a three- to four-foot head of water for its power. Among the woods utilized by the Moravians were oak and black walnut for building timbers and supports, while white pine was used for outbuildings and lighter purposes such as flooring and windows. Oak bark left from the timber was subsequently utilized in the tanning process, leaving little of the tree to go to waste.

10. In addition to the first gristmill, Antes was also involved in the design and building of several other early Moravian mills and buildings, although not all were located in Bethlehem. In May 1747, he supervised construction of the combination saw- and gristmill at Gnadenhuetten, and in November 1747 the saw- and gristmill at Christian Spring. In 1750, Antes built the mill at Friedensthal that had two waterwheels and two sets of millstones. He probably also played a role in the design of the Single Brethren's House

(1748), and the Whitefield House in Nazareth was completed with his advice but not his direct supervision. Thus, some of the earliest Moravian buildings reflected a knowledge of construction and millwrighting gained, at least in part, here in Pennsylvania, rather than from Europe directly. Antes lived in Bethlehem from 1745 until late 1750 when he returned to his farm.

11. Levering, *History of Bethlehem*, 236.

12. "Bethlehem Diary," 12 Feb. 1745, 363, located in the Moravian Archives, Bethlehem, Pa.

13. The Bethlehem oil mill, especially the 1766 complex, is important historically, if for no other reason than because of the extensive documentation available including construction drawings, account books and diaries, and operating accounts that still exist, in contrast to most such mills where little or no evidence survives. A detailed history of the Bethlehem oil mill is contained in Litchfield, et al., *Bethlehem Oil Mill*.

14. Litchfield, *Bethlehem Oil Mill*, 22, provides a list of almost twenty mills, including Bethlehem's waterworks, in which Christensen played an active role in construction before he died from consumption in 1776.

15. "Bethlehem Diary," 18 Nov. 1763, 225.

16. Ibid., 9 Oct. 1765, 192-93.

17. See Litchfield, et al., *Bethlehem Oil Mill*, 31, for a useful tabulation of the profitability of the combined industries operating in the oil mill building for the years 1767-1814.

18. See ibid., 51-56 for a discussion of the hemp and tanbark mill technology. Arbo's advertisement from the *Pennsylvania Gazette*, 20 Mar. 1766, 4, is reproduced on page 30.

19. Wilkinson, "Brandywine Borrowings from European Technology," throughout, but esp. 12-13.

20. Report of John Cammerhoff, March 1748, quoted in Erbe, *Bethlehem*, 65-66.

21. Von Marschall to the Direktorial Kolleg, 1 June 1759, in Erbe, *Bethlehem*, 55 and noted by Gollin, *Moravians in Two Worlds*, 167.

22. J. Leander Bishop, *A History of American Manufactures from 1608 to 1860* (Philadelphia: E. Young, 1861), 1:445.

23. See Peter C. Welsh, "A Craft that Resisted Change: American Tanning Practices to 1850," *Technology and Culture* 4 (1963): 303, for a brief discussion of the several dictionaries of the arts and sciences then available.

24. In the 1790s, tanners developed new processes for heating tanbark and water in kettles, thereby creating a tanning liquor which when heated could be poured directly into the vats

through a pipe called a "liquor log." This technological advance eliminated the strenuous task of individually layering each vat with hides and tanbark, and it further allowed the increased concentration of the tannic acid. The hole in the south wall of the Bethlehem tannery may have been an opening into the vat area for just such a "liquor log." The mention of pumps in the tannery inventories suggest they may have been used to pump water out of the vats, either into the creek or to other vats for further use.

25. A small log building known as the "Weissgerberey," or white tannery, which likely utilized fish oil, probably cod oil, instead of oak bark as the tanning agent, was first included on a 1752 Bethlehem map. Whether this was the same building as the original tannery is unclear from the records, but it is likely that the terms tawry and white tannery were used somewhat interchangeably, for both can refer to the process which produced a leather white in color, hence the name. Whatever the specific processes utilized, the original log building remained in use until 1768 when a new two-story, 20' x 47' brick tannery was erected adjacent to the spring house. Although the records regarding this mill are scanty, it likely remained in operation until the second quarter of the nineteenth century. For details, see Charles LeCount, "Short History on Bethlehem's White Tannery," unpublished ms., Historic Bethlehem Partnership Archives; and for a more general description of white tanning, see R. Reed, *Ancient Skins, Parchments and Leathers* (London: Seminar Press, 1972), esp. 61-72.

26. In 1747, Church records indicate the Moravians, approximately 300 in number, consumed over 15,000 pounds of meat, much of which came from their extensive cattle herds. John Cammerhoff to Count Zinzendorf, 17 Mar. 1748, Moravian Archives, Bethlehem, referenced in Gollin, *Moravians in Two Worlds*, 163.

27. This section draws heavily for background on Karen Zerbe Huetter, *The Bethlehem Waterworks* (Bethlehem, Pa.: Historic Bethlehem Inc., 1976); Stephen G. Young, "They Have a Sett of Pumps, *Old Mill News* 13, no. 4 (Fall 1985): 3-5; Historic Bethlehem Partnership, "Museum Teacher's Handbook"; and Brooke Hindle, *The Meaning of the Bethlehem Waterworks* (Bethlehem, Pa.: HBI, 1977).

28. The building may have initially had a wood shingle roof, but when the oil mill caught fire in 1763, fire spread to the roof of the waterworks and may have been the occasion of its replacement with tile.

29. Robert Rau, *Historical Sketch of the Bethlehem Water Works, Bethlehem, Pa.* (Bethlehem, Pa.: Press of D.J. Godshalk & Co., 1877), includes Christensen's apprentice John David Bischoff's description of the mechanics of the waterworks.

30. Single Brethren's Diary, 29 June 1786, quoted in Huetter, *Bethlehem Waterworks*, 6.

31. Hindle, *Meaning of the Bethlehem Waterworks*.

32. Memorandums of Augustus Spangenberg, 14 Mar. 1752 and 26 Feb. 1753, quoted in Erbe, *Bethlehem*, 67-68.

33. See, for example, the table of annual profitability for the oil mill, which shows only two years of modest profit out of twelve for the years 1794-1805, in Litchfield, et al., *Bethlehem Oil Mill*, 31.

34. In contrast to the Single Brethren, the Single Sisters fared better. Even though by the early 1800s the importance of the nuclear family had taken hold and most young women thought it better to be married than single, the Single Sisters' Choir held together formally until 1841.

35. Erbe, *Bethlehem*, 80-84 and Gollin, *Moravians in Two Worlds*, 178, 195-96.

Religious Conflict and Violence in German Communities during the Great Awakening

AARON SPENCER FOGLEMAN

A SIGNIFICANT LEVEL OF RELIGIOUS CONFLICT and violence erupted in the German communities of British North America during the Great Awakening,[1] and the Lehigh Valley – home of the Moravians in the mid-Atlantic colonies – was one of the centers of these developments.[2] These events were part of an ongoing transatlantic evangelical awakening, in which many participants in Europe extended their agendas, rivalries, and conflicts to North America from the late 1730s to the beginning of the French and Indian War.[3] Among the most aggressive and active European religious groups in North America during this period were the Moravians, who arrived in Georgia and Pennsylvania in the 1730s and were an important part of radical Protestant evangelical movements developing on both sides of the Atlantic during this era. "Radical" refers to those who deviated from traditional, core beliefs in fundamental, controversial ways. With their critiques of society and alternative models of religious-social organization, the radicals challenged the roots of power, authority, and legitimacy of orthodox Christian belief and practice. Many radical groups rejected traditional hierarchies in gender or class relations, while others altered understandings of marriage and the family or economic relations within the community.[4] After their initial failures in Georgia and Pennsylvania, the Moravians built closed communities in Nazareth and Bethlehem in the Lehigh Valley and sent scores of men and women preachers, teachers, and missionaries south to Virginia and as far north as New England, focusing primarily on the German Lutheran and Reformed communities.[5] Many welcomed the Moravians, but many did not, and a religious war erupted in the German communities of the mid-Atlantic colonies, as anti-Moravian factions in Reformed and Lutheran congregations, supported by religious establishments in Europe, fought to keep the Moravians out of their churches. This essay will focus on how and why the conflict developed in and around Pennsylvania, who won, who lost, and why, as well as the kinds of tactics employed by the Moravians and two of their most formidable enemies in Europe and North America, the Lutheran pietists from

Halle, Germany, and the German Reformed preachers sponsored by the state church of the Netherlands.

The religious war in the Lutheran and Reformed communities of the mid-Atlantic colonies was connected to events and tensions involving the Moravians in Europe. Since the late 1730s, the Dutch state church had been embroiled in a bitter campaign to stop the Moravian movement in the Netherlands and in their overseas colonies. In the 1740s they extended the struggle to the Dutch Reformed congregations they supported in North America and also to German Reformed congregations in and around Pennsylvania. This was possible because no Reformed governing bodies in the German territories offered any significant support in America, even though the settlers had been asking for it for years. Also, the Halle Lutherans battled against the Moravians on many fronts, especially in Denmark, Schleswig-Holstein, and Lower Saxony in the late 1730s and 1740s. Since the 1690s the Francke Institutes in Halle had become the most influential center of German pietism. Here Lutheran spiritual leaders worked to reform, revitalize, and renew the state church, society, and individual lives – to finish the Reformation, as they believed. By the 1730s and 1740s, after a long generation of conflict with orthodox elements of the Lutheran church, the new leadership in Halle began to emphasize overseas missions and the expansion of their by then famous school system. And they also became increasingly confessional and intolerant of radicals, separatists, and others, especially Moravians. While this was happening thousands of German Lutheran and Reformed inhabitants from southwestern Germany and Switzerland settled in the North American colonies and began organizing congregations (see Table 1). These were secular, not religious migrations, in which few properly ordained and called pastors participated. This meant that religious authorities in Europe provided little or no oversight of the new immigrant communities. Instead, most religious life in those communities was directed by lay leaders and a few "irregular" pastors. It was an active religious culture, but many wanted more: They wanted access to the sacraments, liturgy, and authority similar to what they had known in Europe.

Table 1:
German and Reformed Congregations in the "Pennsylvania Field," 1727-1748
(includes Pennsylvania, New York, New Jersey, Maryland, and Virginia)

	Lutheran	Reformed	Total
1727	3	14	17
1736	12	22-23	34-35
1742	22-26	30-35	52-63
1748	53	55	108

Source: Glatfelter, *Pastors and People*, vol. 2, for 1742 and 1748 (see tables on 52-53, 138-39). The earlier numbers were calculated from individual community entries in Glatfelder, *Pastors and People*, vol. 1.

The ecumenical Moravians responded first to this new situation in and around Pennsylvania and began sending dozens of men and women preachers throughout the 1740s to serve these new Lutheran and Reformed communities. Eventually the Lutheran pietist center in Halle and the Classis of Amsterdam (the governing body of the Dutch state church) responded. They began sending a small number of pastors to organize and serve these congregations, and also to report on and resist the Moravians. The shorthanded Hallensians and Amsterdamers were in a difficult situation, however, because the Moravians had them outgunned when it came to the number of preachers who could work in these rapidly expanding Lutheran and Reformed communities (see Table 2).[6]

Table 2:
German Lutheran, Reformed, and Moravian Preachers
in the "Pennsylvania Field," 1742-1754
(includes Pennsylvania, New York, New Jersey, Maryland, and Virginia)

	Lutheran		Reformed			
	Hallensian*	Other	Amsterdamers^	Other	Moravian+	Total
1742	1	8	2	11	46	68
1748	6	13	9	11	73	112
1754	8	25	11	22	122	188

* Those sent by Halle, including unordained assistants.
^ Germans sent by the Classis of Amsterdam, or associating with them, including unordained pastors.
+ Includes some non-Germans who did not preach to Germans, but excludes a few who joined the Moravians in America and did preach to Germans.

Sources: Glatfelter, *Pastors and People*, on Lutherans and Reformed, and Fogleman, *Hopeful Journeys*, 206n14.

European religious authorities considered the Moravians a threat for a number of reasons, the most important of which were the Moravians' activist ecumenism and their new, radical spirituality. The Moravians insisted that anyone from any confession who wanted intimate communion with the Savior could live, work, and worship with them without losing their status in their original church. This was problematic to Lutheran and Reformed authorities in Europe (and later in North America) who were becoming increasingly confessional, denominational, and intolerant during this period.[7] Further, the expansionist Moravians were just then in a period of spiritual innovation that alarmed their enemies.[8] Among their many spiritual innovations was their regendering of the Trinity – God the Father was made less important (they believed Jesus was the Creator), the Holy Spirit became a mother, and Jesus acquired female characteristics.[9] They used this altered view of dichotomized gender relations as justification for elevating the role of women and making other changes in gender norms and boundaries in their communities. These changes ranged from the mystical and metaphorical to the tangible: All souls became female, gender transformations occurred during certain ceremonies, and marriage and sex became a sacrament. Further, women could and did preach, and married couples in their inner circles evaluated marital sex as a sacred (not sinful) event which they discussed and practiced openly in most unusual ways. All of this was celebrated in hymns, verse, sermons, discourse, and iconography that emphasized graphically the blood and wounds of Christ on the Cross, especially the side wound.[10]

While these events unfolded in some of their inner circles in Europe and North America, the Moravians sent men and women throughout the colonies to preach to "everyone" – Native Americans, African-American slaves, Germans, and non-Germans.[11] Lutheran and Reformed settlers often welcomed them because they were good preachers, because they presented a recognizable liturgy, and because they did it all for free. Indeed, dozens of Moravian diaries describe the work of their male and female preachers and missionaries in virtually every Lutheran and German Reformed parish in the mid-Atlantic colonies – preaching, teaching, baptizing, marrying, forming women's groups, building churches and schools, and getting into trouble as they did so. All of these events were an important part of the Great Awakening in the Lutheran and Reformed communities of North America. Meanwhile there were few "properly" ordained European clergy, and they were often perceived as arrogant, expensive, and incompetent – and they were rarely there. As an alternative, many lay leaders and independent preachers operated in the colonies and were sometimes effective, but this was not enough for many settlers, who wanted more organization, European connections, and support. The Moravians impressed them with their energy, piety, and resources – something the Lutheran and Reformed authorities could not or would not offer in America.[12]

The struggle against the Moravians began in Europe and spread to North America, first to Georgia and then to the mid-Atlantic colonies, where a religious war erupted in the 1740s. All sides used military rhetoric to describe the course of events. Count Nicolaus Ludwig von Zinzendorf (the Moravian leader) established a *"corps de reserve"* in Philadelphia in 1742 to assist any threatened Moravians. Johann Philip Fresenius, the Lutheran polemicist in Frankfurt am Main, described people in Philadelphia who had fled the "Herrnhuters," yet were still plagued by them: "some began shaking in their arms and legs, some began to wail and cry out in their sleep, and as they awoke said that Count Zinzendorf was there and was trying to get them into his clutches. Others said that troops and crowds of Herrnhuters stood before them and terrified them."[13] Heinrich Melchior Mühlenberg described the battle for Pennsylvania as such:

> For the last twelve years the lot has fallen to me to be in their neighborhood, to note their movements, plans, writings, and attacks, and to observe the defense and preparations of our Lutheran church. With sadness I have learned that we

did not seem to be a match for their strategems of war and their serpentine deviousness, because they advanced mightily and like a plague creeping in the dark they gained the upper hand. The commanding officers and generals of our church were in part badly trained to stand against such a crafty enemy, because they had learned only the theoretical part of the divine knowledge and had not encountered the praxis; also they had more military exercises on paper than in their hearts.

Consequently they often beat the air, and when they thought they were on target they lacked the right judgment, insight into the point of the controversy, the most essential truths, and the power of godliness. Thus, they often opened the door and gate to the enemy, put the sword into his hand, or themselves fought against the heart of our Christian religion when they dared to do battle and attack.[14]

The participants fought over several key, high-profile battleground communities, including Philadelphia, Lancaster, Tulpehocken, York, Coventry, and Muddy Creek in Pennsylvania, and Raccoon (the Swedish Lutheran community in Gloucester County, New Jersey), but a typical pattern of conflict at the local level emerged throughout the region: Moravians preached and were accepted, but later tensions, conflict, and schism followed. In many cases pro- and anti-Moravian factions fought violently for control of their communities.

German Lutheran and Reformed men and women in the mid-Atlantic religious communities had many choices among independent preachers and movements that they might adopt and support in what Patricia Bonomi has called a "free market of theistic beliefs and practices,"[15] but the three most important in the 1740s and early 1750s were the Moravians, the Halle Lutherans, and the Amsterdam Reformed preachers. The Moravians worked out of the Lehigh Valley, and the Halle Lutherans out of the Philadelphia-New Hanover-Providence area. The Amsterdam Reformed operated out of the New Hanover-Whitpain area early on under Johann Philip Boehm, and later out of the Philadelphia-Germantown area under Michael Schlatter. Other Lutherans and Reformed were involved, but they were even smaller than the Halle and Amsterdam groups and did not shape the larger course of events and the future of these three denominations. Also, many of the small, radical German groups played a critical role in stopping the Moravian movement in the early 1740s, but they were essentially separatists defending themselves against the Moravians, rather than competing for control of the German congregations. Of all these groups, only the Moravians had anywhere near enough preachers to serve the growing number of Lutheran and Reformed immigrant congregations.

The Moravians had many advantages and gained the upper hand early in the struggle. They came to America with a plan, and their leadership in Europe enthusiastically supported them. In 1740-42 an elite group of Moravian women (Benigna von Zinzendorf, Anna Nitschmann, and Johanna Sophia Molther) carried out high-profile preaching tours throughout Pennsylvania, especially in Quaker meetinghouses. They intended the tours to get people's attention, and they did –

which both helped and hurt their cause. From 1741 to 1743 reenforcements arrived, including Count Zinzendorf. The Moravians quickly built closed communities deep in the backcountry at Bethlehem and Nazareth. From there they sent women and men out to German and other settlements (including Native American villages) throughout the mid-Atlantic colonies, from northern Virginia to New England.[16]

Essentially, the Moravians tried to send out more preachers and build more churches and schools than their enemies possibly could – at little or no cost to the local community. They sometimes called this highly organized movement "The Plan," or "The Wheel" (which was set into motion), and called the preachers "Fishers." The home base in Bethlehem provided much more support than the Halle Lutheran and Amsterdam Reformed leaders Mühlenberg or Schlatter ever had, including a place of rest, recuperation, communion, and instruction for the preachers. Further, trusted Moravians moved into strategically located houses across the countryside, providing safe havens for weary and sometimes frightened preachers. Also, the preachers often met on the trail, exchanging information, mail, and greetings. They possessed maps marking communities, trails, and the location of Moravian allies. The preachers were flexible and changed their plans based on intelligence received from their colleagues. The Moravian leadership held synods and other meetings in the field at key positions, hoping to attract support in contested areas. All of this impressed many Lutheran and Reformed settlers, who began welcoming them into their communities and supporting them.[17]

With everything apparently in favor of the Moravians in the 1740s, how and why did they lose the religious war for the Lutheran and German Reformed communities, and how did the Hallensian and Amsterdam ministers, with their small numbers, eventually win? Or, put another way, why did the thousands of men and women in those communities stop supporting the Moravians and begin supporting their enemies?

Crucial to the war against the Moravians were the polemical writings against them which their numerous enemies published and circulated on both sides of the Atlantic. They warned the innocents of the dangerous "Moravian threat" and provided fodder for rumors and sermons by enemy preachers who railed against them from the pulpit. Dietrich Meyer has cataloged 385 anti-Moravian books, pamphlets, and magazines published in Europe and America from 1727 to 1764, of which 316 (more than eighty percent) appeared in the years 1738 to 1752, during the peak period of conflict. Writers designed their polemics to stop the Moravian movement on both continents by portraying the group as authoritarian antinomians, irrational lunatics, scandalous predators of women and children, blasphemous liars in league with Antichrist and the Pope, and evil, oversexed perverts who believed Jesus and the Holy Ghost were women. They compared the Moravians to dangerous, radical sects that had plagued southwestern Germany earlier in the century before authorities had repressed them. Publishers in Halle, Frankfurt am Main, Leipzig, Amsterdam, London, New York, Philadelphia, and Germantown printed and reprinted the polemics. European religious authorities shipped them to America and circulated them in sophisticated networks, making them widely available in German communities where the Moravians were working. (The Halle Lutherans Heinrich Melchior Mühlenberg and Peter Brunnholtz, and the German Reformed minister Johann Philipp Boehm, for example, applauded and supported their circulation.) This anti-Moravian propaganda skillfully discredited the group in the eyes of many and helped undermine their efforts.[18]

Religious violence also played an important role in defeating the Moravians. The conflict turned violent in many communities like Lancaster, Pennsylvania, where a series of incidents took place in late 1745 and early 1746 involving about eighty pro-Moravian Lutheran families who fought with about seventy anti-Moravian Lutheran families for control of the church. On December 8, 1745, the anti-Moravian faction began a "riot" outside the courthouse while the Moravians held a synod inside. According to one account, the crowd broke inside the courthouse and pelted August Gottlieb Spangenberg (one of the most important Moravian leaders) with stones while he was preaching. Later they beat a member of the pro-Moravian faction attempting to enter the Lutheran church. Thereafter people began attending services carrying flintlocks and swords. At one point a brawl erupted in front of the entrance to the church, as the pro-Moravian group literally pushed its way into the building and held a service. Later the tide turned against them, and when they tried again to force their way in, the Moravian preacher was beaten by an anti-Moravian crowd. In the ensuing court case all members of the anti-Moravian faction were acquitted.[19]

The religious conflict turned violent in a number of other Lutheran and Reformed communities, as pro- and anti-Moravian factions struggled for control of sacred space. In 1742 an anti-Moravian Reformed faction attacked the Moravian pastor Johann Christoph Pyrlaeus while he preached in Philadelphia, dragging him from the pulpit and into the street, where they beat him. The violence spread to New Jersey in late 1743 and 1744, including the Swedish Lutheran congregation at Raccoon in Gloucester County. At one point fifteen Swedes, Germans, and Irish clubbed and dispersed a crowd of pro-Moravians attempting to enter the church there. Indeed, throughout the mid-Atlantic colonies tensions increased in Lutheran and Reformed communities, as the Moravian preachers began working there and congregations split into factions and fought over whether they should be allowed to stay.[20]

After many early victories, the Moravians began succumbing to the pressure, rumors, conflict, and violence, and many of their preachers could be seen running terror-stricken back to Bethlehem after encounters with their enemies. The Moravians gained influence in congregations by sending one or more preachers who worked regularly and won acceptance from most if not all of the elders and church council members, as well as the congregants themselves. Often they convinced a hard core of upstanding community members and elders who supported them later when opposition and ultimately conflict and schism wracked the congregation. As long as enough members did support them, the Moravian preachers kept returning to the community. From 1743 to 1745, for example, Jacob Lischy, Johann Brandmüller, and their assistants worked in twenty-eight German Reformed communities in Pennsylvania, reporting big crowds and at least some conflict in fourteen of the twenty-eight. According to them the Moravians were winning influence and support in twenty of the twenty-eight communities and losing in only four. (Four were undecided.) Two years later the situation changed, and they were losing ground. Leonhard Schnell and Christian Rauch worked in twenty-six Reformed congregations and reported conflict in eighteen of them. The Moravians were winning in only twelve of the twenty-six, while they were losing in seven, and the status of the rest was either mixed or unclear. Support for the Moravians continued to wither in the late 1740s and early 1750s, while their enemies grew stronger. Though Moravian preachers had served in at least 102 German-speaking congregations and at least 38 others from 1740 to 1748, they served in only 48 and 20 of each during the period 1749 to 1755, and many of these were either brief visits or visits to small congregations that would ultimately become separate Moravian communities instead of Lutheran, Reformed, or something else. In the end the Moravians could and did field enough preachers to care for most of the German communities, but they were unprepared to handle the resistance and violence they encountered in many of those places.[21]

In the midst of the war against the Moravians, two alternatives – one Lutheran and the other German Reformed – emerged and led to a future for the German communities that was much different than what the ecumenical, radical Moravians had planned. The Halle Lutherans and the Amsterdam Reformed preachers benefitted enormously from the anti-Moravian polemics and violence in the mid-Atlantic colonies and provided an alternative that most congregations ultimately accepted, although to a significant degree on their own terms. Let us first look at how the Hallensians built their establishment and then the Amsterdam Reformed preachers.

From 1742 until the beginning of the French and Indian War, Halle sent eight pastors and assistants to the mid-Atlantic colonies. (See Table 3 below.) Their published and unpublished journals, correspondence, and polemics document how the Hallensians operated during this early period and go well beyond what we know from reading Heinrich Melchior Mühlenberg's correspondence and journal.[22]

Table 3:
Pastors and Assistants Sent by the Pietist Center in Halle
to work in Lutheran Communities in the Mid-Atlantic Colonies
of British North America, 1742-54

Name	Dates of Service	Congregations Served to 1754
Heinrich Melchior Mühlenberg	1742-87	Philadelphia, New Hanover, Providence, Germantown, Trinity (NY)
Johann Nicholas Kurtz	1745-89	New Hanover, Tulpehocken, Lancaster, Earl
Peter Brunnholtz	1745-57	Philadelphia, Germantown
Johann Helfrich Schaum	1745-78	Philadelphia, Raritan (NJ), York, Tohickon, Conewago, Pikestown, Frederick, Bermudian
Johann Friedrich Handschuh	1748-64	Lancaster, Beaver Creek, Earl, Germantown
Johann Albert Weygand	1748-70	Raritan (NJ), Pluckemin (NJ)
Johann Diedrich Matthias Heintzelmann	1751-56	Philadelphia
Friedrich Schultz	1751-56	New Hanover, Providence, Indianfield, New Goshenhoppen, Tohickon

Note: Does not include congregations visisted. Unless otherwise noted, all congregations were in Pennsylvania.

Sources: Glatfelter, *Pastors and People*, vols. 2, 107-108 and 190.

Because they had so few ministers (only six in the Pennsylvania field during the period of peak conflict with the Moravians), the Hallensians stationed themselves in key battleground communities and did their best, taking advantage of the polemics and violence wherever possible. Mühlenberg worsened the odds against the Halle cause early on by stubbornly refusing to work with a number of Lutheran preachers from Europe already in the colonies, including some who were ordained and did not like the Moravians either. His early diaries and correspondence suggest that he was a hard-working, competitive, territorial man who was sure he knew the right course and insisted on following it, even when flexibility might have been a better solution at times. One tactic Mühlenberg and the other Halle pastors employed was to ride in groups as a show of force when moving into an area – essentially to disguise their weakness. In April 1748, for example, when Johann Friedrich Handschuh was scheduled to move into troubled Lancaster, where the Moravians were still strong, he stayed the night before in Tulpehocken with the Hallensians' ally, the well-known government Indian agent Conrad Weiser. Weiser kept Handschuh up until midnight, telling him tales of woe about the Moravians. The frightened Handschuh recorded in his diary that he did not want to go to Lancaster, but the next day he rode through the countryside and into the town with Weiser, Johann Nicholas Kurtz, Johann Helfrich Schaum, Peter Brunnholtz, and Friedrich Vigera (the teacher who joined them in Pennsylvania) in a show of force designed to intimidate the Moravians and their supporters, as well as anyone else who might challenge them.[23]

The Hallensians established an umbilical cord of support that stretched from Halle to London to Peter Brunnholtz in Philadelphia (who played a critical role in distributing communications and publications between Europe and America), to Mühlenberg in Providence, to Handschuh in Lancaster, to Schaum in York, Kurtz in Tulpehocken, and Johann Albert Weygand in Raritan, New Jersey. Halle channeled pastors, books (from Bibles to polemics), and medical supplies through the tenuous supply line. The Hallensians preferred to stick together (often two per parish), in or near the battleground communities, and they usually did not stray very far for very long from their line of support. They visited surrounding families and congregations, held meetings in the field, and often traded places with each other. The Hallensians reacted slowly and deliberately to formal calls by congregations for a minister because they did not have very many and wanted to be sure that those they sent would be well taken care of and might serve a functioning congregation. They did send ministers on numerous occasions to help resolve disputes and schisms throughout the Pennsylvania field, but those ministers returned to their home congregations as soon as possible. Thus their coverage was much more limited than that of the Moravians and progress was slow. By 1748, six years after Mühlenberg began, the Hallensians worried constantly about what the Moravians and other foes were doing as they worked regularly in only fourteen of fifty-three known Lutheran congregations in the Pennsylvania field, and six of these were contested (see Table 4).[24]

Table 4:
Number of Lutheran Congregations in the Pennsylvania Field Where
Hallensian Pastors Were Active, 1742-1752

Year	Pastors*	Congregations			
		Under Control	Contested^	Visited	Total
1742	1	2	1	0	3
1745	4	4	2	5	11
1748	6	8	6	8	22
1752	8	16	2	16	34

* Including unordained assistants.
^ Not necessarily contested with Moravians.

Sources: Diaries and correspondence of the Halle pastors in the Lutheran Archives Center (Philadelphia) and the Archives of the Francke Foundations (Halle, Germany), as well as Glatfelter, *Pastors and People*, vol. 1.

But the umbilical cord was stretched to the limit and sometimes snapped, such as when Handschuh failed in Lancaster and the Hallensians lost this key parish in 1751 – a stunning defeat that set them back in surrounding parishes as well. In the 1740s and early 1750s the Hallensians failed to organize most of the Lutheran congregations in and around Pennsylvania and bring them under their influence, in part because support from Halle was insufficient. They did not have enough pastors (Mühlenberg constantly complained of being outnumbered by the Moravians), and Halle refused to send a printing press and other materials that Mühlenberg wanted badly to carry out the struggle. The Hallensian ministers simply could not cover all of the rural parishes. They even lost some key town parishes like Lancaster and Germantown, and sometimes found themselves retreating. The umbilical cord system had allowed the Hallensians to make inroads into the mid-Atlantic colonies, but with it alone they could not defeat the Moravians and other enemies, and they could not control most of the Lutheran congregations.[25]

Ultimately the Hallensian ministers did help defeat the Moravians, not only by exploiting the anti-Moravian polemics and violence, but also by changing their own tactics. They moved away from the umbilical cord system and began building an apparatus less dependent on Europe. They accomplished this by becoming more flexible about taking on experienced teachers and preachers already in America who had not been sent by Halle. The formation of the Lutheran ministerium in 1748 was a crucial turning point. The Hallensian ministers dominated the ministerium, yet it remained independent from Halle. This impressed many non-Hallensian preachers and lay leaders, who began to see the new ministerium led by the Halle ministers as the way of the future for the Lutheran Church in America. Further, the Moravians began withdrawing from the Lutheran communities as the fight with the Hallensians and others took its toll and the group's agenda changed. Thus the new ministerium had no serious, organized rivals by the outbreak of war. Six pastors and twenty-five other delegates from ten congregations attended the first meeting of the ministerium, a small portion of all the Lutheran communities and preachers working in them. But by 1752 twelve pastors and sixty-eight other delegates attended (see Table 5 below). Under Mühlenberg's leadership the organization continued to grow, the restrictive umbilical cord system ended, many other battles were fought against other foes, and the new ministerium became the basis for the denominational Lutheran establishment that eventually controlled most of the Lutheran posts in North America.[26]

Table 5:
Numbers of Pastors and Other Delegates Attending the Annual Meetings of the Lutheran Ministerium of North America, with Number of Congregations Represented, 1748-1754

Year	Pastors	Other Delegates	Congregations Represented
1748	6	25	10
1750	6	61	15
1752	12	68	?
1754	16	?	?

Source: *Documentary History of the Evangelical Lutheran Ministerium.*

The impetus for stopping the Moravians and building a German Reformed establishment in the colonies came not from religious authorities in the German territories but rather from the Netherlands. For years German Reformed settlers in the colonies had appealed to various religious governing bodies in the German territories for support, but these authorities proved unwilling to start a mission, send pastors or significant aid, or otherwise build and support an apparatus in North America. Ultimately the Dutch state church agreed to do so, at first hoping to combine the German Reformed apparatus with that of the Dutch Reformed colonists there. When the German colonists refused to join with the Dutch, the Classis of Amsterdam sponsored each separately. Amsterdam moved slowly at first, but then rushed in more aid and reacted more significantly than Halle ever did. They recognized the German lay preacher Johann Philip Boehm as early as 1728 when they began corresponding with him, and in the 1740s they charged him to carry out the fight against the Moravians in the German Reformed communities. Boehm zealously pursued the anti-Moravian cause in Pennsylvania, eagerly devouring the polemics Amsterdam sent and even wrote two himself.[27]

With rumors, sermons, and polemics Boehm hurried about the numerous German Reformed congregations in the colony and warned his audiences of the Moravian dangers and probably played a significant role in keeping the Moravians from influencing even more congregations than they did in the early to mid-1740s. Many suspected that he had incited the Reformed crowd that attacked Pyrlaeus in Philadelphia in 1742, and he was directly involved in the violence at Coventry, Pennsylvania in 1743. In 1744, Amsterdam sent Peter Heinrich Dorius to Philadelphia to gather information and try to implement a union between the Dutch and German Reformed settlers, and maybe even the Presbyterians, but he did not preach or care for any parishes. Johann Bartholomäus Rieger and Caspar Ludwig Schnorr came under Amsterdam's tutelage, along with Boehm, but Schnorr came under fire for immoral conduct and left for New York in 1746, and Rieger was asked to leave the German Reformed coetus in 1762 because of his long history of improper conduct. By the mid-1740s the union effort had failed, and the Moravians continued to gain ground – they were winning the contest for the Reformed parishes throughout Pennsylvania and beyond.[28]

From 1746 to 1752 Amsterdam sent eleven German Reformed pastors to North America (see Table 6), beginning with Michael Schlatter, who initiated formal organization among the Germans in North America, but their tactics were different than those of the Halle Lutherans. While Mühlenberg was initially competitive, chauvinistic, and territorial regarding other Lutheran pastors in Pennsylvania, rejecting the few who were there, Schlatter quickly organized many Reformed preachers already in the colony and brought them under the tutelage of Amsterdam. Further, he itinerated from northern Virginia to New York to achieve broad coverage – something Mühlenberg never did. Like Halle, Amsterdam sent hymnals, religious books, and anti-Moravian polemics to North America, but unlike Halle they also sent a printing press with German type, and more importantly, they sent ten additional pastors within six years of Schlatter's arrival. Indeed, within a year Schlatter had organized a coetus (a year before the Lutheran ministerium was organized) under Amsterdam's direction, with four pastors and twenty-eight other delegates from nineteen congregations attending the first meeting in 1747 (see Table 7). This paralleled the establishment of the Dutch Reformed coetus in New York in 1747, also at the direction of Amsterdam. In 1752, thirteen pastors representing twenty-two congregations attended the annual meeting. The coetus in Pennsylvania, led early on by Schlatter and heavily supported by Amsterdam, became the framework for building the Reformed denominational establishment and winning the battle against the Moravians. Like the Hallensians trying to develop their denomination, the Amsterdam pastors had many problems other than those with the Moravians, but they slowly made progress and extended their influence in the German Reformed communities in and around Pennsylvania. In the 1740s their numbers were too small to defeat the Moravians, but the polemics and the violence held the Moravians in check while the Reformed leaders slowly built up an establishment that increasingly won the support of the Reformed congregations. By 1752 the Amsterdam pastors themselves controlled twenty-six congregations, and visited many others (see Table 8). The Amsterdam method of building a flexible network worked better than relying on a tenuous umbilical cord as the Lutherans had done initially.[29]

Table 6:
Pastors and Assistants Supported or Sent by the Classis of Amsterdam
Working in the German Reformed Communities in the
Mid-Atlantic Colonies of British North America, 1729-54

Name	Dates of Service	Congregations Served to 1754
Johann Philip Boehm*	1729-49	Falkner Swamp, Skippack, Whitemarsh, Philadelphia, Providence, Coventry, Whitpain, Tulpehocken, Oley, Egypt
P. H. Dorius*	1737-48	New and Old Goshenhoppen, Egypt
C. L. Schnorr*	1744-48	Lancaster, Tulpehocken, Eastcamp/Germantown (NY)
J. B. Rieger*	1745-69	Seltenreich, Hill/Schaeffer's
G. M. Weiss*	1746-61	Old & New Goshenhoppen, Great Swamp
Michael Schlatter	1746-90	Philadelphia, Germantown, Whitpain; Amwell, Rockaway, Fox Hill (NJ)
J. D. C. Bartholomae	1748-51	Tulpehocken (Host and Trinity)
J. J. Hochreutiner	1748	Lancaster
J. P. Leydich	1748-84	Falkner Swamp, Providence
J. C. Steiner	1749-62	Philadelphia, Germantown, Whitpain
T. Frankenfeld	1752-55	Frederick, Monocacy, Conococheague (MD), Conewago
H. W. Stoy	1752-1801	Tulpehocken (Host and Trinity)
P. W. Otterbein	1752-1813	Lancaster
J. C. Rubel	1752-84	Philadelphia (one faction)

J. Waldschmidt	1752-86		Cocalico, Muddy Creek, Reyer's, Seltenreich, Blaser's
J. J. Wissler	1752-54		Egypt, Jordan, Heidelberg

*Not assigned by Amsterdam but sponsored by or connected to the Classis after arriving. Only dates of service while connected to Amsterdam included.

Note: This list includes many congregations only visited by the Amsterdam pastors; however, it does not include the parishes where Schlatter itinerated, from northern Virginia to New York, early in his service. Unless otherwise noted, all congregations were in Pennsylvania.

Source: Glatfelter, *Pastors and People*, 2:38-39, 117 and 190.

Table 7:
Number of Pastors and Other Delegates Attending the Annual Meetings of the German Reformed Coetus of North America, with Number of Congregations Represented, 1747-1754

Year	Pastors	Other Delegates	Congregations Represented
1747	4	28	19
1749	5	18	?
1752	13	?	22
1754	12	?	?

Source: Good and Hinke, *Minutes and Letters of the Coetus of the German Reformed Congregations in Pennsylvania.*

Table 8:
Number of German Reformed Congregations Where Amsterdam Pastors and the Assistants Worked by Year to 1754

Year	Number of Pastors	Number of Congregations
1729	1	3
1734	1	4
1742	2	5
1745	4	12
1748	9	23
1752	11	26
1754	11	26

Source: Glatfelter, *Pastors and People*, vols. 1 and 2.

* * *

The story of the Moravian challenge and defeat in the German Lutheran and Reformed communities of the mid-Atlantic colonies during the peak years of the Great Awakening calls into question many views and assumptions about the nature of this intense religious movement that swept through the region from the late 1730s to the early 1750s. Many historians have stressed the importance of lay-clergy relations and tensions, which in some cases involved property issues, but this does not adequately explain the huge conflict with the Moravians during this period.[30] The conflict with the Moravians involved lay-clergy-vestry alliances on all sides struggling with each other. Property issues do not seem to have been at the heart of the conflict either – in one case a violent uproar took place in a dilapidated rental unit in Philadelphia. Instead, this was a conflict over the nature of religious piety, organization, and social order. The Moravians challenged that order in the newly developing Reformed and Lutheran communities, in some ways as the Baptists did in the Anglican communities of Virginia a few years later, and in both cases a violent response followed.[31] However, in the Reformed and Lutheran communities gender was a critical issue, as it had been among these Protestant groups in many cases since the Reformation.[32] With their female or androgynous view of the Trinity, alternative views of marriage, sex, family, community, and women preaching, the ecumenical Moravians attracted many colonists and threatened others, who ultimately chose to support an orthodox, patriarchal social-religious order.

The tactics employed in the struggle reflected colonial conditions and the hopes, dreams, and anxieties of the colonists in the mid-Atlantic communities. Here opportunity and tolerance led to rapid growth, diversity, and ecumenism, with little influence from European religious authorities. Some people liked it that way, but others wanted more European religious authority and liturgy in their lives, in part to protect them and their beliefs from the dangerous sects like the Moravians lurking in the colonies. When opportunities for alternative forms of piety, organization, and power arose, those who either embraced or resisted them fought for control of their communities in an environment where the state intervened little, if at all. In the end, those who supported the orthodox confessional, patriarchal ideal defeated those who supported the ecumenical, more female form of piety and order. Thereafter other battles over other issues shaped the religious landscape of these communities.

Notes

This essay contains material from a much larger study: Aaron Spencer Fogleman, *Jesus Is Female: Moravians and Radical Religion in Early America* (Philadelphia: University of Pennsylvania Press, 2007). However, it includes many details that had to be omitted from the book. I would like to thank the University of Pennsylvania Press for permission to use material from the book in this essay.

RELIGIOUS CONFLICT AND VIOLENCE

1. Jon Butler has raised significant objections to the idea of a "Great Awakening" and has pointed out how problematic the connection between religious events in this era and later political developments can be. I believe, however, that many important, permanent changes occurred in the religious culture of Americans during this era of revivals and conflict. This essay will deal with some of those changes in the German communities. See Jon Butler, "Enthusiasm Described and Decried: The Great Awakening as Interpretive Fiction," *Journal of American History*, 69 (1982): 305-25.

2. By "religious violence" I mean essentially what Natalie Zemon Davis meant in her famous essay on "rites of violence," in which she defines a "religious riot" as any violent action with words or weapons against religious targets by people not acting officially and formally as agents of political or ecclesiastical authority. To Davis, this kind of behavior was more normal than pathological. Both men and women were responsible for preserving sacred values and space, and they could and would legitimately attack religious opponents, violently if necessary, to defend their values and space. See Natalie Zemon Davis, "The Rites of Violence," in Davis, *Society and Culture in Early Modern France* (Stanford: Stanford University Press, 1975), esp. 153.

3. W. R. Ward, *The Protestant Evangelical Awakening* (Cambridge: Cambridge University Press, 1992).

4. See Fogleman, *Jesus Is Female*, 2-3.

5. On the Moravians' early failures in Georgia and Pennsylvania, see Aaron Spencer Fogleman, "The Decline and Fall of the Moravian Community in Colonial Georgia: *Zeitschrift für Geschichte und Gegenwartsfragen der Brüdergemeine* 48 (2001): 1-22; Peter Vogt, "Zinzendorf und die Pennsylvanischen Synoden 1742," *Unitas Fratrum* 36 (1994): 5-62; Rudolf Dellsperger, "Kirchengemeinschaft und Gewissensfreiheit: Samuel Güldins Einspruch gegen Zinzendorfs Unionstätigkeit in Pennsylvania 1742," *Pietismus und Neuzeit* 11 (1985): 40-58; John R. Weinlick, "Moravianism in the American Colonies," in *Continental Pietism and Early American Christianity*, ed. F. Ernest Stoeffler (Grand Rapids, MI: Eerdmans, 1976), 123-63; Erich Beyreuther, *Zinzendorf und die Christenheit* (Marburg: Verlag der Francke-Buchhandlung GmbH, 1961), 207-53; Ernst Benz, "Zinzendorf in Amerika," in *Zinzendorf-Gedenkbuch*, ed. Ernst Benz and Heinz Renkewitz (Stuttgart: Evangelisches Verlagswerk, 1951), 140-61; John Joseph Stoudt, "Pennsylvania and the Oecumenical Ideal," *Bulletin, Theological Seminary of the Reformed Church in the United States* 12 (1941): 171-97; John Joseph Stoudt, "Count Zinzendorf and the Pennsylvania Congregation of God in the Spirit: The First Oecumenical Movement," *Church History* 9 (1940): 366-80.

6. On the struggle between the Moravians and the state church in the Netherlands, see John Exalto and Jan-Kees Karels, *Waakzame Wachters en Kleine Vossen: Gereformeerden en Herrnhutters in de Nederlanden, 1734-1754* (Heerenveen: Uitgeverij Groen, 2001); Johannes Van Den Berg, "Die Frömmigkeitsbestrebungen in den Niederlanden," in *Geschichte des Pietismus*, ed. Martin Brecht and Klaus Deppermann, vol. 2, *Der Pietismus im achtzehnten Jahrhundert* (Göttingen: Vandenhoeck und Ruprecht, 1995), 542-87; Paul Peucker, "Der Amsterdamer Hirtenbrief von 1738," (unpublished manuscript, Unity Archives, Herrnhut, Germany); Wilhelm Lütjeharms, *Het Philadelphisch-Oecumenisch Streven der Herrnhutters in de Nederlanden in de Achttiende Eeuw* (Zeist: Zendingsgenootschap der Evang.

Broedergemeente, 1935). On the struggle between the Moravians in Denmark, Schleswig-Holstein, and Lower Saxony see Manfred Jakubowski-Tiessen, "Der Pietismus in Niedersachsen" and "Der Pietismus in Dänemark und Schleswig-Holstein," in *Geschichte des Pietismus*, ed. Brecht and Depperman, 2:428-45 and 446-71. On developments in Halle during this era see Martin Brecht, "Der Hallische Pietismus in der Mitte des 18. Jahrhunderts – seine Ausstrahlung und sein Niedergang," in *Geschichte des Pietismus*, ed. Brecht and Deppermann, 2:319-57; and Ulrike Witt, *Bekehrung, Bildung und Biographie: Frauen im Umkreis des Halleschen Pietismus* (Tübingen: M. Niemeyer Verlag, 1996). On German immigration into the colonies during this period see Aaron Spencer Fogleman, *Hopeful Journeys: German Immigration, Settlement, and Political Culture in Colonial America* (Philadelphia: University of Pennsylvania Press, 1996) and Marianne S. Wokeck, *Trade in Strangers: The Beginnings of Mass Migration to North America* (University Park: Pennsylvania State University Press, 1999). There are numerous studies on religious culture in the middle colonies on the eve of the Great Awakening; some of the more important dealing significantly with Germans are A. G. Roeber, *Palatines, Liberty, and Property: German Lutherans in Colonial British America* (Baltimore: Johns Hopkins University Press, 1993); Sally Schwartz, *"A Mixed Multitude": The Struggle for Toleration in Colonial Pennsylvania* (New York: New York University Press, 1987), 81-119; Patricia U. Bonomi, *Under the Cope of Heaven: Religion, Society, and Politics in Colonial America* (New York: Oxford University Press, 1986), 39-127; Patricia U. Bonomi, "'Watchful against the Sects': Religious Renewal in Pennsylvania German Congregations, 1720-1750," *Pennsylvania History* 50 (1983): 273-83; Charles H. Glatfelter, *Pastors and People: German Lutheran and Reformed Churches in the Pennsylvania Field, 1717-1793*, 2 vols. (Breinigsville, Pa.: The Pennsylvania German Society, 1979, 1981), 2:3-53; Martin E. Lodge, "The Crisis of the Churches in the Middle Colonies, 1720-1750," *Pennsylvania Magazine of History and Biography* 95 (1971): 195-220.

7. On Moravian ecumenism, see Fogleman, *Jesus Is Female*, 105-33; Arthur J. Freeman, *An Ecumenical Theology of the Heart: The Theology of Count Nicholas Ludwig von Zinzendorf* (Bethlehem, Pa.: Moravian Church in America, 1998); Weinlick, "Moravianism in the American Colonies"; Beyreuther, *Zinzendorf und die Christenheit*, 207-53; Lütjeharms, *Het Philadelphisch-Oecumenisch Streven der Herrnhutters*, esp. 5-43; Stoudt, "Pennsylvania and the Oecumenical Ideal"; Stoudt, "Count Zinzendorf and the First Oecumenical Movement."

8. Craig T. Atwood, *Community of the Cross: Moravian Piety in Colonial Bethlehem* (University Park: Pennsylvania State University Press, 2004); Paul Peucker, "'Blut auf unsere grünen Bändchen': Die Sichtungszeit in der Herrnhuter Brüdergemeine," *Unitas Fratrum* 49 (2002); Irina Modrow, *Dienstgemeine des Herrn: Nikolaus Ludwig von Zinzendorf und die Brüdergemeine seiner Zeit* (Hildesheim: G. Olms, 1994), 144-67; Hans-Walter Erbe, "Herrnhaag – Tiefpunkt oder Höhepunkt der Brüdergeschichte?" *Unitas Fratrum* 26 (1989): 37-51; Hans-Walter Erbe, *Herrnhaag: Eine religiöse Kommunität im 18. Jahrhundert* (Hamburg: Wittig, 1988); Hans-Walter Erbe, *Die Herrnhaag-Kantate von 1739: Ihre Geschichte und ihr Komponist, Philipp Heinrich Molther* (Hamburg: F. Wittig, 1982); Jörn Reichel, *Dichtungstheorie und Sprache bei Zinzendorf: der 12. Anhang zum Herrnhuter Gesangbuch* (Bad Homburg: v.d.H., Gehlen, 1969).

9. The Moravians' controversial regendering of the Trinity during this period is still being explored by historians on both sides of the Atlantic. Craig Atwood, Paul Peucker, Gary Steven Kinkel, Peter Zimmerling, Arthur Freeman, Jörn Reichel, and F. Ernest Stoeffler have dealt with the concept of Jesus as Creator briefly and the Holy Spirit as

mother at length. See Atwood, *Community of the Cross*; Peucker, "Blut auf unsere grünen Bändchen"; Gary Steven Kinkel, *Our Dear Mother the Spirit: An Investigation of Count Zinzendorf's Theology and Praxis* (Lanham, Md.: University Press of America, 1990); Peter Zimmerling, *Gott in Gemeinschaft: Zinzendorfs Trinitätslehre* (Giessen: Brunnen, 1991); Freeman, *An Ecumenical Theology of the Heart*, 83-84, 88, and 105-15; Reichel, *Dichtungstheorie und Sprache bei Zinzendorf,* 29-64; F. Ernest Stoeffler, *German Pietism during the Eighteenth Century* (Leiden: Brill, 1973), 137-67, and Stoeffler, *Mysticism in the German Devotional Literature of Colonial Pennsylvania* (Allentown, Pa.: Schlechter's, 1950), 67-90. Additionally, there is evidence that Moravians assigned female characteristics to Jesus in their hymnology, iconography, verse, and other writings during this period. For many Moravians their savior remained quite male, which suggests that, like many mystical groups through the ages, the Moravians may have opted for an androgynous solution to the old problem of how both male and female believers could have a sensual, mystical relationship with Jesus. See Aaron Spencer Fogleman, "Jesus Is Female: The Moravian Challenge in the German Communities of British North America," *William and Mary Quarterly* 60 (2003): 295-332, and Fogleman, *Jesus Is Female*, 74-86.

10. For the impact of the feminized Trinity on the role of women in Moravian communities see Fogleman, *Jesus Is Female*. On the status and role of women in Moravian communities in general see Peter Vogt, "A Voice for Themselves: Women as Participants in Congregational Discourse in the Eighteenth-Century Moravian Movement," in *Women Preachers and Prophets through Two Millennia of Christianity*, ed. Beverly Mayne Kienzle and Pamela J. Walker (Berkeley: University of California Press, 1998), 227-47; Beverly Prior Smaby, "Female Piety among Eighteenth-Century Moravians," *Pennsylvania History* 64 (supplement) (1997): 151-67; Beverly Prior Smaby, "Forming the Single Sisters' Choir in Bethlehem," *Transactions of the Moravian Historical Society* 28 (1994): 1-14; Katherine M. Faull, ed. and trans., *Moravian Women's Memoirs: Their Related Lives, 1750-1820* (Syracuse, N.Y.: Syracuse University Press, 1997); Otto Uttendörfer, *Zinzendorf und die Frauen: Kirchliche Frauenrechte vor 200 Jahren* (Herrnhut: Verlag der Missionsbuchhandlung, 1919).

11. Defining what is meant by "preaching" in the eighteenth century is not an easy task. The terms "prophesying" or "exhorting" are often used to describe the work in the early modern period of unordained men and women who had no permanent posts as heads of congregations, yet spoke to groups about such topics as faith or the power of God and Jesus. I am using the term "preaching" to refer to Moravian women (some of whom were ordained) who traveled with their husbands to Lutheran, Reformed, and other communities and met with groups of women outside church services, and also to women like Anna Nitschmann, who spoke before groups of non-Moravian men and women, sometimes in meetinghouses. In North America, informal lay "preaching" by men was common and carried with it significant authority in German communities, where there were few properly ordained European pastors. Thus Moravian men and women performing similar roles represented a significant threat to many, and the anti-Moravian polemics severely condemned the group for allowing women (as well as untrained men) to carry out such "preaching" in these communities. For a good explanation of the work of Moravian women preaching, see Lucinda Martin, "Möglichkeiten und Grenzen geistlicher Rede von Frauen in Halle und Herrnhut," *Pietismus und Neuzeit* 29 (2003), 80-100. On the Moravian worldwide mission movement see Dietrich Meyer, "Zinzendorf und Herrnhut," in *Geschichte des Pietismus*, ed. Brecht and Deppermann, 2:5-106, esp. 30-34; J. Taylor Hamilton and Kenneth G. Hamilton, *History of the Moravian Church: The Renewed Unitas Fratrum, 1722-*

1957 (Bethlehem, Pa.: Moravian Church of America, 1967), 52-59; Karl Müller, *200 Jahre Brüdermission*, vol. 1, *Das erste Missionsjahrhundert* (Herrnhut: Missionsbuchhandlung, 1931).

12. See Fogleman, *Jesus Is Female*, 105-30. On the Great Awakening in the German communities see Ward, *Protestant Evangelical Awakening*, 241-95; Roeber, *Palatines, Liberty, and Property*; Schwartz, "*Mixed Multitude*," 120-58; Bonomi, *Under the Cope of Heaven*, 131-60; Bonomi, "Watchful against the Sects"; Glatfelter, *Pastors and People*, 2:55-134; John B. Frantz, "The Awakening of Religion among the German Settlers in the Middle Colonies," *William and Mary Quarterly* 3d ser., 33 (1976): 266-88; Lodge, "Crisis of the Churches"; Dietmar Rothermund, *The Layman's Progress: Religious and Political Experience in Colonial Pennsylvania, 1740-1770* (Philadelphia: University of Pennsylvania Press, 1961), 16-36; Charles Hartshorn Maxson, *The Great Awakening in the Middle Colonies* (Gloucester, Mass.: P. Smith, 1958).

13. Aaron Spencer Fogleman, "Shadow Boxing in Georgia: The Beginnings of the Moravian-Lutheran Conflict in British North America," *Georgia Historical Quarterly* 83 (1999): 629-59. On the Moravian *corps de reserve* in Pennsylvania see "Etliche Pläne von Gemeinen in Pensylvanien," in *Büdingische Sammlung Einiger In die Kirchen-Historie Einschlagender Sonderlich neuerer Schrifften*, ed. Nicolaus Ludwig von Zinzendorf, vol. 3 (Leipzig, 1744-45), 71-76. The original of the quote is: "einige bekamen ein Zittern in allen Gliedern, einige fangen jämmerlich im Schlaf an zu schreyen, und so sie erweckt werden, sagen sie, der Graf Zinzendorf sey da und greife mit ausgestreckten Armen nach ihnen. Andern kommen gantze Truppen und Menge Herrnhuter vor, und ängsten sie." Anonymous (perhaps Johann Adam Gruber), "Ausführliche Nachricht von Zinzendorfs Unternehmungen in Pennsylvania, 1742-43," 97-236 (here 234-35) in "Americanische Nachrichten von Herrnhutischen Sachen," in *Bewährte Nachrichten von Herrnhutischen Sachen*, ed. Johann Philip Fresenius, vol. 3 (Frankfurt am Main and Leipzig, 1748).

14. I have read the original German of Mühlenberg's correspondence for this study: see Heinrich Melchior Mühlenberg to Johann Philip Fresenius, 15 Nov. 1751, in Kurt Aland, ed., *Die Korrespondenz Heinrich Melchior Mühlenbergs aus der Anfangszeit des deutschen Luthertums in Nordamerika*, 5 vols. (Berlin: Walter de Gruyter, 1986- 1996), 1:443-54, here 443-44. The translation reproduced in the quotation above is from the new English version of Mühlenberg's correspondence. See John W. Kleiner and Helmut T. Lehmann, trans. and ed., *The Correspondence of Heinrich Melchior Mühlenberg* (Camden, Me.: Picton Press, 1997), 2:166-79, here 167.

15. Bonomi, "Watchful against the Sects."

16. See Diarium der Schwester Anna Nitschmann Von Ihre Reysse nacher Pennsylvanien, R. 14. A. 26. 65., Unity Archives, Herrnhut, Germany, and Fogleman, *Jesus Is Female*, 96-102.

17. Fogleman, *Jesus Is Female*, 113-130.

18. Glatfelter uses the term "Moravian threat" when discussing these events in the 1740s (see *Pastors and People*, 1:81-96). On the polemics see Dietrich Meyer, ed., *Bibliographisches Handbuch zur Zinzendorf-Forschung* (Düsseldorf: C. Blech, 1987), Section B (267-582), which includes books, pamphlets, and magazines, but not broadsides. See also Meyer's discussion

in "Zinzendorf und Herrnhut." Lütjeharms (*Het Philadelphisch-Oecumenisch Streven der Herrnhutters*, esp. 179-211), Peucker ("Der Amsterdamer Hirtenbrief von 1738"), and Van Den Berg ("Die Frömmigkeitsbestrebungen in den Niederlanden") discuss the impact of these writings on the struggle against the Moravians in the Netherlands. Many of the anti-Moravian polemics were printed or reprinted in North America and are cataloged in Karl John Richard Arndt, Reimer C. Eck, et al., eds., *The First Century of German- Language Printing in the United States of America*, vol. 1 (1728-1807) (Göttingen: Niedersächsische Staats- und Universitätsbibliotek, 1989).

19. For a detailed discussion of the violence at Lancaster, see Fogleman, *Jesus Is Female*, 206-12. Thomas J. Müller discusses many of the problems in Lancaster but not the violence or the Moravian issues. See *Kirche zwischen zwei Welten: Die Obrigkeitsproblematik bei Heinrich Melchior Mühlenberg und die Kirchengründung der deutschen Lutheraner in Pennsylvania* (Stuttgart: Steiner, 1994), 104–56.

20. Fogleman, *Jesus Is Female*, 192-206.

21. Fogleman, *Jesus Is Female*, 110-30 and 185-216.

22. For a good overview of Halle Pietism during this period that includes the overseas mission see Martin Brecht, "Der Hallische Pietismus in der Mitte des 18. Jahrhunderts–seine Ausstrahlung und sein Niedergang," in *Geschichte des Pietismus*, ed. Brecht and Depperman, 2:319-57; and Ward, *Protestant Evangelical Awakening*. On the work of the Halle pietists in the colonies see Müller, *Kirche zwischen zwei Welten*; Roeber, *Palatines, Liberty, and Property*; Renate Wilson, *Pious Traders in Medicine: A German Pharmaceutical Network in Eighteenth-Century North America* (University Park: Pennsylvania State University Press, 2000); Leonard R. Riforgiato, *Missionary of Modernity: Henry Melchior Muhlenberg and the Lutheran Church in English America* (Lewisburg, Pa.: Bucknell University Press, 1980); Theodore C. Tappert, "The Influence of Pietism in Colonial American Lutheranism," in *Continental Pietism and Early American Christianity*, ed. Stoeffler, 13-33. For Mühlenberg's correspondence, journal, and reports, see Theodore G. Tappert and John W. Doberstein, eds. and trans., *The Journal of Henry Melchior Muhlenberg*, 3 vols. (Philadelphia: Evangelical Lutheran Ministerium of Pennsylvania and Adjacent States and Mühlenberg Press, 1942-58); Aland, ed., *Korrespondenz*; Johann Ludewig Schulze, *Nachrichten von den vereinigten Deutschen Evangelisch-Lutherischen Gemeinen in Nord-America: absonderlich in Pensylvanien*, 2 vols. (Halle: In Verlegung des Waisenhauses, 1787), and the expanded edition of the same title edited by W.J. Mann, B.M. Schmucker, and W. Germann, eds., 2 vols. (Vol. 1: Allentown, 1886, and vol. 2: Philadelphia, 1895). The *Hallesche Nachrichten* contains reports, letters, and diary segments from the other Halle pastors in North America; however, they are heavily censored and omit many important passages on the conflict with the Moravians. This is not only true of the eighteenth-century published editions, but even for the nineteenth-century edition, which is expanded, but still incomplete. I have consulted the manuscript diaries in the Lutheran Archives Center in Philadelphia and the Archives of the Francke Foundations in Halle, Germany.

23. For Mühlenberg's attitude toward other Lutheran ministers during this period see his numerous letters to Gotthilf August Francke in Halle and Friedrich Michael Ziegenhagen in London, e.g., those dated 3 Dec. 1742, 22 Sept. and 25 Nov. 1743, and 6 Mar. 1745, as well as his letter to Caspar Stoever, 20 Jan. 1747, in Aland, ed., *Korrespondenz*, vol. 1. For

Handschuh, see entries for April 1748, esp. 17-24 Apr.: Pastor Handschuchs Diaria von 13. Jan. 1748 bis 2ten Martii 1753, AFSt/M 4 H 10, Archives of the Francke Foundations, Halle, Germany.

24. Glatfelter found thirty Lutheran congregations in 1742, the year Mühlenberg began the Hallensian work in the Pennsylvania field, and fifty-three in 1748 (see *Pastors and People*, 2:52-53 and 139). On the Halle pastors' intervention in Lutheran church community disputes see Müller, *Kirche zwischen zwei Welten*, 104-56 and Paul A.W. Wallace, *The Muhlenbergs of Pennsylvania* (Philadelphia: University of Pennsylvania Press, 1950), 48-55.

25. Fogleman, *Jesus Is Female*, 164-71.

26. On the establishment of the ministerium see *Documentary History of the Evangelical Lutheran Ministerium of Pennsylvania and Adjacent States: Proceedings of the Annual Conventions from 1748 to 1821* (Philadelphia, 1898).

27. Johann Philip Boehm, *Getreuer Warnungs Brief an die Hochteutsche Evangelisch Reformierten Gemeinden und alle deren Glieder, in Pensylvanien, Zur getreuen Warschauung, vor denen Leuthen, welche unter dem nahmen von Herrn-Huther bekandt seyn* (Philadelphia: Andrew Bradford,1742) and Boehm, *Abermahlige treue Warnung und Vermahnung an meine sehr werthe und theurer geschätzte Reformirte Glaubens-verwandte* (Philadelphia: Cornelia Bradford and Isaiah Warner, 1743).

28. Glatfelter, *Pastors and People*, vol. 2; James I. Good and William J. Hinke, trans. and eds., *Minutes and Letters of the Coetus of the German Reformed Congregations in Pennsylvania, 1747-1792, together with Three Preliminary Reports of Rev. John Philip Boehm, 1734-1744* (Philadelphia: Reformed Church Pub. Bd., 1903); William J. Hinke, ed., *Life and Letters of the Rev. John Philip Boehm, Founder of the Reformed Church in Pennsylvania, 1683-1749* (Philadelphia: Sunday School Board of the Reformed Church in the United States, 1916).

29. Good and Hinke, eds., *Minutes and Letters of the Coetus of the German Reformed Congregations in Pennsylvania*; Hinke, ed., *Life and Letters of the Rev. John Philip Boehm*; Michael Schlatter, "A True History of the Real Condition of the Destitute Congregations in Pennsylvania," in Henry Harbaugh, ed. and trans., *Life of Rev. Michael Schlatter* (Philadelphia, 1857), 87-234. Glatfelter, *Pastors and People*, vols. 1 and 2; James Tanis, "Reformed Pietism in Colonial America," in *Continental Pietism and Early American Christianity*, ed. Stoeffler, 34-73.

30. Historians of the Middle Colonies have been especially important in developing this interpretation. See Rothermund, *The Layman's Progress*; Marilyn J. Westerkamp, *Triumph of the Laity: Scots-Irish Piety and the Great Awakening, 1625-1760* (New York: Oxford University Press, 1988); Wolfgang Splitter, *Pastors, People, Politics: German Lutherans in Pennsylvania, 1740-1790* (Trier: Wissenschaftlicher Verlag, 1998). Roeber, *Palatines, Liberty, and Property*, stresses the importance of property issues in this scenario. For examples of general studies of the Great Awakening that include at least part of this interpretation, see Alan E. Heimert, *Religion and the American Mind* (Cambridge, Mass.: Harvard University Press, 1966); Richard Hofstadter, *America at 1750: A Social Portrait* (New York: Alfred A. Knopf, 1971); Bonomi, *Under the Cope of Heaven*; Rhys Isaac, *The Transformation of Virginia,*

1740-1790 (Chapel Hill: University of North Carolina Press, 1982).

31. On the Baptist challenge in colonial Virginia see Isaac, *The Transformation of Virginia.*

32. In recent years a voluminous literature has developed on the role of gender in creating, challenging, and maintaining the social order of Lutheran and Reformed communities from the Reformation to the 19th century. See, for example, Lyndal Roper, *Oedipus and the Devil: Witchcraft, Sexuality, and Religion in Early Modern Europe* (London: Routledge, 1994); Joel F. Harrington, *Reordering Marriage and Society in Reformation Germany* (Cambridge: Cambridge University Press, 1995); Heide Wunder, *He Is the Sun, She Is the Moon: Women in Early Modern Germany*, trans. Thomas Dunlap (Cambridge, Mass.: Harvard University Press, 1998); Witt, *Bekehrung, Bildung und Biographie*; Merry E. Wiesner, *Women and Gender in Early Modern Europe*, 2nd ed. (Cambridge: Cambridge University Press, 2000); Giesela Engel, Ursula Kern, Heide Wunder (eds.), *Frauen in der Stadt: Frankfurt im 18. Jahrhundert* (Königstein/Taunus: Ulrike Helmer Verlag, 2002); Ulrike Gleixner, *Pietismus und Bürgertum: Württemberg 17.–19. Jahrhundert* (Göttingen: Vandenhoek and Ruprecht, 2005).

The Wheels of Commerce: Market Networks in the Lehigh and Musconetcong Valleys, 1735-1800

MICHAEL V. KENNEDY

WHEN LUDWIG NUSPICKEL CARTED A WAGONLOAD of pig iron to Bethlehem, Pennsylvania, in September 1772, he began a relationship with the Durham Ironworks that would last nearly twenty years. Nuspickel was a tenant farmer who lived in Springfield Township, four miles from the Durham Furnace. He transported raw and cast-iron goods for the ironworks throughout the Lehigh Valley, as well as to New Jersey and Philadelphia. Like most farmers who carted goods for ironworks, he did not work full-time, but carried occasional loads, usually in the fall and early winter. He earned between 10 shillings and £2 per trip, depending on the distance he traveled and the weight he carried.[1]

By 1775, the Lehigh River Valley in Pennsylvania and its mirror, the Musconetcong River Valley east of the Delaware River in New Jersey, incorporated a 2,500 square-mile network of commercial markets. Full- and part-time teamsters, many of them farmers like Nuspickel, linked these markets together, moving agricultural commodities, craft goods, and industrial products throughout the area. A proportion of the goods produced there, particularly grains and iron, also went to Philadelphia, Perth Amboy, Newark, and Trenton, and ultimately reached Wilmington, Delaware, New York City, the West Indies, and England.[2]

All roads did not lead to Philadelphia and many rural producers did not look to the great ports for markets. Traditional historiographical emphasis on *direct* connection to major markets has concealed much of the commercial activity of colonists. Most small producers did not keep records themselves, but left evidence of their activities in the books of iron companies, milling complexes, general stores, tanneries and other commercial enterprises. These records reveal the beehive of market activity at the Forks of the Delaware after 1735.[3]

Primary evidence for this study comes from the records of the Durham Ironworks, located at the southernmost point of the Forks of the Delaware in upper Bucks County, Pennsylvania. The records of seven other iron companies, five milling complexes, and four general stores complete the picture. These records include references to other businesses, including 34 distilleries, seven additional ironworks, seven general stores, 130 mills, and 25 inns and taverns. They document the commercial involvement of literally thousands of individuals and households for over sixty years.[4]

Central to this paper are the 362 men who received payment for hauling goods in this 2,500 square-mile market. Also examined are the roads they traveled, how often they traveled them, and the goods they moved. Included are more than four thousand other individuals from the area who appear in existing records, as well as settlement patterns on both sides of the Delaware, production for various markets, and connections between commercial operations. This shotgun approach demonstrates the plethora of commercial activities at the forks of the Delaware in the eighteenth century.

The population of this market region grew precipitously in the second half of the eighteenth century. In 1740, approximately 800 households were scattered in the Greater Lehigh Valley of Pennsylvania, in what was then called Upper Bucks County. By 1775, nearly 2,500 families resided in the area; by 1800, over 6,000 resided there. On the New Jersey side of the Delaware, settlement proceeded more quickly. By 1740, nearly 1,500 families lived there; by 1775, approximately 5,000; and by 1800, over 9,000. In total, therefore, the base of productive, consumptive, and labor markets grew over six decades from approximately 2,300 households to over 15,000.[5]

The settlers who moved into this region were mainly German and Scots-Irish immigrants without the capital to purchase land or establish farms.[6] In Pennsylvania and New Jersey, resident owners of large land tracts could rarely find buyers prior to the American Revolution. By offering leases on relatively easy terms, they secured tenants to improve their land and its value. Absentee landlords also offered leases, but had more trouble with settlers simply squatting on land.[7] While most immigrants sought land either through purchase, lease, or "borrowing," many never farmed independently, but worked for wages throughout their lives in agriculture or industry. On both sides of the Delaware by the 1770s, over 35 percent of adult males were wage workers without land. In the Greater Lehigh Valley in 1775, nearly half the remainder were tenants, and in the Musconetcong Valley between 1720 and the Revolution over 60 percent of farmers leased their land.[8]

Tenants, however, often produced as many agricultural surpluses as farm owners. In fact, the growing market for agricultural commodities encouraged tenants to produce goods for sale. Tenant families comprised most of the farmers who produced surpluses of wheat, rye, oats, barley, buckwheat, corn, flax, hay and straw, vegetables, potatoes, turnips, eggs, butter and cheese, apples, livestock, and other commodities for local markets.[9]

Although a few historians still cling to the myth of the pre-eminence of a simple barter economy in colonial America, the growth of cities and towns, as well as the population of industrial workers in the eighteenth-century mid-Atlantic region belies that argument.[10] Pennsylvania, for example, was consistently fifteen to seventeen percent urban from 1740 to 1790. New Jersey's population was seven to eight percent urban during the same period, and many farmers in the southwestern two-thirds of that colony supplied Philadelphia. With a combined urban population of nearly fourteen percent in the two colonies by mid-century, farmers had to produce a combined fourteen percent annual surplus to support the towns and cities.[11]

Still more agricultural products were destined for export across the Atlantic. While vegetables, fruits, and dairy products went to local and regional markets, grains, seed, and dried meats were exported overseas. Farmers in western New Jersey and in Chester and Lancaster Counties, Pennsylvania, sent flour and whole grain to Perth Amboy and Philadelphia by the 1740s. From there merchants exported these products to the West Indies, England, and later southern Europe. Before the American Revolution, about one-third of the grain, half the flaxseed, and one-quarter of the dried meat – twenty percent of the region's agricultural produce – went overseas.[12]

Finally, while most landless men and women in the colonies worked at least part of the time for wages in agriculture, at least one-fifth of rural adult males worked full-time in industry by the mid-eighteenth century.[13] These full-time employees at ironworks, mills, tanneries, glassworks, blacksmith and cooper shops, and other rural establishments bought food produced by others. Landless workers in the Lehigh and Musconetcong Valleys were no exception. By 1775, the region claimed fourteen iron companies, fifteen tanneries, 61 inns and taverns, at least two dozen commercial distilleries, and nearly 150 commercial mills. These companies employed over 1,600 full-time workers annually. About twenty percent of the households in the region had at least one member working full time in industry; eight percent had two or more.[14] Many of these full-time workers were either landowning craftspeople who deferred farm work to wives, children, or hired workers, or young adults from landowning families whose services on the farm were not imperative. More than half, however, were landless workers.[15]

In order to support this industrial portion of the rural population, the urban population, *and* the export market, the agricultural workforce generated an annual surplus of nearly 50 percent of all commodities (above and beyond any surpluses channeled into non-commercial community exchanges). Individual households, of course, produced widely varying surpluses of specific commodities, sometimes as much as 200 to 300 percent over family needs. And almost all farms contributed to, and profited from, producing commercial surpluses.[16]

Both agriculture and industry in the Lehigh and Musconetcong Valleys depended on good roads to transport commercial products. Business owners and farmers petitioned the Pennsylvania and New Jersey provincial governments to approve new roads and improve existing roads with tax monies. Although many petitioners had political and economic influence, getting governmental road work done was almost impossible. If only roads constructed through the approval of colonial governments had existed, transport would indeed have been limited. Most roads throughout the Lehigh and Musconetcong Valleys before 1775 were old Indian trails that had been improved unofficially through a combination of need and use.[17]

William Penn, always interested in commercial development, wanted to build a network of roads. In his original plans for the colony, he allowed six acres in every hundred to create roads, patterned in parallel lines running from southeastern to northwestern points off the Delaware, and intersected at right angles periodically in settled areas to ease the movement of goods from hinterlands to markets. In 1683, the King's Highway was to be laid out and "made passable for horses and carts" from the Schuylkill River to the Neshaminy Creek.[18] Despite Penn's good intentions, however, a geometric network of roads never developed. Settlement patterns necessitated roads in certain areas before others, while the availability of Indian trails and the inability to raise funds for road construction rendered his plans impractical.

Before 1692, only two roads were laid out officially at public expense. The first was the King's Highway; the second, a narrower wagon path from Philadelphia through Bristol to Middletown in Lower Bucks County. By 1740, of seventeen official roads in Pennsylvania, only the Durham Road and its branches extended into the northern section of Bucks county. The appellation Durham Road began when a road from Bristol in the southernmost part of Bucks was extended in the early 1720s nearly to the forks of the Delaware, where James Logan was building the Durham Furnace.

Over the next twenty years, the Durham Road was extended to the Lehigh River northwest of Durham. Branches of the road were also built and given various names, which changed depending on the ownership of adjacent farms and mills. The two most important branches of the Durham Road were the Easton Fork, which ran northeast to the Delaware and eventually met the Easton Road; and the Bethlehem Fork, which turned northwest three miles north of the Durham Furnace. The Bethlehem Fork continued four miles to Bethlehem, then turned north eight miles to Nazareth by 1745. Before 1760, no other major roads financed by the colony extended north of Bethlehem.[19]

In New Jersey, the Assembly passed its first act dealing with roads in 1716. The act had little impact on the construction of public roads, particularly in the northwest quarter of the colony, the Musconetcong region. Instead, "private interests...improved or constructed roads to serve their own needs."[20]

In both the Lehigh and Musconetcong Valleys before the Revolution, many large landowners, commercial mill owners, and ironmasters cleared wagon trails, used extant Indian paths, and connected their farms and industries to the few major commercial arteries in Pennsylvania and New Jersey. References to "the road to Stover's Mill," "Clymers millroad," and "the Oxford Furnace Road," among hundreds of others, appear regularly in business account books in the 1740s and 1750s, and concern pathways without official standing. All major commercial operations had at least one road that met a highway; some had two or three. As villages and towns grew up around these industries in the late eighteenth and early nineteenth centuries, most of these paths became streets or improved roads. While neither Penn's geometric road network nor the New Jersey Assembly's highways had come to pass by the mid-eighteenth century, a healthy commercial system existed in the Lehigh and Musconetcong region, supplemented by hundreds of sinuous wagon trails connecting farms and industries.[21]

These trails evidently handled traffic as easily as the main roads in the colonies, based on the time and distances carters traveled delivering goods from one location to another. James Lemon has noted correctly that "thirty miles was the maximum distance a loaded wagon could cover in a day under favorable weather conditions."[22] On the best eighteenth-century roads, those leading to Philadelphia, teamsters who traveled forty to fifty miles one-way made the round-trip to the city, including loading and unloading and staying overnight, in three days over 80 percent of the time.[23] Travel times over mill and ironworks roads in the Lehigh and Musconetcong Valleys during the same period are similar. The account books of the fifteen commercial operations document 2,613 trips from 1735 to 1800.[24] Eight hundred and sixty-two (33 percent) referred to day of departure and the day of return.[25] Table 1 illustrates these trips.

The average round-trip covered 29 miles, indicating a market area with a radius of approximately 15 miles. The average trip took 1.28 days, which accords with a 30 mile per day maximum for commercial transport under favorable weather conditions. And while 95 percent of the trips took place between April and December, some doubtless occurred during rain and snow. In fact, twelve percent (103/862) of these trips averaged over 34 miles per day, an indication that hinterland roads were suitable for routine commercial transport.[26]

Table 2 identifies the goods carried around the area, and reflects their sources. Iron forges, for example, shipped cast-iron goods, such as pot ware and stoves, to shops and taverns in the area. Michael Hart, an Easton shopkeeper, bought 117 pots, 56 kettles, 29 skillets, and 20 stoves between 1782 and 1784, while tavern keeper Henry Kooken bought fourteen stoves in one year from Durham. Samuel Lippincott bought several hundred pounds of pot ware each year from the Greenwich Forge for his Hunterdon County, New Jersey store. Gristmills shipped flour to towns, iron companies, and general stores. Carters also carried flour to taverns and inns, such as Bernhart Van Horn's and George Groover's in the Lehigh Valley.[27] Wagoners carted boards, planks, and shingles from sawmills to ironworks, tanneries, and towns between the river valleys, where it was used to build and improve furnace and forge buildings, new mills, shops, inns, and homes. Carpenters, joiners, chair and wagon makers, wheelwrights, and millwrights bought processed wood from the sawmills to use in their own crafts.

The men who hauled freight came from a cross section of society. Wealthy landowners occasionally were paid for hauling goods. Most carters, however, fully two-thirds, were moderate landowners and tenant farmers and their elder sons (including eight free blacks) who transported goods two or three times a year for local businesses. Ninety-three professional teamsters, on the other hand, accom-

Table 1:
Commercial Trips Throughout the Lehigh and Musconetcong Valleys, 1735-1800

Number of Trips	Distance	Round-Trip 1 Day	2 Days	3 Days
645	10-30 Miles	627	18	0
116	31-50 Miles	29	80	7
89	51-80 Miles	0	71	18
12	81+ Miles	0	2	10

Table 2:
Commodities Shipped from Commercial Businesses in Lehigh and Musconetcong Valleys, 1735-1800[28]

Commodity	Wagonloads	Tonnage	Commodity	Wagonloads	Tonnage
Pig Iron	702	1229	Lumber	186	177
Cast Iron	361	622	Flour	676	1057
Bar Iron	316	460	Oil	136	48
Rod/Nails	21	24	Lime	68	71
Bricks	4	7	Sundries	143	136

plished most of the region's hauling, making over 60 percent of commercial trips. Eighteen slaves hauled freight, though no identifiable servants appear, perhaps an indication of the greater possibility of their running away, taking valuable merchandise with them.[29]

Professional teamsters averaged about 39 miles per trip, while farmers made shorter trips – usually about fourteen miles. Some teamsters covered a larger geographic area, even in the 1740s. James Smith, hauling for the Durham Ironworks between 1745 and 1749, carried pig iron and sundry goods from Philadelphia and the Trenton Ironworks to the Oxford Furnace in Hunterdon County and from Bethlehem, Pennsylvania, to the Union Ironworks in High Bridge, New Jersey. His trips covered a 1,900 square-mile area. Four other teamsters worked for Durham in the same years, transporting goods around an 800 square-mile area at the Forks of the Delaware. Durham hired eleven farmers who occasionally traveled a smaller market zone, usually between Durham and Bethlehem or a New Jersey forge, a range of approximately 250 square miles.[30]

Similarly, in the 1740s, Jacob Janeway, who owned a gristmill in New Jersey twenty-five miles from the Musconetcong River, hired farmers to carry goods to destinations less than ten miles distant. He hired teamsters, however, to cart goods to and from Union Forge, over twenty miles away.[31]

By the 1760s and 1770s, on the other hand, farmers like Ludwig Nuspickel often made longer trips to more varied locations. Nuspickel carried bar iron, cast iron, and stoves to Philadelphia, and returned to Durham with items such as sugar, tar, and linen. He also traveled to Northampton Town with kettles, pots, skillets, and stoves for Peter Rhodes's store, and to Upper Saucon Township with ironware for Jacob Ziegenfus's inn. Nuspickel's work for Durham once or twice a year garnered him an extra £1 to £2 annually during lulls in the agricultural cycle. Nuspickel was typical of the dozen or more farmers Durham hired every year as carters.[32]

Other farmers, like Jacob Dehart, combined hauling for ironworks with the sale of farm produce. Dehart, a farmer near High Bridge, New Jersey, sold grain to David Ross's mill store, and carried flour and dry goods back for sale to the Union Ironworks. He sold grain and flaxseed to Mehelm and Berry's Mills in Hunterdon County, New Jersey, and vegetables and hay to Union. He carried nails and pot ware from there back to Mehelm and Berry's Mill Store, and flour (perhaps made from his own grain) back to the Union Works. Because he was paid for carting Union's goods, Dehart was able to realize a greater profit on his own produce, as he bore no transportation costs. Most wagons could carry two tons of iron goods; the average load farmers carted was only 1.3 tons. Farmers, therefore, could complement the paid freight with up to three-quarters of a ton of their own products at no cost to themselves.[33]

Nor were they limited to their own farm products. Some resold goods they purchased elsewhere. Casper Schaeffer, Jr., for example, a miller who lived north of Hackettstown, traveled over twenty-five miles to Greenwich Forge to sell his flour. He did not make the highest possible profits selling his goods there, but he could sell the cast-iron ware he purchased at the forge along his return route. Schaeffer may have made similar transactions at the Oxford and Andover Furnaces, both of which were less than fifteen miles from his mill.[34]

Since farmers rarely carried freight to more than one or two locations, however, teamsters formed the main link among markets in the area. John Tunis moved pig iron from the furnaces in north-central New Jersey to the five forges on the Musconetcong in the 1760s and 1770s. He also carried flour for several mills, including Garret Rapalje's Brooklyn Works outside Hackettstown, Edward Randolph's mills near Round Valley, and David Ross's mill in Elizabeth Town. Tunis carried hoops and staves to Ross's cooper shop, barrels and casks to other mills and stores, and dry goods from these stores. In the 1770s and 1780s, Michael Rosenberg carried oil and leather from Bethlehem to Durham, and pig iron from Durham to Greenwich Forge in New Jersey, along with rice, coffee and cloth from Philadelphia. In the 1780s and early 1790s, John Dennis carried pig and cast iron from Durham to Chelsea Forge and the Union Ironworks, lumber and flour from Randolph's Mills back to Union, rods and nails from there to Coryell's Ferry, near New Hope, and flour from the mills at New Hope, as well as grain and hay from Bucks County farmers back to Durham.

Like farmers, teamsters who hauled goods for ironworks often purchased pot ware and stoves that they resold on their routes. And while farmers carried an average of 1.3 tons of goods, teamsters carried an average of 1.6 tons in larger wagons capable of hauling 2.5 tons. Joseph Fry regularly purchased stoves and pot ware from the Durham Ironworks' store just before hauling freight for the company. He made 24 trips in 36 months, during which time he purchased twelve stoves and 800 pounds of pots and pans. Philip Harple worked as a teamster for Durham in 1783 and made nine trips around the Lehigh Valley, selling six stoves and nearly 500 pounds of pot ware he had purchased on his own account. Michael Rosenberg bought 22 skillets from Greenwich Forge in 1782-83, four or five whenever he hauled goods for the company throughout the Musconetcong Valley. Although most of David Stover's travels took him to Philadelphia, he purchased 39 stoves and two tons of pot ware from Durham during the ten months he made 92 deliveries for the ironworks. More than half the teamsters who worked for Durham bought cast iron at the time of their trips. Certainly, some of these purchases were for personal use, but the size of most of them, including multiple stoves, indicate resale activity.[35]

Teamsters and farmers could profit from sales of ironware on their routes, because the prices they paid at iron company stores were 25 to 50 percent less than a consumer twenty or more miles away would pay at a store for the same item. Store owners, of course, added both transport costs and their profits to the price of goods. Teamsters could charge farm families ten to 20 percent over their cost for the iron and make a profit. Rural people who purchased ironware neither had to travel to ironworks themselves nor pay higher prices at local stores. The teamsters incurred no transportation costs for these goods because they were being paid to carry other freight over the route. These resale transactions, therefore, increased market activity in the countryside beyond the evidence in ironworks' store accounts. While teamsters did not record the extent of their activities, the process was routine.[36]

The teamsters' sales, however, could satisfy the consumer needs of only the small percentage of rural households located on their routes. Accounts of ironworks, mill shops, and general stores demonstrate that at least 50 percent of households within a 300-mile radius of these marketplaces bought goods from the companies every year. In more densely populated areas where several stores competed, nearly 70 percent of households made consumer purchases at one or more locations. The available evidence shows that most families made between five and ten such purchases a year. As less than five percent of eighteenth-century store records from the Lehigh and Musconetcong Valleys survive, it is reasonable to assume that over 90 percent of the region's rural population engaged in at least one commercial transaction a year.[37]

Fewer local families sold (rather than bought) agricultural or craft goods at individual stores in the area, but between five and ten percent of all families did so at each store. Most rural households had the opportunity to sell goods locally, given the eighteenth-century proliferation of stores they could reach in a half-day or less.[38]

Indeed, the store records in this study alone contain entries for 21,485 sales of commercial products by farmers, craftspeople, and others. Table 3 lists the various goods delivered and sold to the stores, including grains, dairy products, wood, and vegetables.[39]

Farmers most often sold small shipments of grain. Company records note 7,613 separate sales of grain – most between eight and 30 bushels – to ironworks and gristmills. Some farmers sold more than one type of grain annually, and often made separate trips to do so. Richard Compton, for example, made three to four trips each year between 1735 and 1746 to Jacob Janeway's mill on Bound Brook in New Jersey with loads of wheat, oats, and flaxseed. None of the loads included more than 29 bushels, but his yearly totals averaged 61 bushels. Less than one percent of farmers sold more than 100 bushels of grain in a single year, even when they sold lots to more than one operation. Similarly, of the 73 farmers who sold grain to Samuel Hartshorne's mill in Milford, Pennsylvania, in 1772, 66 made between two and four deliveries, and sold an average total of 52 bushels. The large number of farmers who sold lots of 30 bushels or less indicates however, that most farmers in the region readily engaged with commercial markets.[40] Only the largest farms could produce commercial quantities of grain that justified a four- or five-day trip to Philadelphia. While transportation costs eliminated small producers from contention in long-distance markets, their activity in local markets was routine.

Dairy and vegetable products, usually delivered by men, were produced by women on farms across the region. Farmers made more than 2,400 sales of such items between 1735 and 1800, usually in small lots; eight to fifteen pounds of butter or fifteen to twenty eggs constituted a typical sale. Potatoes, turnips, and onions were usually sold seven or eight bushels at a time. Individual farmers rarely sold more than 100 pounds of butter or a total of twenty-five bushels of vegetables to any one market in a year. The average household, however, sold 66 pounds of butter and seventeen bushels of vegetables annually, or 88 and fourteen percent (respectively) above average household consumption.[41]

Table 3:
Commodities Sold to Commercial Businesses/Number of Transactions in the Lehigh and Musconetcong Valleys, 1735-1800

C=sold by craftsperson/ I=sold by industry/ others sold by farmers

Product	Transaction	Product	Transaction	Product	Transaction
FOOD:		DRY GOODS:		EQUIPMENT:	
Butter	1004	Thread-C	369	Bellows-C	8
Beef/veal	1556	Stockings-C	209	Candles	36
Pork/bacon	784	Shoes-C	267	Tools	33
Flour	1406	Clothing-C	337	Coal	768
Potatoes	228	Cloth-C	177	Glue	6

THE WHEELS OF COMMERCE

Turnips	178	Flax-C	16	Paper-I	2
Eggs	305	Linen-C	10	Oil-I	25
Vegetables	359	Hats-C	12	Wood	639
Fowl	139	Blankets-C	14	Cordwood	1188
Cheese	97			Iron-I	85
Mutton	30	LIVESTOCK:		Bricks-C	21
Fruit	229	Hogs	315	Cooperage-C	142
Beans	116	Sheep	123	Boards-I	369
Parsnips	124	Cattle	162	Shingles-I	56
Honey	49	Chickens	19	Wheels-C	101
Venison	16	Horses	17	Axles-C	49
Molasses	11			Buckets	4
Salt	10	MISC:		Lime	71
Nuts	4	Patterns-C	15	Tallow/Fat	19
		Offal	17	Ashes	34
GRAINS:		Tobacco	10	Baskets	169
Wheat	4071	Vinegar	7	Hides	102
Rye	1103	Chairs-C	5	Livery-C	47
Oats	472	Bowls	2	Leather-I	33
Corn	411	Locks-C	4		
Buckwheat	506	Squirrels	2	POTABLES:	
Bran	15	Paint	2	Cider	129
Straw/hay	356	Stones	81	Whiskey	33
Flaxseed	661	Sundries	484	Rum	11

Families also found markets for the timber they cut on newly established or expanding farms. Sawmills typically purchased trees and logs from surrounding farms to complement the wood cut on their own property. The accounts of Stephen Brant's (1772-1775) and Edward Randolph's (1789-1800) sawmills and the mill attached to the Hanover Furnace include 639 sales of timber from area farmers. Mill owners (as in most transactions) paid farmers with a combination of cash and store credit. Ironworks also bought wood from local families, usually as cordwood cut for charcoal. The extant records of Hanover and Durham Furnaces and Greenwich, Union, and Chelsea Forges reveal 1,188 purchases, more than 145,000 cords of wood. Farmers received payment for the wood itself and their labor in cutting it. The most common lot was 100 cords, although a number of farmers contracted to deliver between 200 and 500 cords in a single year.[42]

Markets for various commodities evolved over time, particularly at ironworks, as the structure of the industry changed. In 1744, for example, nineteen local families sold 606 pounds of butter to the Durham Ironworks, which used it as part of the diet of the company's full-time workforce of 61 men (including twelve slaves and two servants). In the same year, only three farmers sold wood to Durham. The Durham records for 1784, on the other hand, reveal no purchases of butter, but 34 farmers from as far away as 22 miles sold over 3,800 cords of wood, mainly in lots of 100 to 300. The market for butter had disappeared and the market for wood had grown precipitously, as the organization of the Durham works changed. In 1744, after seventeen years of operation, the Durham Company still owned large tracts of woodland, and employed its own workers, some full-time, some part-time, to cut wood on its property. The works did not seek other sources of cordwood. In 1744, however, Durham did not have farms that raised dairy cattle, so it purchased butter, among other foodstuffs, from local farmers.

By 1784, on the other hand, most of the Durham tract had been denuded of forest and made into farmland. Durham established a company farm that raised hay, flax, and cattle, and where the company produced some of its own butter. Other Durham land was leased to tenants, whose contracts required them to supply butter as part of the rent: outside farmers no longer found a market for butter at Durham. Durham had, since the 1760s, however, been forced to buy the cordwood necessary for charcoal from local farmers. In 1784, Durham purchased 86 percent of the wood it used to make charcoal for its furnace, and wood had replaced butter as a key marketable commodity in the Lehigh Valley.[43]

Few farmers butchered meat for sale to company stores, but those who did sold small lots of between 125 and 150 pounds a year, about fifteen percent above household consumption. On average, at least six farmers supplied meat to ironworks and milling complexes to feed each full-time employee. Ironworks managers, moreover, often bought young livestock, and raised some meat for employees' consumption. In all, the records include 2,796 deliveries of meat and 636 sales of livestock.[44]

Craftspeople also sold goods occasionally to ironworks and mills. Wheelwrights, for example, made and sold axletrees, wheels, and hitches for wagons that moved goods around company property; bellows makers and tanners sold bellows, the leather to repair them, and harnesses; and brick makers sold bricks. Women spun large quantities of thread and sold it to company stores, along with shirts and breeches, mainly for slaves. Women also spun thread and yarn for local weavers, who sold cloth and blankets to nearby businesses.[45]

Altogether, 269 farmers like Ludwig Nuspickel and 93 teamsters drove through the extant records of the central Delaware basin. More than 1,000 farmers delivered commodities to company stores. As the industrial records are limited, these numbers only hint at the thousands of people who sold surpluses and moved freight around a small section of the mid-Atlantic colonies of British North America in the eighteenth century. Certainly industrial activity, movement of commercial goods, and connections to longer distance markets increased over time, as did the population, but to deny extensive colonial market awareness and commercial production by the majority of households is to deny the tangible records themselves.

The Lehigh and Musconetcong Rivers that constituted the Forks of the Delaware, the valleys that surrounded them, and the markets they touched were alive with commercial activity by 1735. The growth of the population and the

THE WHEELS OF COMMERCE 219

increase in the number of manufactories, shops, inns, taverns, and towns over the ensuing six decades enhanced the movement of goods over both official and company roads. Hundreds of carriers moved the products of thousands of industrial employees and tens of thousands of farm households over a 2,500 square-mile regional market. Other commodities generated in the valleys reached urban markets further afield and trans-Atlantic markets as well. The commercial history of this area is complex because of the number of small markets it contained, but it should not be ignored in favor of larger, more cosmopolitan places. At times, one misses the *trees* for the *forest.*

Notes

1. Durham Ironworks Collection 1727-1794, Bucks County Historical Society (hereafter BCHS); Durham Receipt Book, 1772-1789, Northampton County Historical Society (hereafter NCHS); Durham Ledger 1744-1749; Richard Backhouse Ledger, 1775-1782, Historical Society of Pennsylvania (hereafter HSP). Few carters carried loads of less than one ton or over three tons. A one-ton load carried between five and ten miles (one way) usually generated a 10 shilling wage for the carter. A two-ton load carried between thirty and forty miles generated £2.

2. Durham Ironworks Collection, 1727-1794, BCHS; Greenwich Forge Ledgers, 1778-1789; Elk Forge (Wilmington, Del.) Ledgers 1771-1789, HSP; Union Ironworks Ledger, 1773-1774; Samuel Hartshorn Grist and Oil Mill Ledgers, 1772-1781; Thomas Lea Grist Mill Accounts, 1773-1788, Eleutherian Mills and Hagley Library (hereafter EMHL). The region I have included in this study covers the interior geographic area between the Lehigh and Musconetcong Rivers south of the Pocono Mountain Range in Pennsylvania and south of Lake Hopatcong in New Jersey. Also included are the market areas west and east of the respective rivers approximately one day's travel (25 miles) from the farms, towns, and industries located along the rivers.

3. Winifred Rothenberg, "The Market and Massachusetts Farmers, 1750-1855," *Journal of Economic History* 41 (1981): 283-314; Rothenberg, "The Emergence of a Capital Market in Rural Massachusetts, 1730-1838," *Journal of Economic History* 45 (1985): 781-808; Rothenberg, *From Market-Places to a Market Economy: The Transformation of Rural Massachusetts, 1750-1850* (Chicago: University of Chicago Press, 1992); James T. Lemon, "Household Consumption in Eighteenth-Century America and its Relationship to Production and Trade: The Situation Among Farmers in Southeastern Pennsylvania," *Agricultural History* 41 (1967): 59-70; Lemon, *The Best Poor Man's Country: A Geographical Study of Early Southeastern Pennsylvania* (Baltimore: Johns Hopkins University Press, 1972). Direct connection to long-distance markets has been the key to recognized commercial production in the British colonies of North America for over a quarter of a century. Historians whose goal is to deny active participation in commercial markets by the great majority of colonists seek to show limited contact with major market centers, from Philadelphia, New York, and Boston, to London and Bristol. Even historians who recognize market awareness by rural colonists use primarily direct linkages to large market cities as proof of increasing commercial interest in the countryside during the second half of the eighteenth century. Winifred Rothenberg's excellent study of

Massachusetts farmers is an example of this well-meant, but limited approach. Rothenberg uses examples of farmers who weigh market price against transportation cost to justify one-way commercial trips of up to 175 miles in order to turn a profit. Journals and account books from 54 Massachusetts farmers covering the period 1750 to 1850 revealed a total of 1,827 market trips, usually one or two a year, to major market towns such as Springfield and Worcester, or to the primary port of Boston. Certainly the conscious production of market crops and their transport to centers 50, 100, or more miles away reveals an avid market orientation among some Massachusetts farmers. Closer to home for this paper, James Lemon's work on southeastern Pennsylvania similarly concentrates on the Philadelphia market, and farmers with over 125 acres of land. Both studies essentially ignore the fact that the majority of farmers with smaller holdings and much smaller means were also actively involved in commercial market activity.

4. Durham Ironworks Collection, 1727-1794; Aaron Musgrove Store Accounts (Greenwich Forge), 1782-1783; Greenwich Forge Day Books, 1780-1782; Richard Backhouse Wood, Charcoal, and Hauling Book 1780-1789; Chelsea Forge (Fragmentary) Ledger (includes Bloomsbury Forge), 1780-1783; Chelsea Forge Ledger, 1783-1784, BCHS; Union Ironworks Ledger, 1773-1774; Hartshorne Mill Ledgers, 1772-1781, EMHL; Edward F. Randolph Ledger (including mill accounts), 1789-1800; John Bryan General Store Ledger, 1793-1798; Janeway and Broughton General Store Accounts, 1735-1747; Jacob Janeway Mill Ledger 1735-1747, Alexander Library, Rutgers University (hereafter ALR); Mehelm and Berry Store and Mill Accounts, 1772-1774; Stephen Brant Store Ledgers, 1748-1753; Brant Mill Accounts 1772-1797; George Smock General Store Account, 1786-1799; James Parker Diary, 1778-1782, New Jersey Historical Society (hereafter NJHS); Durham Ledger 1744-1749; Hanover Furnace Ledgers, 1793-1795; Mount Hope Forge Ledgers 1784-1789; HSP; Durham Ironworks Scrap Book, 1772-1789, NCHS; Rockaway Forge Ledger, Berks County Historical Society (hereafter Berks). Hereafter, collective references to all of these business records will be cited as Forks Business Papers.

5. *Historical Statistics of the United States: Colonial Times to 1970* (Washington, DC, 1975; repr.White Plains, N.Y.: Kraus International Publications, 1989), Z:1-19, 91-97; Evarts B. Greene and Virginia D. Harrington, *American Population Before the Federal Census of 1790* (New York: Columbia University Press, 1932), 105-20; *Pennsylvania Archives* (Harrisburg, PA, 1897), ser. 3, 13:3-820, and 19:5-400; Terry A. McNealy and Frances Wise Waite, *Bucks County Tax Records, 1693-1778* (Doylestown, Pa.: Bucks County Genealogical Society, 1982); *New Jersey Archives* (Paterson, N.J., 1916), ser. 1, 5:164, 6:242-44, 10:452; Peter O. Wacker, *Land and People, A Cultural Geography of Preindustrial New Jersey: Origins and Settlement Patterns* (New Brunswick, N.J.: Rutgers University Press, 1975), Appendices 2-7, New Jersey Censuses of 1738, 1745, 1772, 1784, 1790, and 1800.

6. Marianne S. Wokeck, "A Tide of Alien Tongues: The Flow and Ebb of German Immigration to Pennsylvania, 1683-1776" (PhD diss.: Temple University, 1982); Wokeck, "German and Irish Immigration to Colonial Philadelphia," *Proceedings of the American Philosophical Society* 133 (1989): 128-43; and Wokeck, *Trade in Strangers: The Beginnings of Mass Migration to North America* (University Park: Pennsylvania State University Press, 1999) are meticulous examinations of origins, migrations, and effects of immigrants to Pennsylvania, and speak to conditions elsewhere in the Mid-Atlantic as well.

7. Peter O. Wacker, *The Musconetcong Valley of New Jersey: A Historical Geography* (New Brunswick, N.J.: Rutgers University Press, 1968), 34-35.

8. *Pennsylvania Archives*, ser. 3, 13:3-98, 19:5-78, 24:107-77, 26:25-211; McNealy and Waite, *Bucks County Tax Records*, 56-57, 64-74, 79-81; Michael V. Kennedy, "An Alternate Independence: Craft Workers in the Pennsylvania Iron Industry, 1725-1775," *Essays in Economic & Business History* 16 (1998): 113-125; Michael V. Kennedy, "Working Agreements: The Use of Sub-Contracting in the Colonial Iron Industry, 1725-1795," *Pennsylvania History* 65 (1998): 492-508; Peter O. Wacker and Paul G. E. Clemens, *Land Use in Early New Jersey: A Historical Geography* (Newark: New Jersey Historical Society, 1995), 92-93; Wacker, *Musconetcong Valley*, 33-37, 68; and Wacker, *Land and People*, 356-65.

9. Lemon, *Best Poor Man's Country*, 150-54; Wacker, *Musconetcong Valley*, 55-64, 132-33; Michael V. Kennedy, "Furnace to Farm: Capital, Labor and Markets in the Pennsylvania Iron Industry, 1716-1789" (PhD diss.: Lehigh University, 1996), 249-70.

10. From an extensive literature concerning agricultural support of urban areas, see Karen J. Friedman, "Victualling Colonial Boston," *Agricultural History* 47 (1973): 189-205; Christopher Clark, *The Roots of Rural Capitalism: Western Massachusetts, 1780-1860* (Ithaca, N.Y.: Cornell University Press, 1990); Richard L. Bushman, "Family Security in the Transition from Farm to City," *Journal of Family History* 6 (1981): 238-56; and Bushman, "Markets and Composite Farms in Early America," *William and Mary Quarterly* 3d ser., 55 (1998): 351-74; Bettye Hobbs Pruitt, "Self-Sufficiency and the Agricultural Economy of Eighteenth-Century Massachusetts," *William and Mary Quarterly* 3d ser., 41 (1984): 333-64; Diane Wenger, "Delivering the Goods: The Country Storekeeper and Inland Commerce in the Mid-Atlantic," *Pennsylvania Magazine of History and Biography* 129 (2005): 45-72; Daniel Vickers, "Competency and Competition: Economic Culture in Early America," *William and Mary Quarterly* 3d ser., 47 (1990): 3-29; and Vickers, *Farmers and Fishermen: Two Centuries of Work in Essex County, Massachusetts, 1630-1850* (Chapel Hill: University of North Carolina Press, 1994). The literature opposing this position, also extensive, has grown more slowly in recent years. For a sampling, see Michael Merrill, "Cash is Good to Eat: Self-Sufficiency and Exchange in the Rural Economy of the United States," *Radical History Review* 3 (1977): 42-77; and Merrill, "Putting 'Capitalism' in Its Place," *William and Mary Quarterly* 3d ser., 52 (1995): 315-26; James A. Henretta, "Families and Farms: Mentalité in Pre-Industrial America," *William and Mary Quarterly* 3d ser., 35 (1978): 3-32; and Allan Kulikoff, *The Agrarian Origins of American Capitalism* (Charlottesville: University Press of Virginia, 1992).

11. *Historical Statistics*, Z:1-19; Greene and Harrington, *American Population*, 105-20. Philadelphia's population was also supported by agricultural produce from northern Maryland and Delaware, but farmers in these colonies also had to support Wilmington, New Castle, Chestertown, Annapolis, and later Baltimore.

12. Lemon, *Best Poor Man's Country*, 181, 27-29, 125.

13. Adult males are those sixteen or older, including heads of households, resident sons, and male inmates. Many fewer women worked full-time in industry.

14. *Pennsylvania Archives,* ser. 3, 13:3-98, 19:5-78; Amelia Mott Gummere, "Forges and Furnaces in the Province of Pennsylvania," *Committee On Historical Research: Pennsylvania Society of Colonial Dames of America Publications* 3 (1914): 1-190; Charles S. Boyer, *Early Forges & Furnaces in New Jersey* (Philadelphia: University of Pennsylvania Press, 1931).

15. Forks Business Papers; *Pennsylvania Archives,* ser. 3, vols. 11-26; *New Jersey Archives,* ser. 1, vols. 5-10.

16. Lemon, *Best Poor Man's Country,* 150-83. Peter Wacker and Paul Clemens have a better handle on this in *Land Use in Early New Jersey,* 89-168, describing the contributions of farms from 20 acres to 2,200 acres.

17. William W. H. Davis, *History of Bucks County, Pennsylvania, From the Discovery of the Delaware to the Present Time,* 2d ed. (New York: The Lewis Publishing Co., 1905), 2:245-46; Wacker, *Land and People,* 57-58; Wacker, *Musconetcong Valley,* 25-27.

18. *Pennsylvania Archives,* ser. 2, 1:121, 146, 383.

19. *Pennsylvania Archives,* ser. 1 & 2; Davis, *History of Bucks County,* 247-53.

20. *New Jersey Archives,* ser. 1, 1:98; Wacker, *Musconetcong Valley,* 134-35, quote on 135.

21. Durham Ledger 1744-1749, HSP; Janeway Ledger, 1735-1747, ALR; Michael V. Kennedy, "'Debtr to the store': The Central Place of Ironworks and Mill Stores in the Mid-Atlantic Market, 1725-1789," unpublished paper presented to the Michigan Seminar in Colonial American History, February, 1998. For an excellent examination of entrepreneurship in the region, see John Bezis-Selfa, *Forging America: Ironworkers, Adventurers, and the Industrious Revolution* (Ithaca, N.Y.: Cornell University Press, 2004), 100-135.

22. Lemon, *Best Poor Man's Country,* 29.

23. Documented trips from eight Pennsylvania ironworks located 40 to 52 miles from Philadelphia reveal the following: Of 1,792 documented trips to the city, 918 (51 percent) relate the timing of the round-trip. The average distance traveled, round-trip, was 88 miles. Six-hundred and eighty-six (74.7 percent) of these trips were completed in three days. Fifty-six (6.1 percent), all from the Durham Furnace, were completed in two days. Durham Ironworks Collection 1727-1794, BCHS; Colebrookdale Furnace Ledgers 1735-1767; Durham Ledger 1744-1749; Elizabeth Furnace Ledgers 1766-1774; Mount Pleasant Ironworks Ledger 1737-1744; New Pine Forge Ledgers 1744-1763; Pine Forge Ledgers 1733-1781; Pottsgrove Furnace Ledgers 1755-1765; Warwick Furnace Ledgers 1747-1762, HSP; Warwick Furnace Ledgers 1789-1792, Chester County Historical Society (hereafter CCHS); Pine Forge Ledgers 1769-1780, EMHL.

24. Forks Business Papers. The 2,613 commercial trips referenced here are limited to the transport of various goods produced by the businesses examined. Not included here are 18,095 separate deliveries of goods to the ironworks, mills, and stores from local farmers and craftspeople in this region. These transactions and deliveries will be addressed later in this essay.

THE WHEELS OF COMMERCE

25. Forks Business Papers. The Durham Ironworks Collection is the most efficiently kept set of available documents for the region, and most transactions are cross-referenced in two or more account books. As a result, approximately 70 percent of the documented trips that can be assessed as to time taken in reference to distance traveled come from the Durham records.

26. Forks Business Papers.

27. Durham Ledger 1744-1749, HSP; Durham Ironworks Ledgers 1780-1789, BCHS; Mehelm & Berry Account Book 1772-1774, NJHS; Hartshorne Mill Ledgers 1772-1780, EMHL; *Pennsylvania Archives*, ser. 3, 13:29-91, 19:5-41, 57-90, 184-244.

28. For flour and oil (flaxseed) bushels and gallons have been converted into approximate tonnage. Sundries are miscellaneous unidentified goods, and shipped by the hundredweight or ton.

29. Three hundred and sixty-two men were paid in existing area records for hauling goods off company property. I have separated these from employees paid as "drivers," those who use company-owned wagons and teams to move goods around ironworks and milling operations. The area records contain references to 208 such drivers: 166 free, 31 slaves, and 11 servants. Their activities, however, are not part of this study. Teamsters are identified because of their general lack of connections to farms, other occupations, and the frequency of their trips, between 5 and 42 a year. Teamsters also appear much more often in the accounts of different companies in a single year, as well as carrying goods for a greater number of years. Teamsters appearing in different company records work an average of 8 years, while farmers, who often did not engage in hauling every year, appear on average for 4 years.

30. Durham Ledger 1744-1749, HSP.

31. Janeway Ledgers 1735-1747, ALR.

32. Durham Ironworks Collection 1727-1794, BCHS.

33. Mehelm and Berry Accounts 1772-1774; Ross Mill Accounts 1756-1794, NJHS; Union Ironworks Ledger 1773-1774, EMHL.

34. Greenwich Forge Ledger 1782-1785, BCHS.

35. Durham Ironworks Collection 1727-1794; Greenwich Forge Ledger 1782-1785, BCHS; Kennedy, "Furnace to Farm," 240-42, and "'Debtr to the store.'"

36. Durham Ironworks Collection 1727-1794, BCHS; Durham Ledger 1744-1749, HSP; Anne Bezanson, et al., *Prices and Inflation During the American Revolution: Pennsylvania 1770-1790* (Philadelphia: University of Pennsylvania Press, 1951).

37. Forks Business Papers; Michael V. Kennedy, "'Cash for his turnups': Agricultural Production for Local Markets in Colonial Pennsylvania, 1725-1783," *Agricultural History* 74

(2000): 587-608; Kennedy, "'Debtr to the store'"; Kennedy, "Furnace to Farm," 247-70.

38. Forks Business Papers; Kennedy, "Cash for his turnups."

39. Over 10 percent of the deliveries contained more than one commodity, some three or more. Sundries is a catchall for deliveries of "goods" and "provisions" as well as "sundries," which were not specified.

40. Forks Business Papers. For example, a family containing three adults (and two young children) with the ability to harvest an acre and a half a day could, in the week before spoilage set in, garner a maximum of twelve acres of grain. This would generate approximately 150 bushels. If the family worked split harvests, in June and again in September, a total of 300 bushels of mixed grains was possible. The hiring of two harvest workers, which most families could manage, might, if the workers exerted themselves as much as the family, result in another 100 bushels, for a total of 400. According to Lemon, *Best Poor Man's Country*, 151-56, a family of five required 290 bushels of mixed grain to support themselves and their livestock. Estimating 10 bushels as payment to harvest workers, this brings the total to 300. The average family with less than 20 acres in grain, with the help of two harvest workers, would then have 100 bushels of grain above the family's needs, a 25 percent surplus. Those with more acreage, perhaps with servants or slaves available, and a greater ability to hire more harvest workers could generate greater surpluses.

41. Forks Business Papers; Lemon, *Best Poor Man's Country*, 150-83; Joan Jensen, *Loosening the Bonds: Mid-Atlantic Farm Women, 1750-1850* (New Haven: Yale University Press, 1986), 81. Jensen estimates that minimum butter consumption was thirteen pounds per person annually at the time of the American Revolution.

42. Brant Account Book 1772-1797, NJHS; Randolph Ledger 1789-1802, ALR; Hanover Furnace Ledger 1793-1795; Durham Ledger 1744-1749, HSP, Union Ironworks Ledger 1773-1774, EMHL; Greenwich Forge Ledgers 1780-1785; Chelsea Forge Journals 1783-1784; Durham Ironworks Collection 1727-1794, BCHS. Cordwood is listed in Table 3 in items of deliveries, as are other commodities. A wagonload of cordwood, however, would be approximately 2 ½ to 3 cords. It would take approximately 50,000 deliveries to bring all of this wood to the ironworks, and the records are not clear on who actually carried much of if. Some accounts specifically credit farmers for the hauling of cordwood, and others note that company employed carters picked it up on farms and brought it in. The majority of the records simply note the arrival. I have, therefore, left the number of sales as the number of deliveries for this commodity. It should be noted, however, that farmers most certainly made more than 1,188 trips with cordwood.

43. Durham Ledger 1744-1749, HSP; Durham Ledgers, Accounts, Memo and Receipt Books 1783-1785, BCHS.

44. Richard Backhouse Memo Book 1782-1784, BCHS; Forks Business Papers.

45. Forks Business Papers.

III

Politics in the New Republic

From Print Shop to Congress and Back: Easton's Thomas J. Rogers and the Rise of Newspaper Politics

JEFFREY L. PASLEY

THE LOCAL NEWSPAPERS OF THE EARLY AMERICAN REPUBLIC are extremely unimpressive specimens to modern eyes. They were typically only four pages long, and half of those pages were advertisements if the paper was successful. There were no maps, no cartoons, usually no illustrations of any kind besides a stereotyped woodcut or two in the advertisements. Sometimes a printer of unusual visual ambition procured a custom woodcut for his masthead, illustrating the name of the journal. Samuel Longcope, the printer of the Lehigh Valley's first English-language newspaper, the Easton *American Eagle*, had a particularly fierce-looking bird atop a shield on his front page. Unfortunately, Longcope was the Valley's last visually ambitious printer for a long while.[1]

Nor was there anything especially creative about the content of early newspapers, little even that a modern reader would recognize as news. Since a typical small-town newspaper's entire staff often consisted only of the printer in whose shop it was published along with his journeymen and apprentices, all of whom were too busy with ink and type and paper to do much but print, no active reporting or systematic news gathering was done. The reader was presented with a barely differentiated mass of tiny type that, upon closer inspection, turned out to be the raw material of news as we know it today, not "stories" but speeches, government documents, political essays, and programs of recent community celebrations.

Only in the case of foreign events, on which the typical early American newspaper was far more informative than local or domestic happenings, would there be any effort to provide any kind of summary or narrative of the news. Most editorial material of any kind in early American newspapers was usually copied from other newspapers (the London journals in the case of foreign news), or from letters written to the printer or one of his neighbors. Sometimes the printer simply jotted down and printed bits of hearsay he picked up in the street or tavern.[2]

Printers tended to compound the unreliability and uninformativeness of the news in the way they arranged their papers. Headlines in the modern sense were nonexistent, and the reports and documents were usually classed not according to their subject or importance, but according to where the material was found. Thus, if you were perusing a copy of the Valley's second English-language newspaper, the Easton *Northampton Farmer*, you might look under the heading "Philadelphia" and find news of a naval battle in the Caribbean. Someone in New York had gotten a letter saying that the French and the British navies had fought a battle near the port of Santo Domingo in the Caribbean, but the Easton printer clipped the item out of a Philadelphia newspaper, so there it was listed.[3] No wonder even Thomas Jefferson, a tremendous supporter of the press, was exasperated by the low quality of the information he found in the newspapers of his time. "I look with real commiseration on my fellow citizens," wrote Jefferson, "who, reading newspapers, live & die in the belief that they have known something of what has been passing in the world."[4]

And yet this is far from the whole story. Strange as it may seem, pathetic little sheets like the *Northampton Farmer* were considered an immense, almost unstoppable political force in their day. As many Americans saw it, newspapers were the "the only voice that can speak daggers to injustice, and awaken the public mind to tyranny." The partisan press that developed in the 1790s was "an overmatch for any government," growled one conservative Federalist after the election of 1800. Like many if not most observers at the time, he blamed Jefferson's triumph on the support he received from the press, and in particular on the work of the Philadelphia *Aurora*.[5]

Edited by an Irish radical named William Duane who had been kicked out of Great Britain for his views, the *Aurora* developed issue after issue into political sticks that could be used to beat John Adams and the Federalists. Some were clearcut and serious, such as the Sedition Act, but many others were more creative, such as a fire in the Treasury Department building that Duane claimed had been set to destroy evidence of corruption that he was close to exposing. In Philadelphia, Duane developed a strong hold over the Democratic Republican party by furiously denouncing those who deviated from what Duane deemed to be the Republican creed, and by building an organized following in the immigrant neighborhoods and in the city militia.[6]

Thanks to Duane and many other editors who fought with, against, and after him, there was nowhere the press loomed larger in politics than Pennsylvania. In Duane's day, words like "tyranny" and "dictator" were employed in all seriousness to describe the power that Pennsylvania newspapers and their editors seemed to hold over politics and public opinion. By the middle of the 19th century, the language had become, if anything, even more hyperbolic. At that time, Pennsylvania editor-politician Alexander McClure remembered later, there were "half a dozen [local] newspapers of either party whose considerate expression on any public question…was vastly more potent in controlling" the course of politics "than a like expression would be from all the newspapers of Philadelphia today." In those days, he wrote, the press "absolutely dominated political conviction and action" and an editor's "deliverances were accepted as commands." Though 20th-century newspapers were infinitely more elaborate, attractive, and profitable than their predecessors, wrote McClure, the political power of the Pennsylvania press had actually declined since the mid-1800s.[7]

How could this be, given the admittedly lackluster nature of the old papers? The answer lies partly in the uneven development of the antebellum party system. On the one hand, the old political parties were far more popular than today's models: voter turnouts were huge, campaign events were a major form of popular entertainment, and people identified with their parties to the point of naming children after Speakers of the House, Vice Presidents, and failed candidates. Yet though the antebellum parties were competing fiercely in every town, county, and state, the party system had many institutional gaps. Parties were not legally recognized by government and possessed no permanent institutional structures, to say nothing of the large office buildings, permanent staffs, and wads of money that the parties possess today. Formal party institutions like national committees and conventions were recent innovations (and the national committees did little in any case). National, state, and local campaign committees might be formed for a particular campaign, but these tended to go dormant or disappear once the campaign was over and so had no ability to shape the party's response to events as they unfolded between elections.[8]

Newspapers filled many of the gaps left by the party system's uneven development, providing a fabric that held the parties together between elections and conventions, connected voters and activists to the larger party, and linked the different political levels and geographic regions of the country. Newspaper offices were unofficial clubhouses and reading rooms of local parties, and newspaper columns were the major source of party doctrine and strategy for activists and voters alike. In most cases, the local party newspapers were the only corporeal or institutional form that the parties had in a community, and a newspaper subscription the only real form of party "membership" or affiliation that existed in this age before voter registration. No politician or party or faction believed that they could accomplish anything without a newspaper, and the first sign of a factional split in a party was usually the founding of a new newspaper.

Similar observations could be made not just about parties, but about early American political associations of all kinds, including religious revivals, moral reform movements, and even the Cherokee Nation. Thus we should think of the early political parties and the political press as not just intimately associated, but fused, as constituent elements of the same system. This convergence of parties and the press, which I call "newspaper politics," was most evident between the turn of the nineteenth century and the Civil War, but it remained strong in many rural locations until the twentieth century. Both the Republican and Democratic presidential candidates in 1920 were Ohio newspaper editors and, just a few years before that, the Lehigh Valley was represented in Congress by Easton newspaper editor Howard Mutchler.[9]

The importance of newspapers to early American politics naturally placed newspaper editors in a crucial position. While newspapers themselves provided the medium for the linkages described above, it was the editors who controlled them, using their newspapers to direct the affairs of the party and coordinate its message. Each editor was his party's principal spokesman, supplier of ideology, and enforcer of party discipline in the area and political level he served. Often he was chief strategist and manager as well. He and his newspaper defined the party line on issues as they arose and maintained it between party conventions and caucuses. He defended his party's candidates and officeholders and attacked its opponents. His often-bitter rhetoric whipped recalcitrant party members into line and punished apostates by reading them out of the party. One of the major advantages that editors had over other politicians was that they were the most professional politicians in the political system. They actually ran businesses devoted to politics, making their livings from politics in a way that a lawyer who served in Congress a few months out of the year did not. They were on the job all the time. Exploiting their position in the party system, numerous editors eventually found their way into office, in everything from low-level patronage jobs to seats in Congress and high posts in the federal government. For example, there were six former editors in the Senate at one point during the late 1830s and three in Abraham Lincoln's cabinet, including Pennsylvania's Simon Cameron in the War Department.[10]

No one created this system intentionally. Most of the early partisan editors, and a great number of the later ones, were printers by trade, and while literate, printers were artisans, mechanics, manual laborers, to be seen and used politically, but not to be heard and certainly not to take the political lead. Benjamin Franklin was very much the exception. The relatively rare political essays in colonial newspapers were always written by educated gentleman customers of printers, and freedom of the press referred not to the printer's freedom to print what he chose but instead to his customers' freedom to get whatever they wrote printed in his pages. True, printing had often attracted boys of greater ambition and more bookish inclination than other trades, but even Franklin had to make his fortune and quit printing before becoming a political leader; he advised young printers to stay out of politics. None of the Founders thought to make "uneducated printers, shop-boys, and raw school-masters...the chief instructors in politics," as one later said.[11]

Newspaper politics probably had its beginnings just before the Revolution, when ambitious young politicians like John Adams and Thomas Jefferson made very effective use of the press against the British and learned what a wonderful political tool newspapers could be. Jefferson became such an enthusiast that he claimed to prefer "newspapers without a government" to "government without newspapers," meaning that coercive government might be unnecessary if public opinion could be guided through the press. Jefferson began thinking of newspapers as tools of political opposition again, however, once he became Secretary of State and concluded that his cabinet colleague Alexander Hamilton was a threat to the republic. He did not want to resign and leave the government wholly in Hamilton's hands, yet he could also not work openly against an administration of which he himself was a leading member.

This was made especially sticky by the fact that Jefferson and the other Founders, President George Washington most of all, intensely distrusted parties and any other form of sustained opposition to regularly constituted republican government. So Jefferson found a surrogate to fight his battle for public opinion, a newspaper editor and poet named Philip Freneau, who was given a job in the Secretary of State's office so he could start an opposition newspaper. This *National Gazette* lasted only two years, but the pattern it established lasted a century.[12]

After the *National Gazette*'s demise, urban newspapers without direct connections to national leaders, such as the Philadelphia *Aurora* and Boston *Independent Chronicle*, took over as chief critics of Federalist policies. By the end of the 1790s, a whole network of opposition journals had grown up to supplement the city papers, with outlets in most of the significant towns in every state. The administration of John Adams tried to stamp out this network with the Alien and Sedition Acts, only to have it grow larger instead, as young printers radicalized by the Federalist repression rushed to politicize existing newspapers or start new, fiercely partisan journals. When Adams finally fell to Jefferson and Aaron Burr in the so-called Revolution of 1800, it became conventional wisdom that any successful party needed to have such a network, and newspaper politics had arrived.[13]

Very inadvertently, this development brought a certain amount of democratization to American political life, by setting up printers, immigrant radicals, and similar folk as the country's chief political spokesmen. President Jefferson distanced himself from his more radical newspaper supporters and kept them out of his administration, but the political culture had changed irrevocably. Editors now set terms on which other politicians were considered loyal to the Jeffersonian Republican cause, and they had control of weapons that could do great damage to the reputations of gentleman statesmen who crossed them. Jefferson found this out the hard way when editor James Thomson Callender, a former supporter embittered at not being properly rewarded, published the rumors about Sally Hemings for the first time.[14]

Many were horrified at the implications of this change in the control over and occupancy of the new nation's public sphere. The Rev. Samuel Miller spoke for many members of the political gentry, Republican and Federalist alike, when he warned in 1803 to expect the most dreadful consequences "when men of small talents, of little information, and of less virtue, undertake to be...directors of public opinion." One would see "the frivolity of weakness, the errors and malignity of prejudice, the misrepresentations of party zeal, the most corrupt doctrines in politics and morals, the lacerations of private character, and the polluting language of obscenity and impiety, daily issuing from the press, poisoning the principles, and disturbing the repose of society." Unless the "growing evil" was corrected somehow, Miller could only foresee "the arrival of that crisis in which we must yield either to an abridgement of the liberty of the press, or to a disruption of every social bond."[15]

In Jeffersonian Pennsylvania, Republican gentlemen and attorneys led by Alexander J. Dallas launched a rebellion against *Aurora* editor William Duane's effective control of the state Republican party and his radically democratic agenda of constitutional and legal reform. Dallas and friends complained bitterly about what they saw as the dictatorial tactics Duane used to keep control of the party, many of which revolved around his newspaper's ability to set the terms of party loyalty. Dallas complained that "the whole machinery of confidential letters, essays upon the state of parties, anonymous hints, admonitions, and accusations" was set in motion against anyone who disagreed with Duane politically. The editor's personal and ideological rivals were charged with *"heresy," "apostasy,"* or *"political defection,"* and then excommunicated from the party, "arbitrarily enrolled as a *Quid* or a *Federalist,* a *traitor* or a *Tory."* The gentleman schismatics styled themselves the Constitutional Republicans for the 1805 state elections and hoped (fruitlessly, it turned out) that Republican voters disliked following the lead of newspaper editors as much as they did. "The citizens of America have begun to perceive," Dallas wrote, "that advantage has been taken of their just veneration of the liberty of the press to shackle them with the tyranny of printers."[16]

Unfortunately for Dallas and like-minded leaders, combating the "tyranny of printers" usually required the establishment of new partisan newspapers to compete with the alleged tyrants, which tended to have the effect of expanding or even worsening the problem. Indeed, after 1800, the founding of newspapers became a sure sign that a new party or faction of a party was working to build its support in a particular area. Hence the Constitutional Republican schism inspired the founding of several new journals across the state, including the Philadelphia *Freeman's Journal,* the Lancaster *Constitutional Democrat,* and at least three new journals in the Lehigh Valley, as will be seen below. Continuing divisions in Philadelphia led in 1807 to the establishment of the *Democratic Press;* this journal was intended as a more tractable replacement for the *Aurora,* but its editor, John Binns, would quickly become an even more hated editorial tyrant than Duane.[17]

As horrifying as the rise of newspaper politics was to some, it was a godsend to others, namely to young, ambitious printers, who could now aspire to be political mechanics in addition to their work with ink, type, and paper. William Duane well articulated the sense of these new possibilities as a particular kind of American dream fulfilled. It was one of the Republic's great glories, he wrote, that it was possible for a printer, an artisan, to become "a writer on American affairs, a politician...worthy of the regards of men distinguished by their talents and their virtues in an age like this."[18]

It was one pursuer of William Duane's dream who helped bring newspaper politics to the Lehigh Valley. Thomas Jones Rogers was born in 1781 and emigrated with his parents from Waterford, Ireland, as a small child. Like many new immigrants of that day, the Rogers family settled in Philadelphia, which, even before the advent of the *National Gazette* and *Aurora,* had one of the liveliest political and print cultures in the country. By the time Thomas was old enough to enter a trade, his choice of printing was one that would almost inevitably involve him in politics. He served his apprenticeship with Samuel Harrison Smith, a young Republican printer who published the first American edition of Thomas Paine's *Rights of Man.* In 1800, Rogers moved with his employer to Washington

City, where Smith established the *National Intelligencer*, soon to be the Jefferson administration's semiofficial spokespaper.[19]

Little is known about Rogers in this period, but he would have been fully trained by this time and may have worked as some sort of foreman on the *Intelligencer*. Smith had poor reputation as a writer and politician, so in light of the facility that Rogers immediately showed in both areas after setting out on his own, we may surmise that the foreman wrote some of the *Intelligencer*'s political material in addition to his printing duties. By 1805, at any rate, Rogers was back in Philadelphia, working for one of the local Republican newspapers (quite likely the *Aurora*) and participating heavily in the vibrant civic life available to politicized artisans in the city. Besides attending an endless round of public meetings, banquets, and celebrations, Rogers served as a junior officer in William Duane's Militia Legion, as much a political organization as a military one.[20]

While nothing specific is known about how Rogers came to buy the relatively nonpartisan Samuel Longcope's printing office in Easton, Rogers's move was almost certainly part of the nationwide effort after 1800 to expand the Republican press network into areas where its support was relatively weak. The most intense focus of this activity was in Federalist New England, but newspapers were also founded in other locations that were either hold-outs against Jeffersonian Republicanism, resistant to party-driven politics, or simply underserved by Republican newspapers.[21]

To varying degrees, the Lehigh Valley fell into all three of these categories. The Federalists were still strong enough to be competitive, but an even more serious problem was political apathy, a characteristic often ascribed (by frustrated English-speaking politicians) to the Germans who made up such a large part of the local population. German speakers did indeed lag behind other groups in terms of officeholding and understanding of Anglo-American political ideas and institutions, but in politics Pennsylvania Germans were more resistant to strict party loyalty than apathetic. Ethnic, religious, and class differences tended to loom much larger for them than partisan ones, and local control of their own communities was the paramount concern. Generally inclined to defer to authority and social hierarchy, Lehigh Valley Germans had begun to stir in opposition to the Direct Tax of 1798. Their resistance was encouraged by several Philadelphia politicians who had escaped that year's yellow fever epidemic by coming north to campaign in the country. Republican newspapers also played a role: the valley was served remotely by the *Aurora* and the like-minded, German-language *Adler* [*Eagle*] out of Reading, in addition to the *Bothe und Kundschafter* [*Messenger and Intelligencer*], a largely commercial paper published by Easton's longtime German printers, Jacob and Cornelius Weygandt. The Weygandts generally reprinted from other papers in their small editorial space, but they published at least one notable local piece in the controversy, an attack on one of the tax assessors by Lutheran pastor Thomas Pomp. From 1798 on, there was a shift in voting toward the Republican opposition, and civil unrest that peaked with the so-called Fries's Rebellion in 1799.[22]

Even these traumatic experiences did not turn the Lehigh Valley into safe Republican territory. As Philadelphia radicals like William Duane and Thomas J.

Rogers perceived them, German voters were prone to wander back to their particularistic and deferential ways without close newspaper supervision. Northampton County Germans were thought to be a key factor in the closely fought reelection of Governor Thomas McKean, a Republican who had broken with the radicals over legal reform and efforts to muzzle the press and, from 1805 on (in most parts of the state), largely depended on Federalist votes. Running under the "Constitutional" Republican banner, McKean held on to much of his previous German Lutheran vote and added some sectarian German pacifists by opposing radical efforts to tighten the militia laws and create a public education system. In the more simplistic view of the Philadelphia radicals, the county's weakly partisan electorate had gone astray, supporting the man in power without sufficient regard to his political consistency.[23]

The partly failed crusade to oust Governor McKean, and a concomitant effort to fully partisanize the local population undoubtedly explains the sudden surge in Lehigh Valley newspaper politics during 1805. In March, the Weygandts had relaunched their newspaper, whose full title had carried the adjective "Unpartheyischer" or (roughly) "impartial," as the more pugnacious *Der Eastoner Deutsche Patriot*. At the same time, young printer Thomas Rogers in Philadelphia seized the chance to move up in his two trades – printing and politics – by moving out to the Lehigh Valley. Possibly some strategizing state leader suggested the move or helped Rogers find the money (likely a modest sum) to buy Samuel Longcope's tiny, faltering establishment. At any rate, by early November 1805, just after McKean's reelection, Rogers was residing at Easton, in control of Longcope's press, and gathering subscribers for a new newspaper, the *Northampton Farmer*, set to appear in December.[24]

Though his background and later behavior suggest that Thomas J. Rogers moved to Easton intending to establish himself in politics as well as printing, he followed a long printer's tradition by not openly announcing the fact. Issuing the customary handbill of proposals for a new newspaper, he promised readers that the "political complexion" of his new paper would be "strict impartiality at all times." It would "be open to all communications of merit, in the political line, from whatever party they may appear, without being influenced by any." Such disingenuous disclaimers were increasingly unnecessary in areas accustomed to newspaper politics, but Rogers operated on the assumption that Lehigh Valley readers would have to be eased slowly into partisanship. By the time the *Northampton Farmer* debuted, the editor revealed his true intentions a bit more accurately by replacing the *American Eagle*'s masthead quotation from George Washington with a new one from Thomas Jefferson, proclaiming "equal and exact justice for all men, of whatever state or persuasion, religious or political."[25]

While repeating the handbill's pledges of impartiality in the *Farmer*'s opening address to readers, Rogers added a remark that hinted at what the Lehigh Valley's Federalist and renegade Republican politicians were in for: in a republican government, the editor wrote, it was "not only proper, but...absolutely necessary, that the conduct of public men should be investigated with a scrutinizing pen." While this statement might be read as a nonpartisan journalist's pledge to defend the public interest, in Rogers's case it also meant taking an active political role, as a sentinel of the Republican party as well as the "public."[26]

Rogers carefully modulated the politicization of his paper over the course of its first year, not fully emerging as a fire-breathing Jeffersonian editor until the months leading up to the October 1806 congressional elections. Even then, he was always careful to tie his political material to specific issues and elections, resisting the urge to declaim upon every available subject and avoiding extended personal quarrels, two leading and problematic characteristics of Philadelphia Republican editors such as Duane and Binns. Politics first entered the journal in March 1806 with a low-key report on Governor McKean's persecution of Lancaster editor William Dickson. Rogers's first long political essay appeared in April, praising a bill to prohibit certain British imports in retaliation for British violations of American neutrality, especially the impressment of American sailors. After expatiating on the need for the United States to show the world that its rights would be defended with "energy and spirit," Rogers emphasized the near unanimity with which congressional Republicans had supported the measure, refuting Federalist assertions that the Republicans were divided. He ended by noting that an apparently endangered local congressman, Robert Brown, had been "among the supporters of our national rights and dignity."[27]

Saving Brown's seat would be one of the major political projects of Rogers's first year in Easton. A local war hero, Robert Brown apparently had little to offer in the way of charisma and oratorical skills. He had not spoken or led very often in the House, so Rogers plugged Brown's faithfulness to his constituents, ideological consistency, and regular attendance. Readers might never see Brown's speeches in the published congressional proceedings, but if they scanned the "yeas and nays," Rogers argued, they would always find that "the vote of General Brown has been for the benefit of our common country, and for the preservation of our republican institutions." Some Republicans had occasionally strayed in the last Congress, but "our representative was as firm and as immoveable as a rock." For Brown's benefit and out of his own partisan political values, Rogers developed a conception of leadership rather different from that of the virtuous republican statesman rising above party and standing against all political and economic pressures. While still "disinterested" and self-abnegating, Brown's political virtue consisted of subordinating his own wishes and interests to those of the nation, the party, and his constituents. "Has not General Brown, citizens of Northampton, always been your friend and the friend of your country? Has he ever acted contrary to your will or opinion?"[28]

While not especially stirring or romantic, this conception of leadership was highly *democratic* on at least two levels: it enshrined the will of voters as the highest power in the political system, while upholding a form of leadership that any reliable and moderately intelligent person could fulfill, with no expensive education, refined breeding, or superhuman talents required. Rogers also used these ideas in support of an even more colorless congressional candidate named Dr. John Hahn. Rogers praised Hahn's "worth, talents, and integrity," the evidence of which was primarily found in his "firm and undeviating republicanism."[29]

Rogers contrasted Brown and Hahn's homely reliability with the personal and political shiftiness of Brown's challenger, state senator William Lattimore, and Frederick Conrad, a fellow incumbent with Brown of the multi-person congressional seat who was sympathetic to the Constitutional Republican schism in the state party. Lattimore was a politically "doubtful character" and rumored former Federalist. Out of selfish lust for higher office, he had "suffered himself" to become "the *passive tool* of a few designing and ambitious men," accepting a nomination from a committee made up partly of Federalists. The key problem was not Lattimore's ambition for office so much as his willingness to go outside his party and abandon political consistency in order to obtain it.[30]

Similarly, Rogers charged that Frederick Conrad was not a "firm and decided politician," but instead "a political trimmer" and hypocrite who had "no fixed principle" or "decided sentiment of his own." Conrad had been elected by Republican votes, the *Northampton Farmer* reported, but was now saying that he "saw the necessity of supporting *federal principles*, in order to keep the d----d Jacobins down." Jacobin was the Federalists' old slur term for the Republicans, connoting a cabal of potentially murderous radicals whose morals were corrupted and whose principles and loyalties were foreign to America. One of Conrad's chief complaints against the Republican "Jacobins" – he clearly referred to Rogers's radical mentors back in Philadelphia – was that they acted too much like a party, demanding loyalty and consistency from members. "'Tis one grand and striking trait in the republican characters," Conrad had said, "that when once they discover an *apostate*, they are sure to discard him." Rogers was only too happy to endorse this remark, which for him described not wild-eyed Jacobinism but virtuous commitment to democracy and the Republican party. "As the democratic republicans of this district have found Mr. Conrad to be an *apostate*, it is no more than right, just, and fair...that they should *discard* him." For good measure, the *Northampton Farmer* and the other Republican paper in the district, the *Norristown Register*, threw in the charge that Conrad, an incumbent, had gone home for several weeks while Congress was in session and still collected his per diem.[31]

The various aspects of the congressional campaign formed part of Rogers's larger project of schooling the Lehigh Valley's relatively independent voters in appropriate partisan political values and behavior. "Give your votes to none but firm and undeviating republicans," the editor advised his readers, and in issue after issue, he tried to supply them with the necessary information. Like most partisan newspapers of this period, the *Northampton Farmer* played another crucial role in simply identifying which politicians were members of the Republican party. Hence great emphasis was placed on any Federalist connections or support that could be attributed to "apostates" like Lattimore and Conrad, who, along with the statewide Constitutional Republican movement with which they were associated, still claimed to be true Jeffersonian Republicans. To successfully label them Federalists was the same thing, in this era of uninstitutionalized parties, as ejecting them from the Republican party.[32]

Apparently the *Northampton Farmer*'s educational efforts were successful. When the returns were in, Robert Brown was the top vote-getter in a six-way race, and John Hahn missed election by only eleven votes. Frederick Conrad's reelection bid was defeated and William Lattimore finished sixth and last. Unfortunately for Rogers and the Republicans, a Federalist or Constitutional Republican named William Milnor came in just ahead of Hahn, meaning that Conrad was replaced with another enemy. The general pattern of votes across the district's five counties suggests the critical role of newspapers in the campaign. The two counties with Republican newspapers, Northampton and Montgomery (home of the *Norristown Register*), gave Brown and Hahn, respectively, their highest vote percentages; Conrad finished dead last in Montgomery, although it was his own home county. In Bucks County, where there was no political newspaper, Conrad and Milnor led the voting. As we might predict, Milnor received his highest percentage in Luzerne, where the one and only newspaper was Federalist.[33]

Despite Milnor's election, Thomas J. Rogers was able to declare victory, writing that the Northampton Republicans had "made a noble stand" and thrown "apostasy" into decline. In the wake of this success, the newly arrived editor emerged as a power in eastern Pennsylvania. One clear sign of this was his sudden appearance as an officer in the Easton Light Infantry militia company. Rogers would rise from a company lieutenant in 1807 all the way to state brigadier general. Militia officers were elected, of course, and Rogers made sure that company doings always received prominent play in the *Northampton Farmer*, getting his own name before the public as something other and more admirable than a mere printer. Following the example of William Duane in Philadelphia, Rogers used the militia as the base for all his future political endeavors. The militia supplied organizational manpower and votes at election time, and its meetings and musters provided opportunities for various Rogers-inspired political messages to be sent, under a respected, seemingly apolitical imprimatur.[34]

By 1808, Rogers was probably the only man in the Lehigh Valley who actually worked in politics for a living. Though influential and relatively well-stocked with advertising, the *Northampton Farmer* was making very little money. Early American newspapers were notoriously unprofitable enterprises. They were sold almost entirely by subscription, and typically on credit. Printers were thus forced to try to collect hundreds or thousands of individual debts far too small to cover the cost of legal action or even a letter if a subscriber did not pay promptly, as possibly one-third to one-half of them did not. Rogers made matters worse for himself by charging an unusually low subscription price of two dollars and then investing in new type and expanding the paper in late 1806. Like many political editors, his basic objectives – promoting his party, its ideals, and its candidates – worked at cross purposes with his newspaper's bottom line. Rogers's political objectives demanded that he maximize his readership and influence as much as possible, which meant publishing as substantive and respectable-looking a paper, at as low a price, as possible. Effective debt collection tactics such as harassing or cutting off deadbeat subscribers would have meant alienating political supporters.

So Rogers learned to use his political leverage to secure other sources of income. Governments did not possess their own printing services in this period, so contracts to print for the federal, state, and local governments were highly sought after by printers. Newly minted officeholders often heard the argument from friendly printers and editors that their political support and financial sacrifices had earned them the right to print for the government. Rogers printed notices for the county and the militia and angled unsuccessfully for a coveted contract to print the laws of the United States. Rogers was also far more successful than most printers at this early period in gaining another form of political income, salaries from government jobs. Rogers held some kind of office almost continuously from 1808 on. "If it were not for the office I hold," Rogers admitted in 1812, when he was clerk of the Northampton County Orphan's Court, "I could not live by publishing my paper."[35]

Rogers was more precocious than unique in finding that politically obtained offices and printing contracts were the solution to his newspaper's financial problems. His predicament was built into the very structure of partisan journalism. As a group, printers and editors formed one of the most insistent constituencies for political patronage, and the rise of newspaper politics went hand in hand with the growth of the so-called spoils system.

Living off politics rather than printing turned out to confer great advantages that aided Rogers's meteoric rise in Lehigh Valley politics. He was on the job full-time and ready to undertake political tasks for which more casual politicians had no time or interest. When influential state senator Jonathan Roberts wrote to a prominent Republican doctor John Cooper suggesting that a meeting be held in Northampton to denounce Governor McKean, the letter and the task were passed on to Rogers. The editor called the meeting himself and instructed Roberts that all important political correspondence for the Easton area should be addressed to him in the future. "We have no society or even a standing committee of correspondence in this county," Rogers lamented, "and indeed, those Democrats in this county who might help the cause are not active" and felt content to let their young editor do the campaigning. Whenever Dr. Cooper received a political letter, "he generally hands it to me, in order that I may communicate it to the Democrats of the county," and whenever any of the other county Democratic leaders came into Easton, they stopped by the *Farmer* office. Rogers and his newspaper had become the Democratic Republican political hub of the region, and the editor sought to make it more so by installing himself as the area's primary liaison with the outside political world as well.[36]

One key to Rogers's success in this effort was the working relationship he established with Jonathan Roberts, a Republican politician from Norristown who would serve in the state senate and in both houses of Congress over the life of the *Northampton Farmer*. Roberts sent Rogers information and essays from the capital that increased the stature and apparent connectedness of Rogers's newspaper, and amplified the editor's personal influence by consulting him on official appointments. In return, Rogers boosted Roberts in his newspaper and kept the congressman informed on public opinion and political events in his locality. They worked especially closely during the period just before the War of 1812, when both were desperate to vindicate the nation's and their party's honor by declaring war against Great Britain. Rogers sent regular updates about support for the prospective war in Roberts's congressional district, at one point touring the district on Roberts's behalf. When Northampton County's "bawling" flour millers mounted an organized protest against the trade embargo with Britain, Rogers personally mobilized a political response.³⁷

Regarding himself as a colleague of other politicians rather than a mere satellite or supplicant, Rogers was quite self-aware about his role as the party's chief operative in Easton. As a party editor, Rogers saw it as his job not only to influence public opinion in his party's favor, but also to manage the local party itself, working to keep it unified and electorally strong. "As our county is now divided," Rogers told Roberts at one point, "I must double the exertions of my Printing office." Campaigning was uniquely an editor's role, because even in ultra-politicized Pennsylvania, candidates were supposed to stand aloof from their own races. "Nothing can be more disgraceful," wrote the surrogate campaigner Rogers of an opposition candidate, "than to see a man riding around the country soliciting votes for *himself*." Rogers's managerial work went far beyond what was printed in the newspaper. He was always in attendance at local party gatherings and usually the leading spirit. When the Easton Democratic Republicans held a borough meeting, Rogers drafted the resolutions in advance and had alternative sets of resolutions ready to suit whatever the mood of the crowd turned out to be. In order to free his time for politics, the increasingly politics- rather than publishing-focused Rogers hired an assistant to gather news from the papers exchanged with other printers; if the assistant was sick or politics got too intense, the news was left out altogether.³⁸

Newspaper politicians were highly influential in pushing the American political system toward the typical nineteenth-century pattern of popular campaigning, seemingly open conventions, and strong parties. This process was occurring long before the full emergence of national mass-based parties in the 1830s, and Rogers was perhaps its most important exponent in northeastern Pennsylvania. Organized political parties had a place for editors in a way that other modes of conducting public affairs did not. Thus editors placed a high premium on party loyalty, the terms of which their newspapers set. The use of nominating conventions, known as "delegate meetings" or "conferences," had become common in Pennsylvania. Thomas J. Rogers ardently defended the practice, which placed decision-making in the hands of local party organizers like himself.³⁹

Not everyone in politics liked the new system as well as Rogers did. He was outraged during the 1811 election season when, after a ticket had already been nominated by the county delegate meeting (where Rogers himself had been a delegate), a group of renegade Republicans joined with Federalists to form a second ticket. Rogers fumed to Roberts that any politician who would "suffer himself [to] be made use of after the will of the majority has been fairly...expressed, cannot be a democrat, for he would, to obtain office, suffer himself to be made use of by any party." Rogers wished that his erstwhile colleagues had resolved their differences within the bounds of party unity, showing both more commitment to the organization and a greater sense of what can only be called political professionalism. "How much better would it have been for those who did not like the Delegate ticket to have said, 'we will support the Delegate ticket this year, to prevent division, and we will endeavour to select a ticket next year we like better.'" Rogers asked Roberts to write a series of articles defending the legitimacy of delegate meetings so that their nominations would be better respected, restraining individualistic ambitions and making the party a more stable and effective political unit: "If we go on as we have..., the Democrats in this state will be like a flock of lost geese, have no fixed plan, while our enemies will take advantage of our want of *system*, and may succeed through...our divisions."[40]

The quick rise of an interloping printer was bitterly resented by Easton's established families and politicians. Rogers had begun to interfere with the local power structure, particularly antagonizing the leading Germans and lawyers. In the spring of 1807, Rogers excoriated three German assemblymen from the area because they had voted against a bill to improve navigation on the Delaware near Easton. In that fall's election, he got one of the Germans replaced with a non-German newcomer like himself. Unable to take much more, the local Constitutional Republicans (probably cooperating with Federalists) encouraged Christian J. Hütter, a veteran printer who published the German-language *Northampton Correspondent*, first to politicize his existing paper and then to start one in English, which appeared as the *Pennsylvania Herald and Easton Intelligencer* in August 1808. Rogers's success as newspaper politician thus begat more newspaper politics to combat him, as was often the case. A report reached Rogers that the new paper had been founded "for the express purpose of breaking me up." Virtually the day Hütter's proposals came off the press, Rogers warned that his enemies were "miserably mistaken" if they thought he could be silenced.[41]

By way of making good on this threat, Rogers became the region's most potent advocate of Simon Snyder's 1808 race against "his majesty" Governor Thomas McKean. The *Northampton Farmer* successfully attached a Federalist label to McKean's supporters and needled Hütter as a "resplendent genius" whose paper was written by Federalist lawyers, a charge that seems to have some merit. In September, Rogers made lawyer domination of officeholding a major and personally resonant issue of the campaign, labeling the two candidate slates the "Republican Farmers' Ticket" and the "Federal Lawyers' Ticket." The *Herald* writers sneered (not always accurately) about Rogers's background and attacked his placement of commas, but to little avail. Snyder won, paving the way for Rogers's appointment with the Orphan's Court, displacing George Wolf, a prominent German lawyer and the former postmaster of Easton. The *Herald* expressed the feelings of many more established Easton politicians in describing Rogers (on the occasion of his appointment) as "an unprincipled printer...without family or property, and without anything to recommend him but want." This revulsion against the local embodiment of democratization was a sentiment shared by many opponents of rising political editors.[42]

The local establishment's efforts to impede the growth of Rogers's power met with little success. An episode that demonstrated Rogers's decisive role in the local politics was the ouster of Congressman William Rodman, engineered by the editor in 1812. Dissatisfied with Rodman's apparent opposition to strong measures against Great Britain (possibly rooted in his Quaker religious beliefs), Rogers took the opportunity of a trip to Philadelphia to travel through the rest of the congressional district and lay the groundwork for a movement to deny Rodman the next Democratic Republican nomination. As a replacement, Rogers had in mind Samuel D. Ingham, a Bucks County paper manufacturer and former state legislator. As the leading party manager in Northampton County, the other half of the district, Rogers sent word for Ingham to come and visit him in Easton. After the visit, Rogers initiated a stream of anti-Rodman, pro-Ingham newspaper items and meeting resolutions. By August, the editor was convinced the voters would "suffer our former friend Rodman to retire and reflect on his treachery and apostacy... nothing shall be wanting on my part in this quarter to endeavor to oust him."[43]

Nothing *was* wanting, apparently, because in October both Ingham and Roberts gave Rogers the credit for Ingham's landslide victory, led by a thousand-vote margin in Rogers's own Northampton County. Writing to Roberts after the election, the editor implicitly revealed the key to his success as a campaigner: Rogers had politics for his profession, his one overriding concern and main income source, while the millers, his main local opponents in this and other recent battles, "do not care about elections as long as flour is so much in demand." This singular focus had made Rogers the Lehigh Valley's major political manager and at times a seemingly unstoppable political force.[44]

Rogers was now ready to take the next step in his career, running for office himself. He and Ingham worked themselves into the graces of the officeholder-dominated "Family" faction in Philadelphia, named (by critics) after the three brothers-in-law, including future vice president George Mifflin Dallas and Philadelphia postmaster Richard Bache, who headed it. The Family had inherited the mantle of the wealthy, conservative "Constitutional Republicans" who had defended Thomas McKean, opposed reform of the legal system, and competed with William Duane's faction for control of the party. Rogers himself had been a bitter detractor of the Constitutional Republicans, but by the 1810s he was gravitating toward Pennsylvania's burgeoning manufacturing and transportation interests and saw more opportunity with the wealthy, well-connected Philadelphians than the state party's other wing, the base of which was much poorer, and more rural, German, and western. The Family's other appeal, reflecting somewhat more favorably on Rogers, was that they could make the most convincing claim to be the regular Republican organization that had supported the national Republican administrations through all the state's various upheavals.[45]

The war against Great Britain that Republican newspapers like the *Northampton Farmer* had helped bring about gave editor Rogers his opportunity to run for office. More and more heavily involved in the militia, he served in Pennsylvania's 1814 mobilization and found an issue for himself in the mistreatment (especially nonpayment) of the Pennsylvania troops by the federal authorities. In the summer and fall of 1815, Rogers sold the *Farmer*, organized protest meetings for militia pay, and got himself nominated for the state senate. The printers who bought Rogers's paper (renaming it the *Spirit of Pennsylvania*) pledged to favor no particular party and even apologized that "the warm politician will denounce our journal as insipid," yet managed to find room for prominent notices of Rogers's political activities. His opponent was old rival George Wolf, the German lawyer who once lost a valuable county office to Rogers. The voting patterns in Rogers's victory were revealing of where his and his paper's actual influence may have lain. Wolf won handily in the town of Easton, where Rogers had been known as a working printer and patronage appointee, but the editor's strength increased with the distance from Easton. In neighboring towns and rural areas, Rogers was known more impersonally as the editor of a highly regarded newspaper and a popular militia officer. The rural areas of Northampton County had also been the hotbeds of opposition to the Direct Tax where Democratic Republicanism in the Lehigh Valley had gotten its start. The town of Easton, by contrast, contained a number of wealthy English-speaking lawyers and businessmen who had never had much use for the party, in addition to assimilated Germans who were increasingly restive under the leadership of Irish immigrant radicals and ex-radicals like William Duane and Thomas J. Rogers.[46]

In the state senate, Rogers made militia reform his issue and laid the groundwork for higher office. He wrote letters on the legislature's proceedings for the Philadelphia *Democratic Press* and, at the same time, attached himself to State Treasurer William Findlay, who would be the regular (and Family-supported) Republican candidate for governor in 1817 despite grave reservations about his integrity and politics in some circles. This shift was a delicate operation for Rogers, since it involved potentially alienating former allies from the newspaper wars, including *Press* editor John Binns.

Other shifts were in the offing as Rogers bid for the brass ring. At home in Easton, he lost his hold over the *Spirit of Pennsylvania* but soon made common cause with his old editorial sparring partner Christian J. Hütter, who founded a pro-Findlay Republican paper called the *Easton Centinel* in July 1817. Rogers and Hütter joined forces to campaign for Findlay, and in the aftermath Rogers worked hard but carefully, through intermediaries, to place his own supporters on the district nominating conference that would choose a congressional candidate in 1818. Mirabile dictu, Rogers emerged as the conference's consensus choice and, with the *Easton Centinel*'s support, won the election over token opposition, becoming only the second long-time printer-editor (after New Jersey senator James J. Wilson) to be elected to Congress.[47]

Ensconced in Washington, DC, Rogers established the same relationship with Hütter that he had once had with Jonathan Roberts. Hütter reported on political movements and public opinion at home – who planned to run against Rogers at the next election, what local people thought of a proposed tax, the progress of efforts to pass a new militia law. Knowing from experience that editorial support back home was crucial to his political welfare, Rogers inundated Hütter with mail. "I must confess that you are the most faithful correspondent I ever had," Hütter wrote the congressman at one point, struggling to keep up an equally heavy output in return.[48]

Rogers became an influential man in Washington, despite his background as a journeyman printer. Along with now-colleague Samuel Ingham, Rogers became one of presidential candidate and Secretary of War John C. Calhoun's chief northern lieutenants, planting newspaper pieces boosting the South Carolinian's nationalist credentials all over Pennsylvania. Like most other Keystone State politicians, Rogers had become a zealous advocate of tariff protection for American manufactured goods, as manufacturing was becoming a mainstay of the Pennsylvania economy.[49]

At home, Rogers's career as an elective politician would be less pleasant, as his choice of state political factions turned out to be unfortunate. While Rogers was away in Washington, William Findlay's administration descended into a morass of financial scandals, opening the governor and all his supporters to attacks on their integrity and strong challenges at reelection time. Almost simultaneously, the Panic of 1819 unleashed great hostility to the cliques of officeholders that were seen as controlling politics all over the nation, a description that unquestionably applied to the Pennsylvania Findlayites. In some eyes, the power now held by men like Rogers showed just how shamefully the republic had declined since the days of the revolutionary heroes. Seen justly as a tireless political entrepreneur who scrambled atop many more distinguished men of longer residence, Rogers was never especially popular in Easton. Many in the town's upper crust had never reconciled themselves to his rise and would take strong action to reverse it when they could.[50]

The intensity of and the resources behind the hostility to Rogers show most clearly in the fact that each of his bids for reelection inspired the founding of special newspapers devoted almost exclusively to his political destruction. The Easton *Mountaineer* first appeared in January 1820 and looked like a conventional newspaper, with advertisements and news and reprinted essays from other papers. Yet from June until the paper went out of business roughly a year later, hardly an issue was published without some anti-Rogers material, usually several columns of it, sometimes interspersed with slaps at the Findlay administration and Hütter of the *Centinel.* In spite of these efforts, Rogers just barely survived an electoral debacle that swept Findlay out of office. The former editor even added to his laurels, winning an election for brigadier general of the state militia a few months later.[51]

In 1822, Rogers's enemies subjected him to an even more ferocious pounding. A former close ally of the congressman's named Hugh Ross was induced, probably hired or heavily subsidized, to turn coat. Ross established a newspaper called *The Expositor*, which dispensed with all pretenses about its purpose: each issue contained four pages of solid type assaulting Rogers and his associates, with no advertising and only occasional news items to dilute the venom. Much of Ross's material came from information, letters, and documents obtained while working with Rogers. The questionable ethics and malevolent intentions of the whole enterprise were laid bare in its banner motto, *That which the welfare of the people demands, is justifiable.* In his final issue, Ross belatedly announced that he would not exchange his paper with other editors because, frankly, "the matter...in it related merely to local politics, and included nothing of general interest." It existed solely to do in Thomas J. Rogers. It was a testament to Rogers's resourcefulness that he survived even this second onslaught, again winning reelection by a few hundred votes.[52]

In their sheer volume and substance, the *Mountaineer* and *Expositor* attacks on Rogers provide a remarkable window into how political editors were perceived – by rivals for power and potentially the citizenry at large – in their communities. Both papers bored in on Rogers's political professionalism. He had won many battles over the years by simply working harder and more creatively at campaigning than others, but now that he was campaigning for himself, this became a potentially serious demerit. It was said that Rogers was too much "[his] own trumpeter." Allegedly, he spent too much of his time in Congress currying favor with constituents by writing letters home and franking copies of the *National Intelligencer*. He had arranged his own renomination by holding meetings in out-of-the-way places and packing them with his own supporters.

Then there were charges of bribing voters: One of his lackeys had supposedly offered a popular local farmer a Merino ram – this was shortly after a speculative "Merino Fever" had swept the area and inflated prices for the Spanish sheep – if he would support Rogers for Congress. The *Mountaineer* made a major issue out of this anecdote, at one point listing Rogers and his allies as the "Merino Ram Ticket," complete with an illustration of a sheep. (By this time, the Merino craze was mostly regarded as an embarrassing fad of rather shady origins, so the label carried the additional connotations of hucksterism and dishonesty.) Perhaps most damning of all, the *Mountaineer* charged that Rogers had toured the district campaigning for himself: "I never knew an instance before in this district," wrote an *Expositor* correspondent, "that the candidate himself would be continually out begging for votes. Such a course...would be too degrading, too little. If he has not friends that will push him, then he had better not run."[53]

Rogers needed to stoop so low, his enemies argued, because he was an unworthy candidate: an immoral man, an immigrant, a social climber who had risen above his station and lacked the respect of his community. Without aggressive self-promotion and partisan overkill, he was nothing. The *Mountaineer* urged voters to choose "an honest German farmer" native to the county over someone who was "not born in the district, state, or even in the United States" and predicted that Rogers could not win twenty votes in his own heavily Republican neighborhood. Chided for insulting the Irish, one editor hastened to add that Rogers came from "the *lowest class* of Irish," which "every well bred man" would admit were "the most profane and vulgar beings in the human family." Especially in the *Expositor*, Rogers was depicted as a drunken lout who swore incessantly and enjoyed fighting in taverns, when not physically threatening enemies or mistreating his own family.[54]

Even when the prophecies of Rogers's sinking voter support turned out to be wrong, it was said to prove nothing about the congressman's personal popularity or community standing. Utterly lacking in traditional attributes of leadership such as wealth, status, or education, Rogers's electoral success was completely the product of excessive partisanship and exertion, an analysis that was not without merit: "Party spirit obtained for him those offices...he could never have looked or even hoped for. Yes, party spirit placed him on the 'top of the wheel,' passed him from one office to another, and at last ushered him into the National Legislature." Rogers's vulgarity and excessive campaigning had disgusted more respectable men and discouraged them from running: "They are as much afraid of a competition with Gen. Rogers, as a well-dressed gentleman would be of encountering a chimney sweep." Open letters were addressed to John C. Calhoun to the effect that he was disgracing himself by accepting the aid of "miserable and forlorn tools" like Rogers.[55]

Naturally, the *Mountaineer* and *Expositor* argued, a man of such low character was venal and proprietary in his approach to office. This was actually a fairly accurate charge, since unlike many more blue-blooded politicians, Rogers actually lived on his official earnings. The anti-Rogers papers claimed that the congressman had gotten his elderly father appointed as a justice of the peace in Philadelphia, with the agreement that the income of the office would go to his son. This may well have been true. Suffering heavy losses from his congressional travel and living expenses, Rogers allegedly declared that this arrangement was a "damn'd fine thing for him in his embarrassed situation, and would help him; and every man was a damn'd fool for not looking out for himself."[56]

Nor did Rogers make up for his coarseness and greed with political consistency, his enemies charged. He had switched state factions, as we have seen, and embraced onetime mortal enemies such as Hütter. The *Expositor* gave Rogers a particularly well-deserved roasting for his course on the Missouri statehood issue. Initially he had joined other Northern Republican congressmen in supporting the Tallmadge Amendment barring slavery from the new state and written numerous impassioned letters home to Easton expressing his hatred of the South's peculiar institution. Then after a few weeks of deadlock and some strong pressure from Ingham and the Calhounites, he caved in and voted to admit Missouri without restriction. While the vote was understandable in terms of Rogers's nationalism, commitment to party unity, and admiration for Calhoun, it was easy to depict as a violation of his own conscience in the name of selfish, weak-minded partisanship.[57]

No doubt the anti-Rogers newspapers exaggerated, but their overall theme that his life and identity were wholly consumed by politics hit fairly close to the mark. So did the allusions to his personal habits. Printing offices were not exactly schools for good manners and healthy living, and political life took place in an endless series of taverns, banquet halls, and well-liquored outdoor gatherings. One of the *Expositor's* ugliest stories seems likeliest to be true. The allegation was that, in September 1822, Rogers had indulged himself in a weekend-long binge of alcohol and politics, while his family was home sick. The fun supposedly began with a political meeting on Friday night and continued with a quarrelsome bender at the Salt Box Tavern. When challenged about why he had stayed in town all night, Rogers lamely explained that he had been buying meat for his family, so that he could nurse them to health with some mutton soup.[58]

Though the voters twice vindicated Rogers in the face of these attacks, the end of his third term found him with little stomach to go on as an elected official.

His reputation was in tatters, and, after six years of congressional service, so were his finances. This was the fate of most early congressmen without substantial wealth or a profession that they could practice in Washington. In 1824, a new Family governor, John A. Shulze, appointed Rogers as register and recorder of Northampton County, and he quietly resigned his seat in Congress to be replaced by long-time rival George Wolf. For the next few years he worked on a school textbook about the American Revolution and put himself quietly out to pasture, a has-been at age 43.[59]

Rogers's retirement would not last long. The long campaign to replace President John Quincy Adams with Gen. Andrew Jackson in 1828 saw newspaper politics deployed on a scale dwarfing anything that had gone before. While bringing a new wave of recruits into the political newspaper business, the Jackson campaign also reenergized a number of the old Republican printers. So in 1827, Rogers suddenly came out of his early retirement and founded the *Delaware Democrat* to be the Jacksonian organ in Easton.[60]

Jackson's victory marked a major turning point in the history of newspaper politics. Thomas Jefferson and Andrew Jackson were alike in crediting their victory to newspapers. Yet where classical republican scruples and high social and educational standards had caused Jefferson to limit the rewards for his editorial supporters to printing contracts, Jackson felt no such compunction, appointing more than sixty newspaper editors to offices in his administration, in addition to having several editors in his "Kitchen Cabinet" of close advisors, the precursors to the later White House staff. Thomas J. Rogers was not one to be left out of such a bonanza. He folded the *Delaware Democrat* on the very day that the election results were reported and lobbied furiously – and successfully – for a plum assignment as naval officer in the Philadelphia custom house. Rogers moved to Philadelphia, but enjoyed his new perquisites and return to big city life only briefly, dying in 1832.[61]

Like most partisan newspaper editors, Rogers left no lasting fame or major legacies. Historically, he barely registers even in books and archives devoted to the local history of Easton and Northampton County. Living as he did on his official salaries, there was no fortune to bequeath, and his family seems to have pressed on much as he did, with at least one son replicating his father's rise from journeyman printer to congressman, in an era when practical printing was if anything a more working-class occupation than it had been in the eighteenth century.

Twelve-year-old William Findlay Rogers was apprenticed to an Easton printer at the time of Thomas J.'s death, and then followed in his father's footsteps, only more slowly and in diffcrent locations. Like his progenitor, William F. achieved only a common-school education and started a newspaper in rural Pennsylvania, at Honesdale this time. In 1846, he gave this up and went to work as a journeyman printer on a Democratic newspaper in Buffalo, New York, eventually founding one of his own and becoming active in the military, first in the City Guards and then in the New York Volunteers during the Civil War. After the war, William served in a number of political offices, including a term in Congress during the 1880s, before retiring with the only sort of nest egg he or his father could have imagined: a government sinecure, in this case the superintendency of the Soldiers' and Sailors' Home in Bath, New York.[62]

What are we to make of the Rogers family and their family business? Perhaps not many readers of this essay would like their children to grow up to be like Thomas J. or William F. Rogers, "biased" journalists and inveterate office seekers as they were. Andrew Jackson's act of welcoming their ilk into the United States government, which set a precedent followed in ever-larger proportions by later administrations, horrified his opponents and even some of his more high-minded supporters. The Washington *Daily National Journal,* an Adams paper, compared the appointments to Sir Robert Walpole's bribery of the British press and amassed a running roster of the lucky editors to document the extent of the "corruption."[63] Reports came to Jackson from Virginia stating that he was losing his "most respectable and staunch supporters" because of his close association with newspaper editors, and the Senate, refusing to "swallow the printers," denied confirmation to several of what were considered to be Jackson's more distasteful nominees.[64]

This might be seen as a courageous effort to stave off the epidemic of political venality that came in later decades. But another interpretation came from Andrew Jackson himself (although his adviser Amos Kendall, an old Kentucky editor, probably wrote the text). Almost all common white men could exercise all the rights of citizenship in most states by the 1830s, and many were eager to participate fully in political life. Jackson viewed this as a natural and noble impulse. The problem was, common men had to work and earn money to live, and if they were to be able to work in politics, then official salaries after the election might be necessary. "Those who stept forward and advocated the question termed the side of the people" did so out of a "generous and patriotic impulse" and ought not to be punished, Jackson told critics. To appoint newspaper editors to office was merely to make "the road to office and preferment...accessible alike to the rich and the poor, the farmer and the printer." Editors in politics represented a form of democratization, not the rise of "the" common man, but of some relatively common men, like Thomas J. Rogers. For better or worse, common men in politics brought their common problems and values with them.[65]

Notes

1. Easton *American Eagle,* 8 Aug. 1799 ff; William J. Heller, *History of Northampton County (Penn.) and the Grand Valley of the Lehigh* (Boston: American Historical Society, 1920), 1: 289-90; Ethan A. Weaver, "*The American Eagle*: The First English Newspaper Printed in Northampton County, Pennsylvania," *Pennsylvania Magazine of History and Biography* 23 (1899): 69-76; E. Gordon Alderfer, *Northampton Heritage: The Story of an American County* (Easton, Pa.: Northampton County Historical and Genealogical Society, 1953), 181-82. The basic portrait of the form and content of early American newspapers presented in this and the following paragraphs draws on: Charles E. Clark, *The Public Prints: The Newspaper in Anglo-American Culture, 1665-1740* (New York: Oxford University Press, 1994); Stephen Botein, "'Meer Mechanics' and an Open Press: The Business and Political Strategies of

Colonial American Printers," *Perspectives in American History* 9 (1975): 127-225; Milton W. Hamilton, *The Country Printer: New York State, 1785-1830*, 2nd ed. (New York: Columbia University Press, 1964); Rollo G. Silver, *The American Printer, 1787-1825* (Charlottesville: University Press of Virginia, 1967); Clarence S. Brigham, *Journals and Journeymen: A Contribution to the History of Early American Newspapers* (Philadelphia: University of Pennsylvania Press, 1950).

2. Thus one Easton paper "covered" a possible change in British foreign policy by clipping a paragraph from a Philadelphia newspaper reporting the opinions of one Mr. Lyman, a passenger on a ship that had just arrived from Boston. Lyman expected "a speedy restoration of good understanding" between Great Britain and the U.S. and was "incredulous as to the report of an approaching peace between Great Britain and France." Easton *Northampton Farmer*, 30 Aug. 1805.

3. Easton *Northampton Farmer*, 23 Aug., 15 Mar. 1806.

4. Thomas Jefferson to John Norvell, 14 June 1807, *The Writings of Thomas Jefferson*, ed. Paul Leicester Ford, 10 vols. (New York: G. P. Putnam's Sons, 1892-99), 9:73.

5. Fisher Ames to Theodore Dwight, 19 Mar. 1801, in *Works of Fisher Ames, As Published by Seth Ames*, ed. W. B. Allen (Indianapolis: Liberty Classics, 1983), 2:1410-11; "Letter I. To the Freemen of the United States," Philadelphia *Independent Gazetteer*, 8 July 1795; Jeffrey L. Pasley, *"The Tyranny of Printers": Newspaper Politics in the Early American Republic* (Charlottesville: University Press of Virginia, 2001), chaps. 8 and 9.

6. For the definitive works on William Duane, see Kim Tousley Phillips, *William Duane, Radical Journalist in the Age of Jefferson* (New York: Garland, 1989); Kim T. Phillips, "William Duane, Philadelphia's Democratic Republicans, and the Origins of Modern Politics," *Pennsylvania Magazine of History and Biography* 101 (1977): 365-87. Though the party of Duane and Jefferson was the ancestor of today's Democrats, and is most often referred to today as the Democratic Republicans, this essay will generally use the name most common employed by Duane and Jefferson themselves, Republican.

7. A. K. McClure, "Pennsylvania Journalism," in Howard M. Jenkins, ed., *Pennsylvania: Colonial and Federal* (Philadelphia: Pennsylvania Historical Publishing Assoc., 1903), 3: 191-192. On the role of the press in nineteenth-century politics, see Gerald J. Baldasty, "The Press and Politics in the Age of Jackson," *Journalism Monographs* 89 (1984): 1-28; Gerald J. Baldasty, *The Commercialization of News in the Nineteenth Century* (Madison: University of Wisconsin Press, 1992); Jerry W. Knudson, *Jefferson and the Press: Crucible of Liberty* (Columbia: University of South Carolina Press, 2006); Culver H. Smith, *The Press, Politics, and Patronage: The American Government's Use of Newspapers, 1789-1875* (Athens: University of Georgia Press, 1977); Mark Wahlgren Summers, *The Press Gang: Newspapers and Politics, 1865-1878* (Chapel Hill: University of North Carolina Press, 1994); William David Sloan, "The Early Party Press: The Newspaper Role in American Politics, 1788-1812," *Journalism History* 9 (1982): 18-24; William David Sloan, "Purse and Pen: Party-Press Relationships, 1789-1816," *American Journalism* 6 (1989): 103-27; and Pasley, *"Tyranny of Printers."* Where not otherwise cited, general background information throughout this essay is drawn from these works.

8. This paragraph and the next several paragraphs condense arguments made and fully documented in Pasley, *"Tyranny of Printers,"* chap. 1.

9. Kathryn Allamong Jacob and Bruce A. Ragsdale, eds., *Biographical Directory of the United States Congress, 1774-1989*, Bicentennial ed. (Washington, DC: U. S. Government Printing Office, 1989), 1556.

10. Based primarily on information gathered from Jacob and Ragsdale. The three former editors in the Lincoln cabinet were: Cameron, Secretary of War; Gideon Welles, Secretary of the Navy; and Caleb Blood Smith, Secretary of the Interior. In addition, Vice President Hannibal Hamlin had once worked as a compositor.

11. Botein, "'Meer Mechanics' and an Open Press"; Pasley, *"Tyranny of Printers,"* chap. 2; J. A. Leo LeMay and P. M. Zall, eds., *Benjamin Franklin's Autobiography: An Authoritative Text, Backgrounds, Criticism* (New York: Norton, 1986), 9-10; Fisher Ames to Jeremiah Smith, 14 Dec. 1802, in *Works of Fisher Ames, as Published by Seth Ames*, ed. W. B. Allen, 2:1451.

12. Jeffrey L. Pasley, "The Two National *Gazettes*: Newspapers and the Embodiment of American Political Parties," *Early American Literature* 35 (2000): 51-86; Pasley, *"Tyranny of Printers,"* chaps. 2 and 3; Noble E. Cunningham Jr., *The Jeffersonian Republicans: The Formation of Party Organization, 1789-1801* (Chapel Hill: University of North Carolina Press, 1957), 13-20, 24-26. Quotation from Thomas Jefferson to Edward Carrington, 16 Jan. 1787, Jefferson Papers, Library of Congress.

13. Pasley, *"Tyranny of Printers,"* chaps. 4-10; Cunningham, *Jeffersonian Republicans*, 166-74; Noble E. Cunningham Jr., *The Jeffersonian Republicans in Power: Party Operations, 1801-1809* (Chapel Hill: University of North Carolina Press, 1963), chap. 10.

14. Pasley, *"Tyranny of Printers,"* chaps. 9, 11-13; Michael Durey, *Transatlantic Radicals and the Early American Republic* (Lawrence: University Press of Kansas, 1997); Michael Durey, *"With the Hammer of Truth": James Thomson Callender and America's Early National Heroes* (Charlottesville: University Press of Virginia, 1990), chaps. 6 and 7.

15. Samuel Miller, *A Brief Retrospect of the Eighteenth Century* (1803; rept. New York: Burt Franklin, 1970), 2:254-55.

16. [Alexander J. Dallas], "Address to the Republicans of Pennsylvania," 10 June 1805, in *Life and Writings of Alexander Dallas*, ed. George M. Dallas (Philadelphia: J. B. Lippincott, 1871), 214, 219, 217, 233, 216, 215; Pasley, *"Tyranny of Printers,"* chap. 12. For the political background of this conflict, see Richard E. Ellis, *The Jeffersonian Crisis: Courts and Politics in the Young Republic* (New York: Norton, 1974), 157-83; Jacob E. Cooke, *Tench Coxe and the Early Republic* (Chapel Hill: University of North Carolina Press, 1978), chap. 22; Sanford W. Higginbotham, *The Keystone in the Democratic Arch: Pennsylvania Politics, 1800-1816* (Harrisburg: Pennsylvania Historical and Museum Commission, 1952), chaps. 3 and 4; Raymond Walters, Jr., *Alexander James Dallas: Lawyer – Politician – Financier, 1759-1817* (Philadelphia: University of Pennsylvania Press, 1943), 119-46.

17. John Binns, *Recollections of the Life of John Binns* (Philadelphia: John Binns and Parry & M'Millan, 1854), 191-92, 202-11, 232-34; Higginbotham, *Keystone in the Democratic Arch*,

68-70, 108, 130, 133, 136-43, 147-66, 273; Phillips, *William Duane*, 216-22, 229-30, 264-66ff, 300, 347-48, 447; Edward Fox to Jonathan Roberts, 2 June 1812 (1st letter), Jonathan Roberts Papers, Historical Society of Pennsylvania (hereafter HSP).

18. Philadelphia *Aurora*, 1 Sept. 1802; *Salem Register*, 10 Sept. 1802.

19. A different version of the material on Thomas J. Rogers in the rest of this essay appears in Pasley, *"Tyranny of Printers,"* chap. 13. The present essay was commissioned and composed before *"Tyranny of Printers"* was published, but where possible I have tried to update this text to reflect the evolution of my own thinking and the historiography since 2001.

20. Heller, *History of Northampton County*, 1:290-91; Easton *Northampton Farmer*, 3 Sept. 1808; Thomas J. Rogers to Jonathan Roberts, 1 June 1812, Roberts Papers, HSP; Printers File, American Antiquarian Society.

21. Pasley, *"Tyranny of Printers,"* chap. 9.

22. Steven M. Nolt, *Foreigners in Their Own Land: Pennsylvania Germans in the Early Republic* (University Park: Pennsylvania State University Press, 2002), 32-43; A. G. Roeber, "Citizens or Subjects? German-Lutherans and the Federal Constitution in Pennsylvania, 1789-1800," *Amerikastudien/American Studies* 34 (1989): 49-68; Philip Shriver Klein, *Pennsylvania Politics, 1817-1832: A Game Without Rules* (Philadelphia: Historical Society of Pennsylvania, 1940), 5-6; Kenneth W. Keller, "Rural Politics and the Collapse of Pennsylvania Federalism," *Transaction of the American Philosophical Society* 72, part 6 (1982): 1-73; Paul Douglas Newman, *Fries's Rebellion: The Enduring Struggle for the American Revolution* (Philadelphia: University of Pennsylvania Press, 2004), 82-87; Weaver, *"American Eagle,"* 70; Heller, *History of Northampton County*, 1:289-90.

23. Higginbotham, *Keystone in the Democratic Arch*, 73, 93, 100; Newman, *Fries's Rebellion*, 196-99; Kenneth W. Keller, "Cultural Conflict in Early Nineteenth-Century Pennsylvania Politics," *Pennsylvania Magazine of History and Biography* 110 (1986): 509-30; Phillips, *William Duane*, chap. 3. For other perspectives on the Republican divisions in Pennsylvania and the battles over legal reform and the McKean governorship, see Richard E. Ellis, *The Jeffersonian Crisis: Courts and Politics in the Young Republic* (New York: Norton, 1974), chaps. 11 and 12; and Andrew Shankman, *Crucible of American Democracy: The Struggle to Fuse Egalitarianism and Capitalism in Jeffersonian Pennsylvania* (Lawrence: University Press of Kansas, 2004).

24. Heller, *History of Northampton County*, 1:289-90; Alderfer, *Northhampton Heritage*, 181-82; Clarence S. Brigham, *History and Bibliography of American Newspapers, 1690-1820* (Worcester, Mass.: American Antiquarian Society, 1947), 2:843-45; Easton *Northampton Farmer*, 10 May 1805; Easton *American Eagle*, 10 May 1805; Weaver, *"American Eagle"*; *Thomas J. Rogers having purchased the English Printing Office*, Broadside, 12 Nov. 1805, Library Company of Philadelphia.

25. Ibid.; Easton *Northampton Farmer*, 21 Dec. 1805.

26. Ibid.

27. Ibid., 15 Mar., 12 Apr. 1806.

28. Ibid., 12 Apr., 3 May, 20, 27 Sept. 1806.

29. Ibid., 11 Oct. 1806.

30. Ibid., 4 Oct. 1806.

31. Ibid., 4, 11 Oct. 1806.

32. Ibid., 11 Oct. 1806, 3 Jan. 1807.

33. Calculated from election returns published in the *Northampton Farmer*, 25 Oct. 1806. On the newspaper situation in the other counties, see Edward Connery Lathem, *Chronological Tables of American Newspapers, 1690-1820* (Barre, Mass.: American Antiquarian Society & Barre Publishers, 1972), 65-69; and W. W. H. Davis, *The History of Bucks County, Pennsylvania, from the Discovery of the Delaware to the Present Time* (Doylestown, Pa: Democrat Book and Job Office, 1876), 816.

34. *Northampton Farmer*, 18, 25 Oct.; 22 Nov. 1806; 1, 8 Aug. 1807. On Duane's political use of the militia, see Phillips, "William Duane, Philadelphia's Democratic Republicans."

35. Rogers to Roberts, 26 Jan. 1812, Roberts Papers, HSP; *Pennsylvania Archives*, ser. 9, 4:2594, 3115. On use of printing contracts as political patronage, see Smith, *Press, Politics, and Patronage*.

36. Thomas J. Rogers to Jonathan Roberts, 6 Dec. 1807, 3 Jan. 1808 (quoted), Roberts Papers, HSP; Easton *Northampton Farmer*, 22 Nov. 1806.

37. Rogers to Roberts, 17 Nov. 1811; 26 Jan.; 8, 22 Mar.; 5, 20, 26 Apr.; 10, 16 May; 7, 14, 21 June 1812, Roberts Papers, HSP; Jonathan Roberts to Thomas J. Rogers, 30 Mar. 1811; 16 Nov.; 17 Dec. 1812, Jonathan Roberts file, Dreer Collection, HSP; Victor A. Sapio, *Pennsylvania and the War of 1812* (Lexington: University Press of Kentucky, 1970), 73-75.

38. Rogers to Roberts, 1 Dec. 1811; 22 Mar.; 7 June 1812, Roberts Papers, HSP; Easton *Northampton Farmer*, 10 Oct. 1807; 2, 23 Jan. 1808.

39. On Pennsylvania nominating procedures in this period, see Higginbotham, *Keystone in the Democratic Arch*; James S. Chase, *The Emergence of the Presidential Nominating Convention, 1789-1832* (Urbana: University of Illinois Press, 1973), 29-30. The most definite statements on the emergence and characteristics of mass party politics are Joel H. Silbey, *The American Political Nation, 1838-1893* (Stanford: Stanford University Press, 1991); and William G. Shade, "Political Pluralism and Party Development: The Creation of a Modern Party System, 1815-1852," in Paul Kleppner et al., *The Evolution of American Electoral Systems* (Westport, Conn.: Greenwood Press, 1981), 77-111.

40. Rogers to Roberts, 4 Nov. 1811, Roberts Papers, HSP.

41. Easton *Northampton Farmer*, 16 May; 19, 26 Sept.; 10 Oct. 1807; 4 June; 14 Aug. 1808; Rogers to Roberts, 3 Jan. 1808, Roberts Papers, HSP; Brigham, *History and Bibliography of American Newspapers, 1690-1820*, 845-46, 1436; Frank Reeder, *Record of the Family and Descendants of Colonel Christian Jacob Hütter of Easton, Penn'a, 1771-1902* (Easton: Easton Sentinel, 1906), 3-5.

42. Easton *Northampton Farmer*, 2, 23 July; 14, 20, 27 Aug.; 3, 17, 24 Sept.; 1, 8, 15 Oct. 1808; *Pennsylvania Herald and Easton Intelligencer*, 10 Aug. 1808 ff.; 4, 18 Jan. 1809.

43. Rogers to Roberts, 10 May, 1 June, 16 Aug. 1812, Roberts Papers, HSP. On Rodman, see Sapio, *Pennsylvania and the War of 1812*, 154-56.

44. Rogers to Roberts, 1 Nov. 1812, Roberts Papers, HSP.

45. Samuel D. Ingham to Rogers, 27 Dec. 1816, 17 Jan., 21 Dec. 1817, Rogers file, Dreer Collection, HSP. For the political background, see Higginbotham, *Keystone in the Democratic Arch*; and Klein, *Pennsylvania Politics, 1817-1832*.

46. Easton *Spirit of Pennsylvania*, 16 June; 29 Sept.; 6, 13 Oct. 1815; Keller, "Cultural Conflict," 523-28; Newman, *Fries's Rebellion*, 82, 87, 89, 90, 199.

47. Easton *Centinel*, 11, 18, 25 July; 1, 15, 22 Aug. ff.; 17 Oct. 1817; 19 Sept. 1818 ff; John Binns to Rogers, 5 Feb., 7, 23 Dec. 1816, Binns file, Dreer Collection, HSP; Rogers to D. D. Wagener, 19 Jan., 5 Mar. 1818, Nathaniel Michler to Rogers, 18 Jan. 1818, Rogers file, Dreer Collection, HSP. See the companion Web site for my book, *"The Tyranny of Printers,"* at <http://pasleybrothers.com/newspols> for a complete list of printers, editors, and publishers who served in Congress up to 1860, based primarily on the *Biographical Directory of the American Congress*.

48. Christian J. Hütter to Rogers, 16 Feb. 1817, 25 Jan. 1818, 13 Feb. 1819 (quoted), Hütter file, Dreer Collection, HSP. Internal evidence makes it clear that many more letters between the two are missing from the file.

49. Robert L. Meriwether, W. Edwin Hemphill, et al., eds., *The Papers of John C. Calhoun*, 23 vols. to date (Columbia: University of South Carolina Press, 1959), 5:672-73; 7:155, 516, 8: xliv-xlvi, 271; *Carlisle Herald*, reprinted in Easton *Expositor*, 19 Aug. 1822; Rogers to Mathew Carey, 20 Jan.; 27 Feb. 1819; 10, 14 Apr. 1820, Lea and Febiger Papers, HSP; Rogers to Carey, 4 Jan. 1819; 21 Apr. 1820, Edward Carey Gardiner Collection, HSP.

50. Klein, *Pennsylvania Politics, 1817-1832*, 96-105.

51. Easton *Mountaineer*, 7 Jan. 1820-22 June 1821.

52. Easton *Expositor*, 19 Aug.-2 Nov. 1822.

53. Easton *Mountaineer*, 16 June; 7, 22 July; 18 ("trumpeter") Aug.; 22 Sept. 1820; 22 June 1821; Easton *Expositor*, 19, 27 Aug.; 4 Oct. ("begging for votes") 1822. On the "Merino Sheep Fever" in the area, see Heller, *History of Northampton County*, 1:154. This note also covers the previous paragraph. On the persistence of discomfort with partisanship and

classical republican scruples against overly aggressive campaigning, especially by a candidate for himself, see, among others, Ronald P. Formisano, "Political Character, Antipartyism and the Second Party System," *American Quarterly* 21 (1969): 683-709; Michael L. Wallace, "Ideologies of Party in the Ante-Bellum Republic" (PhD diss., Columbia University, 1973); M. J. Heale, *The Presidential Quest: Candidates and Images in American Political Culture, 1787-1852* (London: Longman, 1982); Ralph Ketcham, *Presidents Above Party: The First American Presidency, 1789-1829* (Chapel Hill: University of North Carolina Press,1984); Robert J. Dinkin, *Campaigning in America: A History of Electoral Practices* (Westport, Conn.: Greenwood Press, 1989); Mark Voss-Hubbard, "The 'Third Party Tradition' Reconsidered: Third Parties and American Public Life, 1830-1900," *Journal of American History* 86 (1999): 121-50; Glenn C Altschuler and Stuart M. Blumin, *Rude Republic: Americans and Their Politics in the Nineteenth Century* (Princeton: Princeton University Press, 2000).

54. Easton *Expositor*, 27 Aug.; 3, 10 Sept. ("lowest class"); 1, 4 Oct. 1822. Kenneth Keller ("Cultural Conflict," 523-28) lists nativist hostility toward Irish immigrants as one form of cultural conflict that roiled Pennsylvania politics in the early nineteenth-century, but most of his examples seemed directed at a few very specific Irish immigrants, political editor-bosses such as William Duane, John Binns, and Thomas J. Rogers.

55. Easton *Mountaineer*, 16 June, 5 Oct. 1820, 22 June ("party spirit") 1821; Easton *Expositor*, 27 Aug. ("chimney sweep"); 3, 10 Sept. ("lowest class") 1822.

56. "A Free Elector," ibid., 1 Oct. 1822.

57. Ibid., 10, 24 Sept.; 1, 4, 7, 22 Oct. 1822. Though it does not mention the Rogers flip-flop, crucial context on the power of this issue in the North can be found in Matthew Mason, *Slavery and Politics in the Early American Republic* (Chapel Hill: University of North Carolina Press, 2006).

58. Easton *Expositor*, 3, 10, 17 Sept. 1822.

59. Easton *Centinel*, 24 Sept., 22 Oct., 5 Nov. 1824; Rogers to Coryell, 31 Jan. 1823, Coryell Papers, HSP; Rogers to Condy Raguet, 23 Apr. 1826, Rogers file, Dreer Collection, HSP; Allamong and Jacob, eds., *Biographical Directory of the U.S. Congress*, 1737. Rogers was also bowing to the informal congressional term limits that were established in many localities around this time. See Samuel Kernell, "Toward Understanding 19th Century Congressional Careers: Ambition, Competition, and Rotation," *American Journal of Political Science* 21 (1977): 669-93; Nelson W. Polsby, "The Institutionalization of the U. S. House of Representatives," *American Political Science Review* 62 (1968): 144-68; Morris Fiorina, David Rohde, and Peter Wissel, "Historical Change in House Turnover," in Norman Ornstein, ed., *Congress in Change: Evolution and Reform* (New York: Praeger, 1975), 24-57; Robert Struble, Jr., "House Turnover and the Principle of Rotation," *Political Science Quarterly* 94 (1979): 649-67. On the troubles of common men serving in Congress during the Early Republic, see Pasley, *"Tyranny of Printers,"* 320-29.

60. *Delaware Democrat and Easton Gazette* was begun 10 May 1827 and folded 20 Nov. 1828, with the very issue that reported the election results.

61. Smith, *Press, Politics, and Patronage*, 84–99. Rosters of the editorial appointees were compiled by anti-Jacksonian newspapers. See Washington *Daily National Journal*, 9 Jan. 1829; and Washington *National Intelligencer*, 27 Sept. 1832. My ongoing research has uncovered a few errors and omissions in these rosters, raising the overall number over the 57 listed by the *Intelligencer*. For the current figure, see the companion website to my book, *"Tyranny of Printers"*: <http://pasleybrothers.com/newspols/Jackson_appointees.htm>. On Rogers's campaign for an appointment, see Samuel D. Ingham to Thomas J. Rogers, 16 Mar. 1828, D. H. Miller to Rogers, 5, 10 Apr. 1830, Rogers to D. H. Miller, 10 Apr. 1830, Dreer Collection, HSP; Rogers to Lewis Coryell, 8 June 1828, 5 May, 20 June 1830, Lewis Coryell Papers, HSP; Rogers to Isaac D. Barnard, 14 Dec. 1828, I. D. Barnard Papers, Townsend-LeMaistre Collection, HSP.

62. Allamong and Jacob, eds., *Biographical Directory of the U.S. Congress*, 1738.

63. Washington *Daily National Journal*, 5, 9 Jan.; 3, 9, 14, 18, 21, 28, 29 Apr.; 1, 14 May; 28, 29 Nov.; 3, 4, 5, 23 Dec. 1829; 10, 12, 16, 19, 27 Apr.; 4, 11, 12 May; 28 Aug. 1830. See also extracts from other papers in ibid.; and *Niles' Register*, 13 June 1829. An updated roster can be found in Washington *Daily National Intelligencer*, 27 Sept. 1832.

64. John Randolph to Andrew Jackson, 8 Nov. 1831, John Spencer Bassett, ed., *Correspondence of Andrew Jackson*, 7 vols. (Washington, DC: Carnegie Institution of Washington, 1926-35), 4:370; John Campbell to James Campbell, 23 Apr. [1830], Campbell Family Papers, Duke University; Smith, *Press, Politics, and Patronage*, 96-99, 297n45.

65. Andrew Jackson to T. L. Miller, 13 May 1829, in *Correspondence of Jackson*, ed. Bassett, 4:32.

"Perpetual Motion – Perpetual Change – A Boundless Ocean Without a Shore": Democracy in Pennsylvania and the Consequences of the Triumph of the People, 1800-1820

ANDREW SHANKMAN

EARLY IN 1807 JOHN BINNS, former proprietor of the Northumberland *Republican Argus*, set up shop in Philadelphia with a new newspaper, the *Democratic Press*. From 1803 to 1805 Binns's *Argus* had been the most important rural newspaper in Pennsylvania. Binns had enjoyed the patronage of Speaker of the House and gubernatorial candidate Simon Snyder, and future Speaker Nathaniel B. Boileau.[1]

Binns was well established by 1807, and so his relocation invited comment. The most influential newspaper in Pennsylvania, and indeed the nation, William Duane's Philadelphia *Aurora*, celebrated "a new shield for principles" edited by "a faithful, undaunted supporter of the rights of man."[2] Such praise from Duane and the *Aurora* marked Binns in ways that every contemporary reader understood, for by 1807, Duane was a leading figure in a vitriolic political debate that had splintered Pennsylvania's Jeffersonian party. Since their unchallenged ascendancy in state politics, assured by 1802, Pennsylvania's Jeffersonians, first in Philadelphia and then in the west and south, had denounced each others' political ideals and questioned what they identified as their first principles. Binns as an "*Aurora*-man" was the bitter enemy of leading Jeffersonians such as Governor Thomas McKean and former Secretary of the Commonwealth Alexander J. Dallas.[3]

The debates within the Jeffersonian party prior to 1807 centered on conflicting conceptions of the new, slippery, and vague ideal – democracy. During the first decade of the nineteenth century the Pennsylvania Jeffersonian party split into three groups: a radical city faction the Philadelphia Democrats; their moderate opponents who were also from Philadelphia, the Tertium Quids; and a rural group led by Speaker of the House Simon Snyder called the Snyderites. While each of these groups drew on preexisting beliefs, many of the values and ideological commitments of Pennsylvanian's Jeffersonians were conceived and sharpened through argument and struggle with each other.

This process of ideological formation resulted because of the extreme ideas

The journalist William Duane, engraving by Charles Balthazar
Julian Févret de Saint-Mémin, 1802.

National Portrait Gallery, Smithsonian Institution. Gift of Mr. and Mrs. Paul Mellon.

of the Philadelphia Democrats and the efforts of the Tertium Quids and the Snyderites to respond to that group and function in the political climate that the city radicals created. The Philadelphia Democrats came to believe that democracy could arise only if Pennsylvania's legal and political order was drastically remade. Their proposals would have replaced courts, judges, and lawyers with popularly elected arbitrators. The group sought to return the state constitution to something close to the democratic 1776 document. In general, the Philadelphia Democrats hoped to prevent any office or institution from hindering the majority voice of the state legislature. The Philadelphia Democrats' earliest enemies, the Tertium Quids, feared that only chaos and anarchy would result from such proposals. They struggled to articulate a belief system that could explain why democracy depended on the very legal and political structures that the Philadelphia Democrats insisted would destroy it.

Thus during the first two decades of the nineteenth century, the Snyderites, the primary subject of this essay, found themselves in a difficult position. For reasons discussed below, the Snyderites found the Philadelphia Democrats' fears compelling, and even some of their solutions attractive. But they were not part of the urban milieu hardened by social and economic stratification and Atlantic world radicalism that so shaped the Philadelphia Democrats. Further, by 1804 the Snyderites faced a situation that the city radicals had the luxury of never considering – the real possibility that they might actually have to govern Pennsylvania. Thus between 1804 and 1820 the Snyderites labored to make democracy at once a practicable method of politics and a utopian instrument of equality and justice. The need to conceive democracy so that it met both purposes caused the Snyderites to be among the first Americans to articulate a belief system that bound democracy and capitalism together in ways that would come to be seen, as the nineteenth century progressed, as quintessentially American. The absence of consensus in Pennsylvania during the Jeffersonian era produced bitter conflict that provoked the conception of and commitment to these ideas.

In Philadelphia, shortly after Jefferson's election, men such as Duane and the German Northern Liberties Congressman Michael Leib became the leaders of a group of Jeffersonian partisans, the Philadelphia Democrats. These Jeffersonians began to use the idea of democracy to challenge much of the political and economic order in Pennsylvania and the young republic.[4] These Philadelphia Democrats argued that a truly republican society survived only when its citizens were safe from the coercion of all others, when citizens had direct control over government, including the legislature and courts. Such safety came only with commitment to "that happy mediocrity of condition, which is our greatest security and our best preservative against the gradual approaches of arbitrary power."[5]

Demands for such independence did not lead the Philadelphia Democrats to embrace autarky or isolation, either economically or politically. Citizens had to be active and engaged. Philadelphia's vibrant waterfront and Pennsylvania's thriving manufactures and agricultural commerce provided opportunities for the respectable prosperity and freedom from want that separated sturdy citizens from dependents. But great wealth or concentrated control of productive property had in the past produced inequality and destroyed republican experiments. A dynamic economy had to continue to promote the happy mediocrity of condition. And it would, Philadelphia Democrats insisted, with the proper application of democracy.

The Philadelphia Democrats sought to make more popular and accountable those institutions that they identified as threats to the happy mediocrity of condition. Thus a radical conception of popular sovereignty lay at the core of the group's notion of democracy. For the city radicals popular sovereignty was a perpetual and guiding force in political decision making. Once the citizenry eradicated those places where unaccountable decision making favored some over others, the sovereign people could preserve the equality that allowed their republican experiment to succeed where less egalitarian ones had failed.[6]

After 1802, the Philadelphia Democrats identified many institutions that needed to be democratized or simply expunged. In the courts, English common law should be eliminated because it justified inequality and led to crucial decisions by unaccountable judges. In the place of appointed judges, Philadelphia Democrats argued for arbitrators elected by and frequently accountable to the people to decide cases that could either preserve or undermine social and economic equality. Between 1802 and 1805, the Philadelphia Democrats also demanded that the power of the lower house of the Pennsylvania legislature be increased at the expense of the senate and governor. Finally, they came to mistrust written constitutions serving as fundamental law, labeling them efforts to "control future time" and constrain democratic bodies. Constitutions denied the people democratic instruments in their struggle to preserve equality.[7]

Between 1802 and 1804, many Jeffersonians in Pennsylvania grew alarmed at these ideas. They accepted that the Philadelphia Democrats proceeded from a cherished ideal. But rather than achieve it, their ideas would lead to such economic, social, and political uncertainty that the republican experiment would finally produce a society more impoverished and anxious than any but the worst despotisms. The Philadelphia Democrats' early critics were by no means apologists for untrammeled economic development. Nor were they willing to tolerate dangerous inequalities for the sake of an illusive personal freedom that ignored the needs of the community. Jeffersonian leaders such as Dallas and McKean assumed that there would always be differences in wealth and talents. But they sought a world where those differences would not translate into political power, a world where some naturally had more than others, but where no citizen's economic condition gave him so few options that he had to depend on the will or property of others. Men such as Dallas and McKean agreed that the republican experiment could work only if almost everybody had direct access to productive property. But in the early nineteenth century they feared that the greatest threat to this happy prospect was the ideology of the Philadelphia Democrats themselves.

By 1803 a group of Pennsylvania Jeffersonians had organized to argue against the positions taken by the Philadelphia Democrats. The *Aurora* derisively called them the Tertium Quids, or third whats, and the name became popular. The Quids are a fascinating group; they suggest an important development in early national American society.[8] Generally wealthier and better educated than their opponents, they enjoyed real prominence in their communities. When they confronted the Philadelphia Democrats it was clear that they felt Pennsylvania would be far better off if they were in power. Yet the Quids were just as convinced as their opponents that the people had the ability to shape the best political system and fashion the most appropriate social order. In their private writings and the newspaper they started in 1804, the *Evening Post*, soon renamed the *Freeman's Journal*, the Quids did not imagine an organic social order, a preexisting social ideal that republican citizens had to build. Men like Dallas and McKean were at home with mass addresses, gatherings out of doors, even with Democratic-Republican Societies. Indeed when it appeared in 1800 as if the Federalists would try to thwart popular will and make Aaron Burr President, McKean had offered Jefferson the assistance of the Pennsylvania militia.[9]

The Quids imagined a republic with abundant resources in which most citizens could achieve material independence on a scale unprecedented in the western world. But this sweeping faith in expansive material independence would not turn republican citizens into autonomous, disconnected individualists. They would act together politically to protect and expand the material conditions of social and economic independence that made the new nation's circumstances unique. Citizenship was integral to the Quids' hopes. When worst came to worst there had to be a militia for McKean to assemble. In the less extraordinary times of peace, prosperity, and stability citizens had to place in power men who would judiciously protect and extend the conditions of economic, social, and thus political independence for the greatest number. The Quids were convinced of their right to rule because they understood better than most the need to protect what the incendiary notions of their opponents would destroy – the stable economic development and resultant general prosperity that guaranteed independence.[10]

The Quids believed that the people could responsibly protect the republican experiment. The desired republican society would only be established, protected, and properly governed by the vigorous efforts of the people. And once the people's elected governors solidified a republican social structure, abundant resources and opportunities would preserve an unprecedented degree of independence. Pennsylvanians would create a fluid social structure of opportunity and mobility. This mobility would not allow the consolidation of property and corresponding dependence that marred European societies.

For the Quids, then, the Philadelphia Democrats' reforms threatened disaster. If they led Pennsylvanians astray, the radicals could introduce the conditions that allowed the rights of independent citizens to be trampled. They would produce the chaos that would undermine the energies of the people, waste the nation's resources, diminish opportunities, and so cause dependence and want.[11]

Thus after 1802, Philadelphia Jeffersonians divided. They battled over legal reform, the proper republican political structure, and exactly what democracy meant and how it should be used. Battles between the Quids and the Philadelphia Democrats established the terms of political conflict in Pennsylvania. But to a great extent this conflict was a city fight. People throughout the state were concerned about the issues that sparked the argument, especially complaints about the courts and the conduct of judicial officers. But the Philadelphia Democrats brought extremity to the debate fueled by the greater social and economic inequality of Philadelphia, and their own doctrinaire international republican commitments.[12] In rural Pennsylvania, where economic conditions were not so desperate, few Jeffersonians considered desirable the most radical notions emanating from the city.

Thus it was difficult for potential reformers outside Philadelphia to discuss the issues or frame the debate in terms more useful to them, terms that made more sense in the countryside. This problem was one of the key reasons why forces coalesced around Simon Snyder of Northumberland County. Snyderites would between 1803 and 1810 define themselves as distinct from the Philadelphia Democrats and the Quids. The Snyderites would become the most influential force in early national Pennsylvania politics. Indeed, they were the most successful grassroots radical movement to emerge between the American Revolution and the age of Jackson. The Snyderites put their own stamp on democracy. They played a significant part in establishing the boundaries of permissible thought concerning democracy and political economy in a society where all men were created equal. By doing so they defined where, how, and why democracy and capitalism intersected in Jacksonian Pennsylvania.

Prior to 1805 concerns about the Pennsylvania legal system were not confined to Philadelphia County. Courts, lawyers, and judges in the south and west received much criticism. As population increased, farmers cultivated more acres and consolidated landholdings. Increasing commerce and disputes over land titles drove up the volume of court business, something the state's legal system was ill equipped to handle.[13]

But rural Pennsylvanians focused on the courts for deeper reasons. The Pennsylvania judiciary was quite hierarchical. Supreme Court justices also presided at the appellate level. In a position to overturn inferior court decisions, the high court judges were also part of the general transformation of common law occurring in late eighteenth- and early nineteenth-century America. The Pennsylvania Supreme Court interpreted common law to encourage unshackled alienation of property. Thus the court in general supported holders who pursued the most entrepreneurial uses of land, though many traditional holders increasingly believed that such behavior caused undesirable fluctuation, uncertainty, and dislocation. In the volatile commercial period after 1780, the judges' decisions contributed to an unprecedented inequality in landholdings.[14] Like the city radicals, rural Jeffersonians had good reason to focus on the place and function of English-inspired common law and an unaccountable judiciary in a republic.

By the 1790s, rural Jeffersonians such as Simon Snyder were concerned by the influence of elites in the new republic. But the rural southeast, which became the foundation of Snyder's power, was quite different than Philadelphia. Southeasterners did not share the Philadelphia Democrats' sense that only precisely structured democratic politics could save the United States from the fate of Europe. The southeast had far more reason to be sanguine. The prevailing conception in the southeast was of a fluid social structure in which young men experienced temporary dependence on their way to independence.[15]

Nevertheless, beginning in roughly 1760 consolidation of land ownership and the stratification of wealth had begun to cause this social structure to harden. Rural anxiety grew steadily over the course of a generation, and much of the worry led to criticism of the courts. By 1800 many rural Jeffersonians feared that the courts were allowing land companies and wealthy purchasers to disrupt a social and economic structure that permitted general prosperity and independence.

In 1803 John Binns arrived in Northumberland County. He soon met Snyder, the emerging political leader of Northumberland. Snyder was living proof of the opportunities available in the southeast at the end of the eighteenth century. He had come to Northumberland County in 1784. Largely an autodidact, he rose from journeyman tanner to independent proprietor and became a leading citizen of Selinsgrove, Pennsylvania. By 1803, when he met Binns, Snyder was a rising member of the state legislature, soon the Speaker of the House. Snyder introduced Binns to a new friend and ally, state representative from Montgomery County Nathaniel B. Boileau, whose rise was equally impressive. Compared to the England of the younger Pitt, Binns must have thought he was three thousand miles closer to paradise.[16]

Snyder and his friends helped Binns start the Northumberland *Republican Argus*. The paper provided the primary rural critique of Pennsylvania's legal system. Unlike the Philadelphia Democrats, the Snyderites did not seek to eradicate judges and lawyers. Where the city radicals wanted arbitration to supplant the current legal system, the rural Snyderites believed that arbitrators should supplement it. Nevertheless, the Snyderites were attracted to the idea of shifting a great deal of legal decision making to local figures elected by local voters, and thus to democratizing positions that the Quids insisted needed to be held by executive appointees in good behavior. Thus in 1803 and 1804, when Quid Jeffersonian Governor Thomas McKean vetoed numerous arbitration bills, Binns's *Argus* became an opponent of the Governor as well.[17]

There was, then, ample reason for rural reformers to make common cause with the Philadelphia Democrats; after 1803 the two groups did. Binns reprinted *Aurora* articles denouncing the state's legal system and praising the city radicals' brand of democracy. City supporters of Duane and Leib helped place Snyder in the Speaker's chair.

In 1803 and 1804 this coalition of urban and rural Jeffersonians became one of the most vibrant and radical organized political movements ever to operate within mainstream American politics.[18] Yet the radical coalition was never that comfortable a blend of personalities, ideals, or assumptions. By entering the Jeffersonian debate, southeasterners saw a chance to gain control of state government and remake Pennsylvania in their image. While the Philadelphia Democrats cast their net wide, seeking, it seemed at times, almost perpetual world democratic revolution, southeasterners remained firmly grounded in their fertile Pennsylvania soil.

Initially the differences between urban and rural reform Jeffersonians were muted and subtle. They were overshadowed by the shared commitment to profound changes in the legal order. But from the beginning, demand for reforms such as arbitration could be divided into two categories. The first was a commitment to common sense reforms that would speed the judicial process and make an adversarial legal system more amenable to the steadily increasing needs of a growing economy and its litigious participants. The second category was more a utopian impulse to alter the legal system radically and link this alteration to a general transformation of American society. Reformers in this second category connected their vision to international hopes for a general European democratic revolution. These two strains, at least at first, were not automatically incompatible.

Snyderites denounced the Quids and railed against McKean's veto of arbitration bills. Many editorials used terms that would have been quite at home in the *Aurora*.[19] But the Snyderites emphasized practical concerns. They stressed the delay and expense caused by the courts and argued that arbitration should supplement, not supplant, the overworked judiciary.[20] While the Snyderites tended to fall into the first category of reform, the Philadelphia Democrats were only interested in the second. The Quids took full advantage of the Philadelphia Democrats' extremity and began to equate the entire reform coalition with the Philadelphia Democrats' ideals.

The Quids' campaign was effective, and by late 1804 the Snyderites felt the need to respond to it. For by 1804 they had actually begun to accomplish a great deal. Snyder was Speaker of the House, and they had passed a limited form of arbitration that placed strict monetary limits on the cases that arbitrators could hear. McKean was manifestly unpopular and Snyder had a solid chance of defeat-ing him. By 1804 the Snyderites could realistically hope that they would control state government, the place where they believed the most vital decisions were made.

The Quids' lasting legacy, bequeathed in 1804 and 1805, was twofold. First, by insisting that the Philadelphia Democrats and the Snyderites were indistinguishable, they forced the Snyderites to disprove them. The Snyderites did so. But by succeeding, the Quids estranged willingness to consider fundamental solutions to nagging problems from the practical hardheaded workaday world of state politics and public life. After 1805, few dared offer sweeping alternatives, even if most identified serious concerns that demanded solutions. It was too easy to be discredited as caring more for agitation and discord than the supposed improvements that unruly behavior allegedly brought. But the Quids did not simply cast doubt on one way of considering the problems the state might face in the future. The Quids' second achievement was to provide an alternative vision of that future. They insisted that Pennsylvanians, indeed all Americans, should acknowledge their exceptional material circumstances and use economic growth and development to ensure general prosperity and independence.

During 1805 the Snyderites shifted emphasis. They began to speak far less about the sweeping alternatives so dear to the Philadelphia Democrats. Instead they focused on controlling state government. They reasoned that men with their loyalties and concerns could ensure that a good government in a just and equal society was not misused. The state's political structure, then, would not threaten that society. In 1805 Snyder did challenge McKean. The Philadelphia *Aurora* supported him, arguing that the election would allow the massive changes the paper had demanded for the past three years, changes that would occur all at once at the constitutional convention that the Philadelphia Democrats demanded once democrats took power. But Binns's *Argus* took a different tack. It distanced Snyder from the demand for a constitutional convention. Instead it compared his past favorably to McKean's. Snyder was a common man, a laborer. He had been a mechanic, farmer, and merchant. McKean was an effete lawyer. Snyder understood from direct experience the needs and concerns of Pennsylvania's industrious producers. McKean, a college-educated lawyer and non-producer, far removed from the concerns of the common man, could never capably lead the society Pennsylvania hoped to remain.[21] During the campaign McKean lost his temper and denounced as clodhoppers a delegation of legislators headed by Snyder. The Snyderites embraced the term. Snyder was a clodhopper, a hard worker, and a self-made, unpretentious man. In a democracy, the Snyderites suggested, only clodhoppers could rule the people.[22]

Yet the Quids continued to insist that there was no difference between the Philadelphia Democrats and the Snyderites. And the Philadelphia Democrats continued to denounce judges and lawyers and demand a constitutional convention. Frequently during the gubernatorial campaign the Snyderites had to oppose the views of their supposed allies. Their efforts took valuable time away from seeking McKean's defeat.[23]

In the short term the Quids' campaign succeeded. McKean beat Snyder but his majority of close to 40,000 in 1802 had shrunk to 4,766 by 1805. Having won his third consecutive term, McKean was constitutionally prohibited from running again in 1808.[24] The Quids after 1805 were frightened. They understandably looked at the areas of agreement between the two reform groups. Snyder was now the gubernatorial heir apparent. Seemingly Duane and Leib would be more influential in his administration than they ever could be with Quid rule.[25]

The Snyderites drew a different lesson from Snyder's defeat. They ran a candidate truly of the people. They planned to place in positions of responsibility men who had both ideological and material interest in maintaining the conditions that promised widespread prosperity and independence. Why then had they lost? Because of the ways the Quids had made use of the Philadelphia Democrats. Thus in 1807 John Binns moved his Northumberland County office to the nation's largest city. He came with a mission: to teach Philadelphia that democracy meant the election of men such as Snyder, not the sweeping demands of the city radicals.

In 1807 and 1808, Binns, Boileau, Snyder, and their followers sought an independent voice that could not be mistaken or willfully misconstrued. Their goals were shaped by their unprecedented position. Simon Snyder was poised to become the executive with the most humble roots ever elected in the republic. That fact, and the possibilities it represented, demanded that plans for reform be tempered by something approaching moderation. There was much that needed to be fixed in Pennsylvania. Democracy had yet to be secured. But their near-success in 1805, the Snyderites concluded, meant that there was far less disastrously wrong with the state than the city radicals thought.

By autumn 1807, the Snyderites' concerns had exploded into a full-blown newspaper war between Binns's *Democratic Press* and Duane's *Aurora*. The Snyderites proved quite capable of joining in the rough-and-tumble of the city's democratic politics. They boldly denounced the Philadelphia Democrats and shouted just as loudly that they were democrats and plain common men.[26] The Snyderites were ingenious politicians and managed to create a new category in Philadelphia politics – the democrat who believed the Philadelphia Democrats the greatest threat to democracy. In folksy, even semi-comic, editorials the *Democratic Press* introduced a new character to the Philadelphia region, the sturdy yeoman who saw through cant and sophistry. He possessed no polish or great oratory, but his rugged common sense penetrated the elitism of the Quids and the demagoguery of Leib. At times the *Democratic Press* identified this character as "Simon Easy," at others as "a sturdy and uniform Whig from the commencement of the revolutionary war to the present day."[27]

The *Democratic Press*'s editorial voice helped create a democratic vernacular; it helped imagine what sort of person a democratic citizen was, how he acted, and what he expected. Simon Easy, or the steady Whig, or the average Pennsylvanian mistrusted all airs, lampooned social pretensions, and understood that common sense and common men could resolve the community's difficulties without windy pomposity. The Snyderites were in effect taking the farce out of the world of *Modern Chivalry*, the novel written by Pennsylvanian and Quid Hugh Henry Brackenridge. Farrago was the fool and Teague O'Regan capable of fulfilling the responsibilities thrust upon him.[28]

A democracy properly constituted did not need sweeping reforms; it could even benefit from stable institutions that safeguarded fundamental rights. What it needed above all else was an unquenchable belief that ordinary men who held dear the interests of other ordinary men could govern properly. It followed then that decision-making should occur at the state level where the Simon Snyders of the world had a chance to be influential. With the people truly governing, the primary responsibility of government was to pursue a political economy that provided independence. Then democrats and citizens could laugh at those who sought to be first among equals like the Quids, or saviors of the common man like Leib.

Once Snyder triumphed in the gubernatorial election of 1808, the Snyderites began to develop the economy so citizens could mobilize their own resources and insulate themselves from the actions of others. The Snyderites sought to democratize the sinews of economic growth – banks, credit, roads, and markets. The outcome depended on the sort of society that pursued such development. In an aristocracy wealth and commerce raised distinctions, in a democracy they leveled them. Fundamental to the Snyderites' goals was shifting the nation's energies from the external to the internal market, and allowing producers to control and develop that market. The Snyderites would accomplish this shift by placing productive resources directly in producers' hands.

Central to the Snyderites' thought was making Pennsylvania's dynamic economy an agent of democratic equality and independence. Democracy merely required democrats in power. Once the Snyderites took power, common men could govern

> an extensive and fertile territory, an active, industrious and intelligent population, and a wise and beneficent system of government, [that would] present the materials of opulence and social comfort, which it is the duty of the legislature, by a steady exertion of the common energy of the state, to cultivate and increase. The public purse, entrusted to their care for the common benefit, amply supplies them means – and the public voice, and the public necessity loudly demand their application to the purpose of internal improvement. To bring into a productive state the large masses of land which lie wholly uncultivated; to increase the value of those which are partially improved; to stimulate industry by furnishing it with a motive for activity; increase the public wealth, and distribute it in due proportions through all the parts of the state, and thereby as far as possible to equalize the condition of her citizens: and above all to draw together and bind with the ties of common interest, the citizens of the same community; are the results which the legislature, by a liberal policy, may contribute to produce.[29]

Thus the Snyderites increased the number of banks and promoted turnpikes, bridges, and canals. By doing so they hoped to extend credit and opportunity further down the social ladder to most farmers and mechanics. The solution to inequalities, to disparities in power, was for a democratic legislature to support institutions that would increase capital and distribute it to actual producers seeking to develop the internal economy.

In 1808 and 1809 the Snyderites were not uncritical or unthinking advocates of rapid economic development. They believed that unequal societies produced wealth enjoyed unequally. But in democracies, where ordinary producers made decisions and carefully managed the institutions and sinews of economic development, the productivity of a people could in unprecedented fashion strengthen the bonds of community. Economic development, structured democratically, would ensure a rough equality of condition and so prevent systematic inequalities and dependencies. Supporting proper improvement meant avoiding the extreme notions of the Philadelphia Democrats. Democracy would flourish through careful policies that improved the condition of all, not with extreme and dangerous plans that turned citizens against one another.

The Snyderites' insistence that economic development encouraged and administered by common men created democratic economic and social relations provoked some of the *Aurora*'s sharpest and most compelling writing. The *Aurora* continued to keep alive the spirit of 1805 by denouncing the common law, demanding arbitration, defending a constitutional convention, and even by providing a sympathetic explanation for the origins of the agrarian law.[30] The survival of the Philadelphia Democrats had a critical impact on state politics. The city radicals were a constant voice, a nagging reminder that Pennsylvanians should not wholly embrace the Snyderite vision.

Thus, in response, after 1808 the Snyderites became less and less willing to entertain even sober critiques of their ideas. They insisted ever more loudly and uniformly that legislatures and executives comprised of democrats, producers, and common men were congenitally incapable of harming their fellow citizens. The true interest of producers was for producer legislators to expand their economic opportunities. Those who suggested otherwise were enemies of democracy and the people. The Snyderite response meant that it became increasingly difficult from within mainstream Pennsylvania politics to take a cautious reflective position toward economic development. Economic development meant opportunity, opportunity meant equality, and equality produced democracy. To say otherwise was to expose one's lack of virtue, one's hostility to democracy, one's fatal mistrust of the people.

In the name of democracy the Snyderites began to pursue untrammeled economic development. They shaped a belief system that discouraged them from considering the consequences. Indeed, their ideas became a club with which to bludgeon any who tried. By Snyder's third term, which began in 1814, the original balance – development to sustain and protect a rough equality of condition – was in danger of being lost. In the intervening years economic development had come to be identified so completely with democracy, and so intrinsically a positive good, that emerging Snyderites wondered why anyone would ever seek to contain or direct it. The *Democratic Press* had described the Snyderites' vision as "profitable patriotism."[31] By 1814, newer Snyderites such as Samuel D. Ingham, William Findlay, and James Buchanan were refusing to distinguish between profits and patriotism. As older Snyderites, most notably Snyder and Boileau, grew concerned about the uncritical glee with which their party chartered road and canal companies, and applauded accumulation and private improvements, many began to regroup around Ingham and Findlay. The split became public in 1814 when the legislature chartered forty-two banks. Snyder vetoed his own party's bill, and in a sense things then came to their logical conclusion. Snyderites questioned Snyder's own democratic virtue. The first clodhopper was now thwarting the voice of the people.[32]

By the time Snyder vetoed the bank bill, Findlay and his supporters were ascendant in the legislature. And indeed theirs was the more consistent understanding of the ultimate course, if not initial goals, of Snyderite belief. The legislature overrode Snyder's veto and chartered the new banks. The banks lent irresponsibly over the next several years and played a crucial role in the Panic of 1819 that hit Pennsylvania hard and did much to destroy early dreams of an equal democratic community.[33] One of the unfortunates was Simon Snyder who passed 1819, the last year of his life, lamenting the worthlessness of county paper and seeking loans from friends such as Binns.[34]

The Panic of 1819 and its immediate aftermath offer a better place than many to end a discussion of Pennsylvania politics in the early republic. From 1802 through 1819 Philadelphia Democrats, Quids, and varieties of Snyderites had pursued a shared goal: securing a basic economic equality and freedom from desperation and coercion for as many citizens as possible. The groups had very different ideas about how to achieve this vision. But close to two decades feverishly pursuing the goal ended with economic catastrophe. Obviously the Panic struck the entire nation. But given the ideals that drove Pennsylvania politics, the state's leaders were particularly disappointed.

The story of Pennsylvania politics in the early republic cannot be neatly divided into winners and losers. Given first principles, it is difficult to see who won much at all. But between 1802 and 1819 certain developments became increasingly irreversible. Most crucial were, first, that one could not be politically active without identifying with democracy; and second, that democracy largely meant commitment to economic development and an assertion of faith that this development would produce desired social and economic equality. The Panic of 1819 initially appeared likely to threaten but eventually hardened both the commitment and the faith.

After the Panic, the Philadelphia Democrats expected their fortunes to rise. For a time they did. The group called for policies, mostly hard money and anti-bank, that would become quite popular nationally in the Jacksonian era. But by the mid-1820s, the city radicals had been isolated once and for all.[35] And the reason was the peculiar body of ideas that in Pennsylvania had been bound together as democracy. For when the Philadelphia Democrats tried to revive the ideas of 1805, their Pennsylvania opponents were almost uniquely able to denounce them in the name of democracy. A final look at the *Democratic Press* will show the meaning of democracy in Pennsylvania on the eve of the age of Jackson.

The various enemies of the Philadelphia Democrats, including the Quids and Snyderite factions, confronted the Panic directly. They also closed ranks to a certain extent, agreeing at the very least that they had to combat the ideas once again aired in the *Aurora*. The *Democratic Press* began to publish essays by the Quid Matthew Carey. And Binns and Carey took the lead in articulating alternative ideas that they believed explained the Panic, offered a democratic solution, and exposed the Philadelphia Democrats as demagogues.[36]

A May 31, 1819, article in the *Democratic Press* offers a fine example of these efforts. Written by "A Workman," it purported to speak for the "seven-tenths of the population [who] come into the world without the means of subsisting for themselves." This group was the vast majority of the people, the lifeblood of democracy. The ability of laborers to fulfill the obligations of citizenship was crucial, and therefore so was their capacity to become independent and place themselves beyond want and coercion. This capacity the Panic surely threatened. Without doubt, the article continued, government played an important role in furthering the independence of people whose "labor is the only commodity they possess to offer in exchange for those things necessary to supply their wants." How then did a responsible democratic government respond to the Panic of 1819? It did so by acknowledging once and for all that the most reliable market was domestic. The nation had to commit to protective tariffs, a mixed economy of manufacturing, agriculture, and commerce, and internal consumption of internal production. The dynamic internal market would provide the opportunity that allowed the seven-tenths to secure their independence through their own dignified efforts. The Panic had resulted not from Americans' overindulgence or irresponsibility. Rather it occurred because the nation had incompletely embraced the future. Resources, capital, and labor were not fully used, the internal economy was not fully developed, and thus the workers, the best potential citizens, relied on the vagaries of foreign commerce.[37]

Those who called for extreme solutions, the Philadelphia Democrats, frightened men of standing and capital from supporting the internal market. Such demands kept workers idle and undermined independence and genuine citizenship. Those who attacked the sinews of the domestic economy, banks, paper currency, credit, internal improvements, and protective tariffs were in fact demagogues who would reduce the people to dependence. Such men sought to keep the people angry and desperate so they could ride to power on a dangerous and destructive wave of popular fury.

The answer to the Panic was a great deal more democracy, a more complete commitment to economic development, a stronger faith in the power of the market created and expanded by and for producers. Such a market guided by true democrats would produce the independent condition all Pennsylvanians understood as essential for democracy. Snyderites had been articulating these ideas with increasing coherence for ten years before 1819. By the time economic crisis struck, Pennsylvania was capable of deflecting calls for direct popular intrusion into the economy.[38] Pennsylvania could do so because the Snyderites credibly denounced such popular intervention in the name of democracy and the people.

The legacy of Jeffersonian politics in early national Pennsylvania was a bitter one. All the groups discussed here identified a rough equality of condition, a basic independence of circumstances, as the essential ingredient of democracy. The desire of the Philadelphia Democrats, Quids, and Snyderites for such a condition is beyond question. Yet the sustained battle to define democracy, the need to confront and defeat one's Jeffersonian opponents, above all the fear engendered by the Philadelphia Democrats' extremity, produced a body of ideas and a political economy that progressively destroyed the possibility for such equality.[39] Further, the belief system that emerged from the Jeffersonian battles had a powerful capacity to be self-sustaining. Once Pennsylvanians equated democracy with ordinary men seeking as much profit as possible, it became increasingly easier to brand critics of such a system as enemies of democracy. Thus capitalism came to be defined as more than just a potent economic system. Over the decades its supporters insisted, ever more shrilly, that it was synonymous with justice, decency, and freedom regardless of the dislocation and anxiety market solutions to social ills quickly began to produce. Looking back at the first decades of the early nineteenth century, John Quincy Adams described what he saw to the former Quid turned Democrat Charles Jared Ingersoll. All was, Quincy Adams lamented, "perpetual motion – perpetual change – a boundless ocean without a shore."[40] Pennsylvania's Jeffersonians had dared to imagine a world with many ports and few storms. Their efforts provided Quincy Adams his anxious image for many a future pitiable sailor.

Notes

1. Sanford W. Higginbotham, *The Keystone in the Democratic Arch: Pennsylvania Politics, 1800-1816* (Harrisburg: Pennsylvania Historical and Museum Commission, 1952); and

Andrew Shankman, *Crucible of American Democracy: The Struggle to Fuse Egalitarianism and Capitalism in Jeffersonian Pennsylvania* (Lawrence: University Press of Kansas, 2004), 90-95.

2. *Aurora*, 18 Feb.1807. For the *Aurora's* influence see Michael Durey, "Thomas Paine's Apostles: Radical Emigres and the Triumph of Jeffersonian Republicanism," *William and Mary Quarterly*, 3d ser., 44 (1987): 661-88, quotation on 683.

3. Andrew Shankman, "Malcontents and Tertium Quids: The Battle to Define Democracy in Jeffersonian Philadelphia," *Journal of the Early Republic* 19 (1999): 43-72.

4. The term Philadelphia Democrats is my creation. The group called themselves Democratic Republicans or Democrats; opponents usually called them Malcontents or Jacobins. For the Philadelphia Democrats, see Shankman, *Crucible of American Democracy*, chaps. 2 and 4.

5. *Aurora*, 27 May 1805. See also 23 Jan. 1804, 5 June 1805.

6. The Philadelphia Democrats' view of popular sovereignty, then, was far removed from mainstream and more elite understanding of its uses and workings. See Gordon S. Wood, *The Creation of the American Republic, 1776-1787* (Chapel Hill: University of North Carolina Press, 1969) and Edmund S. Morgan, *Inventing the People: The Rise of Popular Sovereignty in England and America* (New York: Norton, 1988).

7. *Aurora*, 10 May 1805. See also 5 Apr. and 7 May 1805.

8. For the Quids, see Shankman, *Crucible of American Democracy*, chaps. 3 and 4.

9. James Roger Sharp, *American Politics in the Early Republic: The New Nation in Crisis* (New Haven: Yale University Press, 1993).

10. *Evening Post*, 21, 25 Feb., 17 Mar., 22 May 1804. See also Andrew Shankman, "'A New Thing on Earth': Alexander Hamilton, Pro-Manufacturing Republicans, and the Democratization of American Political Economy," *Journal of the Early Republic* 23 (2003): 323-52.

11. *Evening Post*, 16, 19, 28 May 1804. See also Alexander J. Dallas, "An Address to the Republicans of Pennsylvania," *Freeman's Journal*, 11, 12 June; 5 July 1805. The address is reprinted in George Mifflin Dallas, ed., *Life and Writings of Alexander James Dallas* (Philadelphia: J. B. Lippincott and Co., 1871), 211-33.

12. Space constraints prevent exploration of this point. But Duane's international experiences as a radical and Leib's commitments to the French Revolution shaped the tone and character of the Philadelphia Democrats' methods and attitudes. See Shankman, *Crucible of American Democracy*, chaps. 1 and 2; Kim Tousley Phillips, *William Duane, Radical Journalist in the Age of Jefferson* (New York: Garland, 1989); and Kenneth W. Keller, "Diversity and Democracy: Ethnic Politics in Southeastern Pennsylvania, 1788-1799" (PhD diss.: Yale University, 1971), chap. 5.

13. For commerce, landholdings, and population, see James T. Lemon, *The Best Poor Man's Country: A Geographical Study of Early Southeastern Pennsylvania* (Baltimore: Johns Hopkins

University Press, 1972); Lucy Simler, "Tenancy in Colonial Pennsylvania: The Case of Chester County," *William and Mary Quarterly,* 3d ser., 43 (1986): 542-69; Simler, "The Landless Worker: An Index of Economic and Social Change in Chester County, Pennsylvania, 1750-1820," *Pennsylvania Magazine of History and Biography* 114 (1990): 163-99; Simler, "James Lemon's Best Poor Man's Country Revisited: Chester County, Pennsylvania, in the Early Republic," paper presented at the McNeil Center for Early American Studies, Philadelphia, 1 Mar. 1996; Simler and Paul G. E. Clemens, "The 'Best Poor Man's Country' in 1783: The Population Structure of Rural Society in Late-Eighteenth-Century Southeastern Pennsylvania," *Proceedings of the American Philosophical Society* 133 (1989): 234-61; and R. Eugene Harper, *The Transformation of Western Pennsylvania, 1770-1800* (Pittsburgh: University of Pittsburgh Press, 1991). For concerns about the courts, see Richard E. Ellis, *The Jeffersonian Crisis: Courts and Politics in the Young Republic* (New York: Oxford University Press, 1971); James F. Dinsmore, "Courts and Western Pennsylvania Lands: The Origins of the Attack on the Pennsylvania Courts, 1790-1810" (PhD diss.: Temple University, 1990); and M. Ruth Reilly Kelly, "Rightfully Theirs and Valid in the Law: Western Pennsylvania Land Wars, 1792-1810," *Pennsylvania History* 71 (2004): 25-51.

14. For changes in judicial interpretation, see Morton J. Horwitz, *The Transformation of American Law, 1780-1860* (Cambridge, Mass.: Harvard University Press, 1977); R. Kent Newmyer, "Harvard Law School, New England Legal Culture, and the Antebellum Origins of American Jurisprudence," in *The Constitution and American Life,* ed. David Thelen (Ithaca, N.Y.: Cornell University Press, 1987), 154-75; Newmyer, *Supreme Court Justice Joseph Story: Statesman of the Old Republic* (Chapel Hill: University of North Carolina Press, 1985); Dinsmore, "Courts and Western Pennsylvania Lands."

15. Lemon, *Best Poor Man's Country;* Simler, "Tenancy in Colonial Pennsylvania" and "James Lemon's Best Poor Man's Country."

16. For Snyder, see "Autobiographical Notes by Simon Snyder," *Pennsylvania Magazine of History and Biography* 4 (1880): 248-49; *Dictionary of American Biography,* vol. 17, ed. Dumas Malone (New York: Charles Scribner's Sons, 1935), 389-90. John Binns, *Recollections of the Life of John Binns* (Philadelphia: John Binns and Parry and M'Millan, 1854).

17. *Argus,* 22, 29 July; 5, 12 Aug. 1803.

18. John M. Murrin, "Escaping Perfidious Albion: Federalism, Fear of Aristocracy, and the Democratization of Corruption in Postrevolutionary America," in *Virtue, Corruption, and Self-Interest: Political Values in the Eighteenth Century,* ed. Richard K. Matthews (Bethlehem, Pa.: Lehigh University Press, 1994), 103-47.

19. *Argus,* 16 Sept. 1803.

20. *Argus,* 21 Oct. 1803.

21. *Argus,* 16 Aug.; 6, 13, 20 Sept. 1805.

22. Higginbotham, *Keystone in the Democratic Arch,* 85.

23. *Argus,* 6, 27 Sept. 1805 provide good examples of this dilemma.

24. Higginbotham, *Keystone in the Democratic Arch*, 99.

25. *Freeman's Journal*, 3, 30, 31 Aug. 1805.

26. Those wishing to follow the early phase of the conflict should see *Aurora*, 3, 23, 25, 26, 28, 29 Sept.; 5, 7, 9, 12 Oct. 1807; and *Democratic Press*, 25, 28, 29 Aug.; 4, 8, 11, 19, 22, 23, 24, 25, 30 Sept.; 2, 3, 5, 6, 7, 9, 10, 12, 13, 19, and 20 Oct. 1807.

27. *Democratic Press*, 7 Sept. 1807; the "Simon Easy" editorials ran between 1807 and 1809.

28. For a discussion of *Modern Chivalry* and its relation to Pennsylvania Jeffersonian politics, see Shankman, *Crucible of American Democracy*, 138-42. For Brackenridge generally, see Joseph J. Ellis, "Hugh Henry Brackenridge: The Novelist as Reluctant Democrat" in his *After the Revolution: Profiles of Early American Culture* (New York: Norton, 1979), 73-110.

29. *Democratic Press*, 2 Feb. 1808.

30. *Aurora*, month of January and 16 Feb. 1807.

31. *Democratic Press*, 30 Jan. 1808.

32. For Snyder's veto message see *Democratic Press*, 29 Oct. 1818 (a reprint of the original message given to the legislature in 1814.) See also Murrin, "Escaping Perfidious Albion."

33. Murray N. Rothbard, *The Panic of 1819: Reactions and Policies* (New York: Columbia University Press, 1972); Charles Sellers, *The Market Revolution: Jacksonian America, 1815-1846* (New York: Oxford University Press, 1991).

34. Snyder to Binns, 30 Aug. 1819, Society Collection, Historical Society of Pennsylvania.

35. Shankman, *Crucible of American Democracy*, 210-19.

36. *Democratic Press*, 23, 24 Apr.; 7, 15, 20, 25, 26 May 1819. *Economics and Technology in 19th Century American Thought*, ed. Michael Hudson (New York: Garland, 1975) reprints Carey's essays.

37. *Democratic Press*, 31 May 1819; Shankman, "A New Thing on Earth."

38. Rothbard, *Panic of 1819*. This capacity survived the Panic of 1837; see James Roger Sharp, *The Jacksonians versus the Banks: Politics in the States After the Panic of 1837* (New York: Columbia University Press, 1970).

39. It also had a profound affect on the health of antebellum Pennsylvanians. See Timothy Cuff, *The Hidden Cost of Economic Development: The Biological Standard of Living in Antebellum Pennsylvania* (Burlington, Vt: Ashgate, 2005).

40. John Quincy Adams to Charles Jared Ingersoll, 22 Aug. 1832, Charles Jared Ingersoll Correspondence, Historical Society of Pennsylvania.

IV

Industrialization and De-Industrialization in the Countryside

Fine-tuning the Forks: Transformation of the Lehigh River

AUGUSTINE NIGRO

> A culture is not a flow, nor even a confluence; the form of its existence is struggle, or at least debate – it is nothing if not a dialectic.
> Lionel Trilling, *The Liberal Imagination*

IN EXAMINING THE DIALECTICAL NATURE of American culture in the nineteenth century, Leo Marx suggests that the garden and the machine evolve as significant symbols of the two major forces in the myth of the United States: ideal pastoralism inherent in the American landscape and industrial technology to which Americans committed themselves in the nineteenth century. Although these forces operate in American history and culture primarily in the form of Trilling's dialectic, Marx points out that implicit in the ideologies of both symbols is the dream of a middle ground, a point in the landscape where the garden and the machine and the respective forces that they represent, nature and technology, join in a mutually enhancing union.[1]

That dream has been occasionally realized in a limited fashion in both literary and historical narratives: one such historical narrative is the record of the transformation of the Lehigh River into a conduit for the shipping of coal from the upper Lehigh Valley to the Forks of the Delaware at Easton. Once opened, the Lehigh Canal ushered the Lehigh Valley into the industrial age, bringing with it the development of the anthracite, iron, slate, and cement industries. This period of balance, however, proved to be short-lived; the very forces reconciled in this middle ground, nature and technology, would also bring about the decline of the canal as an economic and cultural power in the Valley.

Among all the factors contributing to the development of the Lehigh Canal, perhaps the most significant was the rising demand for coal in Philadelphia. Because of forest depletion surrounding the city and insufficient connections to Virginia coal, the city looked north to the anthracite deposits in the upper Lehigh Valley. The Delaware River already connected the southern Lehigh Valley with Philadelphia; all that was needed was a link from the Forks of the Delaware to the coal fields. The Lehigh River appeared to be a natural conduit, and thus nature itself could resolve the dichotomy between urban demand and rural supply.

The river, however, in its natural state could not provide this link because of its peculiar configuration. It began in the Pocono Plateau and flowed for approximately one hundred miles south through the gap in Blue Mountain to Allentown, where it turned east and met the Delaware River at Easton. In its northern reaches, its drop in elevation was severe; one observer noted that "the river is almost one constructed rapid." In the southern valley, the Lehigh's flow was unpredictable, as it broadened its bed on its way toward Easton. One contemporary noted that although "the Delaware is boatable and much used for 200 miles above [Easton]...we cannot find there is much navigation down the Lehigh."[2]

Regardless of such deterrents, residents of the Lehigh Valley had continually tried to use the river as a conduit for trade. As early as 1746, residents sent mast logs down the river to Philadelphia. Throughout the late-eighteenth and early-nineteenth centuries, demand for navigation on the Lehigh heightened as settlers moved north of Blue Mountain. In 1771, the Pennsylvania state legislature declared the river a common highway and appointed commissioners to improve its navigation. Seven years later, it commissioned a combination of Philadelphia, Northampton, and Luzerne county entrepreneurs to improve the river. It had become apparent to those seeking to develop Pennsylvania's anthracite industry that the Lehigh was the best available waterway to connect the rich supply of middle anthracite fields to the anticipated demand in the Philadelphia market. In expectation of such improvements, valley industrialists organized the Lehigh Coal Mine Company in 1793 to extract anthracite from the upper valley. Failures to improve the river, however, hampered their operation as the river remained largely unnavigable. In the thirty years prior to 1820, local residents made seven different attempts to tame the wild Lehigh, all of which failed.

In addition to addressing local trade concerns, those seeking river improvements were also doing their patriotic duty as Americans. Wrapped up in republican ideology, American citizens fervently believed that they could create a society that would allow them to fulfill the goals of the Revolution. One of the main tenets of this ideology was the belief that the wild, forbidding American environment could be improved upon and controlled. Such mastery, in turn, would bring economic growth to the new nation, which would aid citizens either in the form of economic sustenance or commercial profit. Pennsylvanians believed the state's "rivers, by the bountiful Author of Nature, have been made to flow in every direction, as if on purpose to bear from all parts the wealth and produce of the land, in an easy, cheap and expeditious manner to her principal mart and port in the city of Philadelphia." Such rivers seemed to embody what Tench Coxe believed was a "mechanism" inherent in the pastoral landscape; all that remained was to "improve those natural wonders." For the Lehigh River, this meant continuing the attempt to utilize technology to free the waterway from its natural constraints. This had proven too expensive an enterprise for local residents, but in the years after the War of 1812, some of Philadelphia's leading manufacturers, motivated by the acute demand for fuel, would join in the attempt to improve the Lehigh River and connect the valley to larger markets.[3]

In December 1817, Josiah White and Erskine Hazard, successful Philadelphia industrialists who had developed a nail factory at the falls of the Schuylkill, led an expedition from Philadelphia to survey the Lehigh River valley and determine its transportation potential as well as examine the Lehigh Coal Mine Company's anthracite mines. Regarding their visit, Jacob Weiss wrote that the Philadelphians were "much pleased with the appearance of the mine & river, especially the latter…and will take a lively interest to further its immediate improvement." Along with George Hauto, White and Hazard leased the lands of the Lehigh Coal Mine Company, including 10,000 acres of land and the Summit Hill Mines, for a period of twenty years. In return, White and Hazard promised to deliver 40,000 bushels of coal annually to Philadelphia after three years.[4]

To facilitate these shipments, White, Hazard, and Hauto immediately set out to improve the Lehigh. The investors' first steps were to measure systematically the channel of the river. After White's survey, the three investors were certain that they could tame the Lehigh, allowing their coal to float southward to Philadelphia. White planned to impose new technologies on the river to tame its wild course, utilizing dams, canals, locks, wingdams, open sluices, and artificial freshets to clear, deepen, contract, and straighten the riverbed.[5] These technologies would be used to

> improve the River by contracting the channel funnel fashion to bring the whole flow of the water at each of the falls, to as narrow a compass, as the law we could get would allow, by threwing up the Round River stones into low walls, not higher than we wanted to raise the water…and if we had not water sufficient for the Required depth of 15 or 18 inches in by the natural flow to make Artificial Freshets to secure any deficiencies, that is by ponding up the water say as many acres as we could get, and letting it off periodically say once in 3 days, I supposed we could gather enough water, to ensure our required depth and thus have a regular *descending* Navigation.[6]

White determined that he could "improve" the unpredictable Lehigh river, transforming it into a tame fluvial channel that could sustain a fifteen-inch depth year-round, allowing a continuous flow of coal from the anthracite region to Philadelphia. The cost of improving the Lehigh was estimated to be roughly 50,000 dollars.[7]

On March 20, 1818, the Pennsylvania legislature granted the investors navigation rights on the Lehigh River for a thirty-six-year period. According to one legislator, this gave the entrepreneurs "the privilege of ruining themselves" in a foolish attempt to tame the wild Lehigh. Efforts to improve the river were regarded as "chimerical." There had already been numerous failed attempts to control it, some even having the privilege of lotteries to raise money. To many skeptics, this latest attempt would be no different. Believing that navigating the

Lehigh would be impossible, state officials did not worry about granting White, Hazard, and Hauto extraordinary powers.[8]

The only restriction placed upon the company was to open a twenty-foot wide and eighteen-inch deep channel that would run once every three days.[9] In order to facilitate this transformation, the state legislature generously permitted the investors

> to enter upon the said river Lehigh, to open, enlarge or deepen the same in any part or place thereof,...in the manner which shall appear to them most convenient for opening, enlarging, changing, making anew or improving the channel; and also to cut, break or remove and take away all trees, rocks, stones, earth, gravel, sand, or other material, or any other impediments whatsoever within the said river.[10]

According to the state, White, Hazard, and Hauto were "tenants in common" to the river navigation and held all rights and privileges to it. They were granted the power to occupy any lands needed for building locks, sluices, canals, towpaths, or other devices giving proper compensation to the owners. The investors had free rein throughout the landscape "to enter upon the lands contiguous and near to the said river," to take away "any stone, timber, gravel, sand, earth, or other material," and to compensate the owners. White, Hazard, and Hauto were entitled to all water use from the river and could sell it for profit. In addition, all navigation on the channel would be tolled at prescribed rates.[11]

On August 10, 1818, the Lehigh Navigation Company (LNC) was formed to gain additional investors for the project. In order to achieve that end, it was necessary to ease local concerns regarding the project. The LNC did an excellent job in detailing to valley residents how river improvements would not burden local citizens. Because of its natural characteristics, most people believed that the river would need only slight alterations to provide safe transit. The river was not subject to flooding; most of its numerous "riffles," or rapids, needed no improvement at all, while those that did required little technological adaption. Because the channel could be utilized without the construction of large dams, "all injury to private property is avoided." Any needed construction could be achieved cheaply, for "the stone abounds where it must be used, *already quarried!*"[12] Because of these natural characteristics, it followed that any incursion by the investors on the surrounding community would be slight. The LNC's improvements would not intrude upon the natural world, but complement it.

Potential investors, however, were not as certain as were White and Hazard regarding the ease of improving the Lehigh and thus were reluctant to back the project. In 1820, to attract more investors, the Lehigh Navigation Company was combined with the Lehigh Coal Company, insuring the marriage between the canal and future coal operations, thereby creating a more attractive package to would-be investors. One year later, on May 21, 1821, the firm's name was changed to the Lehigh Coal and Navigation Company (LCNC), emphasizing the role of coal in the new transportation system.[13]

The fears of hesitant investors proved well founded as the LCNC struggled throughout the 1820s to create a safe, reliable transportation system. Integrating the technologies of a canal into the natural river proved more difficult than the investors had originally planned. Work was dangerous, and what could be accomplished was continually threatened by the dangerous fluctuations of the river. Eventually, the LCNC integrated more complex and expensive technologies on the river. Because of these difficulties and the company's tendency to underestimate the power of the river, the transformation of the river into an artificial component of the industrial process took place in three stages. In its first incarnation, the Lehigh Navigation Company used innovative technologies to channel the river course and elevate water levels to facilitate descending navigation from Mauch Chunk to Easton. In its next phase of development, the LCNC extended descending navigation further up the Lehigh River to the lumber regions above Mauch Chunk. Finally, development in the valley, along with visions of potential profits, pushed the LCNC to reconfigure the river to allow for both ascending and descending navigation from Mauch Chunk to Easton.[14]

Construction began in the middle of the valley, with the employment of thirteen laborers. Two boats, nicknamed "Whitestown on the Lehigh," were used as workers' housing, offices, a countinghouse, and a store. The boats traveled up and down the river and proved a base of operations for the company. The scope of the project dictated a level of labor organization unheard of in the valley, forcing a dramatic separation between the managers of the project and their labor force. Unlike White's previous work on the Schuylkill, where he worked side by side with his workers, he found that on the Lehigh "the hands come from all nations and [are] strangers to us." Canal workers were primarily Irish, German, and English and stood out in the "wilderness country" of the frontier. They were a transient group, and the company continually struggled to maintain them as a suitable workforce. A report to the board of managers states that "the migratory disposition of the labourers operated injuriously to the contractors in various ways for they would not be urged at work beyond their own inclination; knowing that their services were in demand, they would take up a line of march at the least supposed provocation."[15]

The "rough culture" of the canal workers was quite different from that of the managers and valley residents. White recalls that "While we boarded at Lausanne, the hands on the first day (being a day of leisure) as usual must needs kill time with sport, as usual, a number of them got drunk and then quarreled; they drove the landlord out of his house, broke his windows, etc." In order to protect themselves from their workers, White found it "most prudent to go clad in similar garbs with our hands" so as to prevent assaults. In addition, White and Hazard made certain that the banks did not cash checks unless signed by the two of them, "so that if any of our wild hands caught either of us alone in the Wilds, he had no inducement to waylay us." Despite the undisciplined nature of such a labor force, by the autumn of 1821, roughly four hundred workers were on the river, giving the managers high hopes of finishing construction before winter.[16]

Originally, White had planned to use funnels to constrain the river's flow, thus raising the water level to allow descending navigation. Once on the river, it became apparent that this would not work, and more elaborate technologies would be needed. There simply was not enough water in the channel. White lamented that in the southern valley, "the river appears more like a valley of bottom land than a navigable stream." A severe drought in 1819 demonstrated to the investors that the natural flow of the Lehigh would be insufficient to fill the channel. In that year, the LCNC applied for the right to raise subscriptions to finance dams to raise the river's water level.[17]

In order to overcome this serious obstacle, the investors turned to innovative hydraulic technologies to transform the river's waterflow. As White realized, "we had but one great experiment to make to give us water, by artificial freshets, and if we failed in this our whole work must be exploded and abandoned." To compensate for the lack of water, the investors decided to build retaining dams that could be released, artificially flooding the river any time the natural water level proved too low. Twelve patented hydraulic sluices, "bear traps," were constructed along the channel to ensure an adequate water level. These sluices would constrict and retain the water flow, emptying only when there was a large enough supply of water to facilitate navigation. To transport an ark downstream, the gates would be closed until enough water was harnessed, and then released, floating a barge to the next gate. To gain even more control over the river, at a cost of $40,000 the LCNC constructed two large stone and cribbage dams with lift locks to control its flow.[18]

After this initial phase of construction, anthracite could be transported directly from northern regions to Philadelphia entirely by water. In June 1820, the company loaded 365 tons of anthracite onto arks and sent them downriver. At Mauch Chunk, nearly one thousand laborers gathered along the shore to watch. Bethlehem officials declared a general holiday, as stores and schools closed so that citizens could watch the arks pass en route to Philadelphia. Similar celebrations occurred in Easton and at Philadelphia. To these celebrants, the LCNC had clearly integrated the technology of the canal into the natural landscape.[19]

Despite such celebrations, the LCNC faced a number of specific problems that required a second phase of construction. Because the canal only facilitated descending navigation, the LCNC constructed arks for each separate shipment of anthracite. With no means of getting them back to Mauch Chunk, the returning boatmen destroyed the arks in Philadelphia and sold the lumber before returning upriver. The amount of lumber harvested for arks in the first two years of navigation was more than the company had foreseen, and the forests around Mauch Chunk rapidly depleted. In 1822, the LCNC decided to improve the Lehigh River for sixteen miles above Mauch Chunk to gain access to the valley's pine forests.

Instead of solving the timber problem, the improvement of the upper Lehigh merely moved it upriver. In fact, demand for lumber continued to increase as the

LCNC's anthracite shipments grew. Estimates suggest that the LCNC cut four hundred acres of timber each year.[20] Although such widespread timbering had profound ecological consequences on the northern Lehigh Valley, the primary concern of the LCNC was the high cost of ark construction and its effect on profits. This consideration brought about a third phase of construction, one designed to completely free the channel of its natural constraints.

In 1827, the LCNC decided to forgo its previous improvements on the Lehigh and create a slackwater system from Mauch Chunk to Easton, enabling both descending and ascending transportation along its length. It would be a hybrid design, using both the navigable lengths of the river and canal channels to bypass rapids and river obstructions. Anticipating larger cargoes, the channel would be sixty feet wide and five feet deep. Because the new channel would hold more water than earlier improvements, the LCNC needed to construct eight artificial pools in the northern valley to provide water for the canal.[21]

The new channel officially opened on July 4, 1829, to the wonder of local residents, who found the scope of the improvements difficult to comprehend. One reporter, who after visiting the Lehigh in 1819 had said "never can these wilds support a civilized population, never can the rapid current of the Lehigh be made subservient," now asked "where was the rugged road, the fearful torrent, the silent glen" of his memory? With the opening of the canal, "All, all was changed; it seemed as if [a] supernatural agency" had smoothed the river and sped up the journey.[22]

To the inquiring reporter, the LCNC had successfully transformed the Lehigh River into an integral part of the industrial process.[23] Rather than being limited by the cyclical nature of the valley, the LCNC imposed technologies on the Lehigh, channeling its flow through the canal. Unlike the free-flowing natural river, the canal conformed to the artificial design of engineers. Anthracite mined at the top of Summit Hill Mountain went down a gravity-powered railway to the landing at Mauch Chunk. Lumber floated to Mauch Chunk through the descending navigation in the upper reaches of the Lehigh River. From Mauch Chunk to Easton, arks traveled along a channel five feet deep, sixty feet wide.[24] Its banks were protected by sloped walls and stone abutments. Eight dams held back a supply of water that could be released into the channel. Ascending navigation was now possible on the Lehigh, allowing the LCNC to bring arks back to Mauch Chunk to be used again, saving them a considerable amount.

Altogether, the river improvements encompassed thirty-six miles of canal and ten miles of pools, with fifty-five separate locks spread throughout its length. Near rapids, the canal "reposed in a black, glittering sheet," as it bypassed the river "bounding over its rocky channel in wreaths of snow white foam." The canal, marked by its calm ribbon of water, was the very symbol of God's order in nature, while the river chaotically jumped across the rocky bottom toward the sea.[25]

While completion of the channel may have been cause for some celebration, the real joy was in the expectation of its effects on the surrounding community. Celebrations of the opening of the canal were purposefully intertwined with the nation's Independence Day festivities. Canal technology had delivered the valley from the restraints of nature and would allow the ideals of the Revolution – freedom and independence – to come to fruition. The canal would transform the region from an economic backwater to a major industrial center, turning "a barren wilderness into a source of wealth."[26]

In his 1826 message to the assembly, Governor John Andrew Shulze spoke of the benefits the Lehigh Canal would bring to the state of Pennsylvania. The canal cultivated the imperfect natural world by giving "value to what would otherwise have rotted on the surface, or lain neglected in the bowels of the earth." *The Pennsylvania Argus*, an Easton newspaper, said that for "the working class...it is, in fact, making for them a home, and procuring the means of subsistence and comfort there." Denying the valley's inferiority complex, the editor of the *Lehigh Herald* remarked that "in the course of a year or two the big folks in the cities won't call us the stupid Dutch again – when they pass along in steam boats from Philadelphia, via Bethlehem and Allentown to Mauch Chunk."[27] The *Mauch Chunk Courier* succinctly wrote of the anticipated effects of the canal:

> we shall soon see a change in the aspect of affairs upon the Lehigh...already are our citizens beginning to feel an increasing confidence in the resources of the region....The Lehigh is now in a fair way of becoming what Nature designed it should be, a region of immense business and wealth.[28]

The LCNC, eager for cargo on its canal as well as purchasers of its waterpower and land, actively fostered the development of the slate, cement, anthracite, iron, and zinc industries in the southern valley. With increased ability to ship anthracite to Philadelphia, coal extraction grew significantly, fostering the development of new towns to accommodate incoming laborers. The Lehigh Crane Iron Company, originator of the valley's anthracite iron industry, was a virtual subsidiary of the LCNC. Industrial-centered towns such as the appropriately named Cementon, Ironton, and Orefield rose up among the older religious-centered communities of Egypt, Nazareth, and Bethlehem, testimony of the growing importance of the valley's resources to its industrial development.

To valley residents, the transformation of the Lehigh River into a navigation system was a "work of peculiar felicitation."[29] Industrialists had created a middle landscape – a site between the natural wilderness and the cultural city – where a new technology brought out the natural wealth inherent in the valley. Rich resources of anthracite could now reach urban markets. The LCNC created the channel with local stone and manufactured cement from local limestone deposits. It used lumber from the northern Lehigh valley in the mines as well as in ark construction. The Lehigh navigation ushered in an age of industrial development in the northern valley as new towns serviced the anthracite, lumber, cement, and iron industries. If the LCNC's navigation on the Lehigh had indeed created a mutually enhancing middle landscape, it proved, however, to be short-lived.

The LCNC's success was not without controversy. Contrary to the glowing testimonies of Lehigh Valley newspapers reported at the canal's opening, many valley residents were unsure that the technologies imposed on the Lehigh River would bring wealth and profits to all. Five months after the canal's opening, the *Easton Sentinel* reported complaints lodged against the LCNC by valley residents, criticizing its high tolls. Throughout 1832, residents of the Lehigh Valley gathered to protest the monopolistic character of the LCNC. While much of the impetus for complaint came from the LCNC's rival, the Beaver Meadow Railroad and Coal Company, the protests also reflected local residents' concern regarding the LCNC's growing control over the landscape. The LCNC was accused of deliberately hindering the industrial development of the valley by keeping the Lehigh River trade for themselves. For these critics, Mauch Chunk was an area purposefully held in submission, not one improved by industrial opportunities and wealth. To local residents, "the country about Mauch Chunk has long remained a howling wilderness without population" because of the LCNC's restraint of trade.[30]

On May 21, 1832, residents of Luzerne, Northampton, Philadelphia, and Lehigh counties met in Allentown to discuss the "navigation of the Lehigh on equitable terms." In granting a charter to the LCNC, the state of Pennsylvania had given the LCNC complete control of the Lehigh River. What had once been a natural part of the landscape, shared by all, had now become the sole property of the Canal Company. To critics of the LCNC's monopoly, the river could not be integrated into the industrial process; the state's actions were "an act of indiscretion scarcely less deplorable than if it were to consent to restrictions upon the common benefits of light and air." The Lehigh, in fact "constitute[s] a part of the inherent and elemental riches of a state, as much as the fertility of the soil or the industry of its inhabitants." In essence, the state legislature had sold "the people's birth-right for a mess of pottage" and had given the LCNC a "premium for oppression." Many thought the LCNC unfairly controlled the natural properties of the river, its flow, its energy, its water supply. To the delegates, "all these advantages are natural advantages – not the creations of the company; and were the property of the Commonwealth."[31] The LCNC did not have the right to hold a monopoly over the river, in that the "whole country had a qualified property in the water of the Lehigh." The Lehigh was no longer "a public highway, which every citizen may use, but only a private road from the Mauch Chunk coal mines to the Delaware river."[32]

In creating the Lehigh Canal system, the LCNC had imposed many technologies on the river to facilitate navigation. For some valley residents, however, the river was more than just a transportation system, it was a resource in its own right. The annual shad runs, which had also marked the cyclical nature of the river, came to an abrupt end with the advent of ascending navigation, due both to the increasing number of locks and dams on the river as well as to the increased pollution spilled into its channel. The fishing industry throughout the Forks of the Delaware, which had once sustained Lenape Indians and early settlers, ceased. During debates concerning whether to build a dam at Easton, one newspaper editor argued that fishing should no longer be a concern in the valley, "from the few fish caught this high up the river, the fisheries on the river, at and above this place, are matters of very secondary consideration."[33] The end of the shad runs remained a bitter symbol of the LCNC's failure to integrate nature and technology through the nineteenth century; in 1869, John Hill Martin, a Philadelphia lawyer and visitor to the valley, urged the valley's citizens to compel "those who have obstructed the course of the stream...to facilitate the free passage of the fish upstream to spawn."[34] In the case of the valley's fishing industry, the Lehigh navigation had destroyed one resource through its use of technology to exploit the wealth of another.

Ironically, the same forces that the Lehigh Coal and Navigation Company brought together to create the Lehigh Canal, nature and technology, would conspire to bring about its decline. While many citizens of the valley suspected that the technologies imposed upon the Lehigh River could not successfully contain its flow, the LCNC held fast to notions that technological progress would overcome the troubling constraints of water travel. The LCNC directors continued to believe in canal traffic and in their ability to control the Lehigh.

To contain the growing power of the LCNC, in 1832, valley residents urged the state to grant concessions to the Beaver Meadow Railroad to build a competing transportation route to Easton. Other groups urged the state to allow the Delaware division of the Pennsylvania Canal to charge the same tolls as those on the Lehigh. In that way, the LCNC would be forced to pay whatever tolls they enforced on the Lehigh.[35]

In the following years, the state senate appointed two committees to investigate the charges against the LCNC. In his 1835 report to the Senate, committee chairman S. J. Packer noted that, although the power granted to the LCNC "was an extensive one; and although at this day it may be viewed by some as an extraordinary relinquishment of sovereignty and a singular encroachment upon the natural rights of our citizens; it was at that time regarded as an inducement scarcely commensurate with the magnitude and the hazard of an enterprise which had long been projected and repeatedly attempted, but which had as long been delayed." The committee could find no evidence that the company in any way violated its charter, no matter how unpopular the charter had become. The company was not at fault, and it recommended that any real complaints should be addressed to the legislature that had granted such broad powers to the company. The committee also recommended that the state purchase the Lehigh navigation. In doing so, "the state will again be put into possession of the valley of the Lehigh."[36] The state, however, never attempted to purchase the company, and the LCNC remained in control of river navigation.

Despite the committee finding for the defendant against the charge of monopoly, the LCNC's control over commercial traffic in the valley was doomed. With the creation of the Delaware, Lehigh, Schuylkill, and Susquehanna Railroad, the LCNC lost its monopoly on the Mauch Chunk to Easton trade route. Ironically, despite its pioneering role in the United States' railroad construction with the nine-mile gravity-powered railroad built in 1826, the LCNC did not become an advocate of railroad expansion, and instead preferred canal transportation.[37] Between 1830 and 1840, the LCNC built a number of "feeder railroads" in the northern Lehigh Valley to bring anthracite deposits to the canal landings. Josiah White continued to believe that canal transportation was superior to railroads.

As early as 1828, in the midst of constructing the ascending navigation, Lehigh Valley newspapers began printing articles discussing the advantages of rail travel. White, however, believed that canals were more closely integrated within the natural environment and therefore more permanent than artificial railroads. In a report to the LCNC's Board of Managers, he argued that the railroad's artificiality and reliance on technology made maintenance more expensive, until "its decay gradually increases to its final annihilation." Canals, on the other hand, worked within the realm of the natural world, requiring less maintenance and were more permanent in structure. The anticipated speeds of rail travel would only exacerbate the wear and tear on the line, as White had seen on the switchback railroad.[38] In an examination of the Erie Canal, the Lehigh managers argued that moving freight by canal cost one-sixth that of railroads. In the case of the LCNC, railroads should be used only when nature prevented the use of canals. What this new railroad technology failed to do – force the LCNC to adopt rail travel as its major route to market – nature would later accomplish.

Freshets regularly damaged the canal improvements and caused breaches of the line. In his 1829 engineer's report, Canvass White lamented the rising costs of canal construction. These problems included difficulties getting materials and laborers, the continual need for rock excavation, and the unanticipated construction of retaining walls and stone embankments.[39] From 1830 to 1833, spring freshets damaged the canal and delayed its opening. Although Josiah White and the remaining managers of the LCNC continued to believe that canals were a better form of transportation than railroads, events in 1840 made many other people change their minds. In that year, a major spring freshet destroyed much of the northern section of the canal, with damages reaching $600,000. In its wake, "all resources of the company except the stock of coal on hand and outstanding debts were cut off."[40] The entire line needed to be rebuilt and no coal could get to market until the canal opening on July 10.[41]

To the LCNC, however, the fact that the canal endured nature's torrents and could be readily maintained through repairs showed the mettle of canal technology.[42] The LCNC Board of Managers compared the flood to forest fires and tornadoes, natural disasters that could not be prevented.[43] Citizens of the valley, however, started to question the dependability of the canal. Investors wondered whether the company could maintain control over the Lehigh's navigation. These fears directly affected the security of the company, whose 1842 annual report noted that "the serious depression in the credit of the company, and the diminution of confidence occasioned by the recent visitation" made it imperative that the company reassure investors in its ability to maintain its navigation.[44]

Lehigh Canal, Lock No. 1, Lower Division, at Mauch Chunk (now Jim Thorpe).

Pennsylvania Canal Society Collection, National Canal Museum, Easton, Pennsylvania.

Both the flood of 1840 and the LCNC's continued monopoly of canal traffic pushed many local residents to increase their demands for an alternative mode of transportation. In 1845, a public meeting in Allentown urged support for a railroad from Easton to the coal regions.[45] A bill was sent to the legislature, and in April of 1846, with the urging of Lehigh County Representative Dr. Jesse Samuel, the state assembly created the Delaware, Lehigh, Schuylkill, and Susquehanna Railroad; its name would later be changed to the Lehigh Valley Railroad. Its new name is evident of its intent to serve as an alternative to the river traffic that previously served the valley. The group sought to break the LCNC monopoly on the anthracite trade, thereby encouraging private mining companies to develop. James M. Porter, an Easton lawyer, was named the first president.[46]

From 1851 to 1855, the railroad was constructed along the Lehigh River from Easton to Mauch Chunk. As White and Hazard had used the valley's resources to build the canal, the railroad engineers also utilized valley limestone, sandstone, and shale, assuming the integration of the railroad into the natural environment. As in the case of the canal, however, high prices, lack of labor, disease, and flooding plagued construction. The first trains arrived in Catasauqua on July 4, 1855. Dignitaries and townspeople gathered in their Sunday best to watch the trains enter the town, with cannon blasts celebrating the occasion.[47] On September 12, 1855, the railroad opened in its entirety from Easton to Mauch Chunk. By 1856, the Lehigh Valley Railroad was actively competing with the LCNC for the anthracite trade, and by 1859, the LCNC reported that the "multiplication of avenues to market and the intensity of competition" forced it to lower tolls.

But once again, nature had an even greater impact on canal transportation than its rival technology, the railroad. On June 4, 1862, rain began to fall on the upper Lehigh Valley and continued for thirty straight hours. Mill dams on the upper waterways limited the amount of water escaping the valley, and water levels rose quickly. Flood waters soared to twenty-seven feet above the Mauch Chunk dam, ten feet higher than they had in 1840. Soon the artificial dams gave out, rapidly emptying their reservoirs into the Lehigh. The river rose above its channel and flooded Mauch Chunk, destroying the LCNC's lumber reservoirs, tenant housing, company warehouses, and wharves. More than 200,000 logs held in the reservoirs escaped into the river, battering the LCNC's dams, retaining walls, and embankments. Bodies were found fifty miles downriver, in Easton and Bethlehem, as the waters eventually receded. Towns along the river, including Mauch Chunk, White Haven, Allentown, and Bethlehem were inundated with water. One to two hundred people died. The flood destroyed eighteen lock houses and swept away approximately two hundred coal arks. Company officials estimated damage on the upper section of the canal at $900,000, the lower section's damage at over $500,000.

Even to boatmen and lumbermen, who had been accustomed to the mercurial whims of the river, the flood of 1862 was unlike any before. The flood's destruction left reporters nearly speechless. The *Easton Sentinel* reported that the scene

The Lehigh River flood of June 5, 1862, from the steeple of the Central Moravian Church in Bethlehem.

Moravian Archives, Bethlehem, Pennsylvania.

along the river was one of "destruction and duress, impossible to portray or describe." Indeed, none could "particularize the losses, as that would occupy columns, aye, pages," to chronicle the damages wrought by the canal.[48] The scope of the damages made people aware of the LCNC's accountability in the disaster.

By retaining and channeling the water's flow, the LCNC prevented the river from naturally easing its own hydraulic tensions. The company dramatically increased the flood's devastation by using the river channel to hold cut lumber, creating a massive debris field tumbling southward, destroying additional dams, homes, and other buildings. The LCNC estimated that the total debris included one million board feet of lumber, over 150 coal arks, along with the numerous uprooted dwellings.

In the public's eye, the reliability of rail over canal transportation was now self-evident. The Lehigh Canal's upper sections were utterly destroyed, while the Lehigh Valley Railroad continued to run regularly between Easton and Slatington, thirteen miles below Mauch Chunk.[49] The following week, the *Easton Sentinel* reported that many believed the upper section of the canal should not be rebuilt, seeing how "nine-tenths of the late destruction...was caused by the breaking of dams above Mauch Chunk." Most valley residents argued that "the Penn Haven and White Haven Railroad be now constructed and no such terrible disaster need be feared."[50]

Though the LCNC stated that the flood was not its fault, but "an act of the Omnipotent," the company reassessed its belief in the benefits of canal trade over railroads. Unlike the flood of 1840, the flood of 1862 forced LCNC managers to rethink the advantages of canal traffic. The considerable expense of rebuilding the upper section of the destroyed canal was indicative of the high cost of controlling the river. In its report on the flood, the managers of the LCNC argued that "it would not suffice...merely to restore the works as they were" since it had already been shown that the canal's technology was not integrated with the river.[51] In a reversal of their earlier opinions, the LCNC's opinions regarding the upper navigation had changed; the managers now saw that

> the upper section of the navigation, a considerable portion of which ought never to have been built, was built only upon legislative compulsion, and need not be rebuilt; was never a source of profit to the Company, but always a source of danger; its stupendous locks and dams having been among the chief causes of the ruin which so suddenly overwhelmed the valley of the Lehigh on the 4th of June last.[52]

A new technology was called for, one that did not attempt to integrate itself with nature, one that broke free from its constraints. In the months after the flood, the LCNC turned to rail traffic to move its anthracite to market. In place of the destroyed navigation, the LCNC made plans to build a railroad. Unlike the canal, which was tied to the Lehigh's unpredictable flow, a railroad would allow year-round transportation. The state assembly must have agreed with the LCNC arguments. Noting that "the severity of [the Lehigh Valley's] floods is thought to have been greatly increased by the destruction, mostly above Mauch Chunk, of dams and other works created by the Lehigh Coal and Navigation Company" and that "it would greatly conduce to the future safety of the persons and property along the line of the said river, if a portion of said works now in ruins on the upper section of the said navigation should not be restored," the state assembly granted the LCNC permission to extend their railroad from White Haven past Mauch Chunk.[53] Later that year, the legislature extended the grant to include all of the Lehigh Valley, from Mauch Chunk to the Delaware.

Although the LCNC argued that the railroad would "aid and develop" the canal, in accepting the grant and deciding to build a parallel railroad along its canal, the company finally acknowledged the canal's failure to sustain an integration of nature and technology. The railroad would allow year-long service and would require less maintenance than the Lehigh navigation. In order to build the railroad as quickly as possible, the canal was closed earlier than usual so that the company could concentrate on rail construction.[54]

Regardless of the state's approval, the Beaver Meadow Railroad and Lehigh Valley Railroad remained committed to keeping the LCNC out of the railway business. In 1864, the two railroads combined to thwart the LCNC's efforts. Ironically, the LCNC portrayed itself as the newcomer, entering the rail business to break the monopoly of others.[55] Both the LCNC and the Lehigh Valley Railroad laid tracks along the river, each seeking to establish themselves by occupying the right of way. This process was repeated from Mauch Chunk all the way to Easton.[56] These attempts to thwart the LCNC were fruitless, however, as the railroad was completed by 1868. In February of that year, the first LCNC locomotive traveled from Mauch Chunk to Easton.[57]

Although eclipsed by competing railroads, the LCNC continued to operate the canal well into the twentieth century. The last boats floated downstream in 1942. A renewed interest in the canal right-of-way occurred in 1964 as surrounding towns began to run out of open green space, and the LCNC sold segments of the canal to become urban recreational parks. Thus, the canal, which more than a century ago had introduced a new technology into the valley, ironically and nostalgically became a natural and rustic respite from an increasingly industrial landscape.[58]

Notes

1. Leo Marx, *The Machine in the Garden* (New York: Oxford University Press, 1965), 23.

2. Thomas F. Gordon, *A Gazetteer of the State of Pennsylvania* (Philadelphia: T. Belknap, 1832), 14; Joshua Gilpin, "Journey to Philadelphia." (July 10, 1802) reprinted in *Pennsylvania Magazine of History and Biography* 46 (1922): 21; Anthony Brzyski, "The Lehigh Canal and its effect on the economic development of the region through which it passed, 1818-1873," 2 vols. (PhD diss.: New York University, 1957), 1:25-27.

3. For the relationship between internal improvements and notions of progress, see Carol Sheriff, *The Artificial River: The Erie Canal and the Paradox of Progress, 1817-1862* (New York: Hill and Wang, 1996), 5; John Lauritz Larson, *Internal Improvement: National Public Works and the Promise of Popular Government in the Early United States* (Chapel Hill: University of North Carolina Press, 2001), 28; Schuylkill and Susquehanna and the Delaware and Schuylkill Navigation Companies, *An Historical Account of the Rise, Progress and Present State of the Canal Navigation in Pennsylvania* (Philadelphia, 1795), iii; quoted in Marx, *Machine*, 163.

4. Jacob Weiss Jr. to Jacob Cist, 7 Jan. 1818, reprinted in H. Benjamin Powell, "Establishing the Anthracite Boomtown of Mauch Chunk, 1814-1825: Selected Documents," *Pennsylvania History* 41 (1974): 251; Donald L. Miller and Richard E. Sharpless, *The Kingdom of Coal: Work, Enterprise, and Ethnic Communities in the Mine Fields* (Easton, Pa.: Canal History and Technology Press, 1998), 22-23.

5. Lehigh Coal and Navigation Company, "Observations on the Lehigh Navigation Bill" (1818), 2.

6. Josiah White, *Josiah White's History Given by Himself* (n.p.: Lehigh Coal and Navigation Company, 1939), 19.

7. Donald Sayenga, "The Untried Business: An Appreciation of White and Hazard," *Proceedings of the Canal History and Technology Symposium* 2 (March 1983): 111.

8. Lehigh Coal and Navigation Company, *A History of the Lehigh Coal and Navigation Company* (Philadelphia: Printed by W. S. Young, 1840), 18; *Acts of the General Assembly of Pennsylvania concerning the Lehigh Coal and Navigation Company together with the Bye-Laws, etc.* (Philadelphia: James Kay, Jun. and Brothers, 1837), 1-17.

9. *A Compendious view of the law authorizing the improvement of the navigation of the River Lehigh together with remarks on the facility of making the improvement, and advantages to be derived from it* (Philadelphia: William Brown, Printer, 1818), 1.

10. *Pennsylvania Legislative Acts, 1818* (Harrisburg: C. Gleim, 1818), 205.

11. LCNC, "Observations on the Lehigh Navigation Bill" (1818), 2; *Acts of the General Assembly of Pennsylvania concerning the Lehigh Coal and Navigation Company.* (Philadelphia: James Kay, 1837), 1-10.

12. Lehigh Coal and Navigation Company, *Statements of the Lehigh Navigation and Coal Mine Company* (Philadelphia: William Brown, Printer, 1818), 6; *A Compendious view of the law authorizing the improvement of the navigation of the River Lehigh*, 6.

13. *Acts of the General Assembly*, 18-29; Brzyski, "Lehigh Canal," 1:114-23.

14. Improvements to the Lehigh began at Lausanne as the investors sought to gain access to coal from the Room Run mines. See Michael Knies, "Industry, Enterprise, Wealth, and

Taste: The History of Mauch Chunk, 1791-1831," *Proceedings of the Canal History and Technology Symposium* 4 (June 1985): 25.

15. White, *Josiah White's History*, 28-29; Anne Royall, *Mrs. Royal's Pennsylvania, or Travels Continued in the United States* (Washington, DC: Privately Published, 1829), 126-27. *Report of the Board of Managers of the Lehigh Coal and Navigation Company, presented to the Stockholders* (Philadelphia, 1829), 12.

16. Peter Way, *Common Labor: Workers and the Digging of North American Canals, 1780-1860* (Baltimore: Johns Hopkins University Press, 1993), 172; White, *Josiah White's History*, 29; Josiah White, Slates, to Elizabeth White, Philadelphia, 19 Sept. 1821, Josiah White Papers, Quaker Collection, Haverford College.

17. Josiah White to Elizabeth White, 17 Dec. 1821, Josiah White Papers, Quaker Collection, Haverford College; Lehigh Coal and Navigation Company, "An Address of the Lehigh Coal and Navigation Company to their Fellow Citizens" (Philadelphia: William Brown, 1821), 4; Brzyski, "Lehigh Canal," 1:126.

18. White, *Josiah White's History*, 36; Miller and Sharpless, *Kingdom of Coal*, 24; Sayenga, "Untried Business," 112.

19. George Korson, *Black Rock Mining Folklore of the Pennsylvania Dutch* (Baltimore: Johns Hopkins University Press, 1960), 52-53; *Democratic Press*, 14 Mar. 1821.

20. Brzyski, "Lehigh Canal," 1:166. *Report of the Board of Managers of the Lehigh Coal and Navigation Company* (Philadelphia: Timothy A. Conrad, 11 Jan. 1830), 12. (These reports are hereafter cited as *Report of the Board of Managers*.)

21. *Report of the Board of Managers, 1829*, 5-9.

22. Quoted in M. S. Henry, *History of the Lehigh Valley* (Easton, Pa.: Bixler and Corwin, 1860), 340.

23. In a fourth phase of construction, the LCNC extended the upper section of the canal to Stoddartsville, adding an additional thirty-eight miles to the length of the canal: Brzyski, "Lehigh Canal," 1:190.

24. LCNC, *Statements*, 3.

25. *Report of the Board of Managers, 1830*, 3-5; *Lancaster Examiner and Herald*, 18 Sept. 1844.

26. *Pennsylvania Argus* (Easton, Pa.), 26 June 1829.

27. George Edward Reed, ed., *Pennsylvania Archives*, ser. 4 (Harrisburg: Wm. Stanley Ray, State Printer, 1900), 5:657; *Pennsylvania Argus* (Easton, Pa.), 2 Mar. 1827; *Lehigh Herald*, 3 July 1828.

28. *Mauch Chunk Courier*, 18 June 1832.

29. "Lehigh Canal," *Pennsylvania Argus* (Easton, Pa.), 2 Mar. 1827, 3.

30. *Mauch Chunk Courier*, 12 Nov. 1829; "Navigation of the Lehigh, Proceedings of the Convention held at Allentown on May 21, 1832," 1, Temple University Rare Book Room.

31. "Navigation of the Lehigh, Proceedings of the Convention," 1-7.

32. "The Proceedings of a convention of delegates elected by the citizens, etc.," 20-21 Dec. 1832. Quoted in Chester L. Jones, *The Economic History of the Anthracite-Tidewater Canals* (Philadelphia: University of Pennsylvania Press, 1908), 21; *Register of Pennsylvania*, 3 May 1834.

33. Robert Halma and Carl Oplinger, *The Lehigh Valley: A Natural and Environmental History* (University Park: Pennsylvania State University Press, 2001), 241; *Pennsylvania Argus* (Easton, Pa.), 22 Feb. 1828.

34. John Hill Martin, *Historical Sketch of Bethlehem in Pennsylvania* (Philadelphia: John L. Pile, 1872), 148-49.

35. "Navigation of the Lehigh, Proceedings of the Convention," 5; Pennsylvania General Assembly, Senate, Committee to whom was referred the memorial on the Pennsylvania Canal, *Counter Report of the minority of the committee to whom was referred the memorials of a number of citizens...*(Harrisburg, Pa.: Henry Welsh, 1832), 1.

36. Pennsylvania General Assembly, Senate, Committee on Coal Trade, *Extract Relative to the importance of Lehigh Navigation to the commonwealth* (Harrisburg, Pa.: Hugh Hamilton and Son, 1835), 5-10.

37. Brzyski, "Lehigh Canal," 1:205.

38. *Pennsylvania Argus*, 8 Feb. 1828; *Report of the Board of Managers, 1829*, 9; *Report of the Board of Managers, 1830*, 14; Brzyski, "Lehigh Canal," 1:224-25.

39. For discussions of freshets, see *Report of the Board of Managers, 1832*, 5; *1833*, 1; *1841*, 18; *1842*, 6; *1846*, 1; *Report of the Board of Managers, 1829*, 9-12.

40. *Report of the Board of Managers, 1843*, 11.

41. *Report of the Board of Managers, 1842*, 6.

42. *Report of the Board of Managers, 1832*, 5.

43. *Report of the Board of Managers, 1842*, 11.

44. Ibid., 6.

45. Alfred Mathews and Austin N. Hungerford, *History of the Counties of Lehigh and Carbon* (Philadelphia: Everts & Richards, 1884), 601.

46. Ibid.

47. James F. Lambert and Henry J. Reinhard, *A History of Catasauqua in Lehigh County, Pennsylvania* (Allentown, Pa.: Searle and Dressler Co., 1914), 358.

48. *Easton Sentinel*, 12 June 1862, 2.

49. Ibid.

50. *Easton Sentinel*, 19 June 1862, 2.

51. *Report of the Board of Managers, 1863*, 21.

52. Ibid., 13.

53. *Report of the Board of Managers, 1864*, 31.

54. Brzyski, "Lehigh Canal," 2:804.

55. *Report of the Board of Managers, 1864*, 13.

56. *Report of the Board of Managers, 1865*, 16.

57. *Report of the Board of Managers, 1868*, 7.

58. Sayenga, "Untried Business," 114.

The Improbable Success of Bethlehem Steel

John K. Smith

THE NARRATIVE OF THE HISTORY of a company can be, and often is, fitted into the structure of biography. As is often the case in biography, the history can be structured as internal growth and development toward some larger goal. Along the path, wrong choices are punished and right ones are rewarded. For example, the decline of Bethlehem Steel in recent decades has been attributed to overpaid, complacent managers or uncooperative union members.[1] It can be demonstrated that there is some validity to recalcitrance of both management and labor. But was this really the cause that led to the effect of declining performance?

The life of a business organization involves innumerable activities by large numbers of people frequently spread over larger geographical areas. The historian is challenged to develop frameworks that give perspective on the evolving corporate beehive. The simplest approach was to make business history biography by exploring the lives of corporate leaders. This was a good place to start since entrepreneurship and leadership are essential for success; however, the approach implied, implicitly at least, that the rest of an organization did nothing that merited much attention. Beginning in the 1960s, Alfred D. Chandler revolutionized the practice of business history by putting organization at the heart of corporate success, which he saw as the driver of economic growth in modern economies.

In Chandler's view, the modern corporation succeeded and persists because it effectively organizes a broad spectrum of skills to accomplish complex and expensive tasks. The railroads in the nineteenth century were the first enterprises to encounter the combination of very high costs combined with complex operations. The managerial response to this situation was the development of the multilayered corporate pyramid. It succeeded in railroads and soon spread to other enterprises such as oil and steel.[2] For Chandler the building of a properly functioning organization is the key event in the history of a company, implying that "they all lived happily ever after." Empirical evidence suggests, however, that they do not. Things change – patterns of competition shift, new technologies pose opportunities and threats to established businesses, and entire industries wax and wane. To thrive or even survive, companies must successfully negotiate their way through a maze of shifting opportunities and challenges.

The discussion below analyzes the evolution of the Bethlehem Steel Company within the context of its competitors and the iron and steel industry generally. This approach puts the story in a framework that makes the company's fate rest substantially in the external environment rather than in a succession of heroic deeds that are often chronicled in company histories. Several times Bethlehem might have suffered the fate of most iron and steel companies, losing its independence and identity through merger with another firm. The most severe crises came in 1880 and 1900. Each time Bethlehem's leadership was willing to sell out and in the latter case eventually did, but remarkably to an individual – Charles Schwab – not to a rival firm.

The two most important events in Bethlehem Steel's history – the formation of U.S. Steel in 1901 and World War I – had nothing to do with the company itself. The former created a protective umbrella under which smaller firms flourished and supplied Bethlehem with a dynamic leader, while the latter provided Bethlehem with resources far out of proportion with its overall place in the industry. In 1904, Bethlehem ranked fifteenth in the industry.[3] In fact, until 1916, Bethlehem was a rather unknown and unrecognized company. The 1912 Federal Bureau of Corporations' study of the steel industry scarcely referred to Bethlehem.[4] During World War I, because of its earlier position in armor production Bethlehem garnered two-thirds of the 450 million dollars of lucrative contracts with the Allies. After the war Schwab and Eugene Grace parlayed these earnings into enough physical plant to make Bethlehem comfortably number two.

Yet, Schwab was ultimately unable to complete the one acquisition he needed to make Bethlehem a rival to U.S. Steel. His attempt to take over Youngstown Sheet and Tube was thwarted by another empire builder, Cyrus Eaton, who was a major stockholder in the target company, and the onset of the Great Depression.[5] The 1930s brought an end to the organizational evolution of the industry; the number of players and their relative sizes stayed essentially the same for decades. Significantly, no true competitor for U.S. Steel had emerged from the earlier mergers. Its role as industry leader was never in doubt. Throughout its life, even before the creation of U.S. Steel, Bethlehem Steel, like most corporations, was not the complete master of its own fate but had to adapt to changes in the larger industrial and economic landscape.

The Bethlehem Iron Company was initially organized in the early 1860s by Asa Packer to supply rails to his railroad enterprises. A boom in railroad construction in the 1850s had pushed up rail prices and led fifteen new mills to be built. Ten of these were built west of the Alleghenies to take advantage of regional markets and the increasingly preferred fuel source – bituminous coal. Packer's Lehigh Valley Railroad transported anthracite coal from the Pocono Mountains region to Philadelphia. Packer appointed the son of a friend and engineer for the canal company, Robert Sayre, in charge of the new company.

To attain the technical skills needed to manufacture rails, Sayre hired ironmaster John Fritz, who had been general superintendent of the Cambria Iron Works in Johnstown, Pennsylvania. One of the most experienced ironmasters in the United States, Fritz had invented an improved rolling mill that lowered the cost and improved the quality of iron rails. The three-story-high rail mill allowed rails to be rolled back and forth through the rollers instead of only being fed from one side. By July 1860, Fritz had overseen the construction of two blast furnaces and a rolling mill in Bethlehem, but the onset of the Civil War delayed the beginning of production until 1863.[6] The new company immediately discovered that its product was about to become obsolete.

As Bethlehem Iron Company began to roll wrought iron rails for Packer's New Jersey Central Railroad, several other companies started to make rails from Bessemer steel, a harder and tougher material. An English inventor, Henry Bessemer, had developed technology to convert molten pig iron into steel by blowing air – to burn out excess carbon – through the molten metal in a converter. In the United States, Bessemer technology became available primarily through his American agent, Alexander Holley, who assisted Fritz in building the tenth American Bessemer converter.

The Bethlehem facility opened in 1873, the year Holley also built a plant near Pittsburgh for another entrepreneur, Andrew Carnegie, who had close connections to the Pennsylvania Railroad. During the depressed business years following the financial collapse of 1873, Carnegie began to compete for orders by price-cutting. His relentless pursuit of lower costs both for raw materials and in processing them in his new Edgar Thompson works in Pittsburgh soon made Carnegie the leading manufacturer of steel rails in the United States.[7] Bethlehem was a mid-sized rail manufacturer in the East. Its sales were about three-quarters those of the eastern leader, the Pennsylvania Steel Company, a subsidiary of the Pennsylvania Railroad. In 1885, Bethlehem had about 12 percent of the nation's rail market, about half of Carnegie's share.[8]

Bethlehem faced a simultaneous crisis and opportunity when Asa Packer died in 1879. The directors of the company no longer felt obliged to concentrate on rails, even though a boom in railroad construction in the early 1880s kept the company strong for a few years.[9] This would turn out to be the peak of the rail business with over 90 percent of rolled steel going into rails. When the demand for rails declined in the mid-decade recession, steelmakers began to look for other markets. By 1890, only half of rolled steel went into rails, and by 1900 that fraction had dropped to one-third.[10] Following the industry trend, Bethlehem developed new products and new technologies to make them. Fritz had already been proposing diversification into structural and plate steel. He also had some interest in building a heavy forging plant to make armor plate.[11]

A few years after Packer's death, the largest stockholder, Joseph Wharton, a highly successful industrialist, committed Bethlehem to this latter business – the construction of steel battleships armed with immense steel guns.[12] The first modern battleship, the British *Devastation*, which was commissioned in 1873, had a displacement of nearly 10,000 tons and four twelve-inch guns weighing 35 tons each. As a naval arms race accelerated in the following decades, battleships would get bigger, faster, and more heavily armed.[13]

In 1881, the United States began to consider building a modern navy. John Fritz was involved in some early studies and trips to Europe. Bethlehem's big

Bethlehem Steel Company in 1900.

Bethlehem Steel Corporation Collection, National Canal Museum, Easton, Pennsylvania.

break came in 1886 when Wharton convinced his friend, Secretary of the Navy William Whitney, to help him land a contract to supply armor plate and big guns for the new steel navy. Bethlehem sold $4 million in bonds to finance the acquisition of forges and presses from British and French manufacturers. Some of this original equipment, such as the giant 125-ton steam hammer, did not work very well. Because of delays in procuring and installing equipment at Bethlehem, the U.S. government also awarded contracts to Carnegie.

Fortunately for Bethlehem, the man who was such a ruthless competitor in rails was willing to cooperate when the government was the customer.[14] In the 1890s Bethlehem became a major manufacturer of steel armor plate and big guns, and competed with Germany's Krupps, France's Schnieder, and England's Vickers and Armstrong in the international armaments business. This business was not hurt nearly as badly as rails during the nationwide depression that began in 1893 and lasted for several years. Moving into the international market, Bethlehem received a contract for 1,200 tons of armor plate for the Imperial Russian Navy in 1894. A year later a visiting ordnance expert from Britain declared that Bethlehem's gun plant was superior to any in the world.[15] In spite of these developments, in 1901 the prosperous armaments manufacturer found itself in an extremely vulnerable situation.

The American steel industry entered a new era in February 1901 when Carnegie sold his company to J. P. Morgan, who now had assembled nearly two-thirds of the industry into one giant company, U.S. Steel. Although Bethlehem's aging directors probably would have sold out to Morgan, the small company, with only one percent of the nation's steelmaking capacity, was left out of the merger. The demoralized Bethlehem directors, led by Wharton, then sought a deal with Vickers. In fact, Wharton had negotiated with the British firm even before the formation of U.S. Steel.

Three months after the formation of U.S. Steel, a deal was struck. However, Bethlehem turned down the offer because Vickers wanted more time to examine the Bethlehem works. Three days later, the President of U.S. Steel, Charles Schwab, agreed to purchase Bethlehem in a personal transaction, for a price only slightly higher than that offered by Vickers.[16] Schwab had been a key associate of Carnegie and had restored operations at the Homestead Plant after the violent strike of 1892. Schwab had also been an architect of the U.S. Steel merger.[17] The details of these negotiations apparently are not known. One can surmise, however, that Schwab did not want to see Vickers establish itself on American soil but was unwilling to meld Bethlehem into U.S. Steel. The latter move would have concentrated most of America's armaments capability in the giant firm, which was already being criticized as a monopolistic trust.

It is interesting to speculate how World War I might have followed a different path had Vickers owned the Bethlehem plant. In late 1914, Bethlehem signed a contract with the British to supply submarines. When President Wilson and his Secretary of State William Jennings Bryan decided that this contract would compromise U.S. neutrality, Schwab had the submarines assembled and shipped from a Montreal shipyard owned by Vickers.[18] Although American firms soon became major suppliers of materiel to the Allies, a strategic British owned steel plant on U.S. soil would have complicated Wilson's thinking on the nation's position on the war. Had American firms such as Bethlehem not become major suppliers to the Allies, Germany might not have engaged in the high-stakes gamble of unrestricted submarine warfare, a gamble that backfired, bringing the United States into the war. In any event Schwab's personal purchase of Bethlehem Steel kept it out of British hands.

In addition to accomplishing this objective, Schwab may have been looking for personal opportunities beyond U.S. Steel. By 1903 Schwab was ready to part company with the conservative leadership of the giant steel firm – or more likely, they were ready to part company with him. Complicating his position at U.S. Steel, he had become involved in the creation of a shipbuilding syndicate, into which he inserted the Bethlehem plant. However, when U.S. Shipbuilding soon experienced financial problems, Schwab refused to let Bethlehem's assets be used to bail out the parent firm.

After highly publicized legal and financial controversies, Schwab emerged with control of Bethlehem and most of the other shipbuilding companies. The notoriety that he obtained in this affair most likely led to his resignation from the presidency of U.S. Steel.[19] The man who had been the head of both Carnegie and U.S. Steel now led a much smaller firm.

As head of Bethlehem Steel, Schwab was able to take advantage of a protective umbrella that U.S. Steel had opened over what was left of the industry. U.S. Steel had to pursue a very cautious business strategy because of growing antitrust sentiment, much of it directed against the steel trust. In 1911, while the government was breaking up Standard Oil, DuPont, and American Tobacco, a government suit was also filed to break up U.S. Steel. To avoid the impression that the company was using its size to thwart competition, it did little to modernize plants, improve manufacturing efficiency, or innovate new products or processes. It also set rather high prices for its products, prices that became the de facto industry-wide prices. Under these conditions, U.S. Steel's few remaining competitors began to grow rapidly, taking considerable market share away from the industry leader. By World War I, U.S. Steel's market share of basic steel production had fallen from two-thirds to one-half.[20] Bethlehem was one of the companies that absorbed some of that market share.

Under the aggressive leadership of Schwab, Bethlehem grew rapidly after 1904. Using his negotiation skills he increased Bethlehem's share within the international arms cartel sixfold to $2 million per year. He took advantage of the shift from Bessemer to open-hearth steel in railroad rails. Bethlehem's armor business used steel made in open-hearth furnaces. Between 1908 and 1915 the market share of open hearth rails increased from 30 percent to 80 percent.[21] He also installed a crucible steel plant to produce high quality alloy steels that were used by the expanding automobile industry.

In 1908, Schwab made a major $5 million investment in a rolling mill for producing wide-flange structural beams. The mill's inventor, Henry Grey, had already built one in Europe and had tried to sell one to U.S. Steel, which was not

Top: Bethlehem Steel worker in the crucible steel plant.
Bottom: Bethlehem Steel workers who produced alloy steels.

Bethlehem Steel Corporation Collection, National Canal Museum, Easton, Pennsylvania.

interested. To pay for the mill Schwab had to borrow money from Carnegie and postpone payments to suppliers.

To install the mill, Schwab entrusted a young Lehigh University graduate, Eugene Grace, who succeeded and became Schwab's protégé. The Grey Mill did not begin to bring in any revenue until 1910 when the company won the contract to supply steel for the new Macy's department store in New York City. Other orders followed and structural steel sales soon were double those of armor plate and guns.[22] Between 1905 and 1913, Bethlehem tripled its sales to $42 million per year while only doubling its investment to $72 million. Schwab, however, had borrowed $26 million to finance the expansion and paid no dividends to the stockholders.

Servicing this debt absorbed half the company's income and made the company vulnerable if profits declined significantly.[23] Willing to gamble against such an outcome, Schwab, displaying uncanny foresight and his usual negotiating skills, in 1913 bought the Fore River Shipyard in Massachusetts for $750,000 in bonds, only one-quarter of its net worth.[24] Among its assets were patents on a new piece of military hardware, the submarine.[25]

Had World War I not occurred, or had it ended in a timely fashion, the history of Bethlehem Steel certainly would have been different. Of the $450 million in munitions contracts from the Allies, Bethlehem got two-thirds. For Britain and France alone, Bethlehem produced 65 million pounds of forged military products, 70 million pounds of armor plate, 1.1 billion pounds of steel for shells, and 20 million shells. For the United States the company would produce 65 percent of gun forgings and 40 percent of artillery shells.[26] In 1917 Bethlehem had $270 million dollars in orders for ships.[27] The impact of the war business on the company's fortunes was astounding.

Table 1:
Bethlehem Steel and World War I

Year	Total Assets (million $)	Total Sales (million $)	Net Income (million $)	Annual Steel Ingot Capacity (1000 tons)	Employees (1000s)
1912	77.4	33.9	4.1	739	12.0
1913	85.6	44.5	7.2	950	15.1
1914	96.1	47.7	7.8	1109	15.6
1915	145.8	147.6	20.1	1109	22.1
1916	220.7	217.9	47.4	1897	47.0
1917	381.5	381.5	48.0	2866	64.8
1918	397.0	452.2	30.3	3228	94.0

Source: Gertrude G. Schroeder, *The Growth of the Major Steel Companies, 1900-1950* (Baltimore: Johns Hopkins University Press, 1953), 216.

The year 1916, even before U.S. entry into the war, turned out to be the best year in the company's history. Sales had increased five times over 1913 and profits nearly sevenfold.[28] In that year Schwab pulled off another remarkable coup by purchasing the Pennsylvania Steel Company, whose assets included a shipyard near Baltimore, for $47 million, an amount equal to that year's earnings.[29] The Pennsylvania Steel Company purchase doubled Bethlehem's steel production capacity, which by the end of war was three times what it was in 1913.

Total assets over that period had gone from $85 million to nearly $400 million, making Bethlehem third behind U.S. Steel and Standard Oil of New Jersey. Yet for all this remarkable growth, Bethlehem still had only about one-tenth of U.S. Steel's output and less than five percent of the industry's total.[30] In the 1920s Schwab and Grace schemed to make Bethlehem a true rival to U.S. Steel.

World War I had doubled the capacity of the American steel industry and endowed it with large cash reserves – U.S. Steel had $800 million.[31] In the 1920s Bethlehem and the industry generally faced the challenge of maturity marked primarily by slowing growth. The railroads had always been the largest consumer of steel – 25 percent of output in the early 1920s – and during that decade automobiles and trucks began to take business away from the railroads. Cars and trucks were a major new market for steel but overall did not completely compensate for declining sales for railroads.[32]

Steel production capacity grew by only 20 percent in the 1920s with output peaking in 1929 at just 25 percent above the wartime maximum. By keeping its output at roughly its wartime peak, U.S. Steel allowed some added growth for its competitors as its market share fell from 50 percent to 40 percent during the 1920s.[33] Overall, in the 1920s the performance of the steel industry was solid but certainly not as strong as growth industries such as automobiles, radio, and chemicals.[34]

To compensate for slowing industry growth, steel company executives considered their options. Generally, companies can expand into new geographic regions, integrate backwards into raw materials, integrate forward into fabricated products, or diversify into new product lines. All of these options except forward integration, which would become a major trend in the 1930s, had some appeal to steel executives in the 1920s.[35] The major strategic focus appears to have been achieving geographic and product diversity. Because steel manufacture requires enormous quantities of coal and iron ore, the industry tended to locate around water transportation, especially in the Great Lakes region. It was fortunate that the greatest U.S. source of iron ore, the Mesabi Range in Minnesota, was adjacent to Lake Superior.

This steel industry in the Great Lakes region received an added benefit when the automobile industry grew up around Detroit. The high cost of transporting steel products also made location critical. To eliminate shipping costs in steel competition, U.S. Steel had instituted the Pittsburgh Plus system which set delivered steel prices based on shipping charges from Pittsburgh. If actual shipping charges were less, companies earned a higher profit. Historically concentrated in the East, Bethlehem enjoyed a wide area in which it earned extra income from Pittsburgh Plus shipping fees.[36] U.S. Steel would not invade the East Coast market until after World War II when it built a new mill northeast of Philadelphia.[37] In the 1920s aggressive executives, especially Grace and Schwab, favored acquisition as the main avenue to geographical diversification.

The first few years of the 1920s marked a critical juncture in the history of the American steel industry. In 1920, considerable uncertainty existed about the future structure of the industry. An antitrust suit, instituted in 1911, had reached the level of the Supreme Court, which appeared to have a majority favoring the breakup of U.S. Steel. Yet, just three years later, the industry was locked into overall industry structure that would survive essentially intact for over half a century. U.S. Steel won its contest in the Supreme Court when two judges who had earlier opposed the corporation abstained from voting.[38]

The Supreme Court argued that just because U.S. Steel had the *potential* to exercise monopoly power that did not mean that it did so. It was not size but behavior that constituted anticompetitive practice. Exonerated, U.S. Steel apparently immediately began to throw its weight around in the industry. The major outcome of this was the elevation of Bethlehem to U.S. Steel's little brother east of Pittsburgh. With acquisition of Lackawanna Steel and Midvale Steel in 1922, Bethlehem established itself geographically and physically as the number-two steelmaker, though still only one-third as large as U.S. Steel. Lackawanna and Midvale had been the number-three and five steel makers in terms of production capacity.[39]

Unprecedented competitive behavior by U.S. Steel during the sharp economic downturn that began in mid-1920 and lasted throughout much of 1921 signaled to steel industry executives that a new era had begun. In the immediate postwar period as inflation pushed up steel prices, U.S. Steel held its prices steady and compiled a large backlog of orders. When the market collapsed, this backlog allowed U.S. Steel to operate at 70 percent of capacity – and continue to turn a profit – when many of the independent steel companies were operating only at the 20 percent level. Many companies, including Midvale and Lackawanna, actually lost money during 1921. One steel executive summed up the situation by saying that "U.S. Steel was almost in control of markets."[40]

A response from the industry was not long in coming. In December 1921, news broke that financier Theodore Chadbourne, who had recently assembled Mack Trucks, was arranging a merger of seven of the twelve major independent steel companies. The new company would have been nearly half as large as U.S. Steel and would have had a strong presence in the East, something the industry leader lacked. The new North American Steel would have been three times as large as Bethlehem, which was not part of the planned merger. Clearly, the vision of North American Steel was a nightmare to Schwab and Grace, who saw themselves as *the* dynamic leaders of the industry.

The details of what happened next are not known; however, on May 11, 1922, Grace announced that Bethlehem had agreed to purchase one of the keystone companies of the proposed combine, Lackawanna.[41] By then a geographical misnomer, Lackawanna had moved from Scranton, Pennsylvania, to Buffalo, New

Women workers during World War I.

Bethlehem Steel Corporation Collection, National Canal Museum, Easton, Pennsylvania.

York, twenty years earlier, giving it a tremendous location with regards to raw materials, markets, and water transportation on the Great Lakes. In the acquisition, Bethlehem increased its overall steel production by nearly 60 percent and acquired four of the nation's eleven rail rolling mills. Although Lackawanna was a diversified steelmaker, rails were its major product, accounting for 30 percent of its output. Perhaps its most valuable asset was its Great Lakes iron ore properties.[42]

Because the evolution of steel production technology was gradual and did not include many dramatic improvements, a major source of competitive advantage was in better and cheaper raw materials. Since the supply of high-quality iron ore was limited, it represented a commodity that could be cornered.[43] Securing iron ore properties was a major objective of Bethlehem's acquisitions. Another was establishing bases in new regions.

The defection of Lackawanna from North American Steel was soon followed by another independent, Youngstown Sheet and Tube. Then three more firms dropped out, leaving only Midvale, Republic, and Inland in the proposed combination. This smaller version still would have been nearly the size of the newly enlarged Bethlehem and roughly one-quarter the size of U.S. Steel. By September, however, this merger attempt collapsed, reportedly due to uncertain financing.[44]

Bethlehem once again came forward with an offer, this time for Midvale, in November. After only three weeks of negotiations a deal was made. This acquisition added 50 percent more steelmaking capability to the Bethlehem-Lackawanna combination, bringing it to one-third the size of U.S. Steel. Midvale's major plant at Cambria, near Johnstown, Pennsylvania, was a factor in the large Pittsburgh market. In addition, Midvale added significant quantities of raw materials and several new products, such as large plates and wire, to Bethlehem's portfolio.[45] These two acquisitions transformed Bethlehem into a diversified company in terms of both markets and products.

These mergers were not sufficient to change Bethlehem's overall performance during the remainder of the 1920s. Although the decade generally was a good one for steel, demand was erratic and prices continued to slide. Bethlehem spent $150 million for plant improvements that cut its costs by about 15 percent but yielded no extra revenue.[46] The company prospered from the 1920s' construction boom, which generated a high demand for structural steel. However, U.S. Steel became more active in that market and constructed its own mill to make wide-flange beams in the late 1920s.[47]

Bethlehem also had limited involvement in the major growth market for steel, automobiles. Steel tonnage consumed by that industry grew from four to seven million between 1923 and 1928. In the latter year steel use for automobiles topped that for railroads for the first time.[48] Generally, Bethlehem was one of the poorest performing steel companies in the 1920s, as even U.S. Steel did better. The most profitable companies were some of the remaining independents, such as Youngstown Sheet and Tube and Inland.[49]

Although the steel industry was becoming somewhat more competitive, U.S. Steel and Bethlehem still accounted for about 60 percent of production. Even though prices fell somewhat during the 1920s, they were high enough to insure that all firms earned profits.[50] The steel industry and especially U.S. Steel's lack of competitive vigor, prompted a group of DuPont investors to begin buying U.S. Steel stock in 1926. The syndicate hoped to be able to buy enough shares to get a seat on the board of directors. When the press discovered this, unfavorable publicity stopped this attempted coup d'état. DuPont already owned 25 percent of GM stock, so the prospect of a DuPont-GM-U.S. Steel syndicate was intimidating even in the merger-friendly twenties.[51] Nevertheless, the DuPont attempt reflected a more widespread belief of the lack of efficient management and competitive spirit in the industry.

In the late 1920s, steel industry executives and financiers continued to pursue the strategy of geographical and product diversification through mergers. The major protagonist for additional realignments was a Cleveland-based financier Cyrus S. Eaton, who owned more steel-industry stock than any other individual in the country. In 1930, he triumphed over Schwab and Grace in a highly publicized battle over Youngstown Sheet and Tube. The failure of this round of mergers left the industry permanently without a true rival to U.S. Steel.

In the late 1920s, Eaton succeeded in merging three smaller companies into the Republic Iron Company to create the Republic Steel Company, the third largest in the industry, though still only about one-third the size of Bethlehem.[52] At the same time he was putting together Republic, beginning in late 1927 Eaton had begun buying stock in Youngstown Sheet and Tube, a major independent that had been formed by the merger of three companies in 1923.[53] For several years Eaton attempted to engineer a merger between Youngstown and Inland, a smaller but very profitable company, but the effort ultimately failed. It was likely that Eaton was considering merging his first creation – Republic – with Youngstown to create what would have been a company that would become a real rival for Bethlehem.[54]

In fact, in a November 1929 meeting with Grace, Eaton had suggested that he might be interested in 800,000 shares of Bethlehem stock that were still in the hands of the underwriter. Grace, it was reported, felt that "this would be unwise, would be misinterpreted by the public," even though the collapsing stock market made selling the stock much more difficult.[55] What Grace really meant is uncertain but whatever the implied threat, Eaton shied away from investing in Bethlehem. At the same time, Eaton later reported, Grace assured him that Bethlehem had no intentions of expanding into the heart of the Midwest.

A few months later, in March 1930, Eaton was informed Grace had reached an agreement for the acquisition of Youngstown Sheet and Tube. This possibility most likely had been discussed during a round of golf in September 1929 when Schwab and Grace visited Youngstown to participate in the 75th birthday celebration for James A. Campbell, who had led the Youngstown company for 30 years. Although a possible merger with Bethlehem was not a consideration at that time, Schwab and Grace presented Campbell with a proposal sometime around New Year's 1930.[56] Youngstown would have added about 30 percent to Bethlehem's output, bringing it to over half that of U.S. Steel, but most important was

Youngstown's Chicago steel mill. The Chicago market for steel was second only to that of Detroit.[57] The Youngstown acquisition would have given Bethlehem a strong presence in this important market.

The proposed merger was, however, not what Eaton had in mind for Youngstown. A very public battle soon ensued between Campbell and Eaton as both tried to influence stockholders to vote for or against the merger. Both sides attempted to buy blocks of stock. Eaton sought court injunctions to stop the merger process. When the vote was finally held, on April 11, Campbell won and the merger was apparently approved. Eaton was not ready to give up and filed suit, claiming that Bethlehem had withheld important financial information from the Youngstown stockholders. In July 1930 hearings, Eaton's lawyers induced Grace to reveal the previously undisclosed details of Bethlehem's executive bonus plan. Schwab's generosity to his managers had been remarkable.

Grace was clearly the best-compensated executive in the country, receiving a bonus of $1.62 million in 1929. This amounted to over 3 percent of the company's gross earnings. Since its inception in 1923, Grace had received nearly $1 million per year bonus on top of his publicly stated salary of $12,000.[58] In the 1920s, Bethlehem was a healthy corporation, but among steel companies it was one of the weaker performers. It was outperformed by the behemoth U.S. Steel and most of the smaller independents, especially Inland and Youngstown. Bethlehem's managers were paid exceptional bonuses for rather mediocre accomplishments. The bonuses of all the executives tallied $13.5 million at the same time the corporation distributed $25 million to the stockholders. Unaware that one-third of their potential stock dividends was being paid to top management, several stockholders filed suits to recover the funds.[59]

Eaton certainly embarrassed Schwab and Grace, and tarnished their image as the dynamic duo of the steel industry. The revelations of the financial legerdemain by Bethlehem prompted the judge to set aside the merger in a decision at the end of 1930. Bethlehem appealed and won a reversal in August 1931, but this time interest in expanding had been replaced by interest in surviving.[60] Bethlehem did not complete the merger and would not enter the Chicago market until the 1960s when it completed its plant at Burns Harbor, Indiana, the last major integrated steel mill to be built in the United States.[61] The Great Depression ended the merger era in the steel industry, freezing it into a basic structure that would survive for decades.[62]

Conclusion

Did Asa Packer imagine that his iron and steel company would become a key part of the international arms industry? Did Joseph Wharton foresee the formation of U.S. Steel and the stranglehold it would have on the industry? Did Charles Schwab know that his strategy to move the company away from munitions would suffer a magnificent reversal during World War I? Did he later realize that his plans to create a rival to U.S. Steel would be thwarted by the worst economic collapse in U.S. history? The answer to all these questions is no.

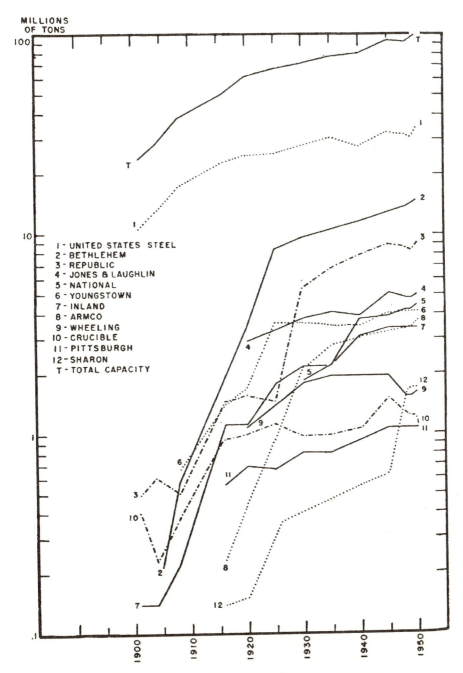

Growth of Steel Production Capacity, 1900-1950

Source: Gertrude G. Schroeder, *The Growth of the Major Steel Companies, 1900-1950* (Baltimore: Johns Hopkins University Press, 1953), 204.

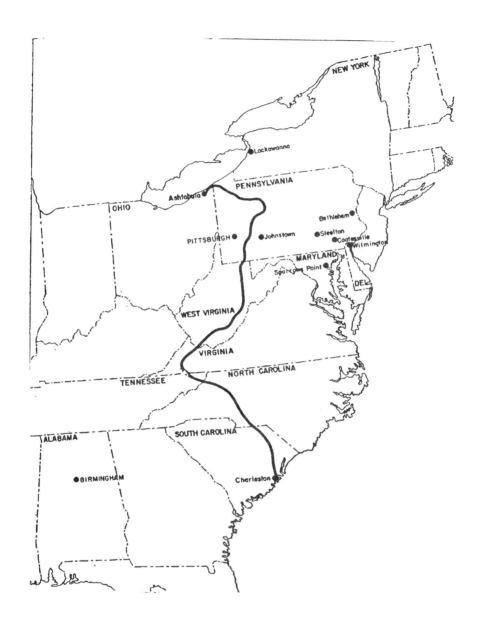

Area in Which Bethlehem Had Shipping Cost Advantage over Pittsburgh.

Source: Temporary National Economic Committee, *Investigation of Concentration of Economic Power, Monograph #13, Relative Efficiency of Large, Medium-, and Small Sized Business* (Washington, DC: G.P.O., 1941), 287.

Thus, the leadership of Bethlehem Steel had only limited ability to discern what the future held for the company. More often management found itself responding to events, such as the formation of U.S. Steel or World War I, that were beyond its control. Until the onset of the Great Depression, Bethlehem's experience had been a seesaw of threats to the firm's existence and opportunities for growth. In this period the only certainty seemed to be uncertainty. Yet, through a combination of skill and luck the company survived and prospered. The Great Depression signaled a major shift in the evolution of the industry. External events that included decades of depression, global war, and unprecedented prosperity brought little structural change to steel. Undoubtedly, the absence of creative responses from the industry to these changes was a factor contributing to its eventual decline.

Notes

1. See John Strohmeyer, *Crisis in Bethlehem: Big Steel's Struggle to Survive* (Bethesda, Md.: Adler & Adler, 1986).

2. On Chandler's approach to business history, see Thomas K. McCraw, ed., *The Essential Alfred Chandler: Essays Toward a Historical Theory of Big Business* (Boston, Mass.: Harvard Business School Press, 1988).

3. Gertrude G. Schroeder, *The Growth of the Major Steel Companies, 1900-1950* (Baltimore: Johns Hopkins University Press, 1953), 96.

4. *Report of the Commissioner of Corporations on the Steel Industry*, Part 1 (Washington, DC: G.P.O., 1911), 65, 109.

5. Mark Reutter, *Sparrows Point: Making Steel* (New York: Summit Books, 1988), 123, 160-69.

6. Lance E. Metz, "The Arsenal of America: A History of Forging Operations of Bethlehem Steel," *Canal History and Technology Proceedings* 11 (1992): 233-37.

7. Ibid., 240-43.

8. Reutter, *Sparrows Point*, 23-24.

9. W. Ross Yates, *Joseph Wharton: Quaker Industrial Pioneer* (Bethlehem, Pa.: Lehigh University Press, 1987), 254-55.

10. Peter Temin, *Iron and Steel in Nineteenth-Century America* (Cambridge, Mass.: M.I.T. Press, 1964), 218-24.

11. Metz, "Arsenal," 246-47.

12. Yates, *Joseph Wharton*, 254-65.

13. Peter J. Hugill, *World Trade Since 1431: Geography, Technology, and Capitalism* (Baltimore: Johns Hopkins University Press, 1993), 141-43.

14. On Bethlehem's entry into guns and armor plate, see Metz, "Arsenal,"243-68; Yates, *Joseph Wharton*, 254-65; and Thomas J. Misa, *A Nation of Steel: The Making of Modern America, 1865-1925* (Baltimore: Johns Hopkins University Press, 1995), 96-106.

15. Metz, "Arsenal," 265.

16. Yates, *Joseph Wharton*, 299-303.

17. On Schwab, see Robert Hessen, *Steel Titan: The Life of Charles M. Schwab* (New York: Oxford University Press, 1975).

18. Reutter, *Sparrows Point*, 94-103.

19. Hessen, *Steel Titan*, 145-62; Metz, "Arsenal," 269.

20. On U.S. Steel, see Schroeder, *Growth*, 36-46; for statistics on market share and production, see United States Steel Corporation, *T.N.E.C. Papers*, vol. 2, *Chart Studies* ([New York?]: U.S. Steel Corporation, 1940), 138-53.

21. Misa, *Nation of Steel*, 153.

22. On Bethlehem Steel before World War I, see Hessen, *Steel Titan*, 163-88 and Metz, "Arsenal," 270-72.

23. Schroeder, *Growth*, 140-41, 217.

24. Ibid., 229.

25. Reutter, *Sparrows Point*, 93-94.

26. Metz, "Arsenal," 274.

27. Reutter, *Sparrows Point*, 123.

28. Schroeder, *Growth*, 217.

29. Reutter, *Sparrows Point*, 107-108.

30. Schroeder, *Growth*, 40-51.

31. United States Steel Corporation, *T.N.E.C. Papers*, 2:15, 139.

32. Ibid., 1:83, 121.

33. Ibid., 2:138-39.

34. Schroeder, *Growth*, 178-81.

THE IMPROBABLE SUCCESS OF BETHLEHEM STEEL

35. Ibid., 105-28.

36. Temporary National Economic Committee, *Investigation of Concentration of Economic Power, Monograph No. 13, Relative Efficiency of Large, Medium-Sized, and Small Business* (Washington, DC: G.P.O., 1941), 241-48, 287.

37. Richard Austin Smith, "Bethlehem and the Intruder," *Fortune* (March 1953): 100-103, 194-99.

38. Reutter, *Sparrows Point*, 166.

39. Ibid., 160-69.

40. T.N.E.C., *Investigation of Concentration*, 223-27.

41. Reutter, *Sparrows Point*, 163-64.

42. William T. Hogan, *Economic History of the Iron and Steel Industry in the United States* (Lexington, Mass.: Heath, 1971), 3:899-910.

43. On the importance of iron ore supplies see Misa, *Nation of Steel*, 155-64. In 1941 *Fortune* commented that "The foundation of U.S. Steel, so far as maintaining its corporate bulk is concerned, was an assured supply of raw materials." "Bethlehem Steel," *Fortune* (April 1941): 150.

44. Reutter, *Sparrows Point*, 167.

45. Hogan, *Economic History*, 3:910-17.

46. Ibid., 3:919-21.

47. Hessen, *Steel Titan*, 267-69.

48. United States Steel Corporation, *T.N.E.C. Papers*, 1:83, 121.

49. Schroeder, *Growth*, 176-78. On the comparative performance of Bethlehem and U.S. Steel, see "Bethlehem Steel," *Fortune*, 64.

50. Schroeder, *Growth*, 175, 204.

51. Charles W. Cheape, *Strictly Business: Walter Carpenter at Du Pont and General Motors* (Baltimore: Johns Hopkins University Press, 1995), 70-73.

52. Schroeder, *Growth*, 151-53.

53. "Clash of Steel," *Fortune* (June 1930): 68.

54. Schroeder, *Growth*, 98-99.

55. "Clash of Steel," *Fortune*, 68.

56. Ibid., 68-69.

57. United States Steel Corporation, *T.N.E.C. Papers*, 1:381.

58. Reutter, *Sparrows Point*, 191-99.

59. Ibid., 202-204.

60. Ibid., 206.

61. Strohmeyer, *Crisis in Bethlehem*, 62. Bethlehem did attempt to merge with Youngstown Sheet and Tube in 1955 but was blocked by anti-trust legal action by the Justice Department. Gilbert Burck, "The Private Strategy of Bethlehem Steel," *Fortune* (April 1962): 246.

62. Schroeder, *Growth*, 196-215.

Bethlehem Social Elites, "The Steel," and the Saucon Valley Country Club

ROGER D. SIMON

THE LARGE CORPORATION IN A SMALL-CITY SETTING can reveal dynamics of class interactions that may be harder to isolate in a metropolitan center. Bethlehem presents an instructive case of how a corporate managerial elite displaced a local upper class and then created an institution designed both to confirm its social position and to advance that corporate culture. This paper will examine the interaction of the established upper class with the new managers and will then focus on the local country club and its relationship to Bethlehem Steel to better understand those dynamics.[1]

In the mid-nineteenth century, a group of industrial entrepreneurs associated with Asa Packer, who built the Lehigh Valley Railroad, relocated from Mauch Chunk to Bethlehem to manage their railroad, iron, and coal interests. The principal figures were Robert H. Sayre, the general manager of the Railroad; Garrett Linderman, Packer's son-in-law and president of Bethlehem Iron in the 1880s; and Elisha P. Wilbur, Packer's cousin, whose bank controlled the Packer estate. They were joined by a few other families with similar interests – Dodsons, Skeers, Cleavers, and Blakeslees – and by the early twentieth century those families were interrelated through a network of marriages and formed the nucleus of a local upper class.[2]

They built mansions along Delaware Avenue in the adjacent borough of Fountain Hill and established their own cultural institutions, including the Episcopalian Cathedral Church of the Nativity and a private Episcopalian girls' school (even though the local Moravian female academy was one of the finest on the east coast). They nurtured Lehigh University, founded by Asa Packer in 1865 to train engineers for the industrializing region. Many of the sons of the local families attended Lehigh and later sat on its Board of Trustees.[3]

With their large homes, immense staffs, white horses, carriages and sleighs, and later chauffeur-driven automobiles, they constituted a local aristocracy, as one of their descendants described them. Stella Wilbur recalled that "everyone had horses." Ms. Wilbur's grandmother had an island in the Thousand Islands, and

Stella traveled to Europe as a young woman, accompanying Mrs. Robert Linderman. Rhoda Thorp, whose father was a prominent doctor and inventor, grew up on Delaware Avenue in the early twentieth century and recalled that everyone had bicycles and went on bike trips, and that everyone had servants. She described the neighborhood as "a gay and glorious place to live." Frances Taylor Martin, whose father was a prominent Moravian attorney and grew up on the north side, recalled that in her youth the social leaders were the Wilburs, Lindermans, Skeers, Cleavers, and Sayres: "The Moravians never had any money and were not social."[4]

The social high point for the Bethlehem upper class occurred on November 25, 1913, when Robert Sayre's son Francis married Jessie Wilson, the President's daughter, in the White House. Although the bridegroom no longer lived in town, all of the extended Fountain Hill relatives attended; it was quite a sensation and source of pride.[5] By the time of that gala event, however, the dominance of the upper-class families was already slipping. They had lost control of both the railroad and the steel company, and they were not even very successful at perpetuating their male line. Asa Packer's sons died childless in the 1880s. By World War I there were only a few Wilburs and Sayres left.[6]

Meanwhile, in 1904 Charles Schwab took control of the local steel plant, and reorganized it as Bethlehem Steel Corporation, or as it was locally known: "the Steel." He purchased the Garret Linderman mansion on Delaware Avenue, and spent much of his time in the city over the next decade. Since he was the most powerful and prominent member of the community, the old elites accepted him. Margaret Dodson Griffin, whose family was part of the upper-class circle, recalled that Schwab regularly played bridge at her home: "no one snubbed Mr. Schwab."[7]

To run the company Schwab quickly assembled a group of younger men known as "Schwab's boys," most of whom were unconnected to the local upper class. Inevitably some resentment resulted; Margaret Griffin recalled a certain "snootiness" and remembered her mother saying: "there's those new Steel people."[8] However, such feelings were probably short-lived and expressed only in private. By their numbers as well as by their wealth and power, the new managers quickly displaced the old guard. By the second decade of the century, old family and Moravian leaders were working together with Steel executives on civic projects.[9]

With a few exceptions, the new Steel managers did not join the old upper-class families along Delaware Avenue. It is not clear whether they were rebuffed in an attempt to buy property, or simply that the street was already built up. Most of the new managers clustered instead on the city's west side, on and near Prospect Avenue where they created their own prestigious residential neighborhood. Since the Steel Corporation paid enormous bonuses, the area soon became known as Bonus Hill. By 1920, Eugene Grace, the corporation president, and six other senior officers all lived within a few blocks of one another. Along the side streets were the homes of aspiring junior executives, professionals, and local businessmen.[10]

In the nineteenth century the American upper class established a number of exclusive institutions both to provide indicators of their social position as well as

Top: The Linderman mansion in Bethlehem, purchased by Charles M. Schwab when he took control of "the Steel."

Bottom: President Woodrow Wilson with Charles Schwab and two riveters at Hog Island Shipyard during World War I.

Bethlehem Steel Corporation Collection, National Canal Museum, Easton, Pennsylvania.

to insure themselves that they were associating with the right people. The first such facilities were the downtown businessmen's clubs that predated the Civil War. They were followed by exclusive summer resorts, boarding schools for boys, finishing schools for girls, societies confirming colonial ancestry, the "blue book" or Social Register, and the country club.[11]

The country club grew out of the convergence of three trends among the upper class: a growing interest in sport, suburbanization, and increased anxiety over the success of non-Protestants. Early private clubs in the countryside focused on cricket, polo, and the hunt, but in the 1880s the upper class eagerly embraced golf, which was safer than polo and better suited than cricket to casual conversation and informal business dealings. Furthermore, the park-like grounds of the golf course were reminiscent of the English country estates the upper class so much envied. Like the exclusive summer resorts, the country club provided a controlled setting for the whole family. Members would be assured, not only that they were playing golf with "gentlemen," but, perhaps more importantly, that their sons and daughters would be socializing with the children of such families.[12]

Until 1920 Bethlehem lacked its own country club. The local upper class was too small to support one, and with their large houses and retinue of servants they preferred to do most of their formal entertaining at home. The local leaders did play a prominent role in the downtown businessmen's club, the Bethlehem Club. In addition, there were the two small country clubs nearby. The Lehigh Country Club, located between Allentown and Bethlehem, had a golf course of no special quality, but it was the venue for many elegant dances and parties. It was built on land originally belonging to the Dodson family, and the Dodsons, Wilburs, and Lindermans were all active members, although the club was considered to belong to Allentown. The Northampton Country Club, between Bethlehem and Easton, had a better golf course and by World War I a number of Steel executives belonged.[13] Eugene Grace, an avid and excellent golfer, was frequently on the course. In September 1920, a reported crowd of eight hundred spectators watched Grace and Chic Evans, "a national amateur champion," play against two British professionals.[14]

By the time of that golf tournament, however, it was clear that the Bethlehem Steel interests were ready for their own club. With enormous profits from the World War, the Steel had absorbed several other companies, enlarging the ranks of its corporate managers who were also flush with large bonuses. The Steel people now had the numbers and the affluence to support their own facilities. To that end, in September 1920, a hundred men convened at the Bethlehem Club, authorized $24,000 to purchase a two hundred acre farm on the outskirts of town, chose the name Saucon Valley Country Club, and selected a board of directors.[15] Full membership was restricted to men and their families. Unattached adult women could be admitted as Special Members with reduced dues and no voting rights. In 1921 the Board added a category of Associate Members for men from Allentown and Easton. Associates paid the same dues and fees as regular members, but could not vote for directors, underlining the intent to make sure that Saucon

Valley would be "strictly a Bethlehem Club and run by Bethlehem people."[16]

High costs for membership and annual dues limited the appeal of the new club. Charter membership was set at $100 and regular memberships at $50, but when the golf course opened the membership fee rose to $100 with annual dues at $50. By 1927 annual dues were up to $100 with golf and locker fees another $40. In 1927, to raise money for a new clubhouse, the board asked members to purchase a $250 bond (see Table 1).[17] Despite the business depression of 1921, membership grew quickly. At the end of that year there were 312 full and associate members, and throughout the decade full membership hovered around three hundred, which represented at most two percent of the city's families (see Table 2).

Tracing the occupations and residential location of members through the city directories provides clues into the kinds of people who joined and how exclusive the club really was. Occupation provides only an approximate surrogate for income and is even less reliable as an indicator of class, but it does offer some insights. Unsurprisingly, considering the fees and the dues structure, the Saucon Valley Country Club drew its membership from upper- and upper-middle-class families. Although the senior Corporation officers took the lead in organizing the club and guaranteed the initial loan, local businessmen, professionals, and corporate middle managers numerically dominated the roster from the beginning. The businessmen included officers of local banks of the Lehigh Coal and Navigation Company, and of the Lehigh Valley Railroad; principals of insurance and real estate agencies; contractors; successful merchants; and local manufacturers. A substantial fraction of local attorneys, physicians, and dentists were members, as well as many engineers, scientists, and accountants who worked at the Steel; there were even a few Lehigh professors in the club. A quarter of the members were superintendents and managers, mostly from the Steel, and salesmen accounted for another ten percent (see Table 3).[18]

Studies of income and family budgets in the 1920s suggest an annual income of over five thousand dollars was needed to sustain a country club membership. In the late 1920s lawyers and physicians, on average, enjoyed that level of income, but college teachers only averaged $3,056. Clerical workers in manufacturing industries earned $2,310 and ministers $1,826, only slightly better than a well-paid skilled male artisan.[19] A 1927 study of the spending habits of "professional class" families in California found their average income to be $6,500, while they spent $378 a year for recreation and entertainment, including all club dues, vacations, concerts, movies, and records.[20] Such families were in the top ten percent of income earners.

The incomes of middle managers at Bethlehem Steel were certainly comparable to those of local professionals and businessmen, but the senior executives were clearly in the upper class. In 1941, Bethlehem Steel superintendents had a base annual salary of $10,000, and made as much as $5,000 more in bonuses.[21] Those may be high-end figures, but it clearly placed superintendents in the upper middle class. In the 1920s, Eugene Grace earned an average of $815,000 a year, while corporate vice-presidents earned over $100,000 a year in the twenties and thirties.[22]

The Country Club leadership adopted admission procedures for new members from standard business and country club practices. A candidate for admission required written nomination by two current members. A secret membership committee investigated the candidate and posted his name in the clubhouse for two weeks. Candidates had to be personally known to two Board members and the Board's approval had to be unanimous. Occasionally a name was withdrawn because of a questionable business reputation, although this was rare. Catholics were accepted in the club, but, not surprisingly, Jews were excluded.[23]

As the membership grew, the club was able to steadily expand its facilities to meet its goals of providing a controlled informal setting for the conduct of business and for family activities among a self-identified group of social elites. The first priority was obviously the golf course and no expense was spared; the first nine holes opened in 1921. Restaurant service began in 1923 when the club sponsored dances for the first time. The clubhouse stayed open through the winter for trapshooting and ice-skating.[24] By the mid-twenties the club serviced the whole family: swimming lessons for children, dances for teenagers, dinner dances for adults, golf and tennis lessons for everyone and tournaments for men and ladies.

Although Bethlehem Steel's employees did not numerically dominate the membership, without doubt Saucon Valley was the company's club. The composition of the Board of Governors revealed the extent of corporation dominance. Ten of the sixteen original Board members were Bethlehem Steel officials. Roy A. Lewis, General Manager of the Bethlehem plant, was the first president, a position he held until 1934. John Sylvester, who worked under Lewis at the plant, was club vice-president, and succeeded Lewis as president; the secretary worked in the real estate department; the first treasurer was an assistant corporate comptroller. Of the other Steel men on the Board, two were corporate officers, three were superintendents and one was in sales. The original board included six other men: two local real estate agents, a lawyer, a bank officer, the vice-president of the city's largest coal company, and Robert E. Wilbur, the sole representative of the older upper class. Wilbur was the publisher of the *Bethlehem Globe Times* and vice-president of a leading commercial bank as well as of the Chamber of Commerce.[25] In the club's first seventeen years, all of its officers worked at the corporation, and at no time were less than half of the Board positions filled by non-corporate personnel.

The Corporation itself made donations of materials, labor, and services. The precise level of that support is unclear, but at one point in the early twenties the club owed the Corporation over $20,000. In 1928, when the old clubhouse burned down, Bethlehem Steel donated structural steel for a new building, a gift Club President R. A. Lewis valued at $15,000.[26] The staff of the Comptroller's office kept the club's books, although after 1925 the club paid for that service. The company print shop produced the club's membership booklets and programs at a reduced rate. In 1930, when Lehigh County raised the assessed valuation of the club property, Lewis asked the Steel Company tax department to investigate. As a result, the county reduced the assessed valuation to less than it had been before.

In at least one instance, Lewis seemed to forget that the Steel and Saucon Valley Country Club were separate entities. In 1924 a club member who worked in Bethlehem's New York sales office was $55.00 in arrears in his dues. Lewis called the man's superior "to see if some pressure could not be brought" to have him pay up, but he had left the company. There are no other instances of this kind in the minutes, but one suspects that the club members who worked at Steel rarely fell behind in their dues.[27]

There was an intangible sense of social hierarchy at the club associated with the corporate ladder. One woman who belonged to both the Saucon and Lehigh clubs recalled a greater egalitarian feeling at the latter because no single firm dominated its membership. A senior Steel official recalled many years later that "some people, particularly wives, get into a race of seeing what the other fellow is doing" and recalled that "it gets pretty competitive." But he also felt that Bethlehem, unlike Wilmington, Delaware, was not really a one-industry town.[28]

During the Great Depression many country clubs around the nation folded, but Saucon Valley managed to survive the crisis with little adverse impact. Ironically, in June 1930, the club decided its membership rolls were filled and began a waiting list for the first time. However, worsening conditions soon affected its members, and by the fall resignations had begun to mount. For the next several years the board cut back expenses to avoid a deficit. They restricted food service and closed the clubhouse during the winter from 1931 to 1934. But in August of 1932, with hungry and unemployed steelworkers all about them, the Board saw fit to spend $1,100 for power lawn mowers, deciding that the savings in labor costs justified the expense. A year later, the Board, to comply with the N.R.A. code for country clubs, increased staff wages fifteen percent and applied for an N.R.A. Blue Eagle.[29]

Finally, in January 1933, recognizing the hardship of its members, the Board cut annual dues from $100 to $60, but also invited those who could to continue paying the higher amount as Sustaining Members. In addition, a special dispensation until the end of 1933 permitted members to rejoin without a new initiation fee.[30] In 1934 the Board pressured members to donate their $250 bonds to the club, but when some held back the Board levied an assessment to retrieve the bonds. By 1934 the club had weathered the storm. Regular membership jumped from 253 to 303. In December 1935, the Board raised regular dues to $75 and to $100 in September 1937.[31]

One might suspect that the delay in reducing dues until it was an absolute necessity was an intentional device to shake down the club's roster and eliminate some of the more socially marginal members. Occupational data do not show any major shift in the character of the membership, but membership records clearly suggest many members suffered from hard times as the number of resignations and terminations for unpaid bills rose sharply while no cut in dues came until January 1933.

In 1947 Bethlehem Steel constructed a new facility near the plant called the

Bethlehem Steel Club. It was a private country club, complete with golf course, pool, and clubhouse with bowling alleys. It was only open to the management personnel of the Bethlehem plant: foremen, supervisors, superintendents, and plant managers. People who worked in the home office division were not eligible. The Corporation was clearly introducing, or confirming, a social split between the home office personnel and the local plant staff. The new club may also have been an effort solidify the loyalty of foremen, who were not eligible for unionization. In the 1950s there was a drop off in the percentage of Saucon Valley members who were managers and superintendents as the club became more exclusive.

Saucon Valley Country Club in 1947

In 1941 *Fortune* magazine did an in-depth article on Bethlehem Steel. They lauded its exceptional management team that in two decades had built the corporation into the nation's second-largest steel company. The editors also concluded that, in many ways, Bethlehem had "more in common with little business than with big business."[32] By remaining in a small city the Corporation kept its managers insulated and, to a degree, isolated. "Bethlehem's management lives in Bethlehem. By day it works together, and by night it strolls across the street to visit itself."[33] The officers, most of whom were corporate directors, ate lunch together almost every business day. Men were literally "on call twenty-four hours." When *Fortune* returned for another look fifteen years later, they found that little had changed. The magazine wrote: "For the most part they create their own society, golf at the Saucon Valley club, or give quiet parties."[34]

No one articulated the dynamic better than Ivor Sims. Sims' father had worked for Bethlehem Steel in Chile; in the 1920s the family relocated to the home office. Sims graduated from Lehigh in 1933 and was lucky enough to get a job with the company that same year. He ascended the corporate ladder to become a director in 1957, vice president in 1963, and executive vice-president from 1966 to 1973. "Success at Bethlehem Steel," Sims argued, was "unquestionably due to its policies, its management, and its fine treatment of its personnel." He emphasized that the executives lived, worked, and golfed together, but he hastened to add "there's no strata here actually. I never felt it that way." He rejected the notion of an "organization man" at Bethlehem. Rather, he strongly emphasized the corporate policy of promoting from within:

> Bethlehem...believes in developing its own personnel; it doesn't go out and hire a new vice-president when someone dies, it has someone who can take the deceased person's place. Internal advancement has meant each employee who wishes to succeed, becomes Bethlehemized, he eats and sleeps and drinks Bethlehem because he loves the company he's working for.[35]

Bethlehem was a small city. In the 1920s the population, including environs, was a little over 50,000; by the 1950s it had grown to 75,000. While corporate managers in large cities also imbibed a distinctive corporate ethos, they had the option of a wider circle of acquaintances and multiple venues for recreation and socialization. In a small city such as Bethlehem, dominated by a single large corporation, the social environment was particularly claustrophobic. Under such circumstances aspiring managers and their wives would readily internalize the values of the corporate leadership and become "Bethlehemized."[36]

Table 1:
Membership Fees and Dues for Regular Members,
Saucon Valley Country Club, 1920-1937

Initiation Fees		Annual Dues**	
1920-21	$ 50	1920-21	$ 36
1921-31	100	1921-23	50
1931-34*	350	1923-27	75
1934-37	250	1927-33	100
		1933-35**	60
		1935-37	75
		1937	100

Notes:

* The membership fees from 1931-34 included a $250 refundable bond. It is not clear whether the bonds represented a pledge or had to be paid up front. Most of the bonds were eventually donated to the club. In 1934 the bond was replaced by the $250 fee.

** Members were invited to continue paying $100 as Sustaining Members.

Source: SVCC Minutes, Saucon Valley Country Club.

Table 2:
Full Members of the Saucon Valley Country Club, Selected Years, 1921-1936

1921	312
1925	301
1927	299
1929	329
1931	306
1933	253
1935	297
1936	310

Source: Annual Reports, Saucon Valley Country Club.

Table 3:
Percentage of Identifiable Members of the Saucon Valley Country Club by Occupation and Employment at Bethlehem Steel

	1925	1931	1937	1950	1950
High Executives	17.2	13.0	6.8	4.6	6.0
Other Executives, Local Businessmen	19.9	18.6	5.4	14.7	17.0
Professionals	25.2	20.1	20.3	24.4	28.6
Managers, Superintendents	23.8	32.1	30.6	20.1	18.3
Salesmen, Foremen	10.3	8.2	12.6	6.6	10.9
Clerks, White Collar Workers	3.0	5.7	18.0	17.5	12.4
Miscellaneous[1]	.6	.6	1.4	4.3	1.0
No Occupation, Retired	1.3	1.9	5.0	7.7	4.9
Worked at Bethlehem Steel	31.7	41.1	34.4	44.5	50.0
Number of Cases	306	318	222	321	469

Source: Saucon Valley Country Club, minutes, Yearbooks; Bethlehem City Directories; Bethlehem Steel Corporation phone books.

1. The city directory listed several men simply as "steelworker" or "machinist." Their residential location, however, makes it unlikely that they were production workers.

Notes

1. The best study of these issues nationally is John N. Ingham, *The Iron Barons: A Social Analysis of an American Urban Elite, 1874-1965* (Westport, Conn.: Greenwood Press, 1978); Ingham refers to Bethlehem briefly, see 51-52,175-76.

2. Burton W. Folsom, Jr., *Urban Capitalists: Entrepreneurs and City Growth in Pennsylvania's Lackawanna and Lehigh Regions, 1900-1920* (Baltimore: Johns Hopkins University Press, 1981), 128. Ruth Linderman Frick, interview with author, 1975. (Recordings of all interviews cited in the paper are in the possession of the author.)

3. W. Ross Yates, ed., *Bethlehem of Pennsylvania: The Golden Years, 1841-1920* (Bethlehem, Pa.: The Bethlehem Book Committee, 1976), chap. 3; Lehigh University Catalogues.

4. Rhoda Edwards Thorpe, interview with author, 1975; Frances Taylor Martin, interview with author, 1975; Ruth Linderman Frick interview, 1975; Stella Wilbur, interview by Donna Coco, 1975; Margaret Dodson Griffith, interview by Donna Coco, 1975. Mrs. Robert P. Linderman was the daughter of Robert H. Sayre and the widow of Asa Packer's grandson. On the cultural meaning of the large mansion, see E. C. Kirkland, *"The Big House," Dream and Thought in the Business Community* (Ithaca, N.Y.: Cornell University Press, 1956), chap. 2.

5. Yates, *Bethlehem*, 231-32. Sixty years later Ruth Linderman Frick (daughter of Robert P. and Ruth Sayre Linderman) still recalled the event with a gleam; interview, 1975.

6. Folsom, *Urban Capitalists*, 136.

7. Margaret Dodson Griffin, interview, 1975.

8. Ibid.; Raymond Walters, *Bethlehem Long Ago and Today* (Bethlehem, Pa.: Carey Printing Company, Inc., 1923), 88. Not all of "Schwab's boys" were newcomers. Among them was Archibald Johnston, an executive of Bethlehem Iron Co., whom Schwab retained. Johnston became a vice-president and director of the Corporation and, in 1917, the first mayor of the merged City of Bethlehem. Although not a native of the city, Johnston moved to Bethlehem as a child, graduated from Lehigh, and married into a prominent Moravian family. Yates, *Bethlehem*, 177-78, 182; *Who's Who in America*, 1922-24 (Chicago: Marquis Who's Who, 1922); Folsom, *Urban Capitalists*, 142.

9. Yates, *Bethlehem*, 299-308.

10. *Bethlehem City Directory*, 1920-37; Bethlehem Steel Corporation, Bethlehem Plant, Phone Directories, 1920-37. Quincy Bent lived on Delaware Avenue and was the exception that proved the rule. Bent joined the Corporation as a vice-president in 1918; he came from an established Philadelphia family, and was listed in the Philadelphia *Social Register*.

11. E. Digby Baltzell, *Philadelphia Gentlemen: The Making of a National Upper Class* (Glencoe, Ill.: Free Press, 1958) and *The Protestant Establishment: Aristocracy and Caste in America* (New York: Vintage Books, 1966); Ingham, *Iron Barons*, chap. 3. The *Social Register* announced in the preface to one edition that it included "those families who by descent or by social standing or from other qualifications are naturally included in the best society," as quoted in Dixon Wecter, *The Saga of American Society* (New York: Scribner, 1937), 235.

12. On the development of the country club see James M. Mayo, *The American Country Club: The Origins and Development* (New Brunswick, N.J.: Rutgers University Press, 1998); Richard J. Moss, *Golf and the American Country Club* (Urbana: University of Illinois Press, 2001); Ingham, *Iron Barons*, 96-98; William Wyckoff, "Landscapes of Private Power and Wealth," in Michael P. Conzen, ed., *The Making of the American Landscape* (Boston: Unwin, Hyman, 1990), 336, 338.

13. Marion Paul, interview by the author, 1976; interviews with Margaret Dodson Griffin, Frances Taylor Martin, Stella Wilbur; *Who's Who in America*, 1922-23; 1928-29.

14. *The Globe*, 27 Sept. 1920, 8. Throughout the twenties local and national golf news received prominent coverage in the *Bethlehem Globe Times*. See, for example, reports on golf matches between Saucon Valley and the Lehigh Club, 18 June 1923, and the game for the Board of Governor's Cup, 23 July 1923. Grace was a championship golfer for many years; see, for example, U.S. Golf Association, "Program of the 51st Annual Championship, Saucon Valley Country Club, September 10-15, 1951," 47.

15. Interview with Marion Paul; Saucon Valley Country Club manuscript minutes of the Board of Directors, 14 Sept. 1920; hereafter cited as SVCC minutes.

16. SVCC minutes, 7 Sept. 1921. In 1924, in response to dissatisfaction from the Associate members, the Board dropped the discrimination, but by then it was clear that locals dominated the club's membership, see SVCC minutes, 8 May 1924.

17. SVCC minutes 7 Sept. 1921; also 13 Sept. 1921, 13 Dec. 1923, 27 Mar. 1927, 11 Feb. 1929, 11 Nov. 1932. Women and Lehigh student members did not have to pay the golf fee. In 1933 the caddy fee was 75 cents, SVCC minutes, 19 Apr. 1933.

18. The Club admitted a few men of lesser prestige. Ben Pflume, for example, was a member from 1921 to 1923. At the time he joined Pflume was a machinist at Bethlehem Steel, perhaps a foreman. About the time he left the club he became the foreman at a local car dealership. In 1927, he became the caretaker at the Masonic Temple where his wife was the cook. SVCC minutes; Bethlehem City Directory; Harriet K. Pflume, interview with the author, 1975.

19. Income figures for lawyers and physicians are for non-salaried professionals only. U. S. Bureau of the Census, *Historical Statistics of the United States to 1957* (Washington, DC: G.P.O., 1957), 91, 97.

20. Daniel Horowitz, *The Morality of Spending: Attitudes Toward the Consumer Society in America, 1875-1940* (Baltimore: Johns Hopkins University Press, 1985), 144–45; the study was done in the San Francisco Bay area where the cost of living was probably higher than in Bethlehem.

21. *Fortune*, 23 (April 1941): 139.

22. Ibid., 142; *The New York Times*, 15 Apr. 1931, 1.

23. SVCC minutes, 25 Oct. 1920 and 18 Oct. 1937. On upper class anti-Semitism generally see Baltzell, *Protestant Establishment*.

24. SVCC minutes, 19 Apr. 1921, 29 July 1921, 23 Aug. 1921, 24 Aug. 1924, 13 Aug. 1925.

25. SVCC minutes, 14 Sept. 1920; Bethlehem Plant, Phone Directory, 1920. In 1921, when the club refinanced a loan of $50,000, fifty-four men guaranteed a portion of the debt; two-thirds of those guarantors were Bethlehem Steel officers or managers.

26. SVCC minutes, 18 Oct. 1925, 10 Dec. 1925, 14 Jan. 1926, 9 Sept. 1929.

27. SVCC minutes, 24 Aug. 1924.

28. Interview with Marion Paul; C.E. Snyder, interview by Lynn Succop, 1975.

29. SVCC minutes, 14 Aug. 1933; N.R.A. stands for National Recovery Administration.

30. SVCC minutes, 9 June 1930, 13 Oct. 1930, 10 Nov. 1930, 9 Nov. 1931, 11 Jan. 1932, 11 Apr. 1932, 9 May 1932, 10 Oct. 1932, 23 Jan. 1933, 14 Aug. 1933.

31. SVCC minutes, 3 Mar. 1928, 9 Apr. 1934, 8 Aug. 1934, 19 Nov. 1934, 11 Dec. 1934,

14 Dec. 1934, 27 July 1936, 16 Dec. 1936, 30 Sept. 1937.

32. *Fortune*, 23 (April 1941): 66, 142.

33. Ibid., 60.

34. Richard Austin Smith, "Bethlehem Steel and the Intruder," *Fortune* 47 (March 1953): 101.

35. Ivor Sims, interview with Lynn Succop, 1975; Sims was also a trustee of Lehigh University.

36. See Diane Rothbard Margolis, *The Managers, Corporate Life in America: Work, Family and Community* (New York: William Morrow, 1979) for an introduction to modern corporate socialization.

Gender and Economic Decline: The Pennsylvania Anthracite Region, 1920-1970

THOMAS DUBLIN and WALTER LICHT

NEWSPAPERS AND MAGAZINES in the United States in recent decades have published numerous articles dealing with factory closings and corporate restructuring. "De-industrialization" and "downsizing" are headline words that tell of contemporary economic shifts and the elimination of millions of jobs, particularly in manufacturing.[1] For the most part, the stories related are centered on men; they are about male loss of employment (and esteem), the male search for new work, and often downward occupational mobility. This treatment of economic decline is thus in a sense gendered, but of course a fully gendered look would examine the differential impact of economic change on men and women, and, equally important, the effect on male and female perceptions, roles, and relations.[2]

De-industrialization in the United States has occurred so precipitously that scholars and other commentators have yet to get a firm handle on the causes of change; the ultimate impact of massive job loss on people's lives also remains unclear as this history is still unfolding. The anthracite coal region of northeastern Pennsylvania in this regard offers a clearer perspective on the consequences of long-term economic decline on individuals and communities. There the process is largely complete. A seventy-year period of mine closings, beginning in the early 1920s, reduced mine employment from upwards of 175,000 men to a scant 1,400 and brought on greater regional economic collapse.[3] The men, women, and children who experienced the abrupt ending of stable employment circumstances are still alive, some remaining in their home communities, great numbers having migrated from the region. They can be tracked and their testimonies help in the writing of the history of economic decline. The oral history method is particularly useful in investigating the gendered nature of the subject, for recent published scholarship offers few clues as to the varied impact of economic disruption on men and women and the ways they relate to each other.

This chapter reports on the results of more than ninety interviews with current and former residents of the Pennsylvania anthracite region, equally divided between men and women.⁴ The interviews show clearly that men and women felt the impact of industrial decline in distinctly different ways and that gender relations were dramatically transformed in the aftermath of regional economic crisis.

Before plunging into our evidence and argument it may be helpful to discuss our sources and methods and to outline at least sketchily the major conclusions that we draw from the evidence. Access to the voluminous employment records of the mining operations of the Lehigh Coal and Navigation Company led to a focus on the Panther Valley, a group of adjoining towns south and west of the upper Lehigh River Valley. We interviewed about seventy lifelong residents of these communities over the course of three years beginning in 1993. Not wanting to limit our perspective to persisters in the region, we interviewed another two dozen outmigrants from the anthracite region who settled in working-class suburbs northeast of Philadelphia and in northern New Jersey. While we gathered life histories of those we interviewed, the focus was primarily on attitudes and behavior in the 1950s and '60s, the period in which anthracite mines closed down and economic pressures on working people and their families in the region were greatest.

A number of themes emerged from our interviews that speak to the impact of de-industrialization in the region and offer insights into thinking about similar phenomena in more recent years. First, working-class men and women were active agents responding to and shaping developments following the closing of the mines. In their actions they adapted traditional values to cope with new circumstances. And while men had predominated as bread-winners in mining communities, women played crucial roles in the strategies families employed in response to the mine closings. Finally, gender relations in working-class families underwent significant change as the mine closings undermined the economic basis for the patriarchal system that had shaped family life in earlier decades.

Ninety-five percent of the nation's supply of anthracite coal lay below a five-county, triangular area in eastern Pennsylvania that extends northeast from Harrisburg to Scranton. Great entrepreneurial activity, transportation innovations, and the hard labor of successive immigrant generations brought anthracite out of the earth to fuel American industrialization and heat the nation's homes and workplaces. Beginning in the 1920s, the efficient, long-burning anthracite lost its market to cheaper fossil fuels. Mines in the region closed; the area experienced with the rest of the country the economic downturn of the Great Depression; a revival of fortunes followed during World War II, but the bottom fell completely out of the market for anthracite thereafter. With the massive loss of mining jobs, businesses dependent on the purchases of miners' families closed their doors and the region entered a general long-term economic contraction. Today boarded-up storefronts mark the business districts of small town and city alike.⁵

To understand the impact of economic decline on individuals and families requires an appreciation of patriarchy within the working class as a basic element in the history of the region. The area developed with the expansion of an industry whose work force was 99 percent male. Women did not work inside mines; in fact, their presence in mines was taboo and held to bring bad luck. By the 1940s and '50s, on the eve of the mine closings, a substantial garment industry had developed in the region that gave employment principally to single women in the years before marriage.

Still, many more men than women were employed outside the home and their earnings dwarfed those of women. Working-class families in the anthracite region depended principally on the earnings of men; male power and authority within the family reflected their superior earnings. Recalling the deprivations she felt growing up during the Depression, one woman remembered a conversation from that period: " And I even said to my mother, 'Why can't I drink this milk?' [Her mother replied,] 'Because that's for your father. That's for your father. He's the one that works; he's the one that has to eat.' "[6]

Just as superior earnings gave men advantages at the dinner table, so too men exercised power in determining how their wages were spent. As one woman recalled, " My father was a gambler and a drinker, too. Whenever he worked, he would just give [my mother] so much money and the rest he kept for himself." Toward the end of the mining period women did challenge men's exclusive control of their earnings, but these developments only underscore male dominance earlier.[7]

The closing of the mines and the subsequent economic collapse of the region reinforced the separate domains that men and women occupied – the mine and the barroom had been the traditional places of men, the home of women. Although increasing numbers of married women found paid employment outside the home as the mines closed down, men and women continued to work in strongly sex-segregated sectors of the economy. Men's and women's respective experiences continued to be defined in gendered terms.

Job hunting after the mines closed provides a useful case in point. The process of job hunting proved to be a collective male endeavor that allowed former miners to maintain the close relations with fellow workers that had characterized their working lives in the mines. Unemployed men sat in bars and clubs exchanging tips on job possibilities in places near and far off. They also traveled together in search of work and remained loyal to each other. Joe Rodak thus described how he and three of his buddies roamed through industrial districts of Philadelphia, knocking on factory doors. Joe had training in electronics and received an offer at the Link-Belt Company, which he refused when his friends were turned down. They all later secured employment together at a General Electric plant (helped by a guard who recognized them as fellow "coal crackers").[8]

With the closing of the mines in the mid-1950s, fathers and sons also traveled together in search of work, and here generational role reversals occurred with sons often securing work for their fathers. Paul Melovich remembered how his older brother took his father on job searching expeditions through southern New Jersey, sleeping together at night in their car. John Zokovitch finally left the mines when his oldest son insisted that he join him looking for work in New Jersey. Economists treat hiring as an arrangement between individual labor suppliers and purchasers, but interview recollections point to the very social nature of the job search process. Job hunting trips were all-male affairs aimed at perpetuating the male provider role that had been so central to family life in anthracite mining communities.[9]

When these job hunting trips were successful, former miners often carpooled and commuted on a weekly basis to jobs in the Philadelphia area or northern New Jersey – the domain of work now 100 to 150 miles from their homes. Men drove down together to Fairless Hills or Levittown, northeast of Philadelphia, to jobs in the Fairless Works plant of U.S. Steel. Similar groups of area men commuted to northern New Jersey and worked at General Motors in Linden, Johns Manville in Manville, or Phelps Dodge in Elizabeth. Commuting men lived in area boardinghouses or boarded with family or friends during the week, returning to their families in the anthracite region every weekend.

The more fortunate ones found work closer to home and commuted on a daily rather than a weekly basis. Even short-distance commuting took its toll on the men involved. Bob Sabol commuted for thirty-one years from his home in Coaldale to Allentown and vividly recalled the perils of winter driving through the mountainous area. Mike Knies would stay at a YMCA in Reading some days during the winter to avoid the drive home in bad weather after his nightshift work. Robert Daniels recalled "sleep[ing] half the way home" after a grueling day at Bethlehem Steel in Bethlehem. Steve Pecha held two jobs; he continued to work in the mines from seven to eleven in the morning and would then drive to Bethlehem to work in the steel mill until 10 at night and drive back to be in bed by 11:30.[10]

Weekly commuters faced additional difficulties. They typically found themselves separated from their families from early Monday morning until late on Friday. Life in the rooming houses could be unsettling. John Pavuk recalled living in Manville, New Jersey, with eight men in a room, the men sharing single beds as each replaced another coming off different shifts at a local factory. Mike Vitek noted that after paying the boardinghouse rent and buying gas for his car, he returned home to the anthracite region on weekends with little of his paycheck left.[11]

Migrants from the anthracite region followed various paths, accommodating to the closing of the area's mines. For some, long-distance commuting lasted just six months; they gave up their new jobs and returned to their hometowns hoping for the best. Others commuted for ten years or more while their families remained in their hometowns; ownership of a home, strong family, ethnic and religious ties, closely knit community life, and love of rural life did keep many in the anthracite region in the face of continued economic insecurity. Lastly, a good number liked the prospects that new jobs and communities offered, saved money, purchased homes, and eventually brought their families to join them. With the growth of commuting, economic decline reinforced the traditional separation of the worlds of working-class men and women in the anthracite region.

While irregular work and the outright loss of employment drove long-distance job searches, commuting, and ultimately migration, interviews also reveal that work injuries and brushes with death impelled men to look elsewhere for work. As mine owners tried to bring out the last of the coal in expiring mines or worked the mines with reduced staffs to cut costs, the perils of mining often increased. "I had an accident," Andrew Andrusko recalled. "I smashed my finger hustling timbers....[T]hat's when I said to myself, 'That's my last day I'll ever work in the mines.'" Subsequently, he moved. The coincidence of the death of an uncle in a mine and an accident of his own similarly convinced Henry Blum to pursue work as a carpenter, work that he could find only outside the region. Don Hunsinger's wife got him out of the mines. After an accident, she insisted, "You're not going to work down there! You're not going to work down there." Hunsinger became an autoworker in northern New Jersey.[12]

The role of Don Hunsinger's wife in his resolve to commute underscores the importance of joint decision making in a period of dramatic economic change. Traditionally women had known very little about men's mining work, but with the closing of the mines husbands and wives both had input as they arrived at decisions concerning employment and family residence. Mary Painter encouraged her husband when he left their hometown for Fairless Hills in May 1954 and later she joined him in a new house they bought. Although Mary Painter had supported the decision to migrate, she remembered other wives who refused to move or who tried it for a stretch and then returned to the anthracite region. "We had one friend," she recalled. "He was a guard at U.S. Steel, and he came home one day, and the house was empty." His wife had taken herself and their children back home. This couple did not talk over the relative merits of their alternative choices, but the wife's decisive action carried the day and led her husband to give up his new job and return to the uncertain prospects of their hometown.[13]

Migration out of the region obviously disrupted relations within families, but even those who remained in the region experienced significant change. Wives of commuting husbands in effect became single parents, totally responsible for raising the children – economic decline again reinforcing their domain in the home. Mary Jasinski's husband commuted on a weekly basis for seven years. During that period, her husband spent little time with their children, typically absent during the week and fatigued on weekends. She was, as she noted, "father" to her children, and her daughter reminded her that it was she who taught and took the children fishing. Irene Gangaware's husband, Grant, was on the road for fifteen years. He had to admit playing little role in his children's upbringing: "I didn't spend the time with my kids, raising my children, it was my wife that really done that." Mike Knies commuted only on a daily basis, but he worked the night shift (for twenty-eight years) and he was driving to Reading right after his children came home from school and was back in the morning just about the time that the new school day began. He, too, lamented the limited time he had spent with his son and daughter during their growing years.[14]

The women of the anthracite region who became de facto single parents with the closing of the mines and the commuting of husbands did rely on each other and relatives for assistance – and the credit of local proprietors when cash resources dwindled – but the experience could be exhausting and dispiriting. Mary Rossi thus remembered the difficulties:

> [I]f you only have one car, he's got the car, you know what I mean? Then you have to walk every place, if you have to go to the store, if you have to take the baby to the doctor, you have to walk to the doctor, because he's got the car. He's in Jersey with the car. So, it wasn't so nice. We didn't have such a good, happy time here.[15]

Just as residence issues became subject to negotiation between husbands and wives, and had dramatic implications for the quality of life for family members, so too were employment decisions matters to be resolved in varied ways within families in the anthracite region. Some husbands refused to allow their wives to work, no matter how desperate the situation. Tom Strohl felt his wife's job was "raising the kids." "I wouldn't leave [her] go to work," he recalled. Even though his wages in a series of jobs were close to minimum wage, he insisted that his wife stay home. Ella Strohl did not mention her husband's opposition to her working outside the home, but did recall the difficulties of stretching her husband's limited income: "We had it pretty rough.... We let the rent go, we let the butcher go, but we explained to them what happened and all." Only when an accident forced her husband's early retirement did Ella Strohl begin working in a garment factory just a block or two from her home. Today she expresses pride in the contribution her earnings made and that her small pension still makes to the family's income.

In contrast to Ella Strohl's positive recollection, her daughter Ruth remembers the bitter arguments her parents had over the work issue, reconstructing her father's opposition vividly: "No way. You're supposed to stay home, this is your job, you stay in the house," she recalled him saying. Eleanor Yelito, also, remembered her father's refusal to entertain the notion of his wife's working. "A woman belongs at home," she remembered him repeating.[16]

The great majority of the interviews indicate, however, that married women in the anthracite region worked outside the home throughout their lives – if intermittently – and not just when the mines closed permanently in the 1950s. Miners made good money, that is, when production of anthracite was high. In slack periods (and there was a feast-or-famine quality to life in the anthracite region), miners' fallen incomes required wives to work. Our interviews also reveal that women secured gainful employment during mine strikes and when men suffered accidents. While married women were reluctant to leave young children to other caretakers, large families forced some women to work even when their husbands were fully employed.

Thus when the mines closed, there was nothing new in the practice of women finding wage work in area garment factories. Lillian Verona had been in and out of employment in local garment factories and she remembered: "I was working part-time, 'cause this was a common thing, to work part-time in any factory." Theresa Mogilski confirmed the persistent pattern: "[Y]ou know, most of the women had been working already at the time."[17] What did change in the period after the mines closed was the prevailing ideology. By the late 1950s and '60s, women (and sometimes men) were more willing to acknowledge the importance of women's earnings for family support than they or their parents would have done.

Married women in the anthracite region then had long experience with the so-called double shift, working outside the home and then fulfilling the role of homemaker; as Mary S. noted, even though she worked full-time, " my house was perfect" – referring to the meals she put on the table and the cleanliness of her home. For working wives with commuting husbands, the term "triple shift" is probably in order for they were decidedly on their own. Mary Daniels in speaking to the tasks fulfilled by women while the men were away during the era of economic decline imparted a heroism to them: "[T]he women, they were ones that kept the valley going."[18]

Economic decline in the anthracite region brought different experiences and burdens for men and women, initial reinforcement of the traditional separation of spheres, but also new roles, especially for wives who were more likely to be regularly employed as their husbands' earnings became more uncertain. Interviews also revealed certain gender role reversals – beyond Mary Jasinski's claim of becoming the "father" to her children. In the immediate aftermath of the closing of the mines, some men remained unemployed for substantial periods of time. They stayed at home taking on homemaking tasks; here a blurring rather than further separating of domains occurred. Mary Kupec described the new situation in her household. "He [my husband] was at home. There was no work – you couldn't get anything. So then I went to work full-time then and he babysat.... The man became a woman and the woman a man." Mary Jasinski remembered a similar development in her household: "I never had a baby-sitter [when my husband was unemployed before he began commuting]. No, every time I worked, he was home." Grace Ferrari similarly recalled her husband's domestic work with some amusement. "When he wasn't working, he washed the clothes. My neighbor next door would say, 'Boy, he hangs the clothes funny.' I said, 'I don't care how he hangs them, as long as he washes them.'"[19]

The assumption of domestic duties was not always easy for the men. Sarah Fibac recalled that when her unemployed husband "was hanging clothes they used to call him sissy, and why is he doing it, that his wife should be doing it." The bitterness persisted. Years later Joe Orsulak depicted a frequent scene in mining communities with the closing of the mines – idle men showing up to pick up their wives after their day's toil in the garment factories:

> In those days when the men lost their jobs the women went to work. But most of them had cars at that time already. And they would line up down at Rosenau Brothers waiting for the wives so as to pick them up at work. That was their main duty of the day.... [H]ere they had to go down there, and she made the money, and he had to bring her home and that's all he did. That was degrading, sure, it was. That's the way they saw it.

Married men found themselves performing work traditionally done by their wives and for some the adjustment was not easy.[20]

Women sometimes earned more money than the men – not just when the men were unemployed – and that too was a source of tension. In fact, interviews reveal that the control of family income and budgets generated conflict in mine families in good times and bad. Commuting added to the difficulties here. Irene Gangaware remembered that when her husband was on the road for months at a time, she made sure that his company sent his paycheck directly to her. He lived on a company expense allowance. When he demanded once that he receive his check, she argued back, "The day I don't see your paycheck, that's the day you go out the door with the old luggage. Because I wasn't drinking his money; I wasn't gambling the money. It was our money.... [W]e never had yours and mine."[21] Irene Gangaware's strong words are emblematic of new kinds of relations between men and women that emerged with economic decline.

Irene and Grant Gangaware and other working-class men and women in the anthracite region of Pennsylvania grew up in patriarchal families with distinct male and female spheres. Their fathers worked in and around the mines, enjoying male camaraderie there and in the bars that dotted the streets of mining communities. Their mothers generally stayed home raising large families; close family ties and neighborhood and church networks offered women close bonds with one another. Children in mining towns before World War II were socialized into these distinct gender roles.

Economic decline initially fortified these separate gender domains, but eventually traditional practices could not sustain families. Those who migrated from the region found less convivial, more heterogeneous communities in working-class suburbs of Philadelphia and New York City. They left behind close-knit extended families and neighborhoods and distinctive ethnic churches. Even those who stayed put found their lives dramatically altered. When the mining careers of the men were abruptly truncated, they could not maintain the world of their parents. Some wives raised their children virtually alone as their husbands commuted to distant jobs. Others worked outside of the home on a regular basis to supplement the lower and uncertain earnings of men. In either case, the formerly unchallenged authority of the wage-earning husband and the subordination of the exclusively domestic wife were modified significantly.

From the perspective of the relatively more egalitarian period fifty years later, the transformation of gender roles in the anthracite region in mid-twentieth century can be viewed in a positive light. That was not always the case at the time. Women had more say in family deliberations, but economic disruption also brought new burdens. As Mary Rossi noted in describing her life as a de facto single mother: "We didn't have such a good, happy time here."

As families coped with declining prospects locally, parents came to develop a strikingly different attitude toward their children. Before the economic collapse, children frequently felt parental pressure to quit school at early ages and work to contribute to their families' immediate needs; in the post-World War II period, parents began to view their children's future work in new ways. They took more interest in the education of their children than had been common earlier. Increasingly many parents saw education and outmigration as keys to their children's long-term economic success – a perspective that differed markedly from the framework in which they had come of age. Their economic resources were limited and they accepted the limits the region's decline placed on their own economic prospects. Instead, they placed their hopes in their children and took great pride in their educational and occupational achievements. They adapted the traditional gender expectations they had inherited from their parents to survive in a changing economic world and sought to prepare their children for lives very different than they had known.[22]

What can be learned by focusing on issues of gender relations in the Pennsylvania anthracite region during the period of economic decline? Area residents were not simply hapless victims, passive in the face of cataclysmic change. They adapted traditional values to cope with new circumstances. And women played crucial roles in the strategies families employed – whether migrating to more prosperous areas or doing the best they could on familiar home turf. Relations between husbands and wives and parents and children changed significantly as the economic bases of a strongly patriarchal working-class family system were stripped away.

A focus on gender thus provides new perspectives on economic decline. The collapse of the Pennsylvania anthracite region affected men and women differently. The crisis both reinforced and changed existing patterns of relations between men and women. Together, though, the men and women who faced such extended adversity did not act as victims; they shaped their new histories. They relied on class- and ethnic-based traditions of mutuality. Those who stayed even chose community over chances for better job opportunities elsewhere. More was at work than purely economic calculations. Even traditional understandings of the roles of men and women served in weathering the storm. Oral history interviews provide rich evidence of the values and behavior that men and women exhibited during a period of economic crisis and transition. They help us understand the cultural significance of economic change. They also offer us ways to think about the impact of continuing de-industrialization in the United States. Whether the experiences of men and women in the Pennsylvania anthracite region in the middle decades of the twentieth century will be repeated in communities now experiencing long-term economic shifts remains to be seen. Still, this analysis of one time and place is richly suggestive of ways that we might understand how people cope with change in our midst today.

Notes

Earlier versions of this article appeared in *Historia, Antropologia y Fuentes Orales* 17 (1997): 59-72 and *The Oral History Review* 27 (2000): 81-98, and the authors thank the editors of those journals for permission to publish a revised version in this volume. A more extended account of our argument appears as Thomas Dublin and Walter Licht, *The Face of Decline: The Pennsylvania Anthracite Region in the Twentieth Century* (Ithaca, N.Y.: Cornell University

Press, 2005). Financial support for research for this project has been provided by the National Endowment for the Humanities and the Ford Foundation. The authors would also like to thank Mary Ann Landis who assisted on the interviews and Melissa Doak for transcription and indexing work.

1. *New York Times* reported on de-industrialization in an extensive week-long series of articles, 3-9 Mar. 1996.

2. Our perspective here draws on insights offered in Linda K. Kerber, Alice Kessler-Harris, and Kathryn Kish Sklar, eds., *U.S. History as Women's History* (Chapel Hill: University of North Carolina Press, 1995), 6. They note there: "To recognize women as historical actors...is to introduce into historical work the analysis of gender relations. The work of women's history expands to include not only those experiences particular to women but also the complex relations between men and women. Asking questions about how men and women construct meaning for their historical experience, historians now understand that gender itself is socially constructed."

3. "Production of Anthracite...1913-1932," RG 9, Box 6065, NRA Anthracite Code materials, National Archives; Bureau of the Census, *1992 Census of Mineral Industries: Coal Mining* (Washington, DC: G.P.O., 1995), 12A-5.

4. Support for the oral history was provided by the Ford Foundation, the Pennsylvania Historical and Museum Commission, and the State University of New York at Binghamton.

5. For the basic history of the anthracite region, see Donald L. Miller and Richard Sharpless, *The Kingdom of Coal: Work Enterprise, and Ethnic Communities in the Mine Fields* (Philadelphia: University of Pennsylvania Press, 1985) and Dublin and Licht, *Face of Decline*. For a collection of oral history interviews with particularly rich recollections of labor struggles in the anthracite region in the 1930s, see John Bodnar, ed., *Anthracite People: Families, Unions, and Work, 1900-1940* (Harrisburg: Pennsylvania Historical and Museum Commission, 1983).

6. Interview with Lillian Verona (pseudonym), October 5, 1994, 6.

7. Interview with Lillian Verona, October 5, 1994, 4; interview with Paul Melovich, June 7, 1995, 16, 19-21. Melovich recounts wives in the Hazleton area accompanying their husbands to work on their paydays to see that they paid their bar tabs and turned over the rest of their earnings. As he recalled: "[The bar tab] was paid. And then [my mother] took all the money. That was her territory (21)."

8. Interview with Joe Rodak, June 6, 1995, 23-24.

9. Interview with Paul Melovich, June 7, 1995, 27; interview with John Zokovitch, June 5, 1995, 22.

10. Interview with Elizabeth Mikovich and Bob Sabol (pseudonyms), October 3, 1994, 14; interview with Mike Knies, July 19, 1994, 12-13; interview with Robert Daniels (pseudonym), May 26, 1994, 19; interview with Steve Pecha, July 29, 1993, 16.

11. Interview with John Pavuk, April 20, 1994, 15-16; interview with Mike Vitek and Mary Vitek, November 24, 1995, 23.

12. Interview with Andrew Andrusko, June 17, 1995, 9; interview with Henry Blum and Dorothy Blum, June 8, 1995, 27-28; interview with Don Hunsinger, May 16, 1995, 13, 31.

13. Interview with Mary Painter, September 16, 1994, 14-15.

14. Interview with Mary Jasinski, August 29, 1994, 5, 9; interview with Grant Gangaware, May 17, 1994, 13-14; interview with Mike Knies, July 19, 1994, 14.

15. Interview with Mary Rossi (pseudonym), October 12, 1994, 8.

16. Interview with Tom Strohl, July 30, 1993, 19; interview with Ella Strohl, July 30, 1993, 4, 6, quote on 7; interview with Ken Ansbach and Ruth Ansbach, September 6, 1993, 9; interview with Eleanor Yelito, August 29, 1994, 2.

17. Interview with Lillian Verona (pseudonym), October 5, 1994, 16; interview with Theresa Mogilski, September 1, 1994, 10.

18. Interview with Mary S. (pseudonym), August 23, 1994, 27; interview with Mary Daniels (pseudonym), May 26, 1994, 16.

19. Interview with Mary Kupec, Isabel Zickler, and Philomena Tout, October 4, 1994, 21; interview with Mary Jasinski, August 29, 1994, 7; interview with Grace Ferrari, August 24, 1994, 10.

20. Interview with Sarah Fibac and Maria Bulgrin (pseudonyms), July 18, 1994, 5-6; Interview with Anna Stone and Joe Orsulak, August 24, 1994, 18-19.

21. Interview with Irene Gangaware, September 5, 1993, 16.

22. The results of this perspective are particularly evident in a study we have done of graduates from six anthracite-region high schools between 1946 and 1960. Of 575 alumni who responded to a survey questionnaire, 43 percent went on to post-secondary school education. Achieving advanced schooling, however, did loosen ties to the community, for we discovered that college education was the strongest predictor by far of whether respondents ultimately migrated from their home towns. College education took these young people out of the region and revealed new possibilities to them. A college degree was a ticket to good employment elsewhere. Parents encouraged their children's education knowing full well that traditional family bonds were endangered. Still, our interviews reveal that these parents remain proud from afar of their children's educational and occupational attainments.

Notes on Contributors

MICHAEL G. BAYLOR is Professor and Chair of the Department of History at Lehigh University. He specializes in Early Modern Europe and Germany, and European Intellectual history. Two of his books are *The Radical Reformation* (1991) and *Revelation and Revolution: Basic Writings of Thomas Müntzer* (1993).

STEPHEN H. CUTCLIFFE is Director of the Science, Technology, and Society Program and Professor of History and STS at Lehigh University. He has published numerous books and articles on the history of technology and the interdisciplinary STS curriculum, including *Ideas, Machines, and Values: An Introduction to Science, Technology, and Society Studies* (2000).

GREGORY EVANS DOWD is Professor of History and American Culture and Director of Native American Studies at the University of Michigan. His most recent book is *War under Heaven: Pontiac, the Indian Nations, and the British Empire* (2002).

THOMAS DUBLIN is Professor of History at Binghamton University, State University of New York. He is the author of many publications, including *Women at Work: The Transformation of Work and Community in Lowell, Massachusetts, 1826-1860* (1979) and, with Walter Licht, *The Face of Decline: The Pennsylvania Anthracite Region in the Twentieth Century* (2005).

AARON SPENCER FOGLEMAN is Professor of History at Northern Illinois University. His research interests include Early America, the Atlantic World, religion, immigration, and gender. His publications include numerous articles and two books, *Hopeful Journeys: German Immigration, Settlement, and Political Culture in Colonial America, 1717-1775* (1996), and *Jesus Is Female: Moravians and the Challenge of Radical Religion in Early America* (2007).

KAREN Z. HUETTER is Director of Development for Visual Impairment and Blindness Services of Northampton County, Pennsylvania. She has authored several books and articles, including *The Bethlehem Waterworks* (1976), and is the co-author of *The Bethlehem Oil Mill, 1745-1934* (1984).

MICHAEL V. KENNEDY, who teaches at Founders College, South Boston, Virginia, has published articles in *Pennsylvania History* and *Essays in Economic and Business History* and, with Christine Daniels, has co-edited *Over the Threshold: Intimate Violence in Early America, 1640-1865* (1999).

NED C. LANDSMAN is Professor of History at the State University of New York at Stony Brook. His many publications include *Scotland and Its First American Colony, 1683-1765* (1985), *From Colonials to Provincials: American Thought and Culture, 1680-1760* (1997), and *Crossroads of Empire: The Middle Colonies and the Making of a British Atlantic* (forthcoming).

WALTER LICHT is Professor and Chair of the History Department at the University of Pennsylvania. He is the author of many books, including *Working for the Railroad: The Organization of Work in the Nineteenth Century* (1983), *Getting Work: Philadelphia, 1840-1950* (1992), *Industrializing America: The Nineteenth Century* (1995), and, with Thomas Dublin, *The Face of Decline: The Pennsylvania Anthracite Region in the Twentieth Century* (2005).

AUGUSTINE NIGRO is Assistant Professor of History and Government at Atlantic Cape Community College. His fields of interest include Nineteenth-Century American history, Environmental history, and the history of Science and Technology.

CATHERINE S. PARZYNSKI, who received her PhD from Lehigh University, is a member of the faculty at Montgomery County Community College in Blue Bell, Pennsylvania. She specializes in early American and women's history.

JEFFREY L. PASLEY is Associate Professor of History at the University of Missouri-Columbia. A former journalist and speechwriter, he is the author of *"The Tyranny of Printers": Newspaper Politics in the Early American Republic* (2001) and co-editor of *Beyond the Founders: New Approaches to the Political History of the Early American Republic* (2004).

ANDREW SHANKMAN, Associate Professor of History at Rutgers University, Camden, is the author of *Crucible of American Democracy: The Struggle to Fuse Egalitarianism and Capitalism in Jeffersonian Pennsylvania* (2004). His article "'A New Thing on Earth': Alexander, Hamilton, Pro-Manufacturing Republicans, and the Democratization of American Political Economy" received the Society for Historians of the Early American Republic Ralph D. Gray best article award and the Program in Early American Society and Economy best article prize.

NOTES ON CONTRIBUTORS

ROGER D. SIMON is Professor of History at Lehigh University. His publications include *The City-Building Process: Housing and Services in New Milwaukee Neighborhoods, 1880-1910* (revised edition, 1996) and, with John Bodnar and Michael Weber, *Lives of Their Own: Blacks, Italians, and Poles in Pittsburgh, 1900-1960* (1982).

BEVERLY PRIOR SMABY is Professor Emerita of History at Clarion University of Pennsylvania. She has published *The Transformation of Moravian Bethlehem: From Communal Mission to Family Economy* (1988) and is currently working on a study of women's leadership among eighteenth-century Moravians.

JOHN K. SMITH is Associate Professor of History at Lehigh University. His books include *Science and Corporate Strategy: Du Pont R & D, 1902-1980* (1988) with David A. Hounshell, and *American Chemical Enterprise* (1995) with Mary Ellen Bowden. His recent work includes the history of catalysis.

JEAN R. SODERLUND is Professor of History and Deputy Provost for Faculty Affairs at Lehigh University. She has written *Quakers and Slavery: A Divided Spirit* (1985) and, with Gary B. Nash, *Freedom by Degrees: Emancipation in Pennsylvania and Its Aftermath* (1991).

MARIANNE S. WOKECK is Associate Dean of Academic Affairs and Professor of History at Indiana University-Purdue University Indianapolis. She is general editor of *The Works of George Santayana*; editor of *Documentary Editing*; an editor and author of *Lawmaking and Legislators in Pennsylvania: A Biographical Dictionary, Volume One: 1682-1709* (1991); and author of *Trade in Strangers: The Beginnings of Mass Migration to North America* (1999).

Index

Adams, John, 161, 174, 177, 228, 230, 231
Adams, John Quincy, 246, 268
Alien and Sedition Acts (1798), 228
Allen, William, 104-6, 109, 111, 114
Allentown, Pennsylvania, 17, 104, 106, 110
American Eagle (Easton, Pa.), 227, 234
American Gazetteer, 161
American Revolution (1775-83), 16, 111, 126, 276; impact on economy, 282; impact on Native American sovereignty, 142-43
Anabaptism, 61, 62, 63
anthracite coal mining. *See* coal industry
Arbo, John, 171, 174, 175
artisans, 25-51

Bacon's Rebellion (1676), 134
Beatty, Charles, 105, 111, 115, 117
Beaver Meadow Railroad and Coal Company, 283-84, 290
Bethlehem Iron Company, 179, 296-97, 315
Bethlehem, Pennsylvania, 17, 55, 66, 74-103, 161-84, 185, 190, 295-328
Bethlehem Steel, 17, 18, 179, 295-328, 332
Binns, John, 232, 235, 242, 255, 261-64
Boehm, Johann Philip, 189, 191, 196, 197
Boileau, Nathaniel B., 255, 261, 263, 266
Brackenridge, Hugh Henry, 109, 264
Bradstreet, John, 135-36
Brethren, Church of the, 12, 53, 61, 63-65
Brown, Robert, 235-37
Bucks County, Pennsylvania, 14, 15, 208, 237, 241

Calhoun, John C., 243, 245
Calvinism, German immigrants and, 53, 56, 57, 59
Canadian Indians, 125-57
canals, development of, 275-94
Carnegie, Andrew, 297, 299, 300, 302
Central Moravian Church, 174, 179
Chandler, Alfred D., 295
Cherokees, 125, 126, 129, 229
Cherokee Treaty of 1730, 134
Chickahominies, 133
choir system. *See* Moravian Church, choir system within
Christensen, Hans Christoph, 168, 171, 174-76, 179
churches, relationship to state, 52-73. *See also* Congregationalist Church; Moravian Church; Presbyterian Church; Reformed churches, German
citizenship, 255-71
class formation, 17, 315-28
clergy, in Germany, 56-60
coal industry, 11, 17, 18, 275-76, 280-82, 285, 287, 329-37
commerce, 208-24
Conestogas, 14, 113-14, 137, 139, 140
confessionalization, 57, 61
Congregationalist Church, 110, 111
Conrad, Frederick, 236-37
Constitutional Democrat (Lancaster, Pa.), 232
Constitutional Republicans, 232, 236, 240, 241
Covenant Chain, 131, 135, 137
Crow Dog, 142-43

345

Daily National Journal (Washington, DC), 247
Dallas, Alexander J., 231-32, 255, 258, 259
Dedham, Massachusetts, 128
de-industrialization, 17; impact on gender relations, 18, 329-37
Delaware Democrat, 246
Delaware, Lehigh, Schuylkill, and Susquehanna Railroad, 284, 287
Delaware River, 26, 104, 208, 209, 211, 275, 276
Delawares, 129, 130, 137, 138, 139, 142
Delaware Valley, 11, 14, 32, 38, 106
democracy, 255-71
Democratic Press, 232, 242, 255, 264-67
Democratic Republicans. *See* Jeffersonian Republicans
Duane, William, 228, 231-33, 235, 237, 241, 242, 255, 257, 261, 263-64
Dunkers. *See* Brethren, Church of the
Durham Ironworks, 14, 15, 208-24

Easton, Pennsylvania, 110, 227-54
Easton (Pa.) Centinel, 242, 243
Easton (Pa.) Sentinel, 283, 287, 289
Eaton, Cyrus S., 296, 307-8
economic development of the Lehigh Valley, 25-51, 161-84, 208-24, 275-328
enslaved labor, 31, 33, 35-36
Ephrata, Pennsylvania, 66
Episcopal Church, 106, 110
ethnicity, and indentured servitude, 39-41
evangelicalism, 61, 111, 185-207
Expositor, the, 243-45

family relationships, 329-37
farmers, 25-51, 208-24
Federalist Papers, 142
Federalists, 16, 227-54
Fenton, William, 131
Findlay, William, 242, 243, 266
Fort Pitt, 138, 142
Franklin, Benjamin, 130-31, 139, 140, 230
French and Indian War. *See* Seven Years' War (1754-63)
Freeman's Journal (Philadelphia), 232, 259
Fritz, John, 296-97

garment industry, 331, 334
Geitner, Johann, 168, 171, 175

General Economy. *See* Moravian Church, General Economy
gender relations, impact of de-industrialization on, 18, 329-37; Moravian ideologies concerning, 74-103
German immigrants, 13, 15, 55, 209, 233-34; indentured servitude and, 25-57; religion and, 185-207
Germantown, Pennsylvania, 139, 195
Gnadenhütten, Pennsylvania, 15, 77
golf, 18, 318
Grace, Eugene, 296, 303, 304, 307-308, 316, 318, 319
Great Awakening, 15, 111, 185-207
gristmills, in Bethlehem, Pennsylvania, 15, 161, 165, 167, 170, 175, 176, 212

Hahn, John, 235-37
Hallesians. *See* Lutherans, German-American
Hamilton, Alexander, 16, 142, 230
Handschuh, Johann Friedrich, 194-95
Hauto, George, 277-78
Hazard, Erskine, 17, 277-79, 287
Herrnhut, Moravian church at, 65, 162, 164, 168
Hochenau, Hochmann von, 64
Holy Roman Empire, 53, 56, 61, 63, 65-67
Hütter, Christian J., 242, 243, 245

immigration, German, 25-51, 55, 209; Irish, 25-51, 104-24; Scottish, 104-124
indentured servitude, 25-51, 55-56
Indian Removal Act (1830), 129
industrialization, 15, 17, 161-84, 275-328
Ingham, Samuel D., 241, 242, 244, 266
Irish immigrants, 25-51, 104-24
iron industry, 12, 296
Iroquois, 126, 134, 135, 136

Jackson, Andrew, 141, 246, 247
Jefferson, Thomas, 16, 142, 228, 230, 231, 233, 234, 246
Jeffersonian Republicans, 16, 227-54. *See also* Constitutional Republicans
Johnson, William, 135, 138
Jüngerhaus Diary, 75, 77, 79

King Phillip's War (1675-76), 133

kinship networks, impact on economic development, 25-51

labor systems. *See* enslaved labor; indentured servitude
Lattimore, William, 236-37
Lancaster, Pennsylvania, 191, 195
Lehigh Canal, 179, 275, 282, 284, 289
Lehigh Coal and Navigation Company (LCNC), 17, 179, 279-85, 287-89, 318, 330
Lehigh Coal Company, 278
Lehigh Herald, 282
Lehigh Navigation Company (LNC), 278-79
Lehigh River, 17, 104, 162, 179, 275-94
Lehigh University, 302, 315, 319, 323
Lehigh Valley, class stratification within, 315-28; de-industrialization of, 329-37; economic development of, 208-24; immigrant communities within, 25-73, 104-24; industrialization of, 275-328; Moravian Church and, 74-103; Native American populations of, 125-57; politics and, 255-71; religious conflict within, 185-207
Lehigh Valley Railroad, 17, 287, 290, 296, 315, 319
Leib, Michael, 257, 261, 263, 264
Lenapes, 14, 15, 283
Logan, James, 109
Longcope, Samuel, 227, 233, 234
Lutherans, German-American, 52, 53, 56, 57, 59, 63, 64, 65, 185-207

Mahicans, 15
Madison, James, 142
markets, eighteenth-century development of, 208-24; immigration and, 25-51
Marshall, John, 14, 125, 126, 136
Mauch Chunk (Pa.) Courier, 282
McKean, Thomas, 234, 235, 238, 240, 241, 255, 258-59, 261-63
Mennonites, 12, 13, 28, 53, 60, 61, 62-63
merchants, 25-51
Meyer, Dietrich, 190
migration, of Scots-Irish immigrants, 104-24
mining industry, gender relations within, 329-37

Minweweh (Minavavana), 127, 133, 136
missionaries, Moravian, 65, 77, 105, 162
Missisaugas, 135
Mittelberger, Gottlieb, 12, 13, 52-73
mobility, of Scotch-Irish immigrants, 108-10
Mohawk Indians, 134
Mohegans, 131
Monocacy Creek, 15, 161, 162, 165, 167, 172, 173, 174, 176, 178
Montgomery County, Pennsylvania, 261
Mountaineer, The (Easton, Pa.), 243-45
Moravian Church, 12, 13, 17, 28, 53, 55, 61, 63-66; choir system within, 15, 74-75, 78, 79, 92, 95, 139, 162-63; Directorate, the, 95-96; economic activities of, 161-84; General Economy, 162-64, 177; gender ideologies of; 74-103; "Sifting" within, 88; Single Brethren, 79, 84, 163, 164, 165, 168, 171, 172, 174, 178; Single Sisters, 75, 79, 80, 84, 85, 86, 87, 92, 162, 165
Mühlenberg, Heinrich Melchior, 59, 188, 190-96
Musconetcong Valley, commercial development, 208-24

Narragansett Indians, 133-34
Natick Indians, 128
National Gazette, 231, 232
National Intelligencer, 233, 244
Native Americans, missionary work among, 15, 65, 105; political sovereignty of, 14, 125-57; politics and, 227-54; violence towards, 114-15
Nazareth, Pennsylvania, 55, 75, 185, 190, 211
Neshaminy, Pennsylvania, 104, 105, 115
newspapers, 16, 227-54
Nitschmann, Anna, 75, 84, 189
Norristown (Pa.) Register, 236, 237
North American Steel, 306
Northampton County, Pennsylvania, 239, 241, 242, 246
Northampton Farmer (Easton, Pa.), 228, 234, 236, 237, 238, 240, 241
Northumberland County, 260, 261, 263
Northumberland *Republican Argus*, 255, 261, 263

Ohio Valley, 15, 127
oil mills, in Bethlehem, 161, 164, 165, 167, 170, 171, 173, 174, 179
Ojibwa Indians, 127, 133

Packer, Asa, 17, 296, 297, 308, 315
Panic of 1819, 243, 266-68
party system, development of, 16, 227-71
Paxton uprising, 14, 105, 106, 111, 113-15, 139, 140, 141
Peace of Westphalia (1648), 56
Peasants' War (1525), 62
Penn, John, 14, 138, 139, 140, 141
Penn, Thomas, 14
Penn, William, 11, 12, 14, 30, 58, 60, 129, 137, 211
Pennsylvania Argus (Easton, Pa.), 282
Pennsylvania Gazette, 171
Pennsylvania Supreme Court, 260
Philadelphia, 11, 16, 18, 25, 26, 30, 32, 34, 41, 55, 65, 104, 110, 113, 126, 140, 179, 188, 194, 210, 216, 228, 233, 234, 237, 241, 246, 255, 260, 275, 284, 296, 330, 331, 332, 336
Philadelphia Aurora, 228, 231, 232, 233, 236, 255, 258, 261, 262, 264, 265
Philadelphia Convention (1787), 142
Piesch, Anna Johanna, 75, 97
pietism, 61, 63, 65, 74, 185-207
politics, print culture and, 227-54
Pontiac, 127, 136
Pontiac's War (1763-66), 14, 126, 127, 135, 136, 139, 141
Presbyterian Church, 13, 104-24
print culture, politics and, 227-54
Proclamation of 1763, 14

Quakers. *See* Society of Friends

railroad industry, 285, 287, 290, 296-97, 300, 303, 316
redemptioner system, 12, 25-51
Reformation, Protestant, 57, 61, 62, 63, 92, 186
Reformed churches, German, 185-207
religion, gender ideologies within, 74-103; German immigrants and, 52-73, 185-207
Renatus, 114, 139
republicanism, 255-71, 275-94

Restoration, the (1660), 106, 113, 115, 116, 134
Roan, John, 115
Roberts, Jonathan, 238-40, 242
Rogers, Thomas J., 227-54
Rogers, William Findlay, 246-47
Roman Catholics, German, 53, 56, 57
Ross, Hugh, 243
Royal Proclamation of 1763, 136, 138, 141

Sagourrab, Laurence, 127, 136
Saucon Valley Country Club, 17-18, 315-28
Schlatter, Michael, 59, 189, 190, 197, 198
Schuylkill Indians, 130
Schwab, Charles, 17, 296, 299-300, 302-304, 307-8, 316
Schwenkfelders, 53, 61-64
Scots-Irish immigration, 13, 14, 55, 209
Scottish immigrants, 104-24
sectarianism, religious, 52-73
Seventh Day Adventists, 66
Seven Years' War (1754-63), 11, 14, 135
Shawnees, 138
Single Brethren. *See* Moravian Church, Single Brethren
Single Sisters. *See* Moravian Church, Single Sisters
Snyder, Simon, 16, 240, 255-71
Snyderites, 16, 255-71
Society of Friends (Quakers), 11, 12, 13, 30, 78, 94, 115, 116
Spangenberg, Augustus Gottlieb, 59-60, 177, 191
Spirit of Pennsylvania, 241, 242
steel industry, 295-314, 316
Supreme Court, 14, 260, 304
Susquehanna Valley, 15, 127, 137, 138, 139
steel industry, 11, 17

Tallmadge Amendment (1820), 245
tanneries, 165, 171, 172-74, 179
teamsters, 208-24
technological development, in Bethlehem, Pennsylvania, 161-84
Tennent, William, 104-6, 111
Tertium Quids, 16, 255-71
trade networks, 25-51

INDEX

transportation, 275-94
Thirty Years' War (1618-48), 56
treaties, 129-31
Treaty of Carlisle (1753), 130
Treaty of Paris (1763), 142
Treaty of Utrecht (1713), 134
Treaty of Westphalia (1648), 13

U.S. Steel, 296, 299-300, 303, 304, 306-308, 311, 332, 333

voluntary associations, 283

Walking Purchase (1737), 14, 55
Washington, George, 16, 231, 234
waterworks, in Bethlehem, Pennsylvania, 161, 165, 167, 168, 174-76, 179

Wharton, Joseph, 297, 299, 308
Whiskey Rebellion (1794), 114
White, Josiah, 17, 277-80, 285, 287
Whitehall, Pennsylvania, 129, 141
Wilson, Woodrow, 299-300
Wolf, George, 242, 246
women, Moravian ideas concerning, 74-103
World War I, 17, 296, 299, 300, 302, 303, 308, 311

Youngstown Steel and Tube, 296, 306, 307-8

Zinzendorf, Nicholas Ludwig, 13, 15, 65-66, 162, 164, 177, 188, 190; ideas concerning women, 74-103